Women under Communism

Women under COMMUNISM

Barbara Wolfe Jancar

The Johns Hopkins University Press/Baltimore and London

To John, always

Manufactured in the United States of America

The Johns Hopkins University Press, Baltimore, Maryland 21218
The Johns Hopkins Press Ltd., London

Library of Congress Catalog Card Number 77–16375
ISBN 0–8018–2043–X

Library of Congress Cataloging in Publication data will be found on the last printed page of this book.

Contents

Acknowledgments

It is impossible to thank all who made this book a reality. For fear of forgetting some person or institution, I am hesitant to begin. I am most deeply grateful for the help, encouragement, and advice I have received from many friends and colleagues, both at home and abroad. Certain of these deserve particular mention for the special part they played in the writing of the book.

For the analysis of women in the Central Committees of Eastern Europe I am indebted to the S.U.N.Y. Research Foundation for its grant to me, and to the Archive on East European Elites of the University of Pittsburgh and Dr. William Jarzabek for making the requisite files available. I would also like to express my thanks to the librarians at the Union College Library, Schenectady, N.Y., the Library of the University of Rochester, and the Brockport College Library for their untiring assistance in locating materials, and especially to Ms. Loretta Walker, head reference librarian, and Mr. David Gerhan, assistant reference librarian, at the Union College Library, and Ms. Elsie Hetler of the Brockport Library.

I am grateful to Dr. Robert Sharlet, of the Political Science Department of Union College, and Dr. Robert Getz, of the Political Science Department at Brockport, for their continuing encouragement and support of my work. My warmest appreciation goes particularly to the many men and women in the Soviet Union, Poland, Hungary, Bulgaria, Romania, and Yugoslavia, at institutes and elsewhere, who gave of their time and talents to aid me in investigating a common problem. The views expressed in this book are purely my own. They represent my interpretation of material given to me or my personal observations. If I have in any way misrepresented the opinions of any of the individuals in Eastern Europe and the USSR with whom I talked, the fault is entirely mine and I ask their pardon accordingly.

My sincere thanks go to the University of Rochester computer staff for their help in managing and analyzing the data, particularly that in chapter 5. For their unwearying help on the manuscript itself, including long hours of proofreading and collating, I am indebted to Mr. Robert Duncan, Mr. Robert

Flachbarth, Mrs. Mildred Forgette, Mrs. Della Shiell, and Ms. Calla Bassett.

Last, but not least, my deepest thanks go to Mrs. Catheryn Smith, whose boundless energy, enthusiasm, and tireless work typing the many drafts of the manuscript brought *Women under Communism* to the light of day.

Women under Communism

My workingwoman mother said to me,
    Girl—
years before her rich sudden unreal years
Whatever work you do, always make sure
you can walk out the door, not shut in
    all your hours.

                    Muriel Rukeyser, ''Trinity Churchyard''

1 / Introduction: Equality as a Process

In the mid-1950s, Maurice Duverger's well-known United Nations Educational, Scientific, and Cultural Organization (UNESCO) study revealed that the participation of women in the parliaments of Europe averaged only 5 percent.[1] By the mid-1970s, the participation of women in the top political decision-making positions of Europe, with the exception of Scandinavia, had not increased significantly. As of 1976, no woman was serving as a United States senator, and only 9.0 percent of all state legislators in America were women.[2]

Such statistics come as no surprise to those familiar with the male dominance pattern alleged to characterize "capitalist, bourgeois" politics. What may be of greater interest to students of comparative political systems is that the proportion of women in the highest political decision-making bodies of the Communist world, excluding the People's Republic of China, is no better, if not worse, than that of the United States. The entrance of women in large numbers into the ranks of the legal and medical professions, which in the Western world have been traditionally considered male preserves, is to be applauded in the communist countries. However, after more than sixty years of "socialism" in the Soviet Union and thirty years of the same in Eastern Europe and China, women have not attained representation at the upper levels of society where policies are really made, and which their mobilization in the lower professional and political ranks would seem to demand. Since 1917 only one woman has sat in the Politburo of the Communist Party of the Soviet Union (CPSU). Only one woman, Mme. Mao, has been a full member of the Chinese Politburo since the founding of the People's Republic, and there have been no women in the more powerful Politburo Standing Committee. With a few past exceptions, women are newcomers to the politburos of Hungary, Bulgaria, and Romania.

A comparative investigation of the participation of women in the upper levels of the policy-making process in the Communist world is long overdue.

1

The emancipation of women was one of the central goals of the Russian Revolution, and all communist leaderships since then have pledged themselves to achieving sexual equality. There is no denying that where a Communist system triumphed, an immediate revolution in the life style of women followed the seizure of power. No Western government has been as committed to women's liberation as have the Communist states. Indeed, some adherents to the more radical women's movement in this country would like to suggest that only in a Marxist state can true sexual equality be achieved.[3] Elsewhere, the achievements of women in the Soviet Union and other Communist nations have been objects of admiration and even envy.[4]

The fact remains, however, that the more political or administrative the responsibility attached to a job, the less likely it is that a woman will occupy that position in any Communist country. Two questions come to mind immediately: (1) In view of their advances in the economic sphere, why has there been no large-scale breakthrough of women into higher policy-making positions? (2) Why is it that, despite differences in cultural and economic heritage, women have reached approximately the *same* status level in every Communist country? Are the factors operating within the Communist system to define the limits of advancement of women in these countries unique, or are they common to woman's world-wide experience? The focus here is on similarities, not differences. The aim of this study is an understanding of the impact of the Communist system—in all its various cross-cultural and cross-national manifestations—on the status of women.

An investigation of this kind is not merely academic. It is central to any consideration of the role of women in modernized societies, the majority of which are committed, at least legally, to the principal of sexual equality. The central issue being posed is the relationship between equality and status. Is identical status a necessary and sufficient condition for equality?

I will turn to the question of status first. By status, I am not referring merely to economic function. As Everett E. Hagen has stated, "One's status derives not only from one's economic function, but from all that one does and believes, all of one's relationships to other persons and to the unseen forces in which one believes."[5] Status in this sense is a comprehensive positioning of the individual in his society. It is the ordering of the stimuli received by a person from his environment to form a concept of his place and identity in the world. The statistics cited on female participation in legislative decision-making in Western societies suggest that the level of economic development exerts a minor influence in improving a woman's status. We cannot assume that the more industrialized a nation, the more likely we are to find women in positions of high status and power. There is no automatic process by which the status of women rises in direct proportion to the rise in gross national product. Factors other than economics are patently at work.

Jeane Kirkpatrick has broached the subject quite candidly. In her view, all explanations of why there are so few women in "high" politics everywhere must deal with two fundamental questions: "whether male dominance derives from female preference or male imposition, or both; and whether male dominance is natural or conventional."[6] The way the questions are posed, equating high status with dominance leaves no doubt that equality of status is a central problem in any discussion or investigation of sexual equality.

To put it another way, what difference would it make to men and women, both as individuals and in their relationship with one another, if women did indeed participate significantly in policy-making? If Communist societies are unique in their pioneering efforts to achieve sexual equality, have women in these societies deliberately refused to take advantage of the opportunities offered them? Has the male leadership presented options to them which make it difficult for women to participate? Is the failure of women to rise to the top of the status pyramid symptomatic of a prevailing disinterest among women in status and power, because they feel they have already achieved equality? Is it the product of "centuries of oppression," or is it a consequence of the operation of the Communist system itself? While it may be possible to revolutionize traditional women's positions by fiat, does not the continued operation of government by central directive hamper the onward progress of that revolution?

These questions lead us directly to the meaning of equality. Do we mean arithmetic equality? For example, if a politburo has ten members, should five of these be women if women comprise 50 percent of the population? The Communist states have played the numbers game where power was not one of the stakes. In all the legislatures of the Soviet Union and Eastern Europe (except Yugoslavia, where the legislature appears to wield power more commensurate with that of Western parliaments), women enjoy a much higher proportion of representation than in the United States. Do we mean equality of opportunity? Here the focus would have to be on the sources of unequal opportunity in Communist systems: childhood socialization, government, and Party propaganda. On the more fundamental level, does equality mean women assuming all of men's roles while losing none of their customary female roles? In this case, women in Communist societies have effectively penetrated areas traditionally identified as male. As a result, men move out where women move in, and the feminization of job categories appears. Finally, does equality mean new patterns of behavior that entail a breakdown of differentiation in sex roles and the establishment of role types without reference to sex? Are we to ascribe a positive value to women achieving positions of status and power alongside men? And do we mean, when we say "yes," that they achieve traditional male power positions, or do we anticipate a radical transformation of society in which status and power will come to be defined in new and different ways?

So far no society has succeeded in providing a clear operational definition of equality. As regards sexual equality, Alice Rossi and Carolyn Heibrun have suggested that androgyny may be the ideal value, where both men and women can freely choose their roles and behaviors.[7] I personally prefer this definition. Yet in stating my position I become liable to the charge of cultural bias, for no Communist society has yet admitted the free choice of roles for anyone. It might be more useful to investigate the Communist definition of equality and proceed from there, and thus avoid prejudicing the data.

The problem with this course is that Communist regimes are ambivalent on this very issue. On the one hand, they assert that women are already equal with men. On the other, in every Communist country in the past ten years, scores of articles and books have appeared which demonstrate without a doubt that women in fact are not equal with men. Women earn less and work twice as hard as men because they are constrained to bear the burden of housework. They do not hold administrative positions, are not politically active, and are not joining the Communist party in large numbers. My data for this book come from Communist sources, most of which are surprisingly candid on the position of women in their society. The message seems to be that women may be de jure equal with men, but are not de facto. The wealth of material available in Eastern Europe and the Soviet Union on woman's life style, family, and work suggests that communist leaders are themselves unclear as to why the massive entrance of women into the economy has not brought equality anymore than did the acquisition of suffrage in "bourgeois" countries. Communist regimes talk little about the meaning of equality; but they do talk a great deal about improving social and child care services, increasing the number of washing machines, decreasing the hours of the working day for women, and mobilizing women into the Party.

Because equality tends to be both assumed and recognized as unachieved, it would be as much an exercise in futility to adopt the Communist definition as it would be counterproductive to posit a goal such as androgyny, which does not appear in Communist research, and attempt to demonstrate to what degree Communist systems have or have not measured up to it.

Instead of conceptualizing equality as a goal—arithmetic, androgynous, or otherwise—it would seem more practical to view it as the *process* by which diverse social groups become integrated into the body politic via two fundamental political steps: (1) ability to make demands upon the government; and (2) *actual* participation in policy-making. Both Communist and non-Communist countries can be seen as engaged in such a process. The status position of any group must be understood as central to this definition and critical to a group's integration into the body politic. For status is contingent on the capacity to make and support demands and to participate in policy-making. Equality thus is essentially a political process. It does not come automatically as a result of the interplay of social and economic forces, although these can be instrumental in promoting a demand for equality. To become equal requires participation in the "authoritative allocation of values." Otherwise, the claimant remains a second-class citizen, subordinate to another group or groups that determine his needs for him.

Equality defined as a process permits investigation without forcing normative evaluation on a society different from our own. In this connection, the present study will not attempt to conclude what Communist regimes ought to do as regards their policy toward women. It will, however, attempt comparisons between the countries as to where each Communist country stands in the process. Such comparisons are useful both in identifying problems common to the countries collectively and in distinguishing national idiosyncrasies.

The focus of this study, then, will be on the process of achieving equality for women as a function of their position in the sociopolitical hierarchy. Equality will infer equality of status. Women do become doctors, lawyers, and engineers in far greater percentages in Communist countries than in the West. Yet, it would be unwise to presume that their status vis-à-vis their male counterparts is higher in these countries than in the West. Athena Theodore has shown in her discussion on the United States that women tend to go into those professions or semiprofessions considered appropriate to their sex.[8] These choices are by and large culturally determined and generally do not include professions to which the local culture assigns the highest status. Both the medical profession and the law occupy a much lower position on the professional hierarchical ladder in the Communist countries than they do in the United States, where law is the principal means of access to political power, and the practice of medicine still retains an entrepreneurial character.

As Goode, Merton, Reader, and Kendall have shown, professions, like communities, operate under formal and informal rules. While access to the bottom of the professional ladder may be relatively easy through university ties and assistance, arrival at the top depends far more on the protégé system and "the old boy network." Cynthia Epstein's study suggests that it is far harder for women to make use of the network than it is for men, at least in the United States.[9] The rise of women into high administrative positions in the Communist countries indicates that the same obstacles obtain there. Hence, to say that women are doctors or lawyers is not enough. While the profession itself is some indication of status, to my mind the location of the professional on the status ladder of his own profession provides a more relevant indicator of the real social and political position of that individual. The larger proportion of Soviet and East European women in the labor force as compared to the West, or the greater percentage of women who have entered what are considered in the West male-dominated professions, does not tell us anything about the real status of women in these countries. The key factor in my definition of equality is who makes the decisions about the distribution of goods and services in society. Thus the process of equality may be measured by the degree to which women participate in these decisions, especially at the highest level of political power. If, as Karl Deutsch maintains, modernization *is* politicization, and the political sector plays the primary role in effecting economic and social change,[10] then the activity of women at the highest levels of the political sector becomes the most significant indicator of the process of equality, in terms of making claims upon the government.

The concept of equality as a process may be put in perspective by identifying the main factors involved in a general explanation of the status of any group in time and place. These may then be applied to the specific situation of women in the Communist countries. Figure 1 is the product of earlier research[11] modified by subsequent investigations. It is presented primarily as a tool by which to organize the material under study.

Area A of the figure, the environment, denotes (1) *the economic level of development,* (2) *the demographic features,* (3) *the dominant cultural and ideological orientation,* and (4) *the political structure* of the country under consideration. The number of books that have dealt with women in the economy and the cultural bias against women exhibited in every civilization[12] provide strong justification for considering economics and culture as primary factors in determining a woman's status in any society. Indeed, there would seem to be a reciprocal relationship between the two. Economics may determine status more directly, but culture and/or ideology reinforces or sanctions that determination. Because we are dealing with predominantly ideological societies when we investigate the Communist countries, ideology has been included as a cultural factor. The demographic variable accommodates the physiological constraints imposed on women by virtue of their biology, namely, their ability to bear children, and the relationship between biology and sociopolitical status. Finally, the political structure is seen as the major factor permitting or not permitting the formulation of demands and support for those demands among groups. It goes without saying that it is more difficult to evaluate the role of the Communist political structure in mobilizing and recruiting women to political power; after all, there is no vote and no freedom of assembly which would permit the spontaneous formation of a woman's movement. However, there are data to suggest the degree to which the political structure promotes or frustrates the upward mobility of women.

Within area B of figure 1, political decision-making, lie the factors of (5) *leadership guidance* and (6) the *female self-concept.* The former includes both the prescriptive and promotional functions of leadership in effecting social change. The prescriptive function refers to explicit legislation, Party resolutions, and administrative regulations that aim to clarify social objectives regarding women and justify the measures taken to reach them. Of key interest are decisions regarding labor policy, marriage and the family, health, and the promotion of women. The promotional function refers to the leadership's control and direction of education, the mass media, and other communication mechanisms that induce public consensus for validating current social objectives. At issue here is the socialization process. What role options are being

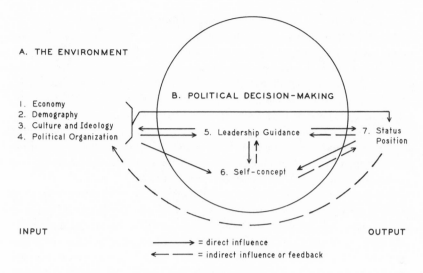

A. THE ENVIRONMENT

1. Economy
2. Demography
3. Culture and Ideology
4. Political Organization

B. POLITICAL DECISION-MAKING

5. Leadership Guidance

6. Self-concept

7. Status Position

INPUT

OUTPUT

———→ = direct influence
←— — = indirect influence or feedback

FIGURE 1. Relationship of Major Factors Determining Status

offered to women, and how are women being socialized into these roles in Communist societies?

The female self-concept refers to the internalization by women of their various role options, including the traditional family childrearing role, the professional role, and the political role. Survey analysis would appear the best approach in this area, but it was not possible for me to conduct a survey in the Communist countries. Happily, however, sociology has come into its own in Eastern Europe and the Soviet Union since the 1960s. Many of these countries have conducted their own surveys on women. The majority of these have to do with women's attitudes toward work and the family. While the surveys were not specifically formulated to elicit responses from women as to the image they have of themselves and their place in society, it has been possible to make deductions from the material available. In addition, I was able to interview women in many of the Communist countries as well as emigrants to the United States and abroad.

The female self-concept is a relevant variable in a model for the explanation of status position. Motivation to make demands and to advance economically and politically is related to the image one has of one's self in terms of (1) the perception of the appropriateness of a particular type of action for a particular person, and (2) belief in a positive outcome of that action for the person. For example, the perception "politics is unfeminine" would be less likely to motivate women to political activity than the opposite perception. Or again, the belief that the probability of a woman being elected president of the United States is very low goes a considerable way in explaining why a particular woman or even women in general do not run for this elective office.

The status of any group is seen as the product of the interaction of the factors identified above. Decisions are not made in a vacuum. As figure 1 suggests, there is a direct flow of information from the environment to the leadership, which in turn directly influences the environment through its decisions. Both the environment and leadership guidance have a direct influence on the female status position (signified by the solid line), while leadership guidance also serves as an intervening variable between the environment and status position. In addition, the environment directly influences the female self-concept through economic and social factors that are important determinants of one's self-image. One's self-image in turn serves as another intervening variable between the environment and status position. The interaction between the female self-concept and the female status position is likewise direct. Achievement of any kind tends to bring about a positive redefinition of self, at least to some degree. Both the female self-concept and the female status position react back on the content of leadership guidance: the former again indirectly, the latter directly, since high status is an indicator of access to participation in the ruling elite. Finally, status provides feedback both to leadership guidance and to the environment for further modification of the system.

Figure 1 attempts to present in graphic form the intricate nature of the system that determines status in society. Status cannot be defined as a linear causal chain; it is rather a plurality of interacting relationships. The underlying assumption of this study is that female status is hard to change precisely because the system that defines it is a complex network of interactions.

A distinction commonly made between a Communist regime and a democratic or open society is that the former, with its monopoly of power, is better organized to coerce change. With its more collaborative attitude toward interests and clients desiring change, the open system more often than not lacks any deliberate, all-inclusive plan to effect change. Those who despair of pluralistic democracy's ability to be an agent of social transformation are tempted to look toward the seemingly greater command capabilities of Communist regimes, expecting Communist leaderships to be able to impose change upon the status of any client group, such as women, with minimum consideration of inputs from the environment. By contrast, less concentration of power is seen as a decisive factor in making open systems more sensitive to environmental input and consequently less able to order change without corresponding inducement from the environment.

This study proposes that rulers and rules in Communist systems are as much the product of their environment as are their Western counterparts. While the Soviet and East European regimes have claimed great progress in making women equal with men, women's political status in these countries has in reality changed little. While the leaderships eagerly sought to give women education and to recruit them into the labor force, they were not firmly committed to sharing power with them. Hence, the paradox between high female participation in the labor force and low participation in the decision-making elites. It is still too early to determine whether the Chinese experience deviates from this norm. What the Chinese example suggests is that authoritarian regimes appear to have greater command capability to change status upon assumption of power. This command capability decreases in proportion as (1) the society modernizes and (2) the regime lengthens its tenure in power.

A corollary to this reasoning, then, is that authoritarian regimes, insofar as they are authoritarian, are unable to change the status of any group over time beyond a certain point. The degree of modernization and length of time a regime remains in power are posited as converging on a threshold beyond which incremental change in status diminishes significantly. A central question posed in this study is whether and to what degree Communist regimes have desired or indeed been able to effect changes in the status of women.

In the following chapters I will try to assess the impact of the Communist political system upon the status of women in the Soviet Union, Communist Eastern Europe, and China, insofar as that is possible. Cuba was originally omitted because of insufficient data. The short section on Cuba (appendix 4) indicates that the status of women in that country parallels that of women in the other Communist countries. Because the analysis focuses on the present-day operation of Communist society, historical material has regrettably but necessarily been relegated to the background. I will first explore environmental factors and then attempt cross-country comparisons of leadership policies and the concept women have of themselves. Much of my material is drawn from Communist sources, although an increasing amount of research, particularly as regards the role of women in the Soviet Union,[13] is being carried on in the United States and in Western Europe. China presents a special problem because the Chinese government has not published statistics since the 1950s. Hence, there are no official data on which to draw as there are in the European Communist countries. I have had to rely on field reports from American visitors, translations from Chinese sources, and the impressionistic studies that have been published in this country by American scholars.

Perhaps a word of caution is needed as regards the evaluation of material from the Communist countries. First, it should be pointed out that survey research there has not yet reached the level of sophistication characteristic of research in the United States. The degree of competency varies from country to country, with perhaps Hungary, Poland, and Yugoslavia ranking, in my estimation, the highest. In the Soviet Union, I found sampling techniques somewhat rudimentary. For example, a survey of women's attitudes toward marriage in a Moscow suburb was based upon data obtained from the arbitrary selection of all the inhabitants of a few apartment complexes instead of a random sample of tenants from every complex. In some cases in which whole populations were said to be recorded, individuals who were not available were simply omitted. The composition of such samples undoubtedly influenced the survey results.

Second, much depends on whether the survey data was obtained by interview or by written questionnaire. In the Soviet Union, there seemed to be a tendency to use university students as survey interviewers. Many times they had had little or no training in the field and were sent out to collect data as part of a summer program.

Third, a closed social system raises the question of reliability of responses, and the questionnaires that I saw frequently did not include questions to test this variable. I was assured by sociologists in all the countries I visited that people generally liked to answer questionnaires and had not become as weary of them as persons in the United States. But eagerness to answer does not equal reliability.

Fourth, there is much greater specialization of function in the Communist countries. Thus, one person may be directing the study, several may be working on the general plan, others may be writing the questionnaire, an entirely different group may be doing the computer programming, and a final group may analyze the results. When I wanted some clarification of a computer print-out, it was not uncommon for me to be told I would have to see a third person who was competent in the subject. This differentiation of project function makes difficult the coordination of any one project from start to finish.

Last, but not least, there is the enduring problem of ideology. While dogmatic ideology is less in evidence in Poland, Hungary, and Yugoslavia, the fact remains that no article or survey published in these countries may claim that the position of women is worse under socialism than under capitalism, or that some alternate form of social organization might better promote sexual equality. Aside from the necessity of taking a positive approach to socialism's ability to solve the problems of women, sociologists in the USSR have to assume the added burden of a unique utopian future: communism. Therefore, much of the research in Communist countries has an instrumental goal: to provide the leadership with information about the way women feel, work, and live, with the aim of improving their performance at work, upgrading family life, or increasing the birth rate. The economic and social goals are set. In no country did I find researchers engaged in projects that would set or *define* goals regarding women. Thus, the objectivity of the surveys and articles published about women must necessarily come into question.

A caveat should also be offered as regards the aggregate statistics given throughout the book. These have been drawn from official domestic, American, and United Nations sources. Often the numbers do not agree across sources, nor do manipulations of the data result in the figures specifically given in one source. The problems of data collection are difficult in any country but are made more so in the Communist countries by the reasons given above.

Once the limits, aim, and direction of research in the Communist countries are taken into consideration, the results can be most helpful in giving us a picture of the problems encountered by women in these societies.

2 / The Socioeconomic Environment

Three main factors may be said to define the position of women in the economies of the Communist countries: the demands of industrialization and economic development; the recruitment of women into administrative and higher-level specialty careers; and the demographic problem. Because of the amount of data presented under the first two categories, the demographic problem will be discussed in chapter 3. Given the absence of recent data from China and Albania, both chapters 2 and 3 will focus on the other countries of Eastern Europe and on the Soviet Union.

THE DEMANDS OF INDUSTRIALIZATION AND ECONOMIC DEVELOPMENT

The huge task of modernizing societies in countries where the Communist Party came to power (except East Germany and Czechoslovakia) posed the problem of mobilizing a primarily manual labor force to offset the limitations of a nascent technology. This period is commonly referred to by East European sociologists and economists as "the period of intensive economic construction." In the absence of immigration, the main sources of labor were the peasantry and, of course, women. Both of these groups had a low level of literacy. The school system was at the beginning ill equipped to handle the numbers pouring into the system, and everywhere women were at a lower educational level than men. As a result, women were generally mobilized into the ranks of unskilled labor.

OVERVIEW OF FEMALE EMPLOYMENT PATTERNS SINCE WORLD WAR II

Soviet female employment patterns are not completely comparable to those of the East European countries, since the USSR has had much longer experience with women working in the labor force. However, the consequences of World War II affected the Soviet Union and almost all the East European countries in similar ways and made the employment of women mandatory in every country. War casualties, as well as population losses resulting from the persecution of the Jews and postwar population transfers, deprived most of the East European countries of a significant part of their male population and labor force.[1] A concerted effort was needed to rebuild the war-torn societies and to transform backward economies where a high percentage of people still worked the land. The massive entrance of women into the labor force was crucial to both economic reconstruction and development.

Table 1 indicates the extent of the recruitment of female workers between 1950 and 1970 in the Soviet Union and Eastern Europe. By 1970, as can be seen in figure 2, essentially 2 out of 3 women working in Eastern Europe (with the exception of Yugoslavia) were between 20 and 55 years of age.[2] The Soviets claim an even higher proportion. By comparison, the proportion of working men in this age group averaged over 95 percent. The substantial increase in the female labor force between 1950 and 1970 indicates unequivocally that women are now an essential part of the Communist working world.

EDUCATIONAL PATTERNS

Initially, women were employed in areas associated with their traditional roles—in textiles, food processing, social services and their delivery—and were at the bottom of the labor scale, as has been admitted by many East European sociologists.[3] However, governments worked hard to draw women into higher education. By the 1970s, every Communist country could boast a pool of highly skilled women, the distribution of which is given in table 2. Unfortunately, no statistics are available for China. Albania also ceased releasing statistics in the 1950s, so it is not possible to compare the Chinese and Albania samples with the European Communist countries.

These figures are impressive for any nation and document the effort to give women equal education with men in the Communist countries. Indeed, if equality were only a matter of years of schooling, one could predict that in a very short time, educational differences between the sexes in every Communist society would be eliminated and women would be on a equal footing with men.

Tables 3–5, however, suggest a different situation. Women are channeled into different types of education than are men. The pattern of this channeling is similar in every Communist country. Without exception, women predominate in those educational areas that a Romanian source assured me are ''more suited to women's inclinations''[4]: health care, education, and accounting. A Bulgarian survey explained the pattern in terms of women's reluctance to

Table 1—Employment of Women as Percentage of Total
Work Force in Eastern Europe, the Soviet Union, and the
United States, 1950 and 1970

Country	1950	1970
Albania[a]		44.9
Bulgaria	34.0	51.9
Czechoslovakia	41.2	48.7
GDR	—[b]	49.1
Hungary	30.0	48.3
Poland	31.9	51.9
Romania	—	54.2
USSR	47.0	51.0
Yugoslavia	24.8	47.9
USA	—	40.8

Sources: "Zhenshchiny v SSSR: Statisticheskie materi-
aly," Vestnik statistki, no. 1 (1974), p. 5; Herta Kührig,
Equal Rights for Women in the German Democratic Republic (Berlin: GDR Committee for Human Rights, 1973),
p. 147; The Working Woman in People's Poland (Warsaw:
Ministry of Labour, Wages, and Social Affairs, 1975), p. 7;
Czechoslovak Socialist Republic, Federal Statistical Office,
Statistická ročenka Republiky československé (Prague: Orbis, 1957), p. 68; idem, Statistická ročenka ČSSR, 1971
(Prague: Orbis, 1971), p. 65; A nökröl (Budapest: Kossuth
könyvkiadó, 1974), p. 8; Nikolina Ilieva, Trifon Trifaniv,
and Nikolina Tsaneva, Izpolzvane na zhenskite trudovi resursi v NRB (Sofia: Partizdat, 1973), p. 26; Women in the
Socialist Republic of Romania (Bucharest: Meridiane, 1974),
p. 28; Ibrahim Latitić, ed., Women in the Economy and Society of the SFR of Yugoslavia (Belgrade: Federal Institute for
Statistics, 1975), p. 11; United Nations, Department of Economic and Social Affairs, Statistical Office, Yearbook of
Labour Statistics, 1973 (Geneva: International Labour Office, 1973), pp. 31–38, 41.
[a]This is a 1960 figure. Albania has not published any
official statistics since that date.
[b]— = data not available.

move into hard-science specialties like computer science or engineering.[5] Yet
it is these specialties which pay the higher salaries upon graduation in the
Communist countries.

A second and more important explanation is the existence of the quota
system for entrance into the various university faculties. These quotas, based
on projected needs set forth in the five-year and yearly plans, determine not
only the number of students to be admitted into the special branches of higher
education, but the percentage of men and women. As was explained to me in
Bulgaria, the percentage quotas are not known to either the parents or the
children. Hence both live in anxiety for fear that a good grade on an exam will
be set aside because the candidate for admission is of the wrong sex.[6]

Tables 3–5 present certain problems for comparison because of the dif-

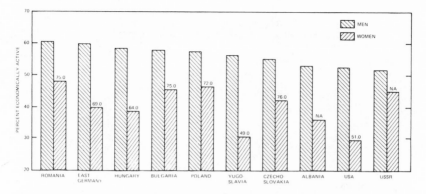

FIGURE 2. Economically Active Population by Sex in Selected Countries, 1970

The histograms represent economically active men and women as a percentage of the total male and female populations. The number at the top of each histogram for women indicates the number of economically active females between the ages of 20 and 55 as a percentage of all the economically active females in the designated country.

ferences in assigning educational categories. While it is possible to restructure the Hungarian data to fit the Soviet categories, the Polish and Yugoslav categories depart so much from the Soviet model that this data must be treated separately. Indeed, including the Hungarian statistics under the Soviet categories is misleading. For example, 52.7 percent of Hungarian medical students at the university level are women, while over 80 percent of all pharmacy students are women. At the secondary level, 100 percent of all nursery school trainees and child care students are women. But because Soviet education categories include art and cinema in the education variable, fitting the Hungarian material into the Soviet model obscures the extent of sex differentiation in the Hungarian case. The Soviet model does not tell the whole story for the Soviet Union either. Although young men are increasingly encouraged to go into elementary education in the USSR through scholarship incentives, I was told that at Tashkent University so far no man had chosen to enter the field. In all the countries women are assumed to be the only proper educators of the very young.

Several findings seem warranted by the data on education. First, there is the perpetuation of traditional sex stereotyping as in the West. A Bulgarian survey made in the early seventies clearly showed that women were underrepresented in the hard sciences. However, a trend seems to be emerging for increasing numbers of women to go into chemistry. Hungarian figures indicate that 82 percent of the students in the chemical-pharmaceutical departments are women. Dodge's figures show that, by 1940, women already constituted 45.3 percent of all chemistry students in the Soviet Union,[7] while Romania re-

Table 2—Enrollment of Women in Secondary and Higher-Level
Schools as Percentage of Total Population of the USSR and
Eastern Europe, 1970

Country	Secondary Schools	Higher-Level Schools
USSR	50.0	50.0
Poland	51.6[a]	48.3
Hungary	50.0	47.0
Yugoslavia	43.4	46.9
Czechoslovakia	—[b]	39.8
GDR	50.2	37.1
Bulgaria	53.8	36.2
Romania	49.0	30.0

Sources: "Zhenshchiny v SSSR: Statisticheskie materialy," Vestnik
statistiki, no. 1 (1974), p. 9; Maria Dinkova, The Social Progress of
Bulgarian Women (Sofia: Sofia Press, 1972), p. 19; Herta Kührig, Equal
Rights for Women in the German Democratic Republic (Berlin: GDR Committee for Human Rights, 1973), p. 150; Statisztikai évkönyv, 1973 (Budapest: Központi Statisztikai hivatal, 1973), pp. 454 and 456; Women in
Poland (Warsaw: Central Statistical Office, 1975), p. 9; Women in the
Socialist Republic of Romania (Bucharest: Meridiane, 1974), p. 24;
Ibrahim Latatić, ed., Women in the Economy and Society of SFR of Yugoslavia (Belgrade: Federal Institute for Statistics, 1975), p. 15.
[a]Refers to the number of female students enrolled. In 1974/1975, 48.6
percent of all university graduates and 45. 1 percent of graduates of vocational schools in Poland were women.
[b]Data not available.

ported a 30 percent increase in the number of women chemists between 1948
and 1975.[8]

Women do, of course, enter the more esoteric fields, and when they do they
are admired much as similar professional women are in the West. In the
Soviet Union, issues of Soviet Life on the role of women in Soviet society,
have listed such noted women scientists as the astronomer Alla Masevich, for
five years vice-chairman of the Astronomy Council of the USSR Academy of
Science,[9] and an outstanding young Uzbek mathematician, Rano Mukhamed-
khanova.[10]

The second trend is also common to women everywhere. While the number
of women graduating from institutions of higher education is higher in the
Communist countries than in the Western world, fewer women than men
complete their higher education. The Bulgarian figures in table 6 give a
representative picture for women alone, while table 7 compares the educational levels of the two sexes in Poland. Despite the educational leveling
process in Poland, men still dominate the upper echelons. A lower level of
education means that women must remain at the middle-professional or
middle-career rung while men continue on.

Finally, women tend to be educated for those professions which do not as a

Table 3—Women Enrolled in Universities, Secondary Schools, and Specialized Schools as Percentage of Total Enrollment, 1969/1970

School	USSR	Bulgaria	Hungary
University Education	48	36.2	47.0
Industry (construction)	37	25.4	—[a]
Transport (communications)	—	—	19.6
Agriculture	29	30.0	19.7
Economics and law	60	50.7	53.2
Public health, physical culture, and sports	55	50.1	52.7
Education, art, and cinema	66	62.2	66.2
Secondary Education	54	53.8	50.0
Industry (construction)	54	28.1	29.0
Transport (communications)	41	—	—
Agriculture	37	36.8	21.0
Economics and law	83	70.8	91.0
Public health, physical culture, and sports	87	—	—
Education, art, and cinema	81	72.2	88.9

Sources: "Zhenshchiny v SSSR: Statisticheskie materialy," *Vestnik statistiki,* no. 1 (1974), p. 9; Maria Dinkova, *The Social Progress of Bulgarian Women* (Sofia: Sofia Press, 1972), p. 19; and *A nökröl* (Budapest: Kossuth könyvkiadó, 1974), pp. 18–19.

[a]— = data not available.

Table 4—Female Graduates of University and Vocational Schools by Field of Study: Poland, 1974

Field of Study	Female Graduates as % of Total Graduates
University	48.1
Humanities, mathematics, natural sciences, and pedagogy	71.0
Medicine	67.5
Economics, law, and administration	55.1
Agriculture	43.6
Other	43.0
Technology	21.3
Vocational Schools	45.1
Health service	96.0
Economics and administration	91.5
Pedagogy	75.3
Agriculture and forestry	64.5
Other	60.7
Technology	27.9

Source: Women in Poland (Warsaw Central Statistical Office, 1975), p. 9.

**Table 5—Female Graduates Secondary and Higher-Level Schools
by Type of School: Yugoslavia, 1973/1974**

Type of School	Female Graduates as % of Total Graduates
Secondary	43.4
Teacher-training and art	65.6
General	54.8
Technical and vocational	53.6
Skilled workers and vocational training	32.3
Other	32.2
High	39.2
Medical	54.4
Natural science and Mathematics	51.2
Social work	46.2
Agriculture and forestry	22.0
Technical	19.7
Higher	46.9
Medical	83.7
Social work	68.8
Pedagogy	65.0
Administration and economics	44.8
Technical	15.1
Agricultural	10.6
Other	5.7

Source: Ibrahim Latitić, ed., *Women in the Economy and Society of the
SFR of Yugoslavia* (Belgrade: Federal Institute for Statistics, 1975), p. 15.

rule provide access to political power. Political-elite recruitment patterns for
the Soviet Union and Eastern Europe indicate that doctors and teachers are not
expected to become political leaders in Communist countries (see chapter 5),
but that a political future is more likely for engineers. Table 8 shows the
proportion of women enrolled in all types of engineering in the Communist
countries in 1970.

Clearly, if engineers tend to become enterprise administrators and top leaders in the Party and government, and women do not go into the engineering
fields, the chances for women reaching these positions are limited because of
education. Perhaps most significant in the data of table 8 is that female
representation in engineering does not appear to be based on any level of
economic devleopment. Czechoslovakia, which has one of the most highly
developed economies, has the lowest number of women engineers; Poland,
which has a less developed economy than Czechoslovakia, runs second. The
three countries with the most backward economies that embarked on the road to
socialism—the USSR, Bulgaria, and Romania—show the highest percentage
of women engineering students. One possible explanation for this discrepancy
is that job differentiation by sex was less marked in the pre-Communist

Table 6—Distribution of Women by Level of Education and Type of Work: Bulgaria, 1969

Level of Education	Average (%)	Blue-Collar Workers (%)	White-Collar Workers (%)	Farm Workers (%)
Higher	5.7	0.2	17.7	0.6
Secondary specialized	15.3	6.9	38.3	1.6
Secondary general	14.6	11.7	28.5	2.3
Professional-technical	4.1	7.8	1.3	0.9
Basic (before gymnasium)	32.0	47.7	3.6	38.6
Elementary	22.8	20.6	0.6	42.6
No schooling	5.1	5.1	10.0	13.4

Sources: Violeta Samardshieva, "Naucho-technicheskata revoliutsiia a efektivnoto izpolzvane truda na zhenata," in Zhenata-maika, truzhenichka, obshchestvenichka, ed. Atanas Liutov et al. (Sofia: Partizdat, 1974), p. 61.

"bourgeois" society of the less developed nations; so women went more willingly into this profession after the Communists took power.

FEMINIZATION OF JOB CATEGORIES

If education has impeded women in their advance to the high-status decision-making jobs, the feminization of job categories has been equally responsible. This phenomenon has been noted by Dodge, myself, and East

Table 7—Comparison of Educational Achievements of Male and Female Employees in Poland, 1956 and 1973

Level of Education	Sex	1956	1973
University	M	4.0	6.2
	F	3.2	5.3
Secondary vocational	M	5.0	12.0
	F	10.8	20.1
General secondary	M	3.3	2.9
	F	6.5	8.9
Primary vocational	M	9.9	22.2
	F	4.7	14.6
Primary	M	39.8	44.1
	F	42.8	38.8
No schooling	M	38.0	13.5
	F	32.0	12.3
Total	M	100.0	100.0
	F	100.0	100.0

Source: The Working Woman in People's Poland (Warsaw: Ministry of Labour, Wages, and Social Affairs, 1975), p. 8.

Table 8—Women Enrolled in Engineering Institutes in Selected
Communist Countries, 1970

Country	% of Total Enrollment
Romania	43.2
USSR	39.0
Bulgaria	27.1
Yugoslavia	19.7
Hungary	19.6
Poland	16.0
Czechoslovakia	15.0
GDR	—[a]

Source: "Zhenshchiny v SSSR: Statisticheskie materialy," Vestnik
statistiki, no. 1 (1974), p. 9; Atanas Liutov, ed., Zhenata-maika, trushe-
nichka, obshchestvenichka (Sofia: Partizdat, 1974), p. 61; Czechoslovak
Socialist Republic, Federal Statistical Office, Statistická ročenka ČSSR,
1969 (Prague: SNTL-ALFA, 1969), p. 484; Statisztikai évkönyv, 1973
(Budapest: Központi Statisztikai hivatal, 1973), p. 460; Women in Poland
(Warsaw: Central Statistical Office, 1975), p. 9; Romania 26, no. 4 (1974):
13; Ibrahim Latitić, ed., Women in the Economy and Society of the SFR
Yugoslavia (Belgrade: Federal Institute for Statistics, 1975), p. 15.
[a]Data not available.

European sociologists,[11] and deserves only statistical recording here. Once
again, the process runs across all the communist countries, as seen in
figure 3.[12]

The most striking feature of the data is the high proportion of women
engaged in agriculture. Women predominate on the farms in every country of
Eastern Europe and the Soviet Union. In Romania, 3 out of 4 women work in
the fields, while less than 1 out of 10 are employed in industry. In Bulgaria
and Yugoslavia, half of all working women are in agriculture. The feminization of agriculture has been one of the central concerns of the East European
regimes, especially in Czechoslovakia, Poland, and Romania. Dr. Mattei of
Romania's Institute of Sociology asserts that the failure of women to become
urbanized as rapidly as men is a key factor hampering their progress. He
stresses the point that while the number of individuals working in agriculture
has decreased since 1960, the percentage of women in that number has increased from 53 to 59 percent. In Poland, the proportion decreased slightly
from approximately 55 percent in 1960 to 53.5 percent in 1974, while the
Hungarian figure has increased by 3 percent in the same time span. The
problem, in Dr. Mattei's view, is twofold. On the one hand, men leave the
farm to seek more lucrative jobs in the cities and leave the women behind to
manage the land. Certain direct benefits accrue to women from this situation,
as they are forced to take part in the administration of the farm. Polish
estimates in 1975 indicated that just under half of the 3.4 million individual

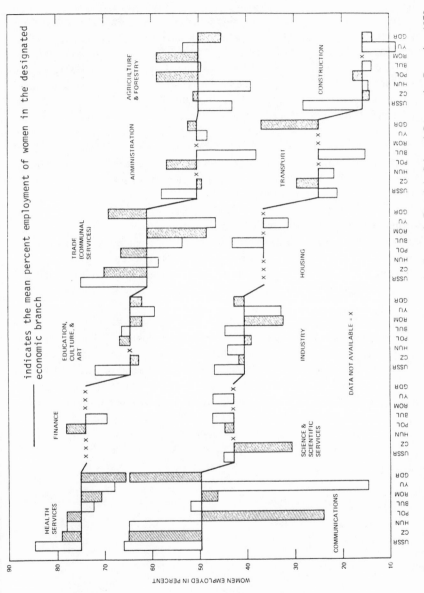

FIGURE 3. Employment of Women as Percentage of Total Employment by Economic Branch in Selected Communist Countries, 1970

farms in Poland were run by women.[13] By contrast, women represent only 5.3 percent of the membership of the agricultural cooperative councils in Yugoslavia.[14]

The negative side of the situation, however, finds women employed in agriculture by and large at the lowest educational level. They are thus left on the farm to do mainly the heavy manual work. The exception is Poland. As the statistics on education indicate, specialized agricultural training seems popular among Polish women. The paucity of child care facilities means that available free time must be given to the care of children. The Communist governments are well aware of the need for social services in the rural areas. Poland in particular has stressed the need for assisting peasant women in child care. The number of child care centers in rural areas in Poland grew from 14,000 in 1970 to 24,000 in 1974, or roughly 74 percent.[15] Given the number of individual farms, each of which contains a family, such figures serve to indicate how much more needs to be done.

As a result of the dual burden of heavy farm work and childrearing, farm women have no time to learn a skill or to continue their education. The men tend to return from the cities as the agronomists and machinists, reducing the woman's status to that of a lower-class farm laborer. The degree to which women do manual labor is particularly evident in the Soviet Union, where, as Dodge's research indicates, peasant women tend to take care of livestock, the chickens, and intensive farming.[16]

A clearer picture of what the absence of technical skills can mean to women is provided by the Bulgarian example outlined in table 9. While almost 55 percent of the men are operating machinery that requires special skill, 63 percent of the women are concentrated at the lower scale of machine use. It might be argued that in countries of low economic development, such as Bulgaria and Romania, the concentration of women in manual and low-skilled

Table 9—Types of Equipment Operated by Men and Women in Bulgaria, 1969

Type of Equipment	Men (%)	Women (%)
Hand tools	27.17	15.62
Machines operated by hand	3.50	17.40
Nonspecialized equipment	14.22	31.24
Industrial machinery	38.93	32.07
Instruments for assembling	15.41	3.14
Apparati for scientific research and computers	0.49	0.31
Unknown	0.28	0.21

Source: Atanas Liutov et al., eds., Zhenata-maika, truzhenichka, obshchestvenichka (Sofia: Partizdat, 1974), p. 112.

jobs is the result of the former "bourgeois" educational bias against them. This argument cannot be applied to the Soviet Union. The 1970 ratio of men to women in the total population (51 percent), suggests that the *decrease* in female representation in higher education from 58 percent in 1960 to the present 49 percent[17] results from regime design. The high toll taken by World War II on the male population created an imbalance in the educational system which the regime apparently corrected at the expense of women. Competition for the available places was evident weighted in favor of men, to improve the ratio of men to women. The press has given us some evidence that this sort of discrimination continues to exist.[18] *Izvestia* has claimed that since 1939 the number of women with a higher education per 1,000 female population has increased seven times (from 5 to 35), as against an increase of 4 times (11 to 48) for men.[19] Given the initial female educational lag plus the war years and war deaths, one wonders why the increase has not been more and why still proportionately more men are better educated.

The feminization of job categories takes place not only according to economic branch but within the sectors of industry. Table 10 provides representative data for Bulgaria. Women still tend to be concentrated in those industries which reflect the traditional female occupations: the textile industry, clothing, leather and shoemaking, and the chemical and food processing industries. They are underrepresented in such sectors as electroengineering, heating, mining, and metallurgy. In Bulgaria, for example, 87 percent of those employed in electroenergy are men, while 85 percent of those employed un the clothing industry are women. In Yugoslavia, women constitute 69.2 percent of all the spinners, weavers, and knitters; 78.7 percent of the building caretakers, cleaners, and related workers; but only 8.8 percent of the administrative and managerial workers.[20]

The division into masculine and feminine categories in industry does not appear to be accidental. On the basis of the data in table 9 it seems a reasonable hypothesis that men dominate those sectors of industry where technology is more in evidence and women dominate the less technologically oriented fields.

The same trend is evident among professions. In Poland, for example, women represent 7 percent of all mining engineers but 37 percent of all agricultural engineers.[21] In medicine, in Poland, women constitute 50.2 percent of the physicians and 83.1 percent of the pharmacists,[22] a pattern comparable to the Hungarian case cited earlier. In Yugoslavia, 23 percent of all gynecologists are women, while 34.5 percent of the general practitioners are women.[23] In Bulgaria, 41.7 percent of all doctors are women, but nurses are all female.[24] In teaching, the pattern is even more obvious. In Poland, 98.7 percent of the teachers in nursery school are women, but only 33.1 percent of university professors are women.[25]

The pattern of sex stereotyping by job is not unique to the Communist

Table 10—Employment of Women by Industrial Branch in Bulgaria, 1970

Industrial Branch	%
Electroenergy	13.0
Fuel	20.2
Heavy metallurgy	26.8
Light metallurgy	16.7
Machine production	29.9
Chemical and rubber	42.5
Construction materials	28.8
Wood-working	25.4
Cellulose and paper	48.1
Glass, porcelain, and earthenware	45.6
Textiles	78.7
Clothing	85.2
Leather and shoe-making	62.0
Publishing	60.8
Food-processing	55.5
Other	57.3

Source: Nikolina Ilieva, Trifon Trifaniv, and Nikolina Tsaneva, *Izpolzvane na zhenskite trudovi resursi v NRB* (Sofia: Partizdat, 1973), p. 187.

countries. All claims to the contrary, they are repeating the identical experience of the "bourgeois" nations. It is unfortunate that no recent statistics are available from the People's Republic of China. A government survey of September 1955 gave the following data regarding the employment of women in China: 21.5 percent of all educational and cultural workers, 18 percent of industrial workers, 16.7 percent of those in banks, and 3.3 percent of those employed in industry were women. Thirty percent of all members of handicraft cooperatives and approximately 31 percent of those working in agriculture were female.[26] Barry Richman has estimated that in 1955, 25 percent of the workers and employees in China's major cities were women, basing this figure on a survey of 35 urban enterprises, while Janet Salaff prefers a slightly lower estimate of 24 percent.[27] By contrast, female industrial workers comprised half of the employees in 28 cities in the 1930s.[28] The discrepancy may be attributed to several factors: (1) the educational lag; (2) the fact that total industrial employment has dramatically increased since 1949, but women are not being hired to fill the new jobs; and (3) the drop in female industrial employment in the late 1950s and 1960s caused by a decline in investment in industry. The third factor is the official explanation, but the second seems to me equally plausible. During the Chinese Civil War and immediately after the Communist takeover, women were urged to move into "productive work." But the First Five-Year Plan concentrated on expansion in heavy industry, where the employment of women was considered unsuitable. Hence, men were hired to fill the jobs.

The situation in China appears to have changed somewhat since the Cultural Revolution. Women are once more being urged into productive work, and a campaign appears to be under way to mobilize women even for heavy labor. The official propaganda speaks of women building railroads, working on high-voltage poles, and of women in the Production and Construction Troops.[29] Yet the Committee of Concerned Asian Scholars in its recent visit noted that "woman's place" was very much in evidence in the Chinese economy and reported that individuals with whom they talked seemed to think the situation "natural." As might be anticipated, the committee observed a concentration of women in the textile industry, the service industries, and in preschool and elementary education.[30] Technically, all jobs may be open to women without exception, but in practice they are not. Indeed, Salaff estimates that the proportion of women now working in industry as compared to the 1950s is probably no higher, due to the overall rate of increase in nonagricultural employment and the shortage of labor in the countryside.[31] If the trend continues, we may anticipate a "feminized" agriculture in China as in Eastern Europe and the Soviet Union.

Sex stereotyping by job has had several negative effects on the sociopolitical status of women in the Communist countries. The first has been lower social status. Manual work is not as important as mechanized work. An agricultural worker is not considered to be doing as valuable a job as the industrial worker. A position as teacher in a nursery school is not as prestigious as a university post, nor is a textile worker considered as highly as a chemical worker. The second consequence relates particularly to the feminization of agriculture. Schools and higher education are not as accessible in rural areas as in cities. Hence, the concentration of women in the countryside deprives them of the opportunity to learn those skills necessary to raise their status. The third consequence is low political status, for women are deprived of access to political decision-making as well. In the Communist countries, as elsewhere, doctors and teachers are not generally candidates for political office. Also, in Communist countries collective or individual farmers are not as a rule politically active. As has been pointed out, engineers and individuals with technical or managerial experience tend to rise to high political levels, and women are poorly represented in these categories.

A fourth consequence of the feminization of jobs is in a lower wage scale for women. The Soviet sociologists I interviewed told me that a doctor beginning medical practice in the Soviet Union receives two-thirds of the salary of a skilled worker, while the pay of a beginning engineer equals that of a skilled worker. Moreover, given opportunities for career advancement, an engineer can expect his salary to increase at least 50 percent over that of a skilled worker. While not as severe as in the United States, the discrepancy in wages and salaries between the sexes has become sufficiently marked so that, except for the Soviet Union, every Communist country has evinced concern. Visitors to the People's Republic of China in 1976 were frankly told that wage discrimination had to be corrected. A Chinese agricultural worker is paid by the piece. If a woman agricultural worker takes time off to take care of her family, she receives no earnings. Domestic work thus automatically lowers her wages. In addition, visitors were told that women are paid less than men, because they are not as skilled.

Figure 4 presents eloquent testimony of wage differentiation between the sexes in Czechoslovakia and Bulgaria.[32] Equally significant are the data in table 11, which show that the average Czechoslovak woman's share in the family income is *less than half* that of her husband.

The reason for the wage discrepancy is obvious. Although no socialist country "discriminates" against women by paying them a lower salary for the same job in the same profession or industrial sector than a man in an identical position, there is, of course, wage differentiation according to industrial branch and level of expertise or skill. The large number of women at the lower end of the wage scale is indicative of their presence in unskilled and semiskilled, paraprofessional occupations. It is also indicative of their dominance of those industrial branches which are not considered as "socially important" as the higher-salaried sectors. (And in many cases the higher-salaried sectors may demand more training or skill with machines and greater danger or risk in doing the job.) One Bulgarian sociologist told me during the course of an interview that the state had not meant to discriminate against women as far as wages are concerned, but had thought mining was a more important industry than textiles and clothing. Now it was taking steps to rectify the inequality.

The sociologist's solution to equalize wages in all the sectors is highly

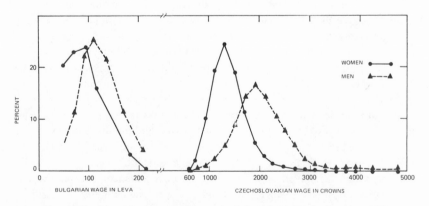

FIGURE 4. Wages Earned by Men and Women in Bulgaria and Czechoslovakia, 1969

Table 11—Income Brought into the Home by Men and Women in Czechoslovakia, 1972

Source of Income	Blue-Collar Worker (%)	White-Collar Worker (%)	Cooperative Farmer (%)
Head of family	49.8	47.7	40.5
Wife	18.1	19.9	14.1
Husband and wife's income as percentage of total family income	67.9	67.6	54.6

Source: Czechoslovak Statistical Abstract, 1972 (Prague: Orbis, 1972), p. 43.

problematic. It was precisely the too equalitarian wage structure that helped precipitate the economic crisis of the 1960s in Czechoslovakia. A more reasonable solution to the problem may lie in opening the "masculine" careers and industrial branches to women and giving them the appropriate training. The difficulty, however, is twofold. First, as will be shown later, the Communist regimes have definite ideas of what constitutes appropriate women's work. These ideas have been institutionalized as laws which forbid a woman employment in high-risk jobs or jobs that might endanger her health. The high-risk jobs which demand certain types of heavy physical labor are defined by law as men's jobs. It could be argued, however, that if old women can be employed in the winter to shovel snow off the sidewalks in Moscow, or to dig ditches in road construction, at least physically they are equally capable of running mining equipment. Similarly, if they can do manual labor on the collective farms, they also should be able to run the machines and tractors. In some countries where women are permitted by law to drive tractors, for instance the Soviet Union, official attempts have been made to encourage farm women to master the mechanized equipment. The attempt has run into male resentment of women's encroachment on their preserve.[33]

The data presented here leave no doubt that women play an inferior economic role in the Communist countries, and that this role is closely allied to their traditional roles in the home. In this connection, a strong case can be made[34] that the inferior position in the working world tends to reinforce a woman's sense of subordination, especially since she is *not* an equal contributor to the family income, but on the contrary is very much a junior partner (see table 11). My discussions with women in Communist countries support Mandel's contention that, regarding their employment, women do not feel themselves inferior.[35] This finding in itself is significant. It suggests that the massive entrance of women into the labor force may be a nonproductive or even counterproductive strategy for female equality, if the economy accepts them only in those areas which are the industrialized counterparts of their traditional roles and pays them accordingly. The European Communist experience underscores the seemingly universal tendency of modernization to perpetuate and enhance sex differentiation by institutionalizing it in the complex hierarchical modern industrial system.

Second, the Communist experience suggests that unless leadership commits itself to changing the trend toward sex differentiation in the economy, the trend tends to be self-reinforcing. There is little question that in the 1920s and 1930s in the Soviet Union, industrialization was the first priority and women were employed where their skills could be used. Their real gains in the skilled labor force did not come about until World War II, when women had to replace men in skilled jobs.[36] Likewise, today, with increased automation and the replacement of the blue-collar by the white-collar worker, the Communist countries' chronic labor shortage demands that women receive adequate technical training. But unless the regimes firmly decide to eliminate sex differentiation through the entrance of women into the "masculine" fields and the entrance of men into the "feminized" areas, the movement of women into the skilled white-collar labor force will have the same result: women will remain subordinate.

In conclusion, it would seem that as long as economic development remains the first priority of the Communist countries, little change in patterns of female employment will occur. Sex differentiation will become increasingly institutionalized. The one country where the pattern may be different is China. Will the new Chinese leaders attempt to find a way to accommodate a radical employment policy by revolutionizing roles for both men and women with rapid economic development? So far, no Communist country, like no Western country, has ever tried.

RECRUITMENT OF WOMEN INTO ADMINISTRATIVE AND HIGH-LEVEL SPECIALTY CAREERS

PROMOTION OF WOMEN INTO THE ADMINISTRATIVE STRUCTURE

The tendency for female participation to decrease progressively the further up one goes on the hierarchical ladder has been well-documented by Dodge and others as regards the Soviet Union. In fact, the tendency prevails in all the Communist countries, as tables 12 and 13 and figure 5[37] attest.

Figure 5 is drawn from a Yugoslav survey entitled *The Influence of Women's Employment on Family Characteristics and Functioning*. Undertaken between 1969 and 1972 by the Institute for Social Research, Zagreb, it received partial support from the United States Department of Health, Education, and Welfare. The aim of the survey was to investigate the influence of

Table 12—Occupational Status of Women in Hungary in 1971 as a
Function of the Total Number of Women Employed

Occupational Status	%
Leading personnel, intelligentsia	6.4
Middle-level professional personnel	27.6
Administrative employees	26.3
Skilled workers	10.3
Semiskilled workers	27.3
Unskilled workers	27.3
Agricultural and manual workers	16.0

Source: Komlós Pálné., ed., A nök a statisztika tükrében (Budapest:
Hungarian Woman's National Council, Kossuth könyvkiadó, 1974), p. 24.

women's employment on family life in Yugoslavia. The sample size was
1,544 families that were selected according to two criteria: (1) the wife was
employed in one of the fifteen occupations listed in the figure; and (2) she
lived in one of the 337 cities within 20 defined demographic regions of
Yugoslavia.

The ratio of male to female administrators is 4:1 in Hungary, 2:1 in Poland,
and 5:1 in Yugoslavia. Even where administrative and clerical workers have
been listed together, as in Bulgaria and Romania, men predominate. In fact,
the Polish example would seem to be unique. The higher Hungarian figure for
management personnel in table 12 may be explained by the fact that the figure
includes the intelligentsia. Nevertheless, Hungarian women, like their counterparts in the other Communist countries, tend to be located either in the
middle administrative levels or at the lower end of the status scale.

In the Yugoslav example, 102 women of the total 1,544 (6.6 percent)
identified themselves as directors of factories or social organizations, while
figure 5 indicates that around 12 percent of the men, or double the percentage
of women, made this identification. By contrast, national Yugoslav statistics
on female participation in the membership of self-management organs, such
as the workers' councils, or in leading councils of organizations performing
social activities, range from 5.3 percent in the agricultural cooperatives to
64.0 percent in social welfare organizations, with a mean of 31.8 percent.[38]
The higher percentage of women on these boards as compared with the low
percentage of women employed in administration is again explained by the
fact that not all women serving on the boards are administrative workers. A
comparison of the two types of data indicates that women are proportionately
better represented in community councils, especially those relating to "women's
work" such as the self-management organs of primary and secondary schools,
public health, and social welfare; but women infrequently assume the leadership of these councils. It is interesting that the leadership statistic for Yugo-

Table 13—Overview of Economically Active Population by Occupation, Sex and Year in Selected East European Countries

Occupation	Bulgaria (1965)		Hungary (1970)		Poland (1970)		Romania (1966)		Yugoslavia (1971)	
	Male (%)	Female (%)	Male (%)	Female (%)	Male (%)	Female (%)	Male (%)	Female (%)	Male (%)	Female (%)
Professional, technical, and related workers	8.6	8.0	10.2	12.6	7.4	8.7	9.3	9.0	6.4	9.8
Administrative and managerial workers	—a	—	0.9	0.2	1.3	0.6	—a	—	1.5	0.3
Clerical and related workers	8.1	6.8	5.6	17.8	6.8	11.9	3.4	2.8	4.7	8.2
Sales workers	2.5	4.5	2.4	5.1	0.6	3.7	1.9	1.6	3.1	3.2
Service workers	3.0	5.5	2.8	9.9	28.6	9.5	4.6	5.3	4.6	8.0
Agricultural, animal husbandry and forestry workers, fishermen and hunters	30.7	54.0	16.2	20.2	28.3	44.5	41.9	71.8	37.8	52.2
Production related workers, transport equipment operators, and laborers	35.6	17.4	61.8	34.1	47.4	18.1	38.9	9.5	32.2	12.1
Workers not classifiable by occupation	11.6	3.7			5.5	3.1	.04	.03	9.6	6.2
Total[b]	100.0	100.0	100.0	100.0	100.0	100.0	100.0	100.0	100.0	100.0

Source: United Nations, *Department of Economic and Social Affairs, Statistical Office, Statistical Yearbook, 1973,* pp. 347–51; statistics were not given for Albania, Czechoslovakia, East Germany, or the USSR.
[a]In Bulgaria and Romania, administrative, managerial, clerical, and related workers are all listed together.
[b]The total may not always add up to 100.0 percent due to rounding errors.

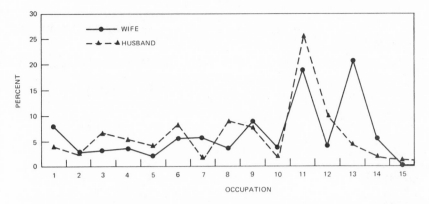

FIGURE 5. Occupations of Wives and Husbands in Yugoslavia, 1973

(1) = primary school teacher, preschool teacher, social worker, secondary school teacher; (2) = university professor, university instructor, artist, cultural worker; (3) = director (manager, administrator) in productive activities; (4) = director (manager, administrator) in nonproductive activities: (5) = university or college educated worker in productive activities; (6) = secondary technically qualified worker in productive activities; (7) = lower vocationally qualified worker in productive activities; (8) = university or college educated worker in nonproductive activities; (9) = secondary technically qualified worker in nonproductive activities; (10) = lower vocationally qualified worker in nonproductive activities; (11) = highly skilled worker and semiski;led worker in productive activities; (12) = highly skilled worker and semiskilled worker in other activities; (13) = unskilled worker in productive activities; (14) = unskilled worker in other activities; (15) = member of representative bodies and elected person in sociopolitical organizations.

The terms "productive activities" and "nonproductive activities" are direct translations of *produktivne djelatnosti* and *neproduktivne djelatnosti*. In the main the former include mining, industry, agriculture, and communications; the latter, education, health, culture, and local and government administration.

Source: Miro A. Mihovilovic, principal investigator, *Reports and Studies: The Influence of Women's Employment on Family Characteristics and Functioning* (Zagreb: Institute for Social Research, University of Zagreb, 1971), p. 67.

slavia is commensurate with the Hungarian figure. It also approaches the 6 percent figure given by the Soviet Union's *Zhenshchiny i deti v SSSR* for 1963 (see tables 14 and 15).

It is difficult to determine the current proportion of women in the top administrative levels of Soviet industry and social services. Included in the 16 percent census figure of 1970 is what the census calls "structural subdivisions," or lower-echelon categories. While the 16 percent figure is a 25 percent increase over the 1959 statistic and, as such, shows improvement, one does not know whether progress has been made at the leadership level or whether there has been a reinforcement of the trend for women to move into the middle administrative ranks. Some indication is provided by comparing the number of female heads of schools. Data for 1970 indicate that 74 percent of the heads of Soviet primary schools, 30 percent of the directors of eight-year schools, and 26 percent of the heads of secondary schools are women. Women constitute 62 and 63 percent, respectively, of the assistant directors in the eight-year and secondary schools.[39] These statistics may be compared to

Table 14—Sample Distribution of Women and Men in the Management Boards and Workers' Councils of Yugoslavia, 1972

	Women		Men	
Type of Management	No.	%	No.	%
Workers' councils	49	3.1	79	4.9
Auxiliary plant	10	0.7	13	1.0
Managerial functions of enterprise management boards	28	1.9	53	3.7
Boards of auxiliary plants	7	0.5	10	0.6
Managers	18	1.2	38	2.7

Source: Miro A. Mihovilovic, principal investigator, *Reports and Studies: The Influence of Women's Employment on Family Characteristics and Functioning* (Zagreb: Institute for Social Research, University of Zagreb, 1971), pp. 218–19.

Yugoslav data for 1972, where women constitute 41.1 percent of the self-management membership at the grade school level, and only 23.2 percent of the self-management membership at the university level.[40] The Soviet data suggest that the USSR probably follows the Yugoslav example in the better representation of women in leadership positions considered "woman's work." The 1963 Soviet statistic of 6 percent represents women in managerial positions and not heads of social organizations.

Dodge has drawn particular attention to the pronounced trend in the Soviet Union for women to remain at the middle administrative levels. This trend has been confirmed by East European sociologists as well,[41] as evidenced by the Yugoslav breakdown of participation of women in the managing boards of enterprises and workers' councils (tables 14 and 15).

Table 15—Sample Distribution of Women and Men in the Self-Management Bodies of Yugoslavia, 1972

	Women		Men	
Self-Management Body	% with function	% without function	% with function	% without function
In the work collective	38.5	61.5	35.6	64.4
In the workers' council	12.0	88.0	21.2	78.9
Management board	5.9	94.1	10.3	89.7
Auxiliary production board	3.4	96.6	5.3	94.7

Source: Miro A. Mihovilovic, principal investigator, *Reports and Studies: The Influence of Women's Employment on Family Characteristics and Functioning* (Zagreb: Institute for Social Research, University of Zagreb, 1971), p. 220.

PROMOTION OF WOMEN WITHIN THE PROFESSIONS

The low representation of women in the highest ranks of the particular professions is the second aspect of the problem of the promotion of women in Communist countries. Figures 6 and 7 give the ratio of men to women teachers employed at all levels of education in Eastern Europe and the USSR.[42] On the average, women outnumber men by twelve to one at the elementary level. The proportion of women to men is almost equal at the secondary level, and men outnumber women on the average by five to one at the university level. Once again, the degree of industrialization does not seem to be a good predictor of improvement in the ratio. Highly industrialized Hungary and Czechoslovakia have the smallest ratio of women to men in higher education, and industrialized Poland has the smallest ratio in elementary education. The pattern is clear. Women predominate in elementary education. High-status university teaching is a male preserve, whether the country be "socialist" or "capitalist," highly developed or developing.

At the present time, 2.1 percent of the members of the Soviet Academy of Science are women.[43] At the far end of the scale, there is only one female Bulgarian academician.[44] Among the East European countries, the Romanian Academy of Sciences has one of the highest proportions of women, counting in 1971 five distinguished Romanian women among its members.[45] One of the

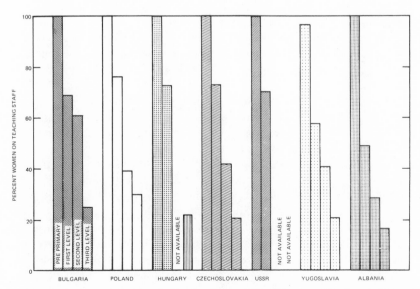

FIGURE 6. Women on Teaching Staff as Percentage of Total Number of Teachers in Selected Communist Countries, 1970

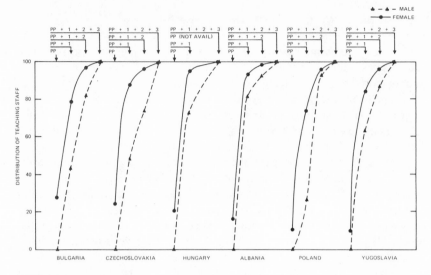

FIGURE 7. Cumulative Distribution of Teaching Staff by Sex in Selected East European Countries (PP) = preprimary level; (1) = elementary school level; (2) = secondary school level; (3) = higher education level.

arguements used by Mandel is that women are not promoted to such prestigious positions because there are so few who qualify. According to 1972 Soviet statistics, 73.9 percent of the candidates of science and 3.7 percent of the doctors of science were women.[46] The 3.7 percent represents a 100 percent increase over 1960 and suggests that there now is a pool of women from which academicians could be recruited. The Polish data presented in table 16 support this contention.

The high percentage of women M.D.'s in the Communist world has received much publicity. Their actual status in the profession, however, can be seen by looking at the percentage of women practicing in the various branches of medicine in Hungary (table 17) and the Soviet Union. Hungarian women rarely become gynecologists or urologists. When I asked sociologists in Budapest why women did not enter these specialties, I was told that surgery and gynecology are considered the most prestigious medical branches in Hungary and therefore are accorded higher male entrance quotas. Apart from their regular salaries, surgeons and gynecologists were seen as demanding and receiving extra honoraria from patients in order to ensure the doctor's closest attention. The material results of this practice were pointed out to me by a young graduate student who gave me a short tour of an area where apparently the "rich doctors" live. Moreover, as Dodge reports, although 70 percent of all Soviet M.D.'s are women (a 5 percent drop from 1960), their representation among administrators is considerably lower (57 percent).[47]

Table 16—Scientific Titles and Degrees Awarded to Women in Poland, 1960-1974

	1960-1969		1970-1974	
Titles and Degrees	No.	% of Total	No.	% of Total
Titles				
Full professor	38	6.1	42	8.6
Associate professor	133	9.3	138	8.9
Degrees				
Habilitated doctor	565	15.6	539	21.3
Doctor	4,554	26.4	3,826	27.3

Source: Women in Poland (Warsaw: Central Statistical Office, 1975), p. 10.

When women in Communist societies do manage to reach the highest administrative ranks, they again tend to be located in industries and professions that have been identified as "woman's work." An unusual and comprehensive Bulgarian survey entitled Woman in the Workworld, in Social and

Table 17—Distribution of Women and Men in the Various Branches of the Medical Profession in Hungary, 1973

Specialty	% Women	% Men	% of Total No. of Doctors
General practice	9.7	11.1	10.6
Surgery	1.5	9.9	6.9
Obstetrics and gynecology	1.0	7.9	5.5
Pediatrics	12.5	4.5	7.3
Lung and pulmonary disease	3.9	3.5	3.6
Skin and venereal disease	2.1	1.4	1.7
Eyes, ears, nose, and throat	1.6	2.1	1.9
Urology	0.1	1.5	1.0
Dentistry and dental surgery	13.9	9.5	11.1
Psychiatry and neurology	3.5	2.6	2.9
Ophthalmology	3.3	1.3	2.0
Roentgenology	2.5	2.7	2.6
Pathology	5.6	2.6	3.7
Geriatrics and aging	0.8	1.3	1.1
Orthopedics	0.3	0.7	0.6
Rheumatology and physiotherapy	1.4	0.8	1.0
Public health and contagious diseases	2.3	2.0	2.1
Industrial medicine	0.6	1.2	1.0
Sports	0.1	0.3	0.2
Other	33.3	33.1	33.2
Total	100.0	100.0	100.0

Source: Statisztikai évkönyv, 1973 (Budapest: Központi Statisztikai hivatal, 1973), p. 428.

Cultural Life, and in the Family was conducted in 1969 among a representative sample of 16,060 women throughout the country. It provides revealing insights into the distribution of women in managerial and supportive jobs in the various sectors of the Bulgarian economy. Only 0.4 percent of the total sample was identified as being employed in managerial functions. Among those in managerial positions, 60.0 percent worked in the education, art, and cultural sector, and were generally heads of schools. By comparison, 11.0 percent were in industry, and 1.8 percent were in transport, communications, or administration. No women in the sample had a managerial job in finance and credit, agriculture, construction, or forestry. The model wage of those employed at the highest level was between 151 and 200 leva a month, [48] a salary that only 3.6 percent of all the women in Bulgaria earned in 1969 but that 11.3 percent of the Bulgarian men received.[49] The evidence is clear that women perform managerial functions in sectors of the economy that pay lower salaries and confer less prestige.

Since 1966 a considerable campaign has been underway in China to promote women particularly to politically important posts. (This campaign will be discussed in chapter 5.) During his trip to China, however, Richman met no women directors of industrial enterprises, although he did meet 7 of 90 assistant directors, and estimates that 15 percent of the department heads were women.[50] Visitors to China in 1975 reported that approximately 10 percent of the members of industrial and agricultural committees were women, but men held the highest positions. Although statistics are lacking, the pattern seems to be developing along the same lines as in the European Communist countries. Criticism in the Chinese press has centered on the fact that only women with the right family connections seem to get promoted while others of merit are by-passed.[51] My own research into the biographies of prominent persons in the People's Republic of China suggests that women tend to rise to high positions in direct correlation with the rise of their husbands.[52] Certainly, the wives of highly positioned Chinese officials tend to be more active in their country's economic and social life than either their Soviet or East European counterparts.

The existence of ''women's'' jobs, together with the failure of women to rise in the administrative and professional ranks, indicates that less competitive positions and therefore less status-valuable positions assimilate women more readily than the more competitive higher-status posts. This chapter has offered several explanations of this phenomenon. Primary among them has been the Communist regime's commitment to economic development. This commitment put women at an initial disadvantage because of the educational time lag, the reason most frequently given to me in interviews for women's present-day inferior economic status in Eastern Europe and the Soviet Union. Data has been presented to suggest that this factor is now no longer operative in the Soviet Union, East Germany, and Czechoslovakia. The priority given industrialization, however, has contributed to a third factor influencing the economic and social status of women in Communist societies: the tension between family and a women's job opportunity, job location, and job choice. This factor will be explored in chapter 3.

3 / The Demographic Variable

The tension experienced by women in Communist societies between the demands of family and work is best discussed under three headings: the demands of work itself; the absence of services planned by the Communist regimes to ease woman's daily work load; and the regimes' concern with demographic trends. Evidence of this tension is to found in the negative correlation between the employability of a married woman and the number of children she has (see table 18). Women with large families, particularly urban women, work in demonstrably fewer numbers outside the home than do women with no or few children.

In an article analyzing the demographic aspects of women in the East European labor force, Jerzy Berent argues that consideration of actual average female employment somewhat weakens this correlation.[1] The number of dependent children has virtually no effect on employment in the rural areas, as indicated by the higher Polish and Hungarian rates. When the figures are broken down by class of worker, the number of children one has appears to have the most significant impact on employment patterns among white-collar workers. In Czechoslovakia, for example, 72.7 percent of all female cooperative farm workers with more than five children were employed in 1961, while only 37.5 percent of all female white-collar workers with the same number of children were employed.[2]

Both the Bulgarian survey mentioned in chapter 2 and Yugoslav research support the finding that industrialization tends to set up a conflict between childbearing and employment, most commonly in urban factory or institutional settings. In the Yugoslav study, there was virtually no correlation between size of family and educational background. But there was substantial correlation between the optimum number of children for employed women and education. The lowest optimum number (1.56) came from skilled and highly skilled workers, or that group which has felt the impact of industrialization most keenly.[3] Women who migrated from rural areas to towns evidenced

Table 18—Female Employment Rates by Age, Marital Status, and Number of Children in Czechoslovakia, East Germany, Hungary, and Poland, 1969

Age of Women	All Women (%)	All Married Women (%)	Childless Women (%)	Women with 5 Children (%)
Czechoslovakia				
17–19	62.9	43.2	83.2	—[a]
25–29	53.7	48.9	84.9	40.4
35–39	63.3	60.3	74.3	40.4
45–49	64.3	59.9	64.7	41.7
55–59	42.5	44.5	41.0	41.0
East Germany				
18–20	84.4	—	92.2	—
25–29	65.4	—	90.8	35.2
35–39	70.5	—	81.0	48.3
45–49	68.1	—	83.0	44.9
55–59	—	—	—	—
Hungary				
15–19	—	37.5	44.2	—
25–29	—	43.5	63.3	18.5
35–39	—	45.6	57.6	30.6
45–49	—	42.0	51.9	31.1
55–59	—	26.4	35.8	19.2
Poland				
15–17	33.3	40.3	43.8	—
25–29	63.8	58.1	76.1	53.3
35–39	68.5	63.9	70.4	66.3
45–49	72.0	65.6	64.3	72.1
55–59	71.4	62.2	60.9	60.0

Source: Jerzy Berent, "Some Demographic Aspects of Female Employment in Eastern Europe and the U.S.S.R.," *International Labor Review,* September 1970, pp. 185–88.
[a]— = data not available.

reaction to stress in the new environment by bearing two children or less, thus reducing their family size to the average two-child family of women who were urban residents from birth.[4]

In the Bulgarian survey, which included both urban and rural women, 46.1 percent of women in the rural sample had three or more children, while only 25.8 percent of women in the urban sample had. Over three times as many women in rural areas had five (7.9 percent) or more children as compared with their urban counterparts (2.4 percent).[5] When the number of children was correlated with the employment of women by job position, the distribution seen in table 19 was obtained. Table 19 shows that while those in high-status

Table 19—Sample Distribution of Number of Children in Family according to Wife's Job Status: Bulgaria, 1969

	No. of Children					
Job Status	0	1	2	3	More than 3	Total
Managers or assistant managers	3.6	31.0	58.2	0.0	7.2	100.0
Managers of sections or chief specialists	5.6	40.6	40.9	1.5	11.4	100.0
Assistant specialists with higher-level or secondary education	7.8	37.9	38.9	1.7	13.7	100.0
Workers in basic position	6.5	26.5	46.3	12.3	8.4	100.0
Workers with secondary education	6.0	28.5	48.7	11.1	5.7	100.0

Source: Adapted from People's Republic of Bulgaria, Ministry of Information and Communications, *Zhenata v stopanskiia, obshchestveniia, kulturniia zhivot a v semestvoto* (Sofia: Central Statistical Office, 1971), p. 51.

and more competitive positions are more likely to have children than any other group, they most probably will have only two. As status is lowered, the likelihood of a woman having more than two children increases. Significantly, women at the mid-specialist level appear most likely to have no children. Apparently, women at the highest status level feel obligated to have some children, but the demands of their position dictate that they severely limit family size. The evidence suggests, then, that job status, in addition to location of work, has an impact on a woman's desire to have children. The more prestigious and demanding the job, the more likely a woman is to restrict family size.

THE DEMANDS OF WORK

The reasons for decreasing family size among urban and high-status working women are discussed by experts in every Communist country. The first reason relates to the job itself. The director of a Bulgarian enterprise in Sofia told me that she generally gets to her office at 8:30 in the morning and seldom returns home before 7:00, and more often after 8:00, in the evening. The mayor of a borough of a large Soviet city said that her job frequently lasted into the evening because of her obligations to meet constituents. In Romania, where Saturdays are full workdays, a woman who holds a high administrative position has only Sunday to spend with her family. Thus, even if she has the advantages of a chauffeur-driven car, a live-in or once-a-week maid, and maybe a mother or mother-in-law to help at home, the demands of work require that she spend most of her time on the job. The manager of a large resort hotel in Dubrovnik, Yugoslavia, left no doubt that a responsible job entailed much sacrifice at home. Part of the sacrifice was the decision to have fewer children.

THE ABSENCE OF SERVICES

The absence of services is the second most frequently cited reason the Communist press gives for the tension experienced by urban working women between home and work. Services here refer to those resulting from government planning: housing, shopping facilities, child care and other communal facilities, and labor-saving devices for the home.

Despite a good deal of educative and propaganda effort by the Communist authorities, women still do most of the childrearing and housekeeping in Eastern Europe and the Soviet Union. The Yugoslav survey undertaken with United States government support in 1969 showed that 69.5 percent of the interviewed wives prepared all the meals and did all the cleaning, washing, shopping, gardening, and feeding of the animals. Only 30.5 percent of the husbands, children, grandparents, or other relatives or friends helped.[6] Interestingly, 88.7 percent of the women divided their time between job and home, while a mere 2.2 percent indicated they worked on the job alone and did no housework.

The Bulgarian survey mentioned in chapter 2 suggests that the urban worker tends to help his wife at home more readily than does his rural counterpart. Responses to the question, "Does your husband help at home?" indeed supported the official Communist contention that the better-educated, urban husband was more likely to participate in housework on a systematic basis. Of the white-collar men, 8.2 percent indicated they helped at home "frequently" as compared with 35.4 percent of the blue-collar men and 24.2 percent of the farm workers. By contrast, 16.3 percent of the white-collar men said they never helped at home, as compared with 19.5 percent of the blue-collar workers and 20.2 percent of the farm workers.[7] Survey data from other Communist countries in Eastern Europe confirm the hypothesis that urbanization and increased education tend to equalize participation in housework.[8]

No woman would argue that housework does not take time or that it does not increase with the number of children. But the amount of time women spend on housework in the Communist countries has been considered by Communist sociologists to be so substantial that experts have named the work done at home "the second shift." A landmark survey on housework was conducted in the Soviet city of Gorky in 1964. The results provide proof of the long hours Soviet women spend on housework as compared with culture and education, or leisure-time activities. More importantly, one child tends to double the time a Soviet woman spends on housework, while three or more children means that a woman spends more time working at home than she does at her paid job (see table 20). One woman on the Moscow subway told me that with three children she went to work "to rest."

In her book *Kobieta pracująca [Working Woman]*, Polish sociologist Magdalena Sokołowska concludes a trenchant chapter confirming the existence of the same "double shift" in Poland with the demand that domestic tasks be restructured. In her view, the married woman with a family performs at least four jobs during the course of her workday: her paid work, housework, childrearing, and work as a wife. Sokołowska's data show that women with young children tend to have a longer illness record and record absenteeism at their place of paid work than do women with either no children or grown children. If the wife is not to become exhausted, she warns, the husband must take on a larger share of the domestic burdens.[9] The data from Bulgaria and Yugoslavia suggest that East European husbands may be actively involved in this restructuring. However, the feminization of agriculture together with the movement of men to jobs in the cities has meant that rural women are as yet only marginal beneficiaries of this process. The relationship of housework and children to work was a question that interested me particularly during my research in the Soviet Union and Eastern Europe. On the one hand, few urban women have a very large home to maintain, and one child would not seem to present large problems as far as care is concerned. However, a closer view of life in these countries indicated that no Communist system is yet in a position to assure the standard of living that would truly alleviate the amount of housework required of women there.

Table 20—Expenditure of Time by Working Women in Gorky Relative to Number of Children in the Family (*hours per week*)

	No. of Children			
Activity	0	1	3	5 or more
Work away from home	49.1	49.0	48.5	47.5
Meal preparation	12.8	13.2	13.8	13.7
Sleep	50.0	47.0	44.3	45.4
Housework	28.1	43.8	48.5	52.4
Leisure-time activities	11.4	5.6	3.9	4.3
Culture and education	16.6	9.4	8.0	4.7
Total	168.0	168.0	168.0	168.0

Source: G. A. Slesarev, "Voprosy organizatsii truda i byta zhenshchin i rasshirennoe vosproizvodstvo naseleniia," *Sotsial 'nye issledovanniia* (Moscow: Izdatel'stvo "Nauka," 1965), p. 159.

HOUSING

The most critical problem is housing. No Communist country has yet solved this problem. Only in the last ten years has the Soviet government begun moving families out of communal apartments into separate (*otdel'nyi*) apartments, but it is doubtful that half of the urban population now lives in these.[10] Communal apartments mean daily queuing up for cooking, washing, and the toilet. They also mean an absence of privacy and living at very close quarters with persons in whom you may have very little interest. The Polish novel *The Eighth Day of the Week* realistically describes the tension and hopelessness produced by such conditions. On a recent study trip to the Soviet Union, Colette Shulman had the opportunity to converse with many Soviet women. Her impression was that many went to work to escape the dreary conditions at home.[11]

East European governments have given housing priority status only within the last decade. Hungarian housing conditions have improved slowly since the fifties. In 1950, 22,596 new apartment houses were constructed; by 1957, the number was 55,434, in 1970, 80,276, and in 1972, 90,194. In 1949–1950, 3.0 percent of all apartments had three rooms or more; by 1971, the percentage had increased to 25.9, and in 1972, it was 34.8. In 1950, 10.5 percent of all apartments had a bath, while in 1970, 31.6 percent had. In 1950, 47.5 percent of all apartments had electricity; by 1970, 92.1 percent had electricity.[12] Table 21 shows that analogous conditions exist in the other East European countries as well. In Czechoslovakia, where World War II wrought the least destruction, 72.3 percent of all apartments in 1960 consisted of a kitchen and two rooms. With averages such as Czechoslovakia's 2.5 rooms per family,[13] conditions are still grim for the typical family.

The failure of the Communist regimes to provide adequate housing lies in two causes. During the period of "intensive economic development" (the intitial phases of Communist economic development, particularly under Stalinism), priority was given to heavy industry—or as the East Europeans express it, "building the material base of communism." Only when this phase was completed in the late 1950s could lesser priorities such as housing be considered. A second cause is the rapid rate of urbanization. According to the 1970 Soviet census, three out of every four persons now living in the city migrated from the countryside. The rate of migration in Belorussia and the Russian Soviet Federated Socialistic Republic (RSFSR) has been as high as 26 per 1,000 population. As a result the Russian Republic's share of rural population dropped from 51 percent in 1960 to 44 percent in 1970.[14] In Romania, the urban population has doubled from 23.4 percent of the total population in 1948 to 42 percent in 1974. Because of restrictions in migration to the capital, Bucharest itself has experienced only a 1.5-fold increase, but the number of towns with populations of 100,000 has increased 2.8-fold. By 1990, official

Table 21—Housing and Conveniences in Eastern Europe and the Soviet Union

	Households			Dwellings			Conveniences			
Country	Year	No.	Average Size (no. of persons)	No.	Average Size (rooms/ dwelling)	Average Density (Persons/ room)	Inside Piped Water (%)	Flush Toilet (%)	Fixed Bath or Shower (%)	Electric Lighting (%)
USSR	1965	50,333,847	3.7	61,658,000	3.0	1.3	—[a]	—	—	—
Albania	1960	279,805	5.8	—	—	—	—	—	—	—
Bulgaria	1965	2,526,635	3.2	2,055,000	3.2	1.2	28.2	11.8	8.7	94.8
Czechoslovakia	1970	4,397,579	3.1	4,284,000	3.1	1.1	75.4	57.6	33.3	99.7
East Germany	1971	6,408,000	2.6	6,068,000	2.7	1.2	82.1	56.6	22.1	100.0
Hungary	1973	3,352,000	3.0	3,346,000	2.8	1.1	44.0	34.1	32.7	94.3
Poland	1970	9,376,000	3.4	8,295,000	2.9	1.4	47.3	32.9	13.9	96.2
Romania	1966	5,954,555	3.2	5,380,299	2.6	1.4	12.3	12.2	9.6	48.6
Yugoslavia	1971	5,375,000	3.8	5,110,000	2.8	1.4	34.0	26.5	—	87.9
USA	1970	62,874,000	3.2	68,679,000	5.1	0.6	97.5	96.0	—	—

Source: United Nations, Department of Economic and Social Affairs, Statistical Office, *Statistical Yearbook, 1974*, pp. 795–96, 804–13.
[a] — = data not available.

estimates set the urban population at 68.7 percent of the total and project the construction of some 300–350 new towns to meet this influx. At such rates of urbanization, it can be expected that the government will have difficulty providing the supportive infrastructure, and housing will necessarily suffer. The Romanian government is well aware of this danger, and the Tenth Congress of the Romanian Communist Party in 1974 put the construction of new housing among its top priorities.[15]

Shopping Facilities

The absence of adequate shopping facilities is the second important factor contributing to the "double shift." In all the Communist countries, shopping is a daily occurrence because refrigerators and freezers are not yet common household appliances. As virtually all the surveys show, the wife is mainly responsible for making the day's food purchases. In the larger cities, getting to and from work can take as much as an hour and a half each way. Because private cars are still a luxury, transportation means the bus, trolley car, or, if the city has one, the subway. At rush hours, these are full to overflowing. In the morning hours, individuals spill out of the public transportation system into offices and factories already nervously exhausted by the press and strain of the ride to work. If a woman has a child, she has to allow enough time to take the child to school or kindergarten before going to work and has to pick him up on the way home in the evening. Only then comes the evening shopping.

East European shopping procedure more or less follows Western habits, and there are supermarkets in the larger cities. However, shopping in the Soviet Union and Bulgaria remains inexplicably complicated. The buyer is forced to stand in one line to select her purchases. She queues up in another line to pay the cashier, from whom she gets a receipt of payment. She then has to stand in a third line to hand the receipt to the salesperson in order to pick up the purchase. Thus, the shopper must stand in at least three lines to make one purchase. Shopping for the evening meal may mean going to three or four stores to buy bread, milk and dairy products, meat, and vegetables. If everyone is shopping at the same hour, the procedure can take a minimum of one hour—and oftentimes more—every evening.

Added to the inherent difficulties of this manner of shopping is the uncertainty of what one may find in the store. It is impossible to go to the store with a shopping list, for many of the desired items may not be available. As one Soviet émigré told me, she tired of her husband always asking her what he should buy when he went to the store. "He would have to buy what was there." Soviet emigrants to Israel have reported that only when they came to that country were they able for the first time to plan a budget for household purchases. In Israel, they found that what was in the stores one week was probably going to be there the next. This is not the case in Eastern Europe and the Soviet Union. Uncertainty of what will be in the stores applies not only to food and drink but also to household items. A woman from Riga told me that right after the 1962 Cuban crisis there was no bread in the stores. No explanation was given. There just was no bread. In Moscow I observed a new shipment of coats arriving in a department store. The line to buy the coats went all the way around the gallery of the store. For fear of missing something that will not be available again, the tendency is for people to form queues. I observed that people would join any line, especially if it looked long. The longer the line, the greater the likelihood that something hard to get was being sold.

The food situation is somewhat better in Eastern Europe, but a wide selection of meats, fruits, and vegetables is not available, and the housewife takes what there is before someone else buys it. In this respect, to cross from a Communist European country into a non-Communist one, even one that is less developed industrially, like Greece, is impressive. In Western Europe, the abundance of food, clothing and items of daily living is striking because of the scarcity in the Communist world.

Émigré women I interviewed cited the inability to budget and plan expenses and menus as a major source of stress in household management. Certainly, time spent on housework, transportation, and shopping was perceived as inordinately long. But the actual hours did not seem to weigh so heavily as the frustration and uncertainty with which they were filled. The psychological factor of the continual struggle to get a meal on the table or keep a house clean is probably as important in the woman's complaint about the "second shift" in the Communist countries as the number of hours the work takes.

Child Care Facilities

A final aspect of the woman's work at home is her primary responsibility, childrearing. The Soviet Union has the widest network of day care, nursery, and kindergarten facilities of all the European Communist countries. By 1972, preschool attendance had increased to almost 10 million youngsters. This increase meant that the system was taking care of approximately 50 percent of the nation's 20.6 million children under the age of five.[16] However, over 78 percent of those attending live in urban areas, which means that children on the collective farm have to be cared for by mothers and grandmothers. Young mothers in the cities told me that they liked the kindergartens but preferred not to use the day care centers, which they thought were overcrowded and not capable of giving sufficient individual attention. They were glad they could rely on their "babushkas" to look after the children while they were at work. (The twenty-odd children I saw in one room in a kindergarten in Tashkent suggested to me that kindergartens also suffer from overcrowding.) In Hungary, Bulgaria, and Romania, the less popular day care centers have enough room for only about 10 percent of the children; on the other hand, kindergartens accomodate from 30 percent of the demand in Bulgaria to 60 percent in Hungary. East Germany has one of the best networks of preschool care. In 1971, its nurseries were able to take care of apporximately 29.6 percent of the demand, while kindergartens took in 73 percent, or three of every four children of preschool age.[17] Once again, however, these institutions are concentrated in the urban centers.[18]

In the Soviet Union, Profs. A. C. Kharchev and S. I. Golod have shown in their study of working women in Leningrad and Kostroma that the main reason women send their children to preschool institutions is that there is no one at home to take care of them.[19] Yugoslav, Bulgarian, and Soviet studies have also revealed that the principal source of child care assistance at home is the husband.[20] Apparently, the "grandmother" is slowly becoming an institution of the past, leaving childrearing entirely to the nuclear couple. During the average week, both husband and wife may share in the care of their children, but when anything unusual occurs, the mother is expected to bear the burden. Preschool institutions understandably lack facilities to keep a child when he becomes ill. One of the parents must leave work to nurse the child. In no country is the husband expected to perform this function.

Moreover, some of the more optimistic survey findings about a husband's participation in child care must be clarified. Dr. Zoya Yankova, of Moscow University's Institute for Applied Social Research, found from her study of 427 women working in Moscow industry between 1965 and 1967 that 65 percent of her sample indicated they were solely responsible for childrearing. When the survey was repeated in 1969–1970, she obtained the same results.[21] All the women I interviewed indicated that the children were primarily their concern. The husband thus tends to become involved in child care only when someone other than the mother is asked to help.

OTHER COMMUNAL FACILITIES

No regime in any Communist country has been in a position to develop communal dry-cleaning, laundry, and eating facilities to the extent that they have been needed, and with the possible exception of China, no regime has succeeded in overcoming the opposition with which these facilities have been met among the female population. The nature of this opposition and the extent of the services are highly relevant to the present discussion.

In their book *Professional Work and the Family* Kharchev and Golod report the findings of their survey of Leningrad and Kostroma regarding the use of dry-cleaning services, laundries, and cafeterias. They conclude that age or number of children has little to do with whether women use the available services, but that education seems to be the most important variable aside from the town itself. I find it difficult to support this conclusion *in toto*. Certainly, the availability of communal services in a town is tremendously important, and Leningrad would be sure to have better distribution than the smaller, more provincial Kostroma. But the most popular services in Kharchev and Golod's survey were the dry-cleaning and laundry facilities. Reasons for not using these services are given in table 22. Clearly, the location of the facilities in relationship to home was an important factor, as was the perceived expense involved. But it is significant that the users of these services in Leningrad, who totaled 81.1 percent of the female respondents, gave poor quality as a major reason for not using them. Only a fraction of the respondents thought it unnecessary to use them. One might conclude, therefore, that if the services were improved and more widely distributed, so as to be more accessible to the home, they would be more highly utilized.

However, when Kharchev and Golod controlled for age as regards food preparation at home, the results were as might be expected. Women under 25 were least likely to eat exclusively at home (58.6 percent), those in the 31–40 age group were most likely to (87.7 percent), and those over 40 were a close second (84.5 percent). The inference is that there is an inverse relationship between age and a positive attitude toward eating out. The older generation here would appear to be resistant to the idea of communal services.

Kharchev and Golod further found that 1 woman in 10 was likely to send

Table 22—Reasons Why Families Do Not Use Communal Services in Leningrad and Kostroma, 1970

Service and Reason	Leningrad (%)	Kostroma (%)
Laundry		
Poor work	13.2	1.2
Period between		
pickup and return too long	13.7	3.0
Too far from home	4.1	18.1
Cafeteria		
Too expensive	35.5	20.4
Poor food; I like to prepare		
the meal myself	29.3	9.9
I don't think it is necessary to		
use these services	1.6	2.0

Source: A. G. Kharchev and S. I. Golod, *Professional' naia rabota zhenshchin i sem'ia* (Leningrad: Izdatel'stvo "Nauka," 1970), p. 85.

her sheets to the laundry, while only 4 in 100 were likely to send the rest of their linen. Women with whom I talked in Eastern Europe and the Soviet Union tended to stress the poor work of the laundry establishments. As far as I could determine, their cost was relatively low. Laundry services in the USSR seem to run about 4 rubles a month, or about the same as having a cleaning woman once a week. With family income for professional couples averaging around 500 rubles a month before taxes, this does not seem exorbitant.[22] The cost of sending out laundry in Bulgaria is approximately the same. My conclusion is that many women choose to do their own laundry at home even when communal services are available. In my interviews, the women stressed the need to have the family wash really clean, and they perceived the communal laundries as unable to meet their high standards. It would appear that ideology has not been successful in replacing the traditional values that equate woman with housewife.

LABOR-SAVING DEVICES IN THE HOME

Given the fact that a great many women still prefer to do the necessary housecleaning, sewing, and laundry at home, what help do they have in the way of mechanical devices? According to Soviet ideologue Vladimir Suslov, as of the 1970 census every second Soviet family had a television set and a washing machine, and every third family had a refrigerator.[23] Kharchev and Golad's figures from their Leningrad and Kostroma survey tell a somewhat different story. As might be expected, the women from the larger city, Leningrad, ranked higher on all mechanical conveniences. The distribution of mechanical devices according to educational level is shown in table 23. Because the salaries of the more educated women are higher, it is not surprising that these women should have more mechanical devices in their homes. In addition, they are probably more adjusted to them than less educated women. Yankova, for example, found that educated women tend to use mechanical devices more and to spend less time on housework.[24]

The discrepancy between Kharchev and Golod's sample and Suslov's statistics may lie in the four-year interval between the survey and the census figures. Still, given the low percentage of Kharchev and Golod's respondents who had refrigerators, it is hard to believe that the average number of owners doubled in 4 years. Suslov does not tell us whether he based his correlation on the number of refrigerators purchased by Soviet families or on the number manufactured. If we accept his figures, it means that over two-thirds of all Soviet families in 1970 were forced to do daily shopping. Moreover, since laundries are located mainly in the large cities, most families were also forced to do their laundry by hand.

In Eastern Europe, the situation is somewhat better. Hungary has steadily

Table 23—Distribution of Labor-saving Devices in Working Woman's
Home by Level of Education: Leningrad and Kostroma, 1966
Kostroma, 1966

		Level of Education	
		---	---
Labor-saving Device	% of Homes	Elementary (%)	Higher (%)
Washing machine	77.0	76.0	78.0
Sewing machine	38.0	37.0	39.0
Vacuum cleaner	30.0	22.0	41.0
Refrigerator	16.0	12.0	22.0
Floor polisher	7.0	6.0	13.0

Source: A. G. Kharchev and S. I. Golod, *Professional'naia rabota zhenshchin i sem'ia* (Leningrad: Izdatel'stvo "Nauka," 1971), p. 79.

increased the number of labor-saving devices per 100 households since 1960. In 1972, official figures showed that there were only 67 washing machines, 46 refrigerators, and 37 vacuum cleaners per 100 households, as compared with 15 washing machines, 1 refrigerator, and 4 vacuum cleaners in 1960.[25] In Bulgaria, 50 percent of all households had washing machines and almost 60 percent had refrigerators in 1975, while in Czechoslovakia the respective figures were 83 and 75 percent; in Poland, 65 and 75 percent; and in the GDR, 70 and 78 percent.[26] In Yugoslavia in 1973, 65 percent of all households had gas or electric stoves, 30 percent had vacuum cleaners, and 35 percent had washing machines.[27]

However, housework still takes a long time. The Bulgarian survey described in table 24 questioned women on the amount of time they spent on household tasks each day. The average was 5 hours and 19 minutes. Men spent half as much time on work in the home.

Magdalena Sokołowska's Polish study estimated 6 hours per day as a woman's minimum daily average for housework in Poland, with 9 hours per day as a maximum when there were children from 14 to 18 years of age in the family.[28]

There is no question that improved living conditions and an increase in household appliances will decrease the amount of time needed for home maintenance. However, as Betty Friedan long ago pointed out in *The Feminine Mystique,* merely having a washing machine or a vacuum cleaner does not necessarily cut down on housekeeping. The machines may generate a compulsion in women to clean more now that their tools are more efficient. The European Communist regimes' efforts to alleviate housework by providing the mechanical conveniences are in this sense counterproductive to a goal of liberating women from housework. Conveniences may in fact put women back in the home. The original Bolshevik argument (as well as that of the female radicals in this country) was that the only way to bring family maintenance into the industrial age was the development of a comprehensive network of communal services. So far this is an area which Communist governments have yet to make a priority.

THE NEGATIVE DEMOGRAPHIC TREND

The regimes' inability to provide a satisfactory quality of life for their people lies at the heart of the twin problems of woman's low economic status and the adverse demographic trends in the European Communist countries. Under communism, Eastern Europe and the Soviet Union have experienced declining population growth rates which the authorities neither expected nor planned.

Between 1963 and 1970, the East German population experienced an annual growth rate of just 0.1 percent. During the same period, Czechoslavakia's population grew 0.5 percent annually, while that of Romania, Yugoslavia, and the USSR increased by 1.1 percent. The highest growth rate was that of little industrialized Albania, 2.2 percent (see table 25). In many of the Communist countries, the birth rate dropped precipitously in the 1950s with the legalization of abortion (Figure 8).[29] In the late sixties Hungary and Romania experienced a negative population growth. The situation was perceived to be so critical by the East German and Romanian regimes that abortion was again outlawed in the late sixties. This step had no immediate effect on the East German birth rate, but the Romanian birth rate forged ahead for two years, only to drop off again in 1969.

The percentage of population change for the period 1970–1974 went down for China and for every European Communist country except the ČSSR,

Table 24—Average Number of Hours Spent on Housework by Women and Men in Bulgaria, 1967

Housework	Women	Men
Total number of hours per day	5 hr., 19 min.	2 hr., 38 min.
Food preparation	1 hr., 33 min.	8 min.
Washing and ironing	40 min.	3 min.
Cleaning the house	1 hr., 24 min.	56 min.
Shopping	41 min.	28 min.
Care of animals or personal garden	30 min.	53 min.
Play with children	31 min.	10 min.

Source: Atanus Liutov et al., eds. Zhenata-maika, truzhenichka, obshchestvenichka (Sofia: Partizdat, 1974), p. 283.

Table 25—Population Growth in the European Communist Countries and China, 1963-1975

	Year			Annual Growth Rate	
Country	1963 (millions)	1970 (millions)	1975 (millions)	1963-1970 (%)	1970-1974 (%)
USSR	225,063	242,768	252,064	1.1	0.9
(Asian section)	55,163	59,685	—ª	1.7	—
People's Republic of China	590,195	771,840	824,961	—	1.7
Czechoslovakia	13,952	14,467	14,738	0.5	0.6
East Germany	16,093	17,058	16,925	0.1	-0.2
Poland	30,691	32,473	33,846	0.8	0.9
Hungary	10,068	10,309	10,509	0.3	0.3
Romania	18,813	20,253	21,029	1.1	0.9
Bulgaria	8,078	8,490	8,647	0.7	0.6
Yugoslavia	19,029	20,371	21,153	1.1	0.9
Albania	1,762	2,168	2,416	2.2	3.1

Source: United Nations, Department of Economic and Social Affairs, Statistical Office, Statistical Yearbook, 1971, 1975; United States, Department of Commerce, Bureau of Census, The 1977 U.S. Fact Book (New York: Grosset & Dunlop, 1977), pp. 867-69; William F. Robinson, "Selected Demographic Data on Eastern Europe," RFE Background Report no. 225, 3 November 1976, Radio Free Europe Research Department, Munich, West Germany (mimeographed).
ª— = data not available.

Poland, and Albania. East Germany averaged a negative growth, despite a slightly improved crude birth rate (10.1 per thousand in 1974), partly because of a relatively high death rate as compared to birth rate, and partly because of outward migration. The most encouraging statistic in table 25 is the 1970-1974 average Chinese growth rate of 1.7 percent. Even with a mean crude birth rate of 33.1 per thousand for that period, the Chinese leadership was evidently able to continue to achieve success in its population limitation program.[30]

A 1968 survey published in Voprosy ekonomiki [Problems of Economics] revealed that in a sample of women in 22 Ukranian factories, only 3 percent of all pregnancies of women who already had one child ended in birth. Women who had two children invariably sought an abortion.[31] A more recent statistic published in the American press indicates that there are more than 10 million abortions a year in the USSR as compared with 4 million births.[32] An article published in the Hungarian periodical Demografia gives a clear picture of what has happened to the Bulgarian birth rate. On the basis of the data, the author concludes that from 1961 to 1974 there was no significant change in birth rate regarding the first and second child as compared to the 1926-1940 period. The significant decrease in the number of births in recent years has been due to the limiting of family size to two children. Thus, while in 1926 the first child accounted for a quarter of the total live births in Bulgaria, in the

1960s the first child represented an average 46 percent of the total live births. By comparison, the ratio of first deliveries to total births in other Communist countries, the United States, and Greece for the same period (1960s) is shown in table 26. The Kaszabov study projects that the current birth rate in Bulgaria is insufficient even to maintain the population at its present level.[33]

Such findings have become a serious concern to the Communist regimes. (The steps they have taken to remedy negative population growth will be discussed in chapter 6.) In the last 10 years, as has been shown, all Communist leaderships have committed themselves to measures designed to improve the quality of life: improved housing, more child care facilities and social services, changes in the period a mother can stay home after childbirth, and studies on the dynamics of family life. Their efforts appear to have been partically successful. While the recent birth rates of Bulgaria and Romania have not equaled the rates recorded in the sixties, the birth rates of Czechoslovakia, Hungary, and Poland have climbed steadily in the 1970s and now stand at 18.4 per thousand in Hungary and Poland, and 19.8 per thousand in Czechoslovakia.[34] The Hungarian leadership in particular has attributed the increase in its population to the expanded program of nursery and child care facilities.[35]

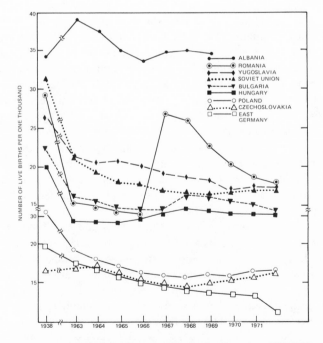

FIGURE 8. Birth Rates in European Communist Countries, 1938–1972

Table 26—Ratio of First Deliveries to Total Number of
Births in European Communist Countries, the USA,
and Greece

Country	Period	Ratio of First Deliveries to Total No. of Births
USSR	1963-1968	35
Ukrainian SSR	1963-1968	46
Czechoslovakia	1961-1970	43
East Germany	1958-1967	40
Poland	1961-1970	37
Hungary	1959-1968	46
Romania	1962-1971	37
Bulgaria	1961-1971	45
Yugoslavia	1961-1970	37
USA	1959-1968	38
Greece	1958-1967	42

Source: Vladimir Szt. Kaszabov, "Bulgaria népessege
születesgyakorisaganak kerdesehez," Demografia (Budapest), no. 2 (1974), p. 177.

A decrease in birth rate as a country industrializes has been a general
pattern of modernization. A birth rate which threatens the maintenance of the
population at a minimum level is a phenomenon which only the Communist
countries have experienced, and reflects a policy aimed at the total employment of the adult female population. Do the data presented on the Communist
experience demonstrate an inevitable and unsolvable conflict betwen a woman's childbearing and working roles? My answer is negative. I believe the
data suggest that the Communist regimes' *present* need to ensure a positive
demographic trend conflicts with the economic and social conditions necessary for women to obtain high-status positions. The regimes have indicated
that the optimum number of children is three to a family. Given the existing
child care and living arrangements in the Communist countries, a three-child
family makes it impossible for a woman to spend the time necessary to work
for advancement to the higher echelons of any professional category. Already,
the various leaves accorded women before and after childbirth mean that
women must interrupt their work. And especially at the higher professional
and career levels, lack of association with colleagues and the work place can
mean an irretrievable loss of the necessary information and skills to do one's
job properly.

Certainly the dilemma of home and work is not unique to the Communist
countries, but it is more apparent there because virtually all women work. It is
also more apparent there because it cuts across all the European
Communist countries without exception. The pattern seems to be circular: (1)

the economy needs women in the labor force for the task of modernization and industrial growth; (2) women are employed where their skills can be used; (3) initially these skills were low, and the jobs women got were low in status; (4) as women moved into the white-collar jobs, the demands of home life encouraged them into the middle-echelon, less competitive positions; (5) thus, certain types of manual and industrial white-collar jobs became "feminized", (6) women remain in these categories because of the burden of the "double shift," which reinforces their acceptance of "woman's place" in the economy. Without seeking higher skills and higher education, it is unlikely that women will move into positions of responsibility and decision-making in the working world. So, the economy continues to employ them where their skills can be used: in low- and middle-status occupations.

Dr. Yankova's findings from a 1970 study[36] offer a new direction to the question of home versus work. This survey revealed that there is a measurable relationship between a woman's professional life and her family life. The more educated women spend less time on housework and are more likely to use mechanical conveniences. Yankova stresses that home habits depend not upon salary but upon educational level, implying that educated working women make better homemakers and mothers. Such findings suggest that education may be a key factor in reducing the strain between family and jobs that now exists for women in the Communist system. But one should not underestimate the degree of strain. In the Communist countries, women have to work. The wage structure is such that the family needs the second income. If the family wants to enjoy any of the frills a higher standard of living brings, the wife must add her money to the family budget.

In the Communist countries, because of the demands of the economy and demography, the woman is not free to pursue role options. She cannot choose not to work and she cannot choose not to have children. It is no wonder, then, that she is channeled into work that makes fewer demands upon her and where her identity as a woman is not subject to challenge.

The data on Communist China do not seem to present any exceptions to these general conclusions. The major difference is China's need to decrease fertility rather than increase fertility. This factor argues in favor of the campaign that has been under way since the Cultural Revolution to mobilize women into productive work and higher administrative responsibilities. However, the concentration of women in agriculture and the lack of services in the countryside result in most Chinese women being forced to concentrate on home maintenance and child care at the expense of social and political status.

The structure of priorities presented to the Communist countries of Eastern Europe and the Soviet Union by the need for economic development has historically argued against women getting into high-level decision-making positions. Because of educational lag, the initial phase of Communist industrialization brought women generally into low-status, nonmechanized jobs.

Women's massive entrance into these positions feminized certain industries such as mining and metallurgy. Women's sizable representation in the feminized industries and social services as well as their tendency to locate in middle-level administrative positions, has reinforced traditional concepts of woman's subordinate role. The second (and in today's world more persistent) factor militating against women in high-status jobs is demography. Where negative demographic trends obtain, particularly in the East European countries, the regimes have attempted to channel women into the dual role of work and family. The inability of women so far to combine home and work responsibilities at an equal level of intensity in the Communist countries has been one of the foremost stumbling blocks to finding equal status with their male counterparts in the economic world.

4 / The Ideological-Cultural Environment

The previous chapters support the conclusion that the admission of large numbers of women into industrial society as workers does not produce a change in female status unless change in status is a primary objective. In the case of the Communist countries, economic development and recent demographic trends have taken precedence over other considerations. Women's entrance into the Communist economies has thus been seen to reinforce traditional sex-role differentiation, particularly where falling birth rates obtain. In this chapter, we will examine the survival of pre-Communist culture, as well as the reinterpretation of that culture by the Communist leaderships, in an effort to determine how Communist ideology has challenged traditional sex-role images.

Great care has to be taken in defining what is meant by "woman's traditional role." In essence, what we are talking about are the unwritten rules and myths embedded in family structure that have been passed down from previous generations and modified over time. Perhaps the most pervasive and oldest social myth about women is that of female weakness and female power. Women are most powerful when they are weak, childlike, and submissive. Only in this condition can they dominate their men, as a mother dominates a child.[1] Because of their weakness and helplessness during childbearing and childrearing, they require a special place or sphere in which to perform their child-related functions. They further require special protection from a dominant male, who, if he is powerful enough, encloses them (Islamic, Chinese-Japanese, and Hindu traditions).

In the West, this enclosure evolved into the bourgeois "home." However, only proportionately few women did not work and stayed at home in the nineteenth-century West. The peasant woman was doing her share on the land. The lower-class working woman was moving into industry. It was the middle-upper-class and upper-class woman who became concerned about the suffrage and challenged the myths and unwritten rules of her male-dominated class. Paradoxically, it was also the upper class, including its women, which imposed the myths of "woman's place" upon the rest of society. Thus, what today is seen as woman's place is in fact the product of Western nineteenth-century social myth-making.

If this myth dies hard in twentieth-century America, it is very much alive in Eastern Europe and the Soviet Union. Indeed, the Communist ideologues, particularly in the USSR, appear to have done everything possible to reinforce it. This chapter develops two propositions. First, while the Communist revolution propelled both men and women into new economic and legal frameworks, it barely touched traditional attitudes regarding sex roles. The two exceptions are Soviet Central Asia and China. When women moved into industry they moved into job categories and industrial branches that were extensions of their roles at home. Where they moved into new areas, the men moved out, and the new areas became associated with "woman's place." This development has been consistently endorsed by Communist ideology.

Second, upon their advent of power, the Communists tried to implement a program that had been part of the general European movement for the emancipation of women, but they did so without consideration of the possible consequences. At the beginning, changes in the life styles of both sexes appeared truly radical, but as industrialization advanced, no new program was developed to meet the changing circumstances. Now, despite the admission by virtually all Communist leaderships that women are not as advanced as they should be, the strategies that are offered only reinforce old traditional attitudes about the role of women at home and antifeminism at work.

WOMEN AT HOME: THE PERSISTENCE OF TRADITIONAL ATTITUDES

Three main factors will be considered in our discussion of the persistence of traditional attitudes in Communist societies: (1) the mode of disintegration of the patriarchal kinship system (primarily in Soviet Central Asia and China); (2) the degree to which women have secured equality of status and decision-making in the home; and (3) the impact of divorce and abortion.

DECLINE OF THE PATRIARCHAL FAMILY

The patriarchal kinship family as an ideal type is identified mainly with societies of the Near and Far East, where a rigid hierarchical structure is embodied in the traditional "five relations" of China (ruler-ruled, father-son, husband-wife, elder brother–younger brother, friend-friend).[2] This structure has never existed in the same way in Europe. Where the family had been the basic economic and social unit, the breakup of the cohesive family into the prototype for industrialized society—the loosely associated conjugal family—required large inputs from the leaderships of China and the Soviet Union. One aim of the revolutionary regimes in Soviet Central Asia and China was to shift loyalty from the family to the Communist Party and state, but this shift was not accomplished without resistance.

Central Asia

Soviet attempts to mobilize Central Asian women for the Revolution involved administrative interventions, propaganda, and consciousness-raising measures. The Soviet administrative effort was climaxed by *khudzum,* an "attack" on the institution of female seclusion. The campaign was launched in 1926 and continued into 1927. In its first phase, emphasis and targets were selected to promote models of behavior among the strata of the population considered most likely to accept them. The second phase aimed at engaging the population as a whole. Particularly in its second phase, *khudzum* was oftentimes marked by violent public demonstrations where women publicly took off the veil and men retaliated with uncontrolled barbarity. Statues of the individual women who died during the *khudzum* campaign stand in the public squares of Central Asia today. The Party's recourse to *khudzum* was determined by the need to raze the basic structure of the old social organization and effect a change in attitude whereby the Party, not the home, would set norms of behavior.[3] *Khudzum* and the mobilization of women were seen as instruments to give the Soviets control of Central Asia.

During the twenties, the Communist Party formed the *Zhenotdel,* or Women's Department, in an attempt to utilize persuasion in gaining adherence to the Party's goals. Curiously, the *Zhenotdel* was the only Soviet effort to develop a systematic consciousness-raising strategy. It was also the only effort made by the Bolsheviks to promote the organization of women under the aegis of the Communist Party. Moslem women who were Party delegates were encouraged to join women's clubs, where they discussed their problems and were taught awareness of their inferior situation and cultural backwardness.[4] But the *Zhenotdel* was hampered by interference from Moscow bureaucrats, who feared an upsurge of "bourgeois," non-Party feminism. The Women's Department was abolished in 1929 with the official statement that Moslem women had been emancipated.

In Central Asia, the Soviet leadership's efforts to revolutionize women ran up against traditional attitudes that were not susceptible of rapid change. To stop the assault on the Moslem family, Moslem men started joining the Party in large numbers. Women lost their incentive to rebel because, in the face of male resistance, the regime was unable to fulfill its promises of liberation.

The strength of the old family pattern is still evident in Central Asia today, where large families are considered a sign of a man's virility and a women's fertility, and family solidarity remains intact. As late as the 1960s, the press was reporting that fathers customarily took their daughters out of school at the age of 12 or 13 to marry them off.[5] When I visited the Central Asian city of Fergana, I was struck by the way near relations and relatives seemed to hold certain clusters of jobs. While there can be no question that the family as the primary *economic* and *social* unit has been destroyed by Soviet power, the kinship system seems to retain its hold as a vehicle for the social and political advancement of its members.

China

In China, the restructuring of the family began with the Chinese Revolution of 1912. At first a slow evolutionary process, it accelerated with the Communist drive for power. Firsthand reports of the arrival of the legendary Seventh Route Army in a Chinese village give graphic descriptions of the strategy used to mobilize women for the cause.[6] First, the woman is persuaded of the injustice of the old system. Then, a "struggle" takes place in which husband and wife confront each other in public, with the wife supported by other like-minded women in her community as well as by the Communists. In many cases the husband undergoes a severe beating if he shows unwillingness to mend his ways.

The Chinese Communist Party attached great importance to the mobilization of women. A Party policy statement of March 1943 stressed that "the mobilization of the vast masses of women to participate in revolutionary struggle is an indispensable force for the winning of the nationwide victory in revolution." However, the same policy statement urged Communists to understand the women's special interests, to have patience in teaching the "vast masses" the meaning of equality between men and women, and in "enlightening" their consciousness. "Abstinence from excessive intervention, compulsion, orders and formalism" was strictly enjoined.[7]

Far more than the Soviet effort, the Chinese thrust in its revolutionary phase was directed at persuasion, education, and teaching, with the aim of enlisting enthusiastic supporters for the Revolution. The authorities encountered resistance similar to what the Soviets had experienced in Central Asia, particularly after passage of the marriage law in 1950, which shattered centuries of tradition. A period of retreat followed. Then the Cultural Revolution renewed the campaign to politicize women and break up family clans. Stories published during the Cultural Revolution had a great deal to say about the continuing cohesiveness of the clans. The clans were identified as "class enemies," and children were encouraged to speak out against their elders as they had done in the 1950s. But the saying, "clans last for hundreds or thousands of years; a government does not last so long,'' may prove stronger than government measures.[8]

Recent evidence suggests that despite considerable government effort, the old ways are still widespread. Myrdal's *Report from a Chinese Village* is full of instances of the survival of traditional family behavior, especially among the older generation. Many peasants, for example, prefer the old practice of purchase marriages, where they marry off their daughter for a price equal to what it costs to bring her up. In the peasant village, men tend to be accepted as rulers of the household, and wives consider themselves just women.[9]

Perhaps the most important tradition of the old family system to survive has been the deference and respect paid to the aged. Significantly, there has been no government campaign against the elderly. Rather, the leadership has apparently made an effort to redefine the relationship of young to old in the concept of a new democratic, united family. Emphasized in this context is not only filial piety in the sense of respect for the aged, but also the younger generation's duty to care for their parents. The newer, liberated position of women, the Chinese regime has been careful to stress, does not permit them to be absent from the household. Every housewife should consider it a patriotic duty to feed the old, teach the young, and make every member of the family feel comfortable.[10]

One should be cautious, however, in reading into the Chinese situation our own Western or American heritage. Francis Li K. Hsu has stressed that the father-dominated Chinese kinship system is characterized by continuity, inclusiveness, authority, and asexuality. By contrast, the husband-wife dominance pattern of the American family exhibits discontinuity, exclusiveness, volition, and sexuality. In China, obedience to authority is readily transferrable from the home situation to the Communist state. The exercise of wifely piety at home becomes identified with fulfillment of duty to the state. Authority itself, however, continues to be unquestioned. While continuity and inclusiveness appear to have undergone some modification, in the sense that the state has intervened in family life, the promotion of women in China still seems more a product of family membership than one of merit. More will be said on this topic in chapter 5.

Finally, as regards asexuality, Hsu observes that sexuality in China traditionally has been specific, confined to a particular area, while in America it has been generalized so as to be virtually ubiquitous. Hence, Chinese women who achieve professional competence are more likely to be treated in terms of that competence than are their American counterparts, who are identified primarily by their sexuality.[11] This does not mean that China is more ready to accept women in positions of authority and dominance. The whole of Chinese history testifies to the contrary. What it does mean is that the reason for female subservience or lack of female participation in high-status positions may be entirely different and perhaps easier to combat in China than in the United States or the European Communist countries. The concept of traditional hierarchy may be challengeable in a cultural revolution, whereas ingrained attitudes regarding the place of sex seem less susceptible of manipulation. Thus, the economic and social bases of the old Chinese family may have been eroded, but the *attitudes* that form social ties both within the family and without have been maintained in such a way as to contribute to the consolidation of the new state.

Eastern Europe and European Russia

In Eastern Europe and the western part of the Soviet Union, family life has generally been that of the Western patriarchal extended form. Contrary to the Asian experience, the conjugal family evolved in the West before industrialization. Consequently, there was less need for the European Communist regimes to break up the intricate network of extended family relationships for the sake of modernization and political power. The need did exist, however, in the less developed rural regions of the western part of the Soviet Union and in the underdeveloped sections of Eastern Europe. Vera St. Erlich's penetrating study of the Yugoslav family in transition traces the problems and difficulties encountered by the patriarchal family as it came into contact with industrialization. She points out the special factor of the loss of protection experienced by women as the patriarchal form was abandoned for the "democratic" family type. With the loss of protection, women tended to be more exposed to ill treatment, and St. Erlich appropriately raises the question whether women in the transitional and modern family are as happy as their mothers were. She suggests that the lack of appreciation of their low status in the patriarchal family might be a product of the closeness and protection that surround women.[12]

The abuse women encountered through dissociation from the patriarchal family has been noted by Sheila Fitzpatrick. In her study of the Soviet literature of the period, she found young Soviet women Communists in the 1920s writing letters to the newspapers asking if their role as Communists committed them to having to sleep with anyone. They feared a loss of prestige and respect if they were identified as casual women.[13] Clearly, the transition from patriarchal to modern family has brought stresses and strains that women in Eastern Europe and the Soviet Union have had to endure, frequently to their great disadvantage.

Paradoxically, traditional family behavior and organization have apparently retained greater vitality in Central Asia and China, where an immense effort was expended to transform the family system, than in either Eastern Europe or European Russia, where the transformation was not regime-sponsored. In both China and Central Asia, insistence on a total revolution in family life would clearly have jeopardized the regime's power position by alienating much of the population. Hence, changes in family behavior were effected slowly. In the European Communist countries, the transformation process was already completed or well underway when the Communists came to power; family organization was not at issue. As a result, the more modernized European family was in a very real sense much less able to defend itself from the social consequences of the Communists' rapid industrial drive than either its Central Asian or Chinese counterparts.

EQUALITY IN THE HOME

The strains evident in family life in all the Communist countries find their focus in the degree to which equality in the family has become a reality and in the ability of the family to maintain stability.

The Soviet Union and Eastern Europe

In Eastern Europe and the Soviet Union, the husband is still regarded as head of the household, although his authority has diminished as compared to that of the patriarchal father. My field observations confirm the findings of Communist sociologists. In a survey of almost 600 families in a Leningrad working district, Soviet sociologist A. L. Pimenova found that 69 percent of the female respondents acknowledged that the husband or some other male member of the family was head of the household, although the percentage indicating acceptance of this arrangement tended to decrease with the age of the couple.[14] According to the 1970 survey by Dr. Yankova of its suburbs, 35 percent of the Moscow respondents admitted the persistence of old patriarchal norms, while 47 percent of a sample in one suburb and 52 percent in another had not yet "adopted the new norms."[15] A figure ranging from 40 to 60 percent as the average proportion of families in European Russia which still practice a modified form of the patriarchal system does not seem unreasonable. This range would approximate roughly the second finding in Yankova's survey, namely, that almost 50 percent of the married couples in the surveyed towns had adopted "democratic equality" in the home. However, caution must be exercised in interpreting these results. To the question, "Whom do you go to for advice in the organization of the home?" well over half of the respondents in each of the survey areas answered, "My husband."[16] Such a response suggests that whether the family form is "democratic" or not, the husband probably retains the final say in most households.

Unfortunately, it is impossible to prepare tables for a comparative analysis of family structure because the surveys conducted in the various East European countries and the Soviet Union are not organized along similar lines. The

Yugoslav survey mentioned earlier offers observations about male dominance in families. The data suggest that there may be some correlation between the number of children and the family authority structure, in addition to the correlation between level of education and authority structure which Soviet research has persistently attempted to prove. According to the Yugoslav study, the "syncratic"[17] or democratic family form is least likely to be present where there are three or more children. However, that survey also shows a higher correlation between religion and authority structure and between a couple's birthplace and authority structure. Moslem families, followed by Catholics, appear to be the least likely to have a democratic authority pattern. Orthodox believers express the highest degree of "syncratic" behavior. Predictably, male dominance is greatest when the wife is from the village and the husband is from the town; it is lowest when both husband and wife are urban bred. As with the Soviet studies, there is a clear relationship between level of education and type of authority in the family, with university- and college-educated couples evidencing the greatest probability of a "syncratic" relationship. But there seems to be little correlation between the differences in educational level of husband and wife and type of authority.[18] Perhaps the most significant conclusion of the Yugoslav study is that the employment of women has indeed brought changes in the family power structure. The three factors considered most important in effecting the change to democratic decision-making are: (1) educational level; (2) size of family; and (3) participation in self-management organizations, particularly the wife's participation in social and political activities. When this conclusion is compared to Yankova's finding that the Soviet couples in her survey tended to be happiest when wife and husband shared power equally, there would seem to be a basis for optimism that the wife can become more heavily involved in her work and community.

This optimism, however, should not be carried too far. When Hungarian sociologist Judit Sas made a study of role expectations of university students in Budapest, she discovered that female students invariably saw themselves in inferior economic roles relative to their prospective husbands, with their husbands earning more. The young women further projected high personal involvement in household management. Male student projections were the reverse: wives were seen as having inferior social roles, earning less, and heavily involved with the care of children.[19] A 1968 study of students and professional people at Leningrad University showed the continuation of a double standard as far as sexual mores were concerned. Girls tended to disapprove of premarital sex except with the loved one, while male students thought casual sex was all right. Again, female students were less likely to condemn their fiancés for previous sexual experience, placing a higher value on emotional relationships. Men, by contrast, were more likely to feel that premarital sex was permissible *for them,* but they cherished dreams of a virgin bride.[20]

If one can draw any conclusion from the literature available from each country, it is that by and large Eastern Europe is more progressive than the Soviet Union as regards the achievement of equality in the home. The strain of Victorian puritanism which played such a significant role in the culture of nineteenth-century Russia runs deep. More important, the onset of Stalinism cut off the Soviet Union both from further experimentation and from access to the intellectual currents of Western Europe during the interwar period. Traditional patriarchism may be ending in the USSR, but a modified form persists. By implication, the woman's job in the Soviet Union is to serve her husband's needs. Female effacement finds its expression at the top levels of Soviet society, where one is at pains to cite the wife of a single major figure, let alone identify her as having made a noteworthy contribution to any aspect of Soviet life. With such a situation persisting among the elite, it is not surprising that the popular attitude that the regime has found least susceptible of change is the male view that wives should stay home to wait on their husbands and that husbands should be exempt from housework.[21]

China

China so far is an enigma. Survey research is unknown in that country, and the observations we do have are observations relative to the minute segment of Chinese society the regime has permitted Westerners to see. The available evidence suggests that the regime has made a concerted effort to change traditional roles, but that these roles are still far from being "overturned." It is hard to eradicate five thousand years of accumulated history in thirty years. The campaign of the early fifties, the Great Leap Forward, the Commune Movement, and the information we have on the period following the Cultural Revolution (such as the "drawing-the-line" campaign of the late 1960s[22]) are all indications of the leadership's continuing effort to promote greater equality within the nuclear family structure. Myrdal quotes one young woman as saying in the early 1970s: "Before the Cultural Revolution, women were too tied to their own homes. Then we discussed the importance of interesting ourselves in state affairs, just as much as the men do.... The young women say, we women must be capable of making up our minds and arriving at decisions.... Now I take part in all discussions."[23] *China News Analysis* reports the case of a patriarchal father in Kiangsi Province whose family "practiced the revolution" and became a "four-good family." A younger daughter became a section leader of the commune, but the father dominated the household, refusing to take criticism from neighbors about his "oppressive" ways with his family. Fearful of losing the "four-good" title, the father apparently became more authoritarian until the study of Mao's works made him see the light and he reformed.[24] The efforts on the part of the regime to encourage women to leave the home in 1973 signifies that the problem is far from solved. In a country as traditional as China, it is especially appropriate that Chairman Mao should have written a letter to his wife at the height of the Cultural Revolution advising her to be humble and not become "over-inflated by success," as she had "many times."[25]

It is also highly significant that the virulent attack on Mme. Mao after her husband's death focused as much on her failings as a woman and wife as they did on her abuse of power. Wall posters alleged she had nagged her husband to death, disobeyed his commands, been indifferent to his needs, and virtually left him to die. She was also accused of having excessive and decadent taste in clothes, and of preferring expensive Western "bourgeois" dress to the prevailing Chinese uniform, a point which Roxanne Witke also makes in her account of Chiang Ch'ing.[26]

In sum, culture and tradition appear to be as powerful in molding attitudes toward women and the family in Communist societies as they are in other parts of the world. In the words of one Bulgarian woman, "How are you going to overcome centuries of oppression in a single generation?" Moreover, tradition seems to reign in an area that most vitally affects the status of woman, the home. The assumption of a subordinate role there carries over into the public world, where women tend to settle for secondary positions.

DIVORCE AND ABORTION

Divorce would seem to be both a blessing and a curse to a woman born in the Communist system. In China and the Soviet Union, it was initially seen as the symbol of women's freedom from the tyranny of her husband. With the passage of time, however, it appears to have become almost universally deplored in the Soviet Union as an undesirable thing. Sociologists in Eastern Europe, however, do not tend to regard divorce in such negative terms. They prefer to cite the tempo of transition and change that the family is experiencing, and frequently they see divorce as evidence of a developing sense of identity on the part of the women.[27]

Divorce in Eastern Europe and the Soviet Union

Significantly, the divorce rate in all the East European countries and the Soviet Union has been rising in recent years. The 1970 and 1974 figures are given in table 27. A rise in the divorce rate is to be expected in industrializing countries, and the Communist nations are no exceptions to the rule. Bulgaria's rate has skyrocketed from 9,905 divorces in 1970 to 10,902 in 1973. "In 10 years, I believe, there will not be a single family left in this country," a Sofia

**Table 27—Divorce Rate per Thousand Population in
Selected Countries, 1970 and 1974**

	Rate	
Country	1970	1974
USA	3.50	4.60
USSR	2.62	2.72
Bulgaria	1.16	1.34
Czechoslovakia	1.74	2.07
East Germany	1.61	2.27
France	0.79	0.95
Hungary	2.20	2.35
Poland	1.06	1.22
Romania	0.38	0.85
UK	1.18	2.14
Yugoslavia	1.01	1.56

Sources: United Nations, Department of Economic and
Social Affairs, Statistical Office, Demographic Yearbook,
1974, pp. 286–88; United States, Department of Commerce,
Bureau of the Census, The 1977 U.S. Fact Book (New York:
Grosset & Dunlop, 1977), p. 51.

judge was quoted as saying by the magazine Zhenata dnes [Women Today]. A decade ago, divorce occurred largely among childless couples. In 1973, 22 percent of all divorces occurred in families with two or more children.[28] Only Romania's rate is low, because divorce was outlawed in 1966.

East European and Soviet studies indicate that the increase in divorce is linked to urbanization and high social mobility, both of which are associated with rapid social and economic change. Published Bulgarian statistics, for example, indicate that 75.3 percent of all divorces occurred in urban areas in 1973, as compared with 62.0 percent in 1960. Sofia accounts for more than a quarter of all Bulgarian divorces.[29] Hungarian sociologists told me that the divorce rate in their country was highest among women who had risen from traditional rural society to the upper echelons of the intelligentsia.

In the Soviet Union, the divorce rate rose from 3.2 per 100 marriages in 1950 to 26.3 per 100 in 1971. Part of the increase can be explained by the easing of divorce restrictions in 1956 and again in 1968. However, the rate has almost doubled in the last 10 years, with 636,000 divorces registered in 1970 alone in a country reckoned to have 60–70 million families; that is 1 divorce for every 3 families. According to Literaturnaia gazeta, these figures are probably low, since not all divorces are registered.[30] The lowest incidence of divorce was reported in those areas where traditional family ties have not been broken, i.e., in Central Asia and in the villages. The highest incidence was in the large cities with over 500,000 inhabitants.

The aforementioned Bulgarian article in Zhenata dnes cited four major causes of divorce: adultery (31.1 percent of all causes in 1973); physical and mental harassment (20.5 percent in 1973); alcoholism (9.7 percent in 1973); and "frivolous behavior" (12.03 percent in 1973).

In his study of the Soviet family, A. Gorkin identifies two basic reasons for divorce: "thoughtless marriages," where young people marry without considering the consequences, and marriages based on "self-respect." In the first category, the marriage is generally short-lived and is the victim of outside pressures, such as housing shortages or insufficient income. The "self-respect" marriages generally last for at least five years. Symptomatic of the tension in these types of marriages is the prevalence of alcoholism[31] and the lack of communication between husband and wife.

Alcoholism appears to be a major factor in divorce. The *Zhenata dnes* study reported that alcoholism had moved from fourth place on the list of causes of divorce in 1965 to third place in 1973, while physical and mental harassment jumped in the same time span from an unspecified point lower down the scale to second place. Official Soviet statistics list alcoholism as the cause of over 40 percent of all divorces. In most cases, the divorce is instigated by the woman, although the incidence of women alcoholics is on the rise.[32]

Increasingly, Communist sociologists are turning from the obvious economic and social conditions contributing to marital conflict to a consideration of the psychological relationships in marriage. Such relationships are the focus of a study of Moscow's Institute of Sociology, which has recently conducted in two neighborhoods of Moscow a survey consisting of two sets of interviews with 200 families (470 individuals). The criteria for selection were that there be children from the marriage and that these children be under 16 years of age. The first interview involved all 200 families and sought to determine the inner structure of Soviet family life. The second interview delved deeper into certain aspects of marital behavior. It was directed at nuclear families and attempted to uncover the pyschosocial dynamics of the family. Half of the second interview sample (i.e., 30 families) had a "happy" marriage according to Institute criteria, half an "unhappy" one. Significantly, the husband's complaints about the marriage centered on such statements as "Marriage limits my freedom" or "I did not expect marriage to bring so much trouble." In unhappy marriages, the husband thought it "better not to discuss my work," while the wives were equally divided on whether to discuss their work at home. The most common complaints of the wives in the unhappy marriages were: "My husband seldom takes account of my mood." "I have many more obligations at home." "My husband talks carelessly about my work." "My husband does not like to go visiting."[33]

Talking about one's work seemed a problem to both partners of the unhappy marriage. The husband's feeling that marriage curtailed his freedom and the wife's feeling that the husband did not consider her moods were cited as indications of different expectations and poor communication in the marriage. The researchers I interviewed felt that on the basis of responses to questions scaled on 10 psychosocial factors, they would be able to determine the likelihood of divorce for a particular couple. It was their opinion that different marital expectations might be a result of socialization, and thus they were strongly in favor of providing better preparation for marriage among young people.

The foregoing discussion suggests that divorce has been something of a two-edged sword in the Communist world. As women move into the labor force and break their ties with the traditional patriarchal family relationships, self-respect becomes of value of them. Divorce thus can be seen as one manifestation of the refusal of women to accept their traditional role unquestioningly. On the other hand, divorce must be seen as symptomatic of more widespread social upheaval, and as such is properly a cause for concern and study by East European and Soviet sociologists.

Divorce in China

In China, as will be discussed in greater detail in chapter 6, the institution of divorce was itself an agent of revolutionary transformation in a country that never had permitted it before. Unfortunately, women bore the brunt of the public protest which attended its legislation in 1950. Female suicides and murders became commonplace in China in the years following 1950. Despite such happenings, divorce was on the increase between 1950 and 1954. As might be expected, two-thirds of the applications for divorce came from couples who had been married for less than one year, and in the majority of cases women appear to have taken the initiative.[34] The high cost Chinese women have had to pay for their "liberation" is exemplary indication again of the severity of the tensions generated by the attempt to restructure sex roles so ingrained that they have become second nature over the course of the centuries. The present Soviet concern over family stability would appear in this light to be a reaction against this process and as such a conservative retreat.

Abortion in Eastern Europe and the USSR

The rise in the number of abortions parallels the rising divorce rate in the Communist countries. Table 28 gives abortion rates for the East European Communist countries. There are no comparable data for China or the Soviet Union. According to the 1970 Soviet census, the average number of children per family, including the more tradition-oriented Moslem families, was 1.5. Yet a Union-wide survey of 33,000 women conducted in 1973 showed that the majority of women thought two or three children the ideal family size.[35] Families surveyed in Yugoslavia and Bulgaria averaged 1.5 children per family. Whatever these women may say, they do not want many children. The

Table 28—Live Births, Fertility Rates, and Abortions in Selected Communist Countries for Selected Years[a]

Country	Legal Abortions (in thousands)			Live Birth Rate (per thousand pop.)			Fertility Rate (live births per thousand women aged 15–49)			Abortion Rate (per thousand women aged 15–49)			No. of Abortions per 100 Pregnancies		
	1953	1967	1973	1953	1967	1973	1953	1967	1973	1953	1967	1973	1953	1967	1973
USSR	—[b]	—	10,000[e]	25.1	17.4	15.5	—	76.6	48.7	—	—	—	—	—	—
Albania	—	—	—	40.9	35.6	33.3	202.8[d]	—	—	—	—	—	—	—	—
Bulgaria	17.4	119.5	137.4	20.9	14.9	16.3	59.5	50.4	63.4	8.9	56.8	62.4	10.2	49.3	49.6
ČSSR	30.6	121.2	81.2	21.2	15.1	18.9	57.3	62.2	75.8	9.6	35.1	22.4[e]	10.1	36.0	22.9
GDR	1.0	20.0	—	16.8	14.3	10.6	—	76.0	52.4	—	—	31.7[f]	—	—	37.6
Hungary	42.7	222.4	169.7	21.6	14.6	15.0	50.9	57.7	58.2	16.9	85.5	63.3[e]	17.1	59.7	52.1
Poland	103.0[g]	222.2	210.7	29.1	16.7	17.4	94.2	65.0	68.0	14.3	28.5	23.6	11.5	30.5	25.8
Romania	112.2[h]	115.0	—	23.8	27.4	18.1	79.2	105.5	70.4	—	53.7	—	—	—	—
Yugoslavia	—	276.2[i]	—	28.8	18.8	15.5	76.5	75.2	67.9	—	—	—	—	41.7	—

Sources: United Nations, Department of Economic and Social Affairs, Statistical Office. Demographic Yearbook, 1961, 1968, 1974, and Statistical Yearbook, 1974; Charles Gati, ed., The Politics of Modernization in Eastern Europe: Testing the Soviet Model (New York: Praeger, 1974), p. 371; William F. Robinson, "Selected Demographic Data on Eastern Europe," RFE Background Report no. 225, 3 November 1976, Radio Free Europe Research Department, Munich, West Germany, pp. 14–15 (mimeographed); idem, "Selected Demographic and Economic Data on Eastern Europe," RFE Background Report no. 90, 29 April 1977, Radio Free Europe Research Department, Munich, West Germany, pp. 6–8 (mimeographed).

[a]These statistics must be taken as indicators only, not as absolute figures. Comparison of the United Nations data with Robinson's data and the yearbooks of the individual countries yields different figures depending on the year of issue of the source consulted.

[b]__ = statistics not available.

[c]The USSR has never published abortion figures for the entire nation.

[d]The last data available is for 1950.

[e]Sudden drop is the result of newly imposed legal restrictions.

[f]Abortion made legal again in 1972.

[g]The year for Poland is 1955.

[h]The year for Romania is 1958.

[i]No statistics on abortion available for Yugoslavia after 1968.

abortion problem has become so severe that many countries, including Romania, East Germany, and Czechoslovakia, have taken measures to limit abortions. (These will be discussed in a later chapter.)

Abortion has traditionally been a delicate subject in the Soviet Union and Eastern Europe, as it has been elsewhere. Even the radical Alexandra Kollontai approved of it only as a necessary evil. During its checkered career in the USSR, it has been permitted, outlawed, and then reinstated. When abortion was made legal in the Soviet Union and throughout Eastern Europe in the 1950s, no groundwork for family planning had been laid, nor, apparently, had the effects of abortion on population growth been thought through. Given the unavailability of contraceptives, abortion evidently became the most effective form of birth control.

The rate of abortion is probably highest in the Soviet Union, with Yugoslavia ranking second. Official Soviet data are unavailable, but according to an extrapolation by population expert Henry P. David, there were 1.6 abortions per live birth is the USSR in 1960, and 2.5–3.0 per live birth in 1965.[36] The Population Council's report of 10 million abortions per 4.5 million live births in 1973 indicates that the use of abortion as a contraceptive has probably decreased, but these figures may still make the Soviet abortion rate the highest in the world (180 percent of all live births).

Abortions in Yugoslavia in 1967 equaled 70 percent of all live births, but with striking regional variations. In Macedonia, for example, abortions equaled only 21 percent of live births; in Boznia-Herzegovina, 30 percent. But in Croatia they were 66 percent, and in Serbia 113 percent, of live births. Incredibly, the Vojvodina, a province of Serbia, reported an abortion rate of 167 percent of all live births for that year. Thus, in the two most populous areas of Yugoslavia abortion is clearly the preferred form of birth control, and, one might add, an effective one. The birth rate for the Vojvodina in 1967 was the lowest of any region in Yugoslavia (13.1 per thousand).[37]

Family-planning and contraceptive information varies throughout the European Communist countries. The discussion of contraception still appears to be socially taboo in the Soviet Union. Birth control pills are available on the market according to Soviet gynecologists, but interviews indicated that they are not procurable in a pharmacy. When an oral contraceptive was introduced in Czechoslavkia in 1965, the red tape surrounding its introduction discouraged both doctors and women from using it. Because of the pill's adverse side effects, a doctor's prescription and six medical visits a year were required for users. Doctors were not eager to assume the extra work, and the visits, plus the fee charged for the pill, did not encourage women to use it.[38] Discussions with medical personnel in Hungary and Bulgaria led me to believe that contraceptives were not widely in use in these countries either. However, in Poland, Hungary, and Czechoslovakia, family planning has now become a part of the governments' pronatalist policies.

In Yugoslavia, the government has been actively pursuing a family-planning program, but with mixed results. Yugoslav officials have been concerned that the population prefers abortion to other types of family planning, despite the existence of a network of family-planning centers and the widespread availability of contraceptives. Even modern, urban Belgrade appears to favor abortions. Surveys have indicated that young women have little interest in contraceptives. A recent sampling of university students recorded such attitudes as "Contraceptives take all the fun out of it," or women "would rather take a chance." Efforts to arouse personal concern for the world-wide population explosion and the development of a proper national population policy have met with minimal response.[39] Yugoslav sociologists explain these attitudes as part of what they term a second of four developmental phases in family planning, i.e., when the acceptance of birth control has reached only a small portion of the population and abortion is seen as a positive approach to family limitation. The fourth phase is total acceptance of birth control.[40]

Abortion in China

Contraceptives and abortion were made available to Chinese women as soon as was medically possible. The campaign to lower the birth rate was launched during the first days of Communist power and involved education, abortion, the employment of local health workers and women "cadres" to disseminate information, and the mobilization of public opinion against large families. The pill was introduced in 1964. The campaign has had its ups and downs, with 1959–1961 being years of little progress, 1962–1963 showing an upward trend, and 1971 marking the beginning of the latest effort. According to Han Suyin, personal propaganda proved to be a more effective campaign method than blasting information from public loudspeakers and invading the sensibilities of the people. In addition, every street committee, neighborhood committee, commune, brigade, and productivity team formed its own family-planning staff. Marriage was encouraged at age 25 for girls and 28 for men. Ruth Sidel indicates that the continuing campaign has been such a success that recourse to contraceptives rather than abortions is now the normal way for women to hold down family size. Statistics are limited, but in 1972 there were 1.2 million women of childbearing age in the Shanghai area (population, 11 million). Of these 80,000 had abortions that year, 400,000 had been sterilized, and the birth rate was given as 0.6 per thousand. Sidel saw a chart in a health center in Hanchow which stated that 46 percent of the women under its jurisdiction were using contraceptives. No abortions were reported for that year (1972).[41]

The differing experiences of the European Communist countries and China in abortion policy reflect the different cultural heritages of Europe and China. The former, with its Christian culture, has looked on birth control and abortion as "unnatural" and potentially or actually murder. In China, however, infanticide has long been customary as a solution to chronic overpopulation.

Hence, the need to regulate family size in China appears not to have raised the same type of moral issue as it has in the West, where the Communist countries are no exception to the general rule. Still, as a *method* of birth control, the Chinese appear to be discouraging abortion in favor of contraceptives.

It would be misleading to interpret the East European abortion statistics as an assertion by women in those countries of the right to control their own bodies on the conscious level. Nevertheless, a common response to my asking why a woman had had recourse to abortion was, ''Why shouldn't I have an abortion if I don't want the child?'' In the light of such statements, abortion may be interpreted as a woman's act of refusal to be burdened with more than she can handle in terms of work and home. The fact that abortion is so widespread amounts to women saying, ''Under the circumstances, we refuse to be childbearers as we have been in the past.'' The prevalence of abortion may thus be seen in this limited sense as a protest on the part of women against their traditional role.

COMMUNIST IDEOLOGY AND TRADITIONAL VALUES REGARDING WOMEN AT HOME

The role ideology has played in changing ingrained attitudes regarding sex roles is ambivalent. Soviet bolshevism claimed to have ushered in a new world for women, but Lenin refused to accept the view that having sex was the same as drinking a ''glass of water'' and he censured Clara Zetkin for permitting sex to be discussed at women's meetings.[42] Alexandra Kollontai insisted that sheer physical attraction was unacceptable unless accompanied by at least a ''temporary passion.''[43] Tension between the conventional and the radical has characterized Communist ideology toward women down to the present time.

THE MARXIST HERITAGE

The views of Marx and Engels on the nineteenth-century oppression of women were essentially unsystematic. Engels's thesis that the first class division was made on the basis of sex in the family[44] provided a useful framework within which to explore the problem of woman's liberation, but the problem was never central to the main body of Marxist thought. In their private lives, Marx and Engels were products of their times. Both abhorred the idea of promiscuity. Yet Marx treated his wife and daughter with a typically ''bourgeois'' lack of sensitivity and Engels showed a preference for women of lower-class origins.

Perhaps personal experience spawned in Marx and his followers an unwillingness to posit an independent woman's movement apart from the Revolution. A firm distinction was drawn between "bourgeois" and "proletarian" women; a woman was labeled proletarian only if she adhered to the socialist movement. Thus, the male socialists subordinated women to the Revolution and relegated the "woman question" to second place after the Revolution had been accomplished.[45] This position found expression in the Bolshevik view that proletarian women were not competitors but worked side by side with their proletarian men for the Revolution.

Lenin, of course, was a firm believer in the subordination of women to the Revolution. For him there were only two classes of women: the good proletarian and the decadent "bourgeois." The difference between the two was essentially a distinction between the good woman and the fallen woman in the Victorian moral code.[46] "Too much talk of sex," he told Clara Zetkin, "leads to excess. It takes two people to make love and a third person, a new life, is likely to come into being. This deed has a social complexion and constitutes a *duty* to the community."[47] The duty of the proletarian woman was to fight for the Revolution and to bear revolutionary children.

It is to be expected that male Marxists should hold to theories of male acquisition and domination of power. What is remarkable is the extent to which female Marxists supported the same theories in both work and deed. Eleanor Marx, Krupskaya, and Inessa Armand are exemplary of the exploitation of women by "progressive" leftists in the pursuit of their own power. Female Russian revolutionaries of the ninteenth century believed that revolutionary action precluded any thought of a personal family life. Catherine Breshkovskaia gave up her marriage, not for sexual license, but for a higher and nobler calling. For a female revolutionary, love between man and woman had to be of purer stuff than the "bourgeois" marriage.[48] The success of a male-led revolution was viewed by most female Marxists of the period as the *sine qua non* for any true emancipation of women. Rosa Luxemburg went so far as to deny that there really was a woman's problem. The only Bolshevik woman who actively espoused the cause of woman's liberation as a value in itself was Clara Zetkin, but she too believed in the primacy of the Revolution. Those like Lily Braun, who insisted that the woman's movement came first, left the Party.[49] Thus, when the Soviets came to power, the women's movement in Russia was deprived of a basis for arguing the validity of female interests, the independence of these interests, or the need for organized support for them. Russian female revolutionaries were as much the products of their nineteenth-century culture as were their male peers.

THE SOVIET EXPERIENCE

The conservatism of both male and female revolutionaries augured poorly for any fundamental change in male-female relationships when the Bolsheviks came to power. A "bourgeoisification" of sexual values and female behavior quickly followed the Revolution and received its benediction under Stalin. There was no official plan to abolish marriage and the family and insititute free love in the twenties. While guidelines as to sexual behavior were unclear, the discussion surrounding the 1926 marriage law leaves little doubt that not only was the country conservative but the Communist Party was as well. Any program affording women greater sexual freedom would have run headlong into the urban-rural conflict. The peasants sharply opposed the law's approval of de facto marriages, the equal distribution of property in the case of divorce, and the obligation of the entire household to pay alimony. The 1926 marriage law, much like the controversy over the Equal Rights Amendment in this country, challenged deep-rooted attitudes and so brought to the surface the Pandora's box of fears and anxieties that a transition to new behavior inevitably brings. In point of fact, however, as Kollontai's lone battle bore witness, the marriage law in essence reinstated and legitimated marriage as a valid social institution in a socialist country, contrary to Marx's prophecy regarding its future under socialist conditions. Although Western observers tended to interpret the law as spelling the virtual end of marriage in the Soviet Union, Kollontai argued that classifying women as wives, registered or unregistered, and casual lovers was a violation of community privacy.[50] However, she was powerless against both the more moderate Bolshevik group headed by Smidovitch and the conservatism of the country at large. The Party leadership appeared to be more concerned that the fruits of the Revolution would be sexual chaos. As its spokesman, Smidovitch decried the image of new socialist woman as promiscuous and came down hard on the side of the "responsible mother."[51]

A close reading of the debate indicates that all the Soviet leadership, and indeed most women in the Party, upheld the institution of marriage. In fact, the reaction to Kollontai's "radicalism" demanded a firmer commitment to it. There seems to me no clearer evidence of the imposition of traditional culture upon Communist ideology than the leaders' concern that sexual anarchy might win the day. The conservative trend that exercised such influence in the passage of the 1926 law eventually triumphed in the Stalinist reaction of the 30s, when socialist marriage became virtually no different from its "bourgeois" variant, except in the absence of a church ceremony.[52]

Clearly, Marx's and Engels' vague generalizations about the kind of new relationships socialism would bring about between men and women, and between parents and children, found no response except among a minority of Russian Bolsheviks. The leadership apparently saw no alternative to the "bourgeois" nuclear family as the basic social unit of the new society. To this they gave the name "socialist marriage," as if by changing the adjective one could change the content and structure. The Stalinist marriage law was the legal embodiment of the old cultural attitude toward marriage, the family, and woman's place in both. Henceforth, the nuclear family would be the focus of Communist propaganda. Motherhood was raised to a noble patriotic and socialist duty in 1944 with the institution of "The Order of Motherhood" for mothers of ten children or more and with a lesser order for those who bore fewer children. That same year, divorce was put out of bounds for most couples because of severe financial and social sanctions (i.e., the requirement of public advertisement to the community).[53] Today, the nuclear family occupies a cardinal place in official thinking about the transition to communism. While communism has seen a transformation of the family from its feudal to "bourgeois" form, and has tried to argue that the socialist marriage is in some way an improvement upon the "bourgeois" form, the nuclear family, as I was told everywhere on my trip to the European Communist countries, is regarded as a permanent institution, with women at its center. This form will carry the socialist state into communism. In place of a church ceremony, there is the marriage palace, but the long white dress remains, together with the ritual reception, honeymoon, and other trappings that attend a Western marriage.

EAST EUROPEAN AND CHINESE CONTRIBUTIONS

I have gone at some length into the Bolshevik-Soviet Communist position regarding women and the home because that ideology was transferred to Eastern Europe when the Communists came to power. Yugoslavia differs little from the general norm. In fact, when one compares Soviet and East European family sociology with the Western product, it is difficult to detect much difference between the two, despite Communist claims that marriage in the Communist countries is superior in being a "socialist" phenomenon. The concept of the future family as nonauthoritarian—democratic or "syncratic"—bears a close resemblance to the "bourgeois" model. The distinguishing feature of Western sociology is that the model is not uniform. The nuclear family is not seen as the only mode of family or sex life. Hence, one can have an organization such as Parents without Partners in the United States, but not in the Soviet Union, where ideology links sex and fertility so strongly.

The evidence suggests that the European Communist contribution to the subject of marriage and the family has been at best unoriginal and at worst only a transference of the norms of the "bourgeois" culture communism is supposed to replace. In the main, Communist ideology has simply absorbed the dominant European tradition. At no time, with the possible exception of Bebel's work, was there a serious effort to investigate the premises upon which male dominance was based, nor was there any coming to grips with the culturally conditioned attitudes that identify women with the home and support the legitimacy of the nuclear family. As will be shown in a later chapter, contemporary sociological investigations of women and the family assume the nuclear family as given. All suggestions for alleviating women's burdens depart from the axiom that the present family structure will remain.

China so far has offered no permanent radical solution or approach to the problem. Modernization of the feudal patriarchal kinship family became national policy with the passage of the 1950 marriage law, which made marriage a matter of public interest for the first time in Chinese history. As with the Soviet marriage law of 1926, the Chinese counterpart found opponents not only among the rural peasantry but also among Party members and government officials. Enforcement of the law could come about only if the full weight of Communist power was exercised. The tactic was to indoctrinate leaders of society and send them out among the general population. By 1953, the Chinese claimed to have trained 3.5 million lower-level leaders in the new law. These were sent out to some 1,200 countries and 111 cities.[54] The task confronting the leadership was enormous. Many of the local leaders were newly recruited peasants who were by and large illiterate, having had no schooling of any kind. Thus, the government's first effort ended in retreat. But a new assault was launched in the late 1950s, this time in the form of the commune experiment, which established separate dormitories for men and women and attempted to abolish private family life. The commune may have been Mao's idea of the proper living unit for a Communist industrial society. One reason for such regimentation was economic. In 1959, reports were published proclaiming the organization of women into "street factories," street production units, and mess halls.[55] The ideological focus of the communes was the creation of a situation whereby men would not have to give up their time-honored prerogatives by participating in housework, but women who were of childbearing age would be free to work because of the existence of communal dining halls, nurseries, and kindergartens. In addition, the commune system completely obliterated the family as a production unit by eliminating private plots and replacing home industries with collective industries. The commune experiment was short-lived, however, and family life was reinstated. The family now seems to be re-forming around the nuclear pattern, and is maintaining such "Chinese" traditions as the authority of the head of the household, respect for the elderly, and the discouragement of sexual intercourse prior to marriage, particularly on the part of young women. According to Ruth Sidel, the discouragement of premarital sex reflects both traditional norms of female behavior and the need to regulate contraception.[56]

After reviewing both Eastern and Western ideologies concerning women, the researcher is impressed by the unanimity of official endorsement of the nuclear family by Communist and non-Communist countries alike. All regimes promote it. However, in the Communist states no other alternative is permitted. In the Soviet Union it is the only acceptable institution for sex and fertility. Lenin said that the community must therefore regulate it. Any type of spontaneity in these matters is inadmissible. Let one admit the principle, but it still does not explain the insistence on the nuclear family form. If nuclear households have been typical of family life throughout history, as demographic data suggest, surely they will endure without excessive ideological intervention. If their time is past, then the ideology that supports them can only become increasingly irrelevant.

COMMUNIST IDEOLOGY TODAY

The traditional cultural emphasis on women in the home seems to have increased as the Communist regimes have moved farther from the Revolution, or takeover. A recent study undertaken on a collective farm near Moscow purports to prove that the mother's presence is absolutely essential during the first four years of a child's life, and thereby calls into question the whole network of preschool institutions.[57] The study argues that precisely because it is the sacred duty of a woman to bear children, she is paid to stay at home, although not at full wages, for fear she will not return to her place in industry and the social services where she is also desperately needed.

However, responsibility for the survival of traditional values regarding the role of women in the home cannot be attributed solely to the strength of male preferences reinforced by official ideology. As the Soviet experience in the debate over the 1926 marriage law showed, women also played a conservative role. The tendency of women everywhere to be more conservative in their values than men has been well documented in polls and studies[58] and is understandable in the greater alienation of women from the intellectual and technological currents of the day. Certainly, in the case of the Soviet Union in 1926, most of the female population was illiterate. But literacy and increasing participation in the working world do not appear to be destined to reverse female conservatism (witness the voting patterns of women in the West).[59] In the European Communist countries women are highly visible in all aspects of social and economic life, yet conservatism is entrenched.

There are practical bases for this phenomenon. In the USSR, Poland, Hungary, and Romania, World War II took a heavy toll of the male population. Only recently in the USSR has the imbalance between the sexes finally been corrected. According to the 1970 census, in 1959, 27 percent of all males between the ages of 20 and 25 were married, while 50 percent of all females in that age bracket were married. In 1970, 29 percent of all males were married as compared to 56 percent of all females. By contrast, in 1959, 91 percent of all males between the ages of 60 and 69 were married, but only 36 percent of all females of that age were. In 1970, 92 percent of all males and only 37 percent of all females of that group were married. The discrepancy diminishes in the 30–34-year-old group. In 1970, 88 percent of all males in this age bracket were married as compared to 85 percent of all females.[60] Clearly, the dearth of males over the past 30 years has meant that a primary concern of many women has been to get and keep a man. The strictures on feminine dress began to be relaxed everywhere in the European Communist world upon Stalin's death. A visitor to Moscow today cannot help but be impressed by the number of beauty salons that seem to be in every apartment complex. Cosmetic counters are common features in the department stores. Kalinin Street in Moscow boasts an elegant shopping center where the cut and style of women's clothing is beginning to rival that in shops in Western Europe and the United States. Kalinin Street also has an Institute of Beauty, one of the many that are flourishing in the large Soviet cities.

In Eastern Europe, the tourist is struck by the number of Western imports in cosmetics and lingerie, all considerably higher priced than the local products, but nevertheless in large supply in the major cities. Rosalea Speteanu, director of "Miraj," Romania's largest cosmetics industry (over 500 employees), confirmed my impression that the cosmetics business is growing rapidly. Not only does "Miraj" produce a fine line of lipsticks, creams, and facial makeup, but it also manufactures the much-publicized Gerovital cosmetic products (advertised as reducing the process of aging) that are now marketed in Western Europe and South America. Director Speteanu was enthusiastic about the future of her company and spoke of expansion as being inevitable because, in her view, "Women want to look feminine."

The new accent on femininity, however, is more than a reaction to demographic data and regime liberalization. Relaxation of the revolutionary standard of mannish dress has produced a revolution in the appearance of women in Eastern Europe and the USSR. Not only is stylish dress a sign of high status (because few women can afford to buy high-fashion clothes or have them made), but it is also a reaffirmation of traditional womanhood. Students and working women alike will spend up to two months' salary for an elegant winter coat, a pair of boots, or a well-cut dress. Perhaps because clothes are relatively more expensive in Communist countries than in the West, women take more care in making their selection. They cannot afford an extensive wardrobe. While blue jeans may be prized by the young, older women seem to prefer skirts. It is curious that in the countries where the proletariat has taken power, great emphasis is placed on elegance, whereas in the decadent "bourgeois" world, the wealthiest "capitalists" take pride in dressing like the common worker.

Thus, women themselves act as agents to maintain conservative values. A Romanian psychologist indicated that in Romania everyone thinks a woman of 40 is old, and that the only thing left for her is to be a grandmother. A Hungarian sociologist reported that the woman's income is used to buy the frills of existence. The man is still seen as the breadwinner. Such attitudes are not a product of Communist ideology. On the contrary, they have permeated ideology and reinforced the leadership's refusal to question the traditional values of family and motherhood.

China again is a case by itself. The unisex uniform of Mao jacket and pants is not particularly aesthetic, especially when one recalls the elaborate fashion of imperial China. Yet it must be remembered that the vast peasant majority of old China dressed in the present uniform. Furthermore, as Hsu stressed, women's sexuality was traditionally confined to the home.[61] Hence, the present asexual appearance of the population at work does not represent any radical upsurge of industrial puritanism; rather, it expresses continuity with past custom. We do not know what Chinese women would choose to wear if they were given a choice as in the European Communist world. The flash of a ribbon in the hair in photographs of Chinese girls suggests that more variety might be welcome. It is possible that the leadership will follow the European example of relaxing its strict standards once the economy has advanced to a point where the consumer can buy more than the bare necessities of life. But we do not know to what degree women would approve of such a relaxation. In her report on urban life in China, Ruth Sidel paints a picture of conservatism on the part of women as regards divorce and family affairs.[62] The fact that the leadership had to abandon the idea of the commune and return to the family is an indication of the force of tradition and of the central role played by the family in maintaining it. Moreover, what Communist ideology has consistently attacked is not so much the institution of the family itself as certain practices and habilts within it: infanticide, child marriage, foot-binding, contractual marriages, confinement of women in the home, arbitrary authority exercised by the husband.[63] All these were foci of concern in republican China, but it took an authoritarian government, with its firm commitment to change, to end the abuses of "the bitter past."[64] Because it provided the philosophical underpinnings for this attack, Communist ideology in both Central Asia and China may be viewed in a more positive light. But when it comes into contact with the institutions and forms of male-female behavior that characterize industrial society, Communist ideology shows itself to be dominated by the cultural environment.

In sum, the evidence seems to point toward a tendency for ideology to be subjected to the rule of culture. The new Communist woman is a wife, a mother, and a worker, but she is best identified by her traditional role. It should be stressed that no effort is made here to judge this phenomenon. The aim has been descriptive. While Marx and particularly Engels did make some suggestions that challenged the social mystique of woman's place in the home, the ideological trend of Communist regimes that have gained power points toward an increasing departure from revolutionary norms and the ultimate absorption of traditional values. The exception at the present time is China. But China is still a country of revolution. If and when it becomes a country of the status quo, when the revolution has exhausted its potential, we shall have an opportunity to see whether it returns to its past for standards of female domesticity or continues to encourage nontraditional roles for women.

WOMEN AT WORK: EVIDENCE OF ANTIFEMINISM

Statistical evidence of antifeminism at work in the Communist countries is virtually nonexistent. Chapter 2 presented empirical data demonstrating the feminization of job categories and the concomitant lower salaries paid to women because of it. We also showed the failure of women to move above the middle level of the economic hierarchy and to repeat in their public lives the inferior roles that they tend to play in their private lives. These data suggest the existence of pervasive antifeminism, in the sense of a lower "woman's place" in all the Communist countries.

The attitude is subtle and hidden, however. Of the women I interviewed in Eastern Europe and the Soviet Union none admitted that antifeminism existed. Indeed, in my interviews with female Soviet emigrants, they assured me time and time again that they had to go to the West to find real discrimination and bias against women. Certainly, obvious overt antifeminism is more blatant in the West than in the Communist countries. Nevertheless, if antifeminism were a thing of the past, the Communist press would not continue to carry instances of discrimination.

In her visits to Soviet schools, Susan Jacoby noted that the required devotion of two hours a week to "labor" at the seventh-grade level meant metalworking for boys and home economics for girls. When she questioned the principal, he replied that women needed to learn something about sewing, cooking, and caring for their families. Boys would not take such classes. He apparently did not comment on whether girls liked to take the classes, as they were required.[65] (The discussion of socialization will come in a later chapter.)

Individual opinions by school personnel of what female students should and should not do, as compared to male students, testify to the kind of subtle antifeminism that is found in the Soviet Union. The Soviets themselves have published data that confirm discrimination in admissions policies. In her study of the professional level of urban youth, Leningrad's E. K. Vasil'eva found that about 50 percent of the female graduates from secondary school were working, as compared to 35 percent of the male graduates, although only a few of the girls (0.6 percent) indicated they *wanted* to work full time and would have preferred to go to the university. Such statistics suggest official endorsement of the traditional view that it is a man's world and that men have priority in choice of education and career.[66]

I was assured in Bulgaria, Hungary, Romania, and Poland that there was no discrimination in admissions policies there. However, the Bulgarian survey mentioned in chapter 2 makes it clear that women are now being encouraged to enter predominantly masculine fields of study such as mathematics, geology, physics, and computer science. In their study of the employment of women as a labor resource in Bulgaria, Ilieva, Trifaniv, and Tsaneva in fact project the favorable impact of increased numbers of women in these occupations for woman's self-image.[67]

The visitor to the Soviet Union is only indirectly aware of antifeminism. Old women are sweeping the streets. Women are doing the dirty work of cleaning, painting, and maintaining the subway stations. Women are doing manual road work while men drive the trucks. One can distinguish a class differentiation in who drives public transportation vehicles. Female drivers of automobiles are extremely rare. The only one I met was the chauffeur for the mayor (a woman) of one of the districts of Leningrad. When I asked why there were so few women driving automobiles, I was told by male taxi drivers and chauffeurs that the driving test was so difficult that no woman could pass it, or that women were not interested in driving cars. Few women work as bus drivers, truck drivers, or locomotive drivers. Women drive the electric trams that run on tracks, but not the more versatile *trolleibus*. A photograph published in *Pravda* of students solving a problem in traffic control during a driver education course showed an all-male class.[68] The "masculinity" of the gasoline engine dissipates in Eastern Europe, however. Women automobile drivers are much more in evidence, particularly in Yugoslavia, where there is easier access to automobiles. While cars are still very much a status symbol in Eastern Europe, their proportionately greater number as compared with the Soviet Union suggests that women have been permitted to share in this status hierarchy.

Incidents of antifeminism reported in the Soviet press include comments by male officials at the Ministry of Higher and Specialized Education to the effect that female graduate students deliberately get themselves pregnant in order to get married, and that such "unprincipled" behavior should not be encouraged.[69] One of the most frequent female complaints has been that Soviet men like to start their weekends early, so they see to it that women are appointed to the committees that meet on Friday afternoons.[70]

Perhaps antifeminism is most pervasive in attitudes regarding what women can and cannot do. One popular male view that has frequently been noted in Poland and the Soviet Union is that women show little initiative on the job and are less creative than men. They are thus less qualified by nature for positions of administrative responsibility. Ilieva, Trifaniv, and Tsaneva have found that women prefer creative types of occupations but shun "rationalizing," organizing work. The authors cite an experience from a Soviet factory where 13.1 percent of the women and 86.9 percent of the men participated in a movement to streamline factory production. They also cite the results of a Bulgarian survey to the effect that 31 percent of 15-year-old girls chose literature and art as professions they would like to take up, as against 17 percent of 15-year-old boys. By contrast, only 13 percent of the girls liked technology, as against 53 percent of the boys.[71] While the authors make it clear that these choices show preference and not ability, the type of preference women indicate reveals the popular concept of what women can and cannot do. It also suggests that antifeminism is not merely an expression of possible male hostility, but a deeply ingrained attitude among women themselves. One Soviet émigré assured me that men make better administrators than women because women are *by nature* too personal and tend to run their organization or business as they run their home: with a great deal of personal involvement and an inability to delegate authority. This same émigré also tried to convince me that antifeminism does not exist in the Soviet Union. The incident seems a good case of the subordinate class willingly adopting the arguments of the upper class for its inferior position, thereby contributing to the perpetuation of that inferiority. The émigré's comment also testifies to the continuation of the myth that women's inferior position is "natural," derived from her biology.[72]

Soviet sociologists have demonstrated that women consistently choose the easier jobs and evince little desire to advance. In Dr. Yankova's sample of 200 female workers, 60 percent had the same opportunities for advancement as men. Yet women made up only 19 percent of those registered in the evening courses the factory management considered obligatory for promotion. Dr. M. Pavlova has found little evidence that women are incapable of fulfilling high administrative posts. But she concedes that women tend to pay more attention to "human relations" than to purely administrative matters. In other words, the question of subordination and status vis-à-vis male colleagues is a primary issue for women in leadership positions. Dr. Pavlova suggests that one explanation for this type of concern is that men are not accustomed to accepting a woman's authority on the job. According to a Polish sociological study that she cites, "women in authority constantly have to prove that they can work as well as men, since men are convinced that women are more stupid than they."[73]

An editor of the Romanian magazine *Femea* [*Woman*] gave further evidence of the persistence of a discriminatory attitude toward women in administrative positions. Apparently she was assigned to interview female executives on the question of whether men listened to their views as seriously as they listened to their own. Her subjects at first said yes, and then in the course of the conversation indicated that this was not always the case. Men tended to listen when the woman was speaking directly about matters relating to her specialty. But when it came to more general or organizational matters, men listened less carefully. The respondents reported male reactions such as "What has a woman got to do with this?" or "This is not your specialty." In the editor's view, women continue to have problems overcoming male reluctance to accept them as equals.

Moreover, breaking down the status barrier requires a tremendous effort on the part of the woman *and* cooperation from the man at home. "A woman who has a high position has to give everything," the Romanian editor said. "She has to divide herself between work and home. But there is a cost for the man as well. He is used to going to work, then coming home and being waited upon. He does not want to work at home, but now circumstances force him to. If he has character, he will help his wife. This is where equality starts." She felt that if men understood and entered into the problems women have at home, they would be more likely to treat women as equals on the job.[74] Natalija Grzecic, manager of the Hotel Libertas in Dubrovnik, Yugoslavia, expressed the problem in similar terms. "In Yugoslavia," she said, "there is nothing a woman cannot do. But to do it, she must sacrifice. Most women do not want to make that sacrifice, and to make it, you need an understanding husband."[75]

Communist China is not immune to charges of antifeminism in the work place. When the Chinese Women's Federation was in the process of being reconstituted in 1972, a propaganda campaign was launched condemning the old saying about "respecting men and despising women."[76] One of the principal themes of the Cultural Revolution was to "overturn" the traditional idea that women are best placed in the home. Yet ten years later male skepticism of woman's ability to work in the world outside her home seems hardly to have abated. The press in recent years has frequently reported such male views as "Women will be women and are better left in the home." An American woman visiting China asked why there were no women surgeons in the hospital she toured. The response by the hospital director was that women do not have the stamina for long operations under the hot lights.[77] The Committee of Concerned Asian Scholars found sex differentiation in economic roles accepted as natural by both men and women whom they talked. The persistence of campaigns to mobilize women to do productive work indicates reluctance on the part of both men and women to accept wholeheartedly Mao's dictum that "Women hold up half the sky" and "Chinese women form a great reserve of manpower." Women may have been liberated from their former slavery, but they still have a long way to go to overcome traditional male attitudes as to their capabilities on the job.

COMMUNIST IDEOLOGY AND TRADITIONAL ATTITUDES REGARDING WOMEN AT WORK

The Bolsheviks and their East European and Chinese heirs have prided themselves on having consistently advocated a revolutionary, antidiscriminatory policy toward women at work. To put the present in perspective, it is useful to recall the first time an official Communist declaration of policy was made, at the Second Comintern Congress in 1920. The question of women was brought to the congress floor but was not considered of sufficient urgency to merit discussion. It was remanded to committee for study. The committee proceeded to await the work of the First International Conference of Working Women that was being held concurrently with the congress. The conference released a long paper outlining what Communists should do to improve the lot of working women. The essential features were: to bring women out of the home into the economy; to end peasant households that keep women in subservient positions; to provide equal educational opportunities for women; to mobilize women in political work, including government administration; to provide adequate work conditions "to satisfy the particular needs of the female organism and also the physical, moral and spiritual needs of the woman as mother"; and to develop communal services to alleviate housework.[78]

The program presented by the 1920 women's conference was subsequently adopted by the Party congress. With little variation, it has been incorporated as the official policy of every Communist regime upon its assumption of power. The Chinese program for women that was defined during the course of 1941–1943 put greater emphasis on only three points: convincing women that the Revolution would not succeed without them; serving the individual needs of women; and abolishing the cruel feudal practices of the past. But the emphasis on enrolling women in productive work was there as well as the emphasis on involving women actively in their liberation through political work.[79]

Three observations are worth making about the 1920 program as an indication of the attitude with which the Communists have approached the problem of working women. First of all, the program represents the first time a ruling political group attempted to formulate a comprehensive policy as regards the problem of women in industrial society. The policy as such has much merit. However, because it is a Communist policy, the solutions given to the difficulties of working women are dogmatic and hence simplistic. In essence, these solutions are the realization of the demands of the nineteenth-century feminists from the Anglo-American and socialist traditions. The solutions are neither new nor original. They thus represent the end of one stage of the realization of sexual equality, not the beginning of a new.

Second, the program says nothing about the role of men in the transformation of the status of women. All Communist regimes since 1920 have failed to consider the necessity of changes in male roles if female roles are to change. It is impossible, for example, to involve women more in the public sphere if men fail to become more involved in the home.

Third, communal services notwithstanding, the program calls on the one hand for the mobilization of women in productive work, but in the next paragraph speaks of the needs of the "female organism" and the "physical, moral and spiritual needs of motherhood." The first international Communist document directed at women's role in the new society thus focuses on *okh-*

rana byta i truda (the preservation of home and work) for women. Every Communist regime since that time has been been caught in the dilemma of wanting to preserve women for home *and* work. (Note that home comes first.) The employment of women was essential for the consolidation of Communist power and economic development. Yet official Communist pronouncements on marriage and the family increasingly assumed the features of the "bourgeois" arrangement the early Marxists had decried.

In short, the Second Comintern Congress made the first and last comprehensive policy statement on the role of women in the new society and on the ways in which Communists could promote it. This policy statement, which was revolutionary in the comprehensiveness of its approach in 1920, has now become irrelevant. More importantly, it has brought unforeseen consequences in its wake.

As Sokołowska concludes, the concept "women's work"—i.e., the factor of gainful work in the economy—occupies but fourth place in the real work schedule of women in Communist society. In first place come the biological functions of childbirth; second, the nursing and rearing of children; and, third, housework. A woman thus does not play two roles or have a "double shift"; she has four roles, of which the time spent at work is the least important. As a result, a woman's right to work in Communist countries becomes what Sokołowska calls an unbearable burden. The irony of the dilemma is that the limitation of gainful work in terms of hours would not resolve the problem, because it would not decrease woman's burden in the remaining three domains of her life.[80]

The antifeminism latent in the official Communist program comes across clearly in Sokołowska's analysis, unplanned and unsought. The program is completely silent on two issues fundamental to the concept of equality as I have defined it: (1) the coordination of woman's biological and traditional roles with her productive work role in such a way that she is not penalized or made to suffer for her participation in gainful work; (2) an anlysis of sex-role differentiation as the basis of a sexist society. Sokołowska asks science to indicate "the directions of the search." But other Polish sociologists with whom I talked felt that the issue was already dead. Nothing would change.

It is true that every European Communist regime in the past 10 years has expanded its network of communal facilities. It is true that domestic appliances are in greater supply. But it is also true that Communist ideology has insisted on the nuclear family and woman's place in it as the appropriate basic societal unit for building communism. It thus pushes women in two directions: toward achievement at work and toward maintainance of the home. Because of her four roles, in contrast to her husband's one principal one, gainful work, the wife has much less time to spend on self-improvement. Ethel Dunn has observed in her study of women in Soviet agriculture that when a rural woman marries she rarely continues her schooling; she simply does not have the time.[81] Ideological exhortations to increased involvement both at home and at work have evidently provided insufficient motivation for the vast majority of women in Communist societies to assert aggressively a new identification on the job.

In conclusion, ideology may be said to have had a positive effect in breaking down barriers to women's employment and in providing the framework for the legal realization of rights for women in marriage, work, and political life. But it has avoided the difficult area of the fundamental reformation of attitudes and the offering of new answers to the contradictions existing between a woman's biological function and work. In this area, the ideology has shown itself the prisoner of past traditions and culture. The "new" solutions are the old solutions advanced a century ago. The need for what Parsons has termed "pattern maintenance" between the post- and prerevolutionary society has meant ideological reinforcement of the popular traditional attitudes regarding marriage and the nuclear family. Equally important, economic weakness has made it impossible for any Communist regime to realize a communal infrastructure, which was originally viewed as the means of ending woman's enslavement to domesticity.

The essence of communism's antifeminism lies in its failure to address the problem of integrating women's four roles, as defined by Sokołowska, and its focus on the primacy of woman's biological function. Again, it must be stressed that this antifeminism is not deliberate. It is all the more powerful because it is unconscious, a tacit transformation of traditional attitudes into Communist norms. Motherhood is the duty of the Communist woman. Her health must be preserved at work in order to secure future generations; therefore, certain forms of work are closed to her because they are not woman's place. Women who do reach prominent positions find themselves confronted with the culturally conditioned male attitudes regarding women's inferior status. Precisely because the ideology fails to challenge the old female role, but rather adds the new work role to it, women tend to internalize the male-dominance attitudes as their own.

In short, from a potential vehicle for revolutionizing and transforming female behavior, ideology in the European Communist countries has become increasingly a conservative doctrine. That this has not yet occurred in China may reflect the fact that China is still in the first stage of female liberation: breaking down the barriers of the past. Or it may reflect a sincere effort to keep Chinese ideology truly revolutionary. But unless the Chinese make a conscious attempt to resolve the conflict posed by the tension between home and work, the European Communist experience suggests that, as far as sex roles are concerned, culture will vanquish ideology.

5 / The Political Environment

Politics and power have traditionally been a man's world. One of Communism's aims was to provide women with equal access to that world. This chapter proposes to investigate four dimensions of female political participation in the Communist countries: (1) participation in the Party and government of various countries; (2) "woman's place" in Communist politics; (3) the systemic factors in Communist organization that could account for (1) and (2); and (4) female dissenters.

PARTICIPATION OF WOMEN
IN THE COMMUNIST PARTY AND GOVERNMENT

Participation of Women in the Communist Party and in government administration follows a similar pattern in every Communist country. (1) In general, women are more visible at the local level, and less visible in the higher echelons of government. (2) The more powerful a political body, the lower the representation of women in it. The data in table 29 confirm this pattern through a breakdown of the number of women in the ruling bodies of Eastern Europe, the Soviet Union, and China for 1972–1976. But statistics on total female participation at all levels of government in selected East European countries given in appendix 1 reveal several inconsistencies.

It is difficult to explain, for example, why Poland and Yugoslavia have no female members on their parties' national executive committees. In Yugoslavia, however, there is better representation of women at the republican level. The president of the Croatian League of Communists is a woman. When Savka Dubcevic-Kucar was ousted from her position because of her stand on Croatian nationalism in 1971, she was replaced by another woman, Maria Planinc. Similarly, the post of secretary of the Serbian League of Communists is filled by a woman. Of the 59 members of the Yugoslav

88

Table 29—Participation of Women in the Politburo and Government of the Soviet Union, China, and the East European Countries

	Politburo						Government[a]					
	1972		1974		1976		1972		1974		1976	
Country	No. of Women	No. of Posts	No. of Women	No. of Posts	No. of Women	No. of Posts	No. of Women	No. of Posts	No. of Women	No. of Posts	No. of Women	No. of Posts
Albania	1	17	1	17	1	17	1	26	0	21	1	25
Bulgaria	1	17	2	18	2	18	—[b]	41	1	46	2	46
China	2	21	2	25	1	25		—	7	63	7	63
Czechoslovakia	0	13[c]	0	13	0	—						
Czech government							1	25	0	27	0	27
Slovakia	1	11	1	11	1	11	0	16	0	19	0	19
East Germany	1	23	2	26	2	28	0	19	6	18	6	18
Hungary	0	13	0	12	1	15	4	86	1	83	1	78
Poland	0	15	0	16	0	17	1	32	3	35	3	35
Romania												
Permanent Bur.	0	9	1	15	0	5	3	51	4	56	4	58
Executive Com.	—	—	2	15	2	23	—	49	—	52	—	61
Soviet Union	0	21	0	23	—	—	1	75	1	75	0	75
Yugoslavia	0	—	0	30	0	38	—	—	3	52	3	52
Total	7	160	11	221	10	197	13	420	26	547	27	557

Source: Radio Free Europe, "Communist Party–Government Line-up," 23 November 1972, 22 July 1974, 21 February 1976, and 7 December 1976, Radio Free Europe Research Department, Munich, West Germany (mimeographed); *Peking Review*, no. 35/36 (7 September 1973), p. 10; ibid. no. 4 (24 January 1975), p. 11.

[a]These figures refer to all the national ministerial posts, membership in the state councils, and the chairmanships of national assemblies.
[b] — = data not available.
[c]The Czechoslovak figures are for 1969.

republican executive committees in 1972, 12 were women (20 percent), while 46 of the 340 members of the republican party central committees were women (13.5 percent) (see appendix 1). Czechoslovakia has never had any female representation in its Politburo, and its state of semioccupation since 1968 has apparently discouraged any change in that pattern. Bulgaria, which prides itself on its progressive policies toward women, has only 2 female ministers, the second of whom in 1976 replaced a deposed female minister of light industry. In 1975, China, whose women might be considered the least "advanced" of any Communist country, had 2 female Politburo members and 3 female ministers. With the exit of Mme. Mao, just 1 female Politburo member remains, and as of this writing there have been no official releases on the composition of Chinese government bodies.

The types of political posts offered to women in Communist government administration are listed in table 30 and appear comparable to the places women occupy in the economy. Women are represented in the presidia of the national legislatures and state councils in small numbers. Among the ministries and government committees, women are found in Light Industry, Education, Health, Art, and Culture, and in the War Veterans and Invalids Administration. No woman has ever been appointed minister of defense, foreign affairs, or agriculture, or head of any of the government departments central to the security and economy of the country, with the exception of Anna Pauker, Romania's first female Communist minister of foreign affairs and a long-time activist and pre–World War II political leader. The pattern appears to be for women to take secondary positions in the state councils and in the leadership of the legislative bodies.

China presents a deviation from the norm, with a woman heading the Ministry of Water Conservation and Power. One development in the 1970s has been an increased emphasis on the work of the national women's committees. Both of Bulgaria's female Politburo members represent the women's committees, as does Lina Ciobanu in the Romanian Party Executive Committee. Significantly, however, neither Ms. Ciobanu nor Mrs. Ceacescu, the Romanian first secretary's wife, serves on the more powerful Permanent Bureau. The executive director of the Romanian Women's Committee, Maria Groza, is the female representative to the leadership of Romania's legislature. In East Germany, the Women's Department is part of the Central Committee Secretariat, and a woman is naturally secretary of that department. Women do not head any other Central Committee department in any other Communist country.

Communist officials, particularly in East Germany and the USSR, like to point to the number of women deputies to the national legislatures as an indication of the significant participation of women in high councils of government. But a comparison of female representation in the central committees

Table 30—Government Posts Assigned to Women in the Soviet Union,[a] Eastern Europe and China, 1976/1977

Type of Post	Number of Women Holding It	Country
Deputy official in		Yugoslavia (1), China (4),
legislative body	8	Albania (1), Poland (1), Romania (1)
State Council	7	East Germany (5), Poland (1), China (1)
Ministry of Justice	1	Bulgaria
Ministry of Public Education		
and Instruction	2	East Germany, Romania
Ministry of Health and Welfare	3	Poland, Yugoslavia, China
Ministry of Light Industry	2	Hungary, Romania
Chairman, Committee on		
Art and Culture	1	Bulgaria
Chairman, National Council		
of Women	1	Romania
War Veterans and Invalids	1	Yugoslavia
Ministry of Water Conservation		
and Power	1	China
Total	27	

Sources: Radio Free Europe, "Communist Party Line-Up," 7 December 1976, Radio Free Europe Research Department, Munich, West Germany (mimeographed); Peking Review, no. 4 (24 January 1975), p. 11.
[a]Since the death of Furtseva, former minister of culture, in 1974, there have been no women in the top government posts in the USSR.

with that in the national legislatures of the various Communist countries (figure 9) shows where the real power lies.[1]

Yugoslavia provides a case in point. Various constitutional reforms undertaken in 1953 (including the devolution of power to the constituent republics and the decentralization of the League of Yugoslav Communists) served to increase the power of the legislature at the federal and republican levels of government. Interestingly, the participation of women showed no significant increase during this period. In 1971 and 1972, Tito responded to the crisis of ethnic nationalism by recentralizing the Party and, to a certain extent, the government. A new constitution was drafted to strengthen the federal administration and to at the same time guarantee republican rights. But women have been the victims of these latest government reforms. The 1974 constitution provides for the institution of a delegate system based on representation and election from the economic and sociopolitical self-management organizations. There are now no direct elections to the federal government in Yugoslavia. The self-management organizations elect delegates from their groups to the Federal Chamber. The republican and provincial legislative assemblies elect

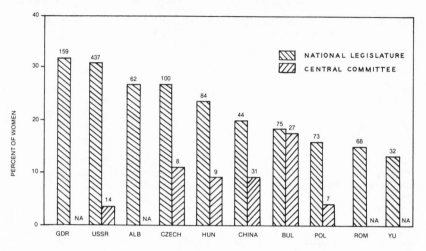

FIGURE 9. Women in the Central Committees and National Legislatures of Eastern Europe, the USSR, and China, 1975

representatives to the Chamber of Republics and Autonomous Provinces. Such provisions eliminate individuals and groups (such as housewives) that cannot or do not have their own self-management associations. Since only about half of Yugoslav women work, half are not eligible for federal office, official disclaimers to the contrary.[2] One may expect, therefore, a decreasing percentage of women in the Yugoslav federal legislature concomitant with the increased functions and powers of that body.

Another dimension to the pattern of female participation is found in data on Communist Party membership (see table 31). While the percentage of women recruited into the various parties has steadily been increasing, the increase has been slow. Indeed, the Soviet press was triumphant when it announced the highest female membership in its history prior to the Party's 1971 congress.[3] In no Communist Party does female representation approximate the proportion of women in the total population. Yet the Party constitutes the principal point of access to high political and administrative office.

Table 32 indicates a correlation in Bulgaria between membership in executives of social organizations and membership in the Communist Party. Despite the larger female membership in the Fatherland Front (64.7 percent of the respondents as compared with a BCP membership of 10 percent), Communist Party members comprised almost a third of those who said they had leading roles. In a comparison by column, the correlation becomes more apparent. Almost 60 percent of the Communist Party members said they held or had held elected leadership positions, while only 17 percent of those who were members of the Fatherland Front indicated that they had held an executive position.

Thus, countries with a low level of female membership in the Communist Party can be expected to have fewer women in executive positions. Those with a high rate can be expected to have more women in such positions, with certain exceptions; Bulgaria, for example, has one of the highest levels of female representation in the Communist Party of any Communist country, 26 percent. Yet women constitute only 18.75 percent of its national legislature, as compared with over 30 percent female representation in the USSR's Supreme Soviet. Again Bulgaria has two female ministers while China has three. These inconsistencies serve to confirm the rule. Membership in the Supreme Soviet is not an indication of the political power of an individual. Moreover, two female ministers in a country that has a smaller total number of ministries compares favorably with the representation of women in China's more numerous high-ranking government organs. Leadership in the Communist countries is rooted in membership in the Communist Party, and women continue to be underrepresented there.

The greater political activity of women at the local level, as evidenced in tables 33–35 and appendix 1, provides confirmation of the tendency for

Table 31—Women in the Communist Parties of Eastern Europe, the Soviet Union, and China, 1972

Country	%
Albania	24.0
Bulgaria	26.0
Czechoslovakia	27.4[a]
East Germany	—[b]
Hungary	25.0
Poland	23.2
Romania	25.0
Soviet Union	22.6
Yugoslavia	16.1
China	—

Sources: Same as for tables 30 and 34, except for *Enhancing the Role of Women in the Building of a Developed Socialist Society* (Sofia: Sofia Press, 1973), p. 17; and *Život strany*, no. 18/ 1966 (21 September 1966).

[a]This is the 1966 figure, which is the most recent statistic available. For a discussion of women in the Czechoslovak Communist Party, see Barbara Jancar, *Czechoslovakia and the Absolute Monopoly of Power: A Study of Political Power in a Communist System* (New York: Praeger, 1971), pp. 111–12.

[b]— = data not available.

Table 32—Distribution of Bulgarian Women in Elected Leadership Offices of Social and Political Organizations by Level of Membership and by Social and Political Organization

Membership	% of Total Sample (16,060)	Social and/or Political Organization				Not a Member of Any Social Organization (%)
		BCP[a] (%)	BZNS[b] (%)	DKMS[c] (%)	OF[d] (%)	
A. By Level of Membership						
General membership	10.0	0.6	18.0	64.7		6.7
Member of the executive	32.4	1.0	16.6	49.3		0.7
Past member of the executive	21.2	0.5	20.1	57.1		1.1
Never a member of the executive	5.1	0.5	18.0	68.1		8.3
B. By Social and Political Organization						
Member of the executive	12.8	41.6	24.2	11.8	9.7	1.3
Past member of the executive	8.6	18.4	8.0	9.6	7.6	1.4
Never a member of the executive	78.6	40.0	67.8	78.6	82.7	97.3
Total	100.0	100.0	100.0	100.0	100.0	100.0

Source: Adapted from People's Republic of Bulgaria, Ministry of Information and Communications, *Zhenata v stopanskiia, obshchestveniia, kulturniia zhivot a v semestvoto* (Sofia: Central Statistical Office, 1971), p. 88.

[a]BCP = Bulgarian Communist Party.
[b]BZNS = Bulgarian Agrarian Union.
[c]DKMS = Dimitrov Young Communist League.
[d]OF = Fatherland Front.

women to concentrate in the lower echelons of the political hierarchy. Apparently, the Soviet Union has made the most concerted effort to recruit women into political office, with East Germany coming second. The higher representation of women in the regional rather than the local councils of Poland, Yugoslavia, and Hungary is to be noted. However, when the Hungarian figures are broken down, as in table 34, the general pattern reaffirms itself. The proportionately higher representation refers only to council members at large, not to executive posts.

The Bulgarian figures in table 35 do not tell the whole story. In answer to the question, "Are you a member of an organ of elected political power?" 0.4 percent said they were councilwomen to the rural collective people's soviet, 0.3 percent said they were deputies to the municipal soviet, 0.3 percent said they were deputies to the regional soviet or to the National Assembly, 1.0 percent indicated that they had been deputies at one time, and 98.0 percent said they had never held an elective office (see table 37).[4] If one compares table 33 to table 34, the figures in the Bulgarian sample suggest that politically active women tend to be office workers. The highest proportion of women in political office come from the urban white-collar strata.[5] However, proportionately more women hold offices in the rural soviets than in any of the other government bodies. While 35 of the female deputies to the rural soviets indicated they were cooperative farmers, 32 said they were office workers. White-collar representation in municipal soviets is, as might be expected, even higher; of a total of 51, 37 said they were office workers, as compared to 14 self-identified blue-collar workers.

In Hungary, by contrast, women are more likely to be members of municipal councils than of rural councils. The Bulgarian survey bears out Ethel Dunn's finding that for the amount of free time they do have, peasant women can be surprisingly active.[6]

A final question on the Bulgarian questionnaire that is worth noting is, "Did you participate in political education in 1969?" Of the respondents, 19.3 percent said they had, as propagandists, and 6.6 percent said they had attended lectures. Apparently, political activity does not extend to political

Table 33—Women in the National and Local Councils of Eastern Europe and the Soviet Union, 1971[a]

Country	National Legislature (%)	Regional Council (%)	Local Council (%)
Albania	26.0	—[b]	—
Bulgaria	18.75	—	25.65
Czechoslovakia	—	—	—
East Germany	31.8	35.9[c]	36.0
Hungary	24.0	30.0[d]	25.1
Poland	15.9	25.3	27.5
Romania	14.6	—	31.0
Soviet Union	30.5	34.8[e]	45.8
Yugoslavia	13.6	16.8[f]	15.2

Sources: Same as for Table 30, with the addition of Komlós Pálné, ed., A nök a statisztika tükrében (Budapest: Hungarian Woman's National Council, Kossuth könyvkiadó, 1974), p. 62.
[a]No such data is available for China.
[b]— = data not available. Albania reported 1,878 women on the people's councils in 1970; see Eugene K. Keefe et al., Area Handbook of Albania (Washington, D.C.: Government Printing Office, 1971), p. 119.
[c]The percentage for town or village councils is 29.8 and for urban assemblies, 35.2.
[d]In Hungary, known as municipal and county councils.
[e]Refers to the percentage of women in the Union Republic Soviets. The figure was 38 percent in the 1969 elections for the Supreme Soviets of the Autonomous Republics. See Barbara Jancar, Women and Soviet Politics (New York: John Wiley & Sons, 1974), p. 126.
[f]Refers to membership at the republic level.

Table 34—Female Council Members and Officeholders in Hungary, 1973

	Local Council			Municipal and County Councils		
	Total No.	No. of Women	% of Women	Total No.	No. of Women	% of Wom
Council members	77,114	16,843	21.8	2,013	604	30.0
Executive council members	10,129	1,908	18.8	191	35	18.3
President	1,660	109	6.6	20	0	0.0
Deputy president	133	12	9.0	59	2	3.4
Secretaries	1,745	520	29.8	20	1	5.0
All officeholders	3,538	641	18.1	99	3	3.0

Source: Komlós Pálné, ed., A nők a statisztika tükrében (Budapest: Hungarian Women's National Counc Kossuth könyvkiadó, 1974), p. 61.

education. The Bulgarian data confirm the more general statistics presented in the earlier tables. Woman's low profile in Communist politics parallels that in most countries around the world.

The highly unsystematic data coming out of China regarding female participation in government administration indicate that a similar pattern obtains there. Ruth Sidel observed on her 1971 trip that women are well represented at the local level. According to Ms. Sidel, 60 percent of the neighborhood committee members in the Kuang Chian district of Shanghai were women, while women were head and vice-head of the Min Kang Residents' Committee in the Fangsheng neighborhood of Shanghai. The first committee is an official organ of state power at the primary level and is subordinate to the district committee. The latter is responsible for family groups living in two or three blocks of a city district. Its functions include the mediation of disputes between family members or neighbors, the organization of study sessions, and the organization of sanitation work.[7]

Female representation at the higher levels of government is much lower. Since the Cultural Revolution several campaigns have been aimed at recruiting more women "cadres," perhaps due to the influence of Chiang Ch'ing. The results indicate an increasing number of female administrators. From the data available, it would appear that these women now represent about 22 percent of the total administration at all levels of government, with higher representation in the Communist Youth Organization.[8] However, female participation in the revolutionary committees probably amounts to no more than 10 percent, a figure that has been publicized in local Chinese papers.[9] Visitors to China confirm that women are still very much in the minority in high-level administrative posts, and Chinese officials are outspoken in admitting that more work has to be done in this area. However, when compared with the

European Communist countries, the proportion of women at the very top of the Chinese political hierarchy is quite respectable, although substantially lower than in the basic administrative units.

A final indicator of the degree to which women participate in the running of Chinese politics is their representation on the urban and provincial committees. As of 1971, 5 of 158 positions (3.2 percent) were held by women. Of these, 3 were deputy heads of revolutionary committees, one was listed as a worker, and one was just a deputy. None was head of a Party committee. All held positions at the bottom rung of the hierarchical ladder.[10] If the Party is the highest authority in the country, women apparently are not very influential in its management, despite the rather favorable percentage of women on the Central Committee.

The proportionately higher representation of women on local and municipal councils cannot be taken to infer a high level of political involvement at the local level by the female population as a whole. The proportionately few women who identified themselves as active members of self-management organizations in the Yugoslav survey described in table 36 may be contrasted with a similar number in the Bulgarian survey data in table 37. The higher percentage of politically active females in the Yugoslav sample is partially explained by the urban and educational bias of the survey. Even given this bias, however, the survey respondents indicated they gave little time to what they termed "social" activities: 65 percent said they spent no time; 15.1 percent, one day; 2.8 percent, three days; and 5.3 percent, four or more days a month. The 196 women, or 17.9 percent of the sample, who spend two or more days in "social" work were women with a secondary or post-secondary education. The least active women were those with no schooling or an incom-

Table 35—Women in Political and Social Organizations by Social Group and Residence: Bulgaria, 1969

Organization	Total (%)	Blue-Collar Worker (%)	White-Collar Worker (%)	Cooperative Farmer (%)	Urban (%)	Rural (%)
Bulgarian CP	10.0	7.6	17.0	5.4	11.8	5.7
Bulgarian Agrarian Union	0.6	0.3	0.5	1.0	0.4	0.9
Dimitrov Young Communist League	18.0	19.0	23.5	9.2	20.9	11.5
Fatherland Front	64.7	65.4	57.0	73.4	62.0	71.0
Not a member of any organization	6.7	7.7	2.0	11.0	4.9	10.9

Source: People's Republic of Bulgaria, Ministry of Information and Communications, Zhenata v stopanskiia, obshchestveniia, kulturniia zhivot a v semestvoto (Sofia: Central Statistical Office, 1971), p. 81.

Table 36—Female Membership in Self-Management Organizations in Yugoslavia, 1970

Organization	Leading Management Position (%)	Active Member (%)	Passive Member (%)	Nonmember (%)
School council	0.5	5.1	1.1	93.2
Council of health institution	0.5	1.8	0.4	97.2
House council	0.8	5.2	2.9	91.0
Voters' meeting	0.6	9.7	12.6	77.1
Community council	0.3	2.1	3.9	93.6
Jury member	0.3	1.6	0.1	98.0
Other	0.3	1.5	0.3	97.8

Source: Miro A. Mihovilovic, principal investigator, *Reports and Studies: The Influence of Women's Employment on Family Characteristics and Functioning* (Zagreb: Institute for Social Research, University of Zagreb, 1971), p. 308.

plete primary education.[11] "Joiners" in Communist countries evidently come from the more educated strata of society, as they do in this country and in Western Europe.[12]

In terms of participation in nonpolitical organizations in the Yugoslav sample, the Red Cross ranked first, with 18.4 percent of the respondents indicating active or passive membership. As regards political organizations, participation in the community council ranked fourth after voters' meetings, house councils, and school councils. However, community councils ranked sixth, or last, in terms of the number of women leaders in the sample. The main reason women gave for not participating in "social" activities was that it was too much work and they were already too burdened with job, house, and children.

The survey noted a marked disinterest in politics on the part of Yugoslav women. Even the percentage of those with a secondary-school education who indicated some political involvement was low. In Bulgaria, the sample showed an even lower degree of participation in terms of election to political office.

A possible trend in political participation may be observed from the data on the age distribution of elected female officials in the Bulgarian sample. The modal ages for membership in the rural soviets were 30–34, and 50–54; for membership in the municipal soviets, 40–44; and for election to the regional and national assemblies, 35–39.[13] In view of the predominance of women in agriculture, it is not surprising to find more younger women running for rural office. Indeed, the largest proportion of those women in the sample who were between 20 and 24 and held any political position, held a position in the rural soviets. However, ranking next in terms of the participation of younger women are the municipal soviets.[14] If the sample is representative, one might expect increasing numbers of young women as deputies at the municipal level to balance their participation in rural government. These women by and large will be married and thus will be bearing the burdens of home and work that have been described. What the data show is that women about the age of 45 in general tend not to be involved in elected office. Their noninvolvement is doubtless a reflection of the tradition that women do not interest themselves in politics. The influx of younger women into urban and rural posts suggests the beginning of a change in this posture.[15] However, it must be remembered that the percentages are low and that the vast majority of the Bulgarian sample never held elected office at all.

The Yugoslav and Bulgarian studies indicate that women in Communist countries continue to be nonpolitically oriented. Politics has remained a man's world. Women tend to get involved in social organizations of an apolitical character, such as the Red Cross in Yugoslavia. Their limited participation in the political sphere suggests two things: (1) that women find politics unattractive, and (2) that the men who dominate politics do not want to let them in. The first line of thought will be discussed in detail in a later chapter. The second leads to the problem of "woman's place" in Communist politics.

"WOMAN'S PLACE" IN COMMUNIST POLITICS

Unquestionably, there is a "woman's place" in Communist politics. Table 30 indicates that, although not well defined, woman's place at the national level is either as deputy chairman or deputy president of the legislative body, or as head of a ministry whose sphere of interest is close to woman's traditional role: Health, Education, or Light Industry. Both China and Bulgaria

Table 37—Women in Elected Offices by Social Group and Residence: Bulgaria

Elected Office	Total (%)	Blue-Collar Workers (%)	White-Collar Workers (%)	Collective Farmers (%)	Urban (%)	Rural (%)
Deputy to the rural soviet	0.4	0.2	0.6	0.9	0.3	1.1
Deputy to the city soviet	0.3	0.3	0.8	—a	0.4	0.0
Deputy to the regional soviet or national deputy	0.3	0.3	0.5	0.1	0.5	0.1
Past member of an elected assembly	1.0	0.7	1.5	0.9	0.9	1.1
Never an elected official	98.0	98.7	96.6	98.1	98.1	97.7

Source: People's Republic of Bulgaria, Ministry of Information and Communications, *Zhenata v stopanskiia, obshchestveniia, kulturniia zhivot a v semestvoto* (Sofia: Central Statistical Office, 1971), p. 81.
aData not available.

have had women as ministers of justice, but both women had had long and distinguished careers. In terms of position on the hierarchical ladder, the data presented in appendix 1 indicate a clear tendency for women to stop at the deputy or secondary leadership level, and table 32 shows that women are better represented in local and regional politics than in the national arena. Table 34 suggests that at the regional and local levels women tend to concentrate in the post of secretary, with participation in higher executive positions falling off sharply.

Another way of understanding woman's place in Communist politics is to look at the types of careers followed by men and women in the Communist political elites. A grant from the State University of New York Research Foundation enabled me to conduct such a study based on the Archive on East European Political Elites held by the University of Pittsburgh. The archive contained biographic and career data for the political elites in four East European countries: Bulgaria, Czechoslovakia, Hungary, and Poland. Participation in the elite was operationalized in the archive to mean membership in the Politburo, Secretariat, Central Committee, or Council of Ministers. Of the 1,341 individuals in the archive, 103, or roughly 8 percent, were women. Poland had the fewest women in the elite, 15; Bulgaria came next with 19; Hungary had 22; and Czechoslovakia, 47.

The hypothesis I wanted to test was that women have not been recruited in large numbers to positions of high political leadership in Communist countries because they have had significantly different career patterns from men. Recruitment was defined as having occurred when a man or woman was elected to the Central Committee of the Communist Party for the last time. For those who never were members, the cutoff point was the last entry in their career. The different events in the lives of each individual in the Archive were collapsed into 12 career categories, five of which were identified as preparatory career activities: education; membership in a Communist or non-Communist (prewar) youth organization; non-Communist prewar political activity; revolutionary underground activity or incarceration; and membership in the Communist Party. Seven categories referred to specific types of careers: military, economic, scientific-cultural, intellectual (SCI), mass organizations; Party; and government. The final category was election to the Central Committee. The six types of careers and the education category were further subdivided into three levels: low, medium, and high. In order to handle the data, five types of analysis were used: (1) a count of the movement of individuals between careers; (2) a count of the movement of individuals *within* careers across the three levels; (3) a count of the movement of individuals from levels within one career to levels in another career; (4) a calculation of the expected value for the movements of individuals between careers as compared with the observed value, and a plotting of career patterns where the expected value differed by more or less than 5–10 percent; and (5) a comparison of the percentage distribution of women in the central committees of the four countries over time.

The results of this study disproved the initial hypothesis. Separate, specific career paths for men and women into the elites of the Communist countries were not found. However, the study did support the contention of a strong male bias to political power in the four countries under observation. Significantly, men had no defined career paths. Women, on the other hand, had a narrow basis of access to power positions and fewer career options. The military, SCI, and government offered the most frequent advancement for men, while careers starting at the lowest level of the economy (worker) and moving though the mass organizations and the Party were characteristic of career progress for women. Male elites tended to follow a routinized path to the top, moving through the three career levels more often than women, who were more likely to be promoted from a low level to the top of the Party or government hierarchy. On the average, men dominated the top career levels. Men and women started off with an equal chance for promotion at a low career level, but women fell off at the middle level and did not regain the advantage with men. The career paths of both men and women started in youth work and/or revolutionary activity, but men were more likely to have participated in non-Communist prewar politics. Of all the careers, the Party appeared to be the major determinant in elite recruitment for women. Men had more equal access across all careers.

While disproving the initial hypothesis, the study did reveal what might be described as a "woman's way" to power in Communist societies. This way appears to be characterized by fewer choices; a reliance on secondary power institutions, such as the mass organizations, for promotion; and fewer opportunities for promotion to the top.[16] The study thus complements an earlier analysis by Joel Moses on women in political roles in the Soviet Union. Moses also found that women have limited political career options open to them in Communist societies. According to his findings, the most likely starting point for a woman in Soviet politics is as an indoctrination official. Because of the nature of the narrow specialty into which she is recruited, a woman's chances for advancement are much lower than those of a man, who has broader skills.[17]

In Eastern Europe and the Soviet Union, I was fortunate to be able to talk to several women in political roles. In the Soviet Union, the district major of Leningrad was an elected offical. The director of the Lenin Museum in Tashkent was a former worker in the peace movement (mass organization). In Bulgaria, Hungary, and Romania I talked with the executive directors of the national women's committees. In Yugoslavia, I spoke with hotel manager Natalija Grzecic, who has been active in regional and national politics since the 1950s.

Mayor Starodub, of the Leningrad district, had majored in linguistics at the university. She then became active in the administration of the Komsomol and subsequently was asked to run for the office of district mayor. She thus had had no prior education or experience that would qualify her for the job. Khudzhume Shukurova had had a general university education, but in this case it fit the type of political activity in which she was engaged. The executive directors in Bulgaria and Romania had degrees in literature. The Bulgarian director came from a worker's family, while Mia Groza was the daughter of the first Romanian prime minister after World War II.

Ms. Grzecic's qualifications for political involvement rested squarely on her knowledge of the hotel industry. For 30 years she managed a restaurant. Then, in 1951, she became director of a hotel management school in Dubrovnik, a post she held until 1971. As economist by training, she obtained a three-month fellowship to study hotel management at Cornell University. In 1963, she was elected to the Federal Assembly for two years as first deputy for the tourist industry. In 1969, she was reelected to represent tourism in the Council on Industry and was one of two women from 120 deputies to serve in the economic sector of Parliament.[18]

At present, Ms. Grzecic is vice-president of the Dubrovnik Executive Committee for Tourism and serves in the Federal Chamber of Commerce, where she represents the hotel industry of Dalmatia. She is also a member of the Yugoslav Tourist Association and is hotel industry representative to the Foreign Trade Commission. To my persistent queries as to whether being a woman had made any difference in her career, she said that perhaps it had, in a positive way. "Because I was the only woman, and because I knew what I was talking about, they perhaps listened to me more carefully than they might have if I had just been another man."

This very small sample provides field confirmation of my more detailed elite study. (1) Women tend to be recruited to limited political careers from limited or limiting educational backgrounds. It is hardly likely that the chairman of a women's committee or a hotel manager will become first secretary. It is more probable that a district mayor will become mayor of a whole city. Of the mayors in East Germany in 1972, 18.6 percent were women.[19] But mayors in Communist politics have not customarily advanced to the top of the political hierarchy.

(2) The decision of where women will be recruited is largely a Party matter. With the exception of Ms. Grzecic, all the other women in my sample had been "asked," appointed, or recruited. The most common response to the question, "How did you reach your present position?" was, "The Party" or "they" came to me and suggested it.[20]

When the Party feels it needs a woman in a certain position, it will recruit one. When you are asked, it may not be wise to refuse. Although even emigrants appeared reluctant to talk about the activities of the Party, some women I interviewed indicated that in their experience, it had happened that a woman did not really want a certain position. But the Party asked her and then, "poor woman, what could she do?" Party activity was also seen as a means to foster one's career, sometimes the only means to reach the top, Thus, the tendency of women to stop at middle-level positions in both economic and government administrative positions, may reflect their lower career aspirations as compared with men, and a reluctance to put themselves in situations where the Party may "ask" them. The impression I derived from conversations with several Soviet and East European emigrants was that the Party commands. If there are women in certain governmental positions, the Party has determined that a woman should be there. By extension, if the Party really wanted women in positions of supreme power, it would put them there as well.

It is possible that here, as elsewhere, China presents a deviation from the rule. Ruth Sidel was told on her recent visit there that the neighborhood committee must be partially chosen by "the masses" in the places where it works. Each "interest group" gets together and elects two representatives, "first by thinking through their own views on neighborhood matters and then evaluating whether the representatives will represent them correctly." But Sidel goes on to say that while the representatives are first chosen by their units, they are then approved by "higher authority." The Fengsheng Neighborhood Committee is comprised of 16 women and 11 men. Seven members are full-time "cadres" who are often but not always Communist Party members.[21] The committee is representative not only in interest but in age. The selection process, the full-time representation of the Party "cadres," and the composition of the committee suggest that in China, too, the Party, as the "higher authority," is the major determinant of who gets into political office. Hence, if women are better represented in the higher echelons of the Chinese government, it is because the Party wants them there.

The statistics presented relative to the participation of women in government at the national and local levels supports this type of explanation. In the case of the Soviet Union, the progression of percentages from 30.5 percent female representation in the Supreme Soviet to 45.8 percent representation in local government seems more a matter of statistical tokenism than anything else. In East Germany the deviation between 31.8 percent female representation at the national level and 36.0 percent at the local level is even smaller. When one compares country to country, Yugoslavia excepted, the spread between the lowest and highest percentage of female representation at the national level is 12 points, with a mean of 23.08 percent. The temptation is to ask whether there is not something special about the 30 percent range toward which the East European countries seem to be aspiring.

By contrast, the percentage of female representation in the central committees of the various countries is much lower than that in government administration and exhibits a larger range, running from a low of 3.5 percent in the

Soviet Central Committee to 18.3 percent in the Bulgarian Central Committee, with a mean of 9. The range of participation suggests that the more internationally powerful a Communist country is, the less likely it is to promote women to its most important decision-making body. This conclusion breaks down in the cases of Poland, which is internationally less powerful and has very few women in its Central Committee, and China, which is becoming increasingly powerful and has proportionately more women in its Central Committee than Poland has.

A second conclusion is derived from the elite analysis mentioned earlier. Where there is flux or an easing of tension in the struggle for political power, the proportion of women in government increases—e.g., in the unsettled conditions immediately after World War I and World War II and during periods of liberalization such as that in Hungary in the mid-fifties and in Czechoslovakia in the early sixties. When the struggle for power intensifies, there is a drop in the participation of women and a concomitant increase in the proportion of men (see figure 10). For example, female representation in the Soviet Central Committee plunged from a high of 7 percent in 1917 to 0 during the Civil War and thence vacillated from crisis to crisis, dipping during Khrushchev's fall from power and leveling off at 3.5 percent in the seventies.

China is apparently an exception, for female representation in the Central Committee has been steadily increasing. An intervening factor here may be that the Chinese Communists themselves insisted that the support of women was essential to winning the Civil War. Hence, the somewhat greater degree

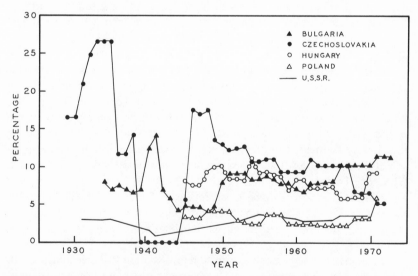

FIGURE 10. Women as Percentage of Total Membership in the Central Committees of the Communist Parties of Bulgaria, Czechoslovakia, Hungary, Poland, and the USSR, 1930–1970

of female involvement at the upper levels of government may reflect to some extent the women's share of the input into the victory of communism. Significantly, during the period of the Civil War, female representation in the Central Committee was virtually nil and has increased only since the Communist accession to power. It will be interesting to see whether the percentage of women in the Central Committee formed under Hua's new political administration maintains the exception or conforms to the political-crisis rule.

In summary, women's political role in the Communist countries seems to be determined by three factors: (1) a concept of her place as analogous with her economic and domestic place; (2) a limited choice of political career options based on limited economic and educational options; and (3) most importantly, the factor of Party recruitment, which appears to support women in high-level political posts during periods of internal stability and to overlook them for such positions during periods of domestic crisis, but which at all times tends to define a woman's political career at the middle rung of the political hierarchy.

SYSTEMIC FACTORS LIMITING PARTICIPATION OF WOMEN IN COMMUNIST POLITICS

ABSENCE OF AN INDEPENDENT POLITICAL ORGANIZATION FOR WOMEN

As mentioned in chapter 4, the Bolsheviks were wary of creating a separate political organization for women that might create a feminist deviation, splitting the revolutionary movement into male and female. There was also the danger of influence from "bourgeois" feminism. The Party was particularly suspicious of the political rights groups because of the support by many feminist organizations of the czarist involvement in World War I.[22] Still, it was generally recognized that women had to be organized or else their very backwardness and oppressed status might become an impediment to the Revolution.

It must be stressed that, in addition to men, women in the Party were skeptical of an independent women's organization.[23] However, the spontaneous organizing by women workers, as well as the activities of the prerevolutionary feminist groupings, apparently convinced the Bolsheviks that they had to appeal to women as a separate group. In March 1917 a women's bureau was set up under the Petrograd Bolshevik Committee. The task of the bureau was purely political agitation. Its lack of independence was indicated by its subordination to the Petrograd Committee, which directed and approved its work.[24] This bureau was a prototype of the *Zhenotdel* created in 1920.

The struggles of the *Zhenotdel* should not be underestimated. The literature suggests that during the first five years of its existence it waged a war on two fronts, the first for its survival, and the second to cater to the very real needs of women at that time. In 1922 the *Zhenotdel* complained of discrimination because its director was not invited to attend sessions of the Party Orgbureau, but was consulted only when "women's questions" came up.[25] At the same time, the Women's Department was engaged in alleviating the high unemployment of women that had resulted from the introduction of NEP and in carrying on its vital literacy program.

The war on two fronts was basic to the whole Bolshevik woman's movement. The women were forbidden to organize themselves. If they made any progress in their own liberation, they were labeled "bourgeois" feminists. Since the Party had a great many other things to contend with, the problems of women had to be relegated to second place. The *Zhenotdel* gradually reverted to a vehicle for Party influence among women and was finally abolished in 1929. My discussion of its activities with Soviet women raised little comment except among Uzbek women, who particularly stressed the work of the delegates' conferences in awakening Moslem women and in combating illiteracy. An older woman in Fergana spoke with pride of having learned to read through the *Zhenotdel* and then told me how she herself had gone on to teach other women. Her daughter, she exulted, was now a teacher in a secondary school.

The early Soviet policies regarding the political organization of women set the pattern for the other countries that subsequently became Communist. An independent women's movement was as inadmissible as an independent trade union movement. "Feminism" was divisive to the Revolution. After some experimentation, however, the eventual solution was to create the women's organizations that exist today. In Albania, China, Czechoslovakia, East Germany, and Yugoslavia a national women's group is organized on territorial lines like the mass organizations but is closely supervised by the Party "cadres"; its membership numbers in the millions.[26] In the Soviet Union, Poland, Hungary, Bulgaria, and Romania, this organization was disbanded during the fifties and replaced by a national committee composed of prominent women who are called on to give advice pertaining to women's problems. The "woman's question" was considered solved. By the mid-1960s, however, all the European Communist countries were aware that the question was far from solved, and Poland led the way in the research to demonstrate why.

The inability of women in Communist societies to organize independently clearly hampers female political participation. The national women's committees cannot be said to represent women. As I was told in Moscow, Budapest, Sofia, and Bucharest, the Party leadership decides what should be done and then the committee undertakes the requisite research or performs the requested task. Representative of the nature of the women's committees is Soviet astronaut Valentina Tereshkova. Although chairman of the Soviet National

Women's Committee, she has never been identified as a specialist on women's problems. She is largely there as a figurehead. The activity of these committees is oriented primarily overseas, although the committees do supervise the publication of the national women's journals. Foreign access to women in the Communist countries, particularly if they are women of any prominence, is channeled through the committees, and committee members are called upon to represent the country at international meetings. The committees further compile data on women and present them to the Party leadership, or to whoever might ask. Basic research on women's problems, however, is not done through the committees but in the institutes and universities, prominent female members of which are represented on the committees.

The appointment of the chairmen of the women's committees to the Politburo in Bulgaria and Romania, and the upgrading of the chairman of the East German women's organization to the status of Central Committee secretary, suggests that some East European leaderships are beginning to consider the role of women in their societies more seriously, no doubt because of the negative demographic trend. But only in Bulgaria did I feel that the members of the Women's Committee saw themselves as having any real initiative. There the executive director told me that the committee was empowered to make recommendations for legislation to the leadership. In addition, if the committee finds that there has been discrimination against women in the sense that the law has not been properly upheld in terms of promotion, pay, or giving women leave for childbirth, the committee is authorized to take the delinquent enterprise to court. As far as I know, this power of enforcement is unique to the Bulgarian Women's Committee. Finally, the Bulgarian Women's Committee believes it has developed a good international image. Its president, Elena Lagadinova, has represented the women's organizations of all the East European countries, excluding Yugoslavia, at Comecon meetings, and has been the champion of a proposal to coordinate efforts to solve women's problems in these countries.

The work of the women's committees cannot be considered analogous to that of the mass organizations, the trade unions, professional unions, or youth leagues, since women are not organized as women on a hierarchical territorial principle. There are women's committees attached to the trade union in every factory and enterprise, and women's organizations in the collective farms, but their allegiance is to the trade union or the local collective, not to the women's organization. Their primary function is to make sure that the law is observed regarding women's legal rights at work. They also have an educative function. They hold meetings on health problems relating to women (pregnancy and child care) and lecture on what women are doing around the world. In Romania, I was told they sometimes give fashion shows. Plainly, their function is not to represent women, but to mold them in the direction of the ideal female worker. Since there is no hierarchical structure as in the mass organizations, the factory women's committee cannot send delegates to a central women's council. Thus, the national women's committees operate as advisory bodies to the Party and government, with no roots in or support from a regional, local, or enterprise unit. Understandably, the chairmanship of such a committee is not a post of political power as is the chairmanship of a trade union, or even the Writers' Union. Indeed, the position would seem to invite a figurehead.

The Chinese example illustrates that the national women's organizations should perhaps not be expected to have a stronger political voice. The All-China Women's Federation and numerous local women's associations played a leading role in mobilizing women to the cause of the new government in the 1950s, mainly in agriculture. But in 1966, at the height of the Cultural Revolution, the organization was broken up and the woman's movement came to a standstill. In 1971, the Party began again to pay serious attention to the question under the slogan, "We must rectify the tendency to neglect work concerning women." First, special education courses were set up to train female Party "cadres" and to educate the female masses in the thought of Mao Tse-tung, and a program was launched to recruit new Party members. Women's representative congresses were reestablished and each brigade, the smallest village unit, was provided with a women's guidance team. Once again, as in the 1950s, the policy was reaffirmed that women should receive equal pay with men. In 1972, the Congress of Women Representatives elected women's committees that were reintroduced into the communes and industries. Finally, 1973 saw the rebirth of the Women's Federeation, whose organization and activities appear to parallel its predecessor.[27]

The history of the Chinese Women's Federation illustrates that the women's movement has been permitted, first and last, by the sufferance of the Party. It cannot claim independence. The same is true of the Czechoslovak organizations. The Czechoslovak National Organization of Women followed the fate of its sister organizations in Eastern Europe during the 1950s on the grounds that the women's question no longer existed. It was reconstituted after 1968 with the stated aim of developing "a fundamentally socialist conception of the solution to the women's question." In the case of East Germany, the appointment of the chairman of the National Women's Organization to be Central Committee secretary provides confirmation of the subordination of women's problems to Party dictates in a manner far more direct than that which other mass organizations have experienced, since neither the head of the trade unions nor the head of the Youth League is a Party secretary.

It might be argued that every mass organization exists at the Party's discretion and that the woman's movement is no exception. The fact is that no other mass organization has been disbanded in the European Communist countries and that the Women's Federation was the last mass organization to be reconstituted by the Chinese after the Cultural Revolution. The reasoning that hampered its rebirth was the classic Marxist argument: "All work includes women. There is no need to grasp women's work separately."[28] I submit that the women's organizations are on much more tenuous ground than their more readily accepted mass movement competitors, even in Yugoslavia, where the Women's Conference shares with the League of Communists, the Socialist Alliance, the Trade Unions, and the army the distinction of being the only institutions in the country to have centralized structures.

The consequences of the uncertainities surrounding the existence of women's organizations and committees are fundamentally two.

First, the other mass organizations are primarily concerned with totally different problems from those that affect the status of women and attitudes about them. In their implementation of Party directives, it is only natural that women's problems should be put in second place. As a result, no matter how much research is carried on about the status of women, without a women's organization, there is no other institution in Communist society that can effectively do anything about women's problems, particularly since the other mass organizations are dominated by men.

There is a Party department for women in East Germany and in China, but there is no similar organ in any other Communist country that focuses exclusively on women's questions. Thus, in the majority of Communist countries, women have no effective political grouping within the Party through which to "lobby" for their interests. True, pressure may be exerted through clients in government and economic administration, among whom women will be represented. But their representation will be as local officials, or management and workers. No group represents women. Thus, women find themselves at a disadvantage at every point in Communist politics where interests form and client-supported demands are made upon the leadership. As Massell showed in the case of Central Asia, or as the lone voice of Kollontai testified in the early days of Soviet power, when a revolution in the life style of women is attempted by an authoritative institution, men move to inhibit the change either by joining the institution, such as the Central Asians did in the case of the Communist Party, or by exerting pressure in other ways. Without their own organization, women have no way of appealing to other women and mobilizing their support for change. Overwhelmed by male dominance and male bonding in these institutions, they either withdraw or acquiesce.

The second consequence follows from the first. "Liberation" has in fact meant the "double shift." In all the Communist countries women are aware that they work harder and longer hours than men. The press is full of accounts or letters in which women request that their men do more housework, or on the contrary stay out of housework because they make more mess than if they did not try to clean up.[29] The classic picture is that of the husband coming home to sit in front of the TV while the wife, who has come in later because of the evening shopping, turns to prepare the meal, feed the family, supervise the children's homework, and do some housecleaning before falling into bed exhausted. Every woman I interviewed in Eastern Europe and the Soviet Union made me aware of the problems she had coping with daily life. What impressed me was the degree to which women seemed resigned to their difficulties and greater burdens. "What is the use?" a Polish woman said. "They have all the information but it will never change. More research will just go over the same old ground."

The explanation for the hold the conservative trends have as regards marriage and family in the life style of women in all the Communist countries lies at least partially in the fact that women have no way to discover the mutuality or universality of their problems, to discover female bonding, to find support and reinforce one another—in short, to mobilize politically.

One of the most important aspects of the present women's movement in this country and Western Europe has been consciousness-raising, a recognition of common experience. Yet even where it is allowed, a broadly based women's political movement seems incapable of getting off the ground. The large majority of women remain in the traditional culture in which they were raised, but the fact that they *are* free to organize means that they can be agents of change. In Communist society, a woman's fragmented life in the family is supported by isolation as a woman at work, where she is merely another worker. Woman's place, then, inevitably retains its "natural" association with the traditional home.

LACK OF A MEASURABLE INDICATOR OF FEMALE POWER

It is hard to equate directly regime response to certain conditions with satisfaction of *group* demands in Communist societies. Jerry Hough has found a correlation between the percentage of women deputies in a local soviet and the existence of an adequate network of nurseries and preschool institutions or health care facilities. The problems of women have also surfaced in the many surveys undertaken in all the Communist countries. Although directed at investigating women as a labor resource, or at understanding the dynamics of family life, the research has uncovered many of women's essential grievances: the lack of services, the need for more preschool facilities, the long hours of work. And the regimes have responded as the documentation in earlier chapters here has indicated.

The question of whether we are witnessing a demand made with client support followed by regime response is problematic, and would require information about the dynamics of research or the nature of the interaction between deputy and constituent. Is it proper to say that recognition of a need is the same thing as acceptance of a demand with its implication of support behind it? I think not. Certainly, there is a difference between being given a car because your need is recognized, and deciding you want a new car and satisying your demand. But admittedly, need and demand can fuse.

If women do exert political pressure in Communist societies, it appears to be indirect at best, localized, and focused on specific "women's" issues. A content analysis of three Soviet newspapers during the first six months of 1974 determined that letters to the editor written by women appeared more frequently in the local *Vechernaia Moskva* [*Evening Moscow*] than in the more national *Izvestia* or the erudite *Ekonomicheskaia gazeta*. The subjects of the letters were overwhelmingly related to matters of education, consumer goods, household, and communal service needs.[30] The editors of *Sovietskaia zhenshchina* and *Rabotnitsa*, as well as the Romanian *Femea*, told me that the bulk of the thousands of letters they receive from women ask questions about education, child care, or problems at work. To the extent, then, that female problems at work and the expansion of day care facilities are given priority by a particular regime, one can probably say that there has been some attempt to satisfy an expressed demand.

There is no way of determining whether female power exerts any influence in policy areas other than those designated as relevant to women. Are women in Communist countries highly concerned about peace, for example, as the leaflets emanating from the women's committees would have us suppose? Since women are represented in the top policy-making echelons only in token numbers, and none are involved in shaping foreign policy, no estimates can be made as to their approach to foreign affairs. What the content analysis mentioned above confirms is an apparently universal tendency on the part of women to interest themselves in the very practical considerations of everyday domestic life.

There are, of course, exceptional examples of individual women influencing political events in the Communist countries. The most obvious and most successful has been Chiang Ch'ing, whose model plays and views on the direction of Chinese culture helped start the Cultural Revolution, in which she played a significant role. Apparently, she managed to develop a sizable power base independently of her husband, among elements of the People's Liberation Army and provincial officials aligned with the "radical" cause. Her personal power, however, could not withstand the organized forces of the new leadership of the Communist Party once her husband was gone. No wife of a European Communist leader has enjoyed a similar amount of influence.

The one woman in a European Communist country to have a popular following and to influence the course of politics in the past decade is Savka Dubcevic-Kucar, past president of the Croatian Communist League. Significantly, she appears to have developed her own constituency, and it was only strong pressure by Tito and the upper echelons of the League of Yugoslav Communists that forced her and the other two members of the Croatian "triumvirate" sponsoring national autonomy within a federal Yugoslavia to resign.

Two other illustrations of influential women in high Communist politics are Chou En-lai's wife, Teng Yin-ch'ao, who was responsible for the drafting of the Chinese Marriage Law of 1950, and the women lawyers who pushed through the Soviet Family Code in 1968. In contrast to Mme. Mao and Dubcevic-Kucar, these women exerted indirect rather than direct political influence.

Along the same lines, Natalija Grzecic stressed her ability to contribute or influence because of her expertise, as did the director of "Miraj" in Bucharest. These examples indicate that some women do have an opportunity to exert influence, particularly the wives of prominent figures in China. But the numbers of women who can do this are few and far between. Clearly, individual influence is not open to the great majority of women in the Communist societies, any more than it is open to women in the West. Because of the inability of women to organize politically, "woman power" in the Communist countries is a bare ripple below the surface of a male-dominated society in which military might and economic progress come first.

BIASES IN THE COMMUNIST POLITICAL SYSTEM AGAINST WOMEN

The question here is whether identifiable biases unique to Communist political systems account for the low level of political participation of women by discouraging them from trying to gain political power. But there is no clear, objective answer to the question. One could ask the same of the so-called democratic systems. The percentage of women in the United States Congress is not that different from the representation of women in the CPSU Central Committee. There are a few notable exceptions to the poor representation of women in high-level positions of political power, such as Mrs. Helen Thatcher, the leader of Britain's Conservative Party. The governors of Connecticut and Oregon are women, as are the vice-governors of other states. But on the whole, it is curious that in democracies, where women control half the vote, they tend to be so little involved politically.

Perhaps the question might be rephrased. Is there something in the structure of Communist political systems that discourages women from entering the political arena? On the one hand, there is the record of the considerable revolutionary activity of Russian women in the nineteenth century. Women, in fact, formed the nucleus of the Nechaev, Dolgushin, and Chaikov groups. These women were remarkable individuals in their own right and were apparently treated equally by men within the group. They frequently performed tasks beyond their strength. Idealists to the core, they would starve if the workers or peasants with whom they came into contact were starving, and they selflessly demonstrated their commitment to the Revolution. Female membership in the Bolshevik Central Committee reached its peak in 1917 at the very moment the old order was collapsing. During the war years, women in Russia, as in England and the United States, demonstrated their courage and fortitude in industry. Then came Soviet power. Since the passing of the old generation of Bolshevik women, there has not been a single woman, with the possible exception of Furtseva, who can be cited for her role in either the Party or the government. True, there are Yadgar Nasriddinova in Uzbekistan and Nizoramo Zaripova, vice-president of the Supreme Soviet in the Tadzhik Republic, but it is doubtful whether these women, remarkable as they may be in terms of Soviet Central Asia, are comparable, in terms of influence and contribution to the country, to the older generation. In Yugoslavia, between 1941 and 1945, 100,000 women are reported to have served in the Partisan Army. Of these, 170 became officers by the end of the war and 91 were later named national heroes. Two million women participated in the Communist-directed National Liberation Movement, and a staggering 620,000 gave their lives for the cause. No women, however were appointed to the Provisional Government in 1943, and only two women, both representatives of the Communist-organized Anti-Fascist Women's Front, were appointed to the 64-member presidium of the provisional legislature, the Anti-Fascist Council of National Liberation.[31] The present political apathy of Yugoslav women has already been noted earlier in this chapter. In the rest of Eastern Europe, one is at pains to cite a single woman of distinction in the younger generation. Of the first generation of ruling Communists, Anna Pauker comes to mind immediately, but she would hardly seem comparable to Rosa Luxemburg or Clara Zetkin. For all the talk about female liberation, women appear to be less visible at the forefront of the political arena under Communist regimes than they were under the so-called oppressive "bourgeois" governments.

Turning to China, we again find the older generation of Communist women playing prominent roles in the new regime (see appendix 2), mainly because of the family relationship of these women to the male politicians. On the other hand, the wives of men who are purged also are purged. The one female newcomer to the Politburo in 1975 was active in the Cultural Revolution. She is virtually unknown and can hardly be equated with the illustrious women of the first generation of Chinese Communists. As in Russia, the "oppressive" climate of imperialism and capitalism appears to have provided a more fruitful ground for female political activists than has the present regime.

The course of Russian, Yugoslav, and Chinese history just prior to and after their Communist revolutions suggests one explanation of this problem.

Female political participation seems to increase during moments of systemic change such as occurred in Russia at the end of the nineteenth century and during the Yugoslav and Chinese civil wars, and to decrease once order has reasserted itself. When society is in a state of flux, old hierarchical structures break down and authority becomes fluid and unstable. In such a situation women have easier access to political roles, since dominant institutional patterns are weak. Moreover, social change affects women directly in every aspect of their lives. Hence, there is a greater likelihood of political interest and political response. Third, role differentiation according to sex tends to diminish as women find they have to perform tasks formally considered male, such as waging guerilla warfare or working in armaments factories while men fight at the front. Finally, because the new order has not yet been established, the real possibilitiy of change still exists. Change was what Vera Figner, Inessa Armand, and Kollontai expected from the Revolution, change that would fundamentally affect the relationships between men and women. Instead, order reasserted itself, family life was reinstated along the "bourgeois" pattern, the demands of daily life engulfed women, and they withdrew from politics.

In this sense, women as a political group in any society may be considered marginal, exerting their influence and becoming involved only when their direct interests are touched. Their participation is marginal because the demands on their time are such as to preclude sustained political activity.

I would stress that female political participation tends to increase in the presence of challenges to an existing political system. It is not coincidental that the present women's movement in the United States got under way during the sixties, in the shadow of Vietnam, the beginning of the crisis of confidence in political leadership, and the start of the economy's slide down to recession. Nor is it a coincidence that women finally got the vote in England, the United States, and France *after* those countries had been through wars that challenged the very survival of their political institutions. Hence, we should not be surprised to find women active in revolutionary movements in pre-Soviet Russia or becoming heavily involved in the Communists' bid for power in Yugoslavia and China.

Certainly, there will be exceptions to this generalization. But the data show that the establishment of Soviet, Yugoslav, and Chinese Communist order inevitably meant the reordering of women out of politics back to their "place" at home and, as it turned out, at work. The contention here is that built-in biases in the Communist system have promoted the depoliticization of women to the degree that female political apathy has become a fundamental characteristic of the system. Four of these biases deserve mention.

The "Command," Educative Nature of the Communist System. Democratic centralism and the leading role of the Party are not mere slogans. They express central facts about Communist political life. Ample description has been given of the official ideological interpretation of the meaning of female liberation, an interpretation that has changed little from country to country. Women are told what to do. Women are to be educated, to be mobilized into industry, to be taught how to participate in public life. Recent statements in the Chinese press have exhorted the Communists to "get the great mass of women . . . to take their place on the labor front."[32] The Communist political and social order is far more rigid and hierarchically structured than its Western counterparts. One Soviet official told me, *"U nas, nash poriadok"* ("We have our own order."). If women find it hard to struggle against the less restrictive political structures of the West, it is no wonder that they are largely apolitical in most Communist countries.

Failure to Teach Women Political Skills. In the entire history of the CPSU as a ruling party, only 84 women have risen high enough to fill any of the approximately 4,600 positions that have been available in the leading Party organs since 1917.[33] Only two women made it to the Orgbureau or the Politburo. Most get only as far as the Auditing Commission or the Control Commission. With the exception of East Germany, there is no woman in the secretariat of any of the ruling parties of Eastern Europe, nor has there been, except for Anna Pauker in Romania. Yugoslavia is somewhat different, but it is significant that as real power has devolved upon its legislature, the participation of women has decreased. In China, women are better represented in the Politburo, but there is no female representation (nor has there been) in the more powerful Standing Committee of the Politburo.

These data, in my opinion, tell us something fundamental about the relation of women to the Communist system, even in its modified form in Yugoslavia. Men who rose to the top of the Soviet power structure devoted their lives to this goal. The unsuccessful were physically or economically liquidated. Brezhnev and Khrushchev rose to the top over the bodies of fallen comrades. The same may be said of men who reached the pinnacles of power in Eastern Europe: witness the fate of Rákosi, Nagy, Gomułka, or even Dubček. In China, Lin Piao did not survive the warfare waged against him. The more bitter the struggle, the more dire the consequences for the loser. It takes time to learn the skills necessary to survive in such a political world. Women traditionally have not developed political skills, except in the aristocratic feudal societies. Elizabeth, Victoria, Catherine the Great, Catherine of Aragon, Maria de Medici all were members of a privileged class in which they could learn the art of politics. Indira Gandhi is a modern-day equivalent. Golda Meir learned her skills in the long, hard struggle for Israeli independence. As in the West, no Communist country is dedicated to teaching women these skills. Contrary to the West, they do not even provide women with the opportunity to learn them. With the possible exception of China, women are being tied down to home and work, with their domestic roles taking precedence over gainful work. The majority of women in Eastern Europe, the Soviet Union, and China are still peasants struggling to make a living off the land, in many instances only one step removed from grinding poverty. In such situations women, no more than men, can be expected to be politically involved voluntarily. They have to be politicized. And the record shows that politicization has been half-hearted at best: active when the regime deems it necessary, as China did in the 1950s and the early seventies, or as the Soviet Union did in Central Asia in the twenties, but lapsing when the need for regime support has passed.

The Ruthlessness of Advance. It takes a certain ruthlessness to advance in the Communist political system. The greater the power at stake, the more ruthless seems the struggle. Hence, the larger percentage of women in the Central Committee of Bulgaria, which does not aspire to be a great power, and the low percentage of women in the Soviet Central Committee. Similarities could be drawn between the Communist countries and the Western democracies, but there is a difference in degree between the ruthlessness of Stalin or Brezhnev and the ruthlessness of Watergate. In the Soviet Union, Eastern Europe, and China, the loser is destroyed, if not physically, at least politically and so-cially. He becomes a nonperson. In the United States, he can return to fight another day. Hence, in the Communist political system, not only is politics a full-time job, but one has to stake one's life upon it.

The Nature of Party Work. Enormous demands are made on the individual who seeks political success in the Communist system. Becoming a Party member means giving up a good deal of your private life. The higher one rises, the more personal sacrifices one has to make at the cost of greater insecurity. Once you lose, there is no way back up again. Such demands are ill-suited to a woman with a family.

In my interviews I tried to determine how much extra time a Party member has to spend as compared with an ordinary worker or professional person. There are, of course, Party meetings at least once a month in every institution or organization. These are obligatory. I attended one of these meetings at the University of Sofia. The subject was a report on the population conference that had just been held in Bucharest. There were five speakers. The meeting started around five in the afternoon. As the speakers took their turns, the dinner hour approached. Some of the participants began looking at their watches. The report ended and questions were solicited from the floor. For a moment there was silence and everyone began making motions toward the door. It was almost seven. Then a gentleman in the front row stood up and talked for fifteen minutes. After him, another stood up to dispute what he had said. Then a woman made a five-minute comment. By this time, the audience was clearly restless. There was some concern lest the dispute between the first two discussants draw more of the comrades in, but fortunately the moderator called the meeting to a close. It was a relief when we all stepped out into the night.

In all fairness the topic, population control, was interesting. A slide presen-tation graphically portrayed the facts of population growth. The trouble was that the hour was late. People had already put in a full day. My women colleagues quickly excused themselves after the meeting because other matters demanded their attention. As Party members, they were required to attend, even if the time was inconvenient.

Aside from the regular meetings, there are extraordinary gatherings when a matter of importance comes up. In addition, each Party member is required to perform what is euphemistically described as "socially useful work," or "one's social obligation." For an academic, such as Zoya Yankova in Moscow, this may mean organizing and arranging lectures on your specialty—in her case, marriage and the family—in nearby factories. From time to time, she may have to prepare a lecture and deliver it herself. But just arranging the program and getting the lecturers can be time-consuming. Then too, a university teacher who is a Party member has a circle of students with whom political discussions must be held at regular intervals. The instructor is not expected to choose the topic; that is chosen by the university Party Committee and distributed through the Youth League. The instructor is not even expected to deliver a talk; the meetings are more like seminars. But the instructor has to assign topics to the students and direct the discussion when the circle meets. One university teacher estimated that she spent about 25 percent of her free time on Party matters.

Other women told me that Party affairs were incorporated into the normal workday and they could not give me an estimate of the time they spent on them. The district mayor of Leningrad said that Party matters and the requirements of her job were all mixed up together. But her day was long, starting around seven in the morning and oftentimes ending late in the evening, if she had meetings with her constituents, as she frequently had. A woman executive in the Soviet trade union movement devoted a Saturday to "volunteer" work. She worked with a brigade raking leaves on Lenin Prospekt. Party members may also be involved in security matters at their place of work. For example, on public holidays, or when there are public parades, the members may spell each other on watch duty at their place of work. For women with children, such demands can make large inroads into the precious time needed on weekends and holidays to do the week's laundry or to make special shopping trips to buy the children's clothes.

If you are a member of the Party apparatus, your work *is* the Party or, as one woman put it, you do not perform "any socially useful work." While such positions bring one the unwritten privileges that accrue to "the New Class," they also involve placing one's self almost permanently on duty, coupled with the necessity to play the chess board of intrigue and politicking that inevitably accompanies any political career. Such a prospect cannot appeal to the majority of women, most of whose time is taken up by family responsibilities.

Another aspect of Party work that respondents who had emigrated from the Soviet Union particularly censured was the fact that a Party member was required to promote the Party line. A rector or chairman of a department in an administrative position in a university was frequently asked to make requests of students that he knew they would not like and that he was not convinced made practical sense. For example, he might have to "request" students to "volunteer" to go to a collective farm to help bring in the harvest, or help on a construction job. He might be involved in a student's dismissal from the university because of some political charge held against him. Knowing you have to do what the Party tells you makes it difficult to sustain open student-faculty relations.

A final factor that must be mentioned, although it is changing in Eastern Europe and obtains mainly in the Soviet Union and possibly China, is that once you become a Party member, you cannot voluntarily resign. To hand in your Party card under Stalin was tantamount to asking for your own liquidation. Even now, Soviet Party members know that resigning from the Party means the virtual end of their careers. To be asked to resign is to put yourself under threat of arrest or worse. At best, you lose your job, maybe your apartment, as well as other privileges you had as a member. Thus, once you become a Party member, you know it is a commitment for life.[34]

In Eastern Europe the situation is somewhat different. After 1968, and before the "review" of Party cards in 1969–1970, which became the largest purge of the Czechoslovak Party (KSČ) in its post-World War II history, many KSČ members turned in their cards voluntarily. While legal prosecution was surprisingly small after the Soviet invasion of Czechoslovakia, the comrades who resigned put themselves permanently under suspicion. No one moves easily in and out of the Communist Party in the Communist countries.

In summation, the absence of a separate woman's organization, lack of a measurable indicator of female power, and the biases of the Communist political system in terms of its authoritarian posture, failure to teach women political skills, the intensity, risk, and oftentimes brutality of the power struggle, and the commitments of Party membership—all suggest that engagement in the Communist political arena demands too high a price for most women. The result has been that women have largely remained outside the political power structure and, as the evidence has shown, have demonstrated a marked passivity toward anything political. The political world remains male, except where, as in China, the males choose to draw women in. Both the economic and ideological-cultural environments appear to militate generally toward the internalization by women of traditional role patterns, with China perhaps being the exception. The political structure would seem to set too great a cost at too little benefit to encourage women to risk changing that situation.

WOMEN IN POLITICAL DISSENT

A concluding comment should be made about women dissidents. Some of the most remarkable women in Soviet history are to be found on the dissident side, women like Anna Akhmatova, Marina Tsvetaeva, Bulat Okudzgava, Tatiana Velikonova, Alla Tsvetopolskaia, Maia Ulanovskaia, Larissa Bogoraz, and Natalia Gorbanevskaia, who risked their lives in Red Square to lead a demonstration against the Soviet invasion of Czechoslovakia in August 1968. This action was reportedly taken against the wishes of male dissidents, who were reluctant to put the women's lives in jeopardy.

In Eastern Europe, women dissidents are also few in number but are exceptional individuals. Many are intellectual and political leaders of no mean stature. Women in the Czech Charter '77 movement include philosophers, journalists, artists, and singers of national reputation. Dissent in Yugoslavia is harder to identify because of the changing nature of Yugoslav constitutionalism,[35] but the stand of Dubcevic-Kucar for Croatian national rights against the decision of the Communist Party would seem to be a clear case of opposition. A leading philosopher, Dr. Zoya Pesic-Golubovic, has been identified with the "Belgrade 8" "anarcholiberal" group condemned by Tito in 1974.[36] If one contrasts these women to those who have not challenged authority in their countries, the dissidents distinguish themselves by the force of their character and originality.

Women have likewise been outspoken in Poland and East Germany, particularly as demonstrators against specific government practices. In Poland, female workers went on strike in 1964 and 1971 protesting wages and working conditions in the huge textile center of Łódź. In 1971, in contrast to the male workers, who chose delegates to represent them in their negotiations with the Party and government, the female strikers apparently did not do so. The government was faced with one of two options: to accede to their demands or to engage in large-scale reprisals. Reportedly, the government chose the former course and increased wages to meet the strikers' conditions. The deliberate choice of nonorganization by the women workers constitutes a new approach in Eastern Europe to the perennial problem of dealing with an all-powerful government.[37]

The reasons why women turn to the dissent movement are not known, but several opinions can be offered. The response of Soviet emigrant women to the question was surprisingly uniform. Women become dissidents because of personal experience. The moment comes in the majority of cases when the injustice of the power structure touches their lives in a direct and personal manner: the desire to emigrate to Israel is frustrated; a parent or close relative is arrested; a man in the dissident movement to whom one has been attached is arrested and sentenced to prison; there is a decision to defy authority by signing a letter in defense of Alexander Ginzburg; personal unhappiness may play a role. Larissa Bogoraz, for example, had just heard of the arrest and imprisonment of her fiancé prior to the Czechoslovak invasion. Her demonstration on Red Square might have been her way of showing her indifference to what happened to her in the face of the harm of her loved one. A young woman may feel isolated at school, or she may be an orphan and seek the companionship of sympathetic friends. Soviet women who become dissidents appear to envision themselves as less immersed in ideological issues and more concerned, like the female revolutionaries of Czarist times, with the age-old issues: injustice, inhumanity, suffering, oppression. The commitment, I was told, is affective rather than intellectual. The adverse position of women in Communist society or the need to develop a new self-concept has little to do with it.[38]

Such opinions should be taken critically, both because of the limited information we have on female dissidents and because of the notable exceptions to this view—Anna Skripnikova, the religious dissidents, the women in the Charter '77 movement, and the Yugoslav female dissenters. In addition, personal experience is also a significant element in turning men into dissenters; witness the cases of Solzhenitsyn, Sakharov, or Ludvík Vaculík. It is important to recognize that whether the individual is male or female, the decision to become a dissident is highly personal and voluntary, bearing the risk of self-annihilation. It is also an assertion of independence. In the latter aspect, it is a totally different kind of decision than that which is made if one is asked to join the Party or has decided on a career in legitimate politics. Because dissident life is essentially individualistic, it is natural that both the men and women in the movement should be those who have broken with Soviet or Communist institutions and are strong individuals in their own right.

As in Czarist times, women appear to form the nucleus of the Soviet dissident circles. Among the Baptists, they are the comforters of the families whose men have been sent to Gulag: they look after the orphans; they help compile the lists that provide information on where every man has been sent; and, of course, they help type the Baptist journal, *Bratsky vestnik*.[39] In my interviews with the women émigrés, I gained the impression that women in the dissident movement continued to play nurturing and supportive roles. Maia Ulanovskaia, for example, who now lives in Israel, helped type some of the *Samizdat* material. She also took in persons sought by the police. As she explained to me, her actions were motivated by humanitarian concerns. One helped one's friends, rather than supported the particular views of one friend over another.

In Eastern Europe, women also appear to be a rallying point for dissenters. Mme. Dubcevic-Kucar was known as "Queen Savka," signifying her central role in the Croatian demands for autonomy in 1971. Czech singer Marta Kubisová focused attention on Charter '77 by asking fellow artists all over the world to support the campaign for human rights in her country in February 1977.[40]

Women, however, do not lead the dissident movement. That is the province of males. I asked Maia Ulanovskaia why this is so. She was unable to offer any explanation except in her own case. Her parents had been arrested and she came rather unwillingly into the movement through meeting young people in similar circumstances. She was subsequently sentenced for five years for having been a member of a "dissident circle." This circle, as she saw it, was merely her group of acquaintances. Upon her return to Moscow after the general amnesty, she met her husband, also a dissident. She insisted she is not, and was not ever, interested in politics. Few women, she believes, are as politically minded as men, and perhaps that is why they are not interested in leadership positions.

Ms. Ulanovskaia's explanation is only one of many. Her insistence on her lack of interest in politics may be the product of both her cultural and political environments. Another explanation could be that the huge problems of injustice in the European Communist countries tend to obscure the question of whether women *should* be in leadership positions among dissidents. A third explanation relates to the dangers involved. According to the women émigrés I interviewed, men in the movement are careful not to expose women to any extraordinary risk. The perceived necessity to protect women dissidents would automatically lead to a supportive rather than an equal female role. A final reason is suggested by the works of Galina Telnikova: "Women's liberation in the Soviet Union means hard labor."[41] The whole concept of equal status as it is discussed in the West is foreign to the dissidents. As a consequence, women do not strive for leadership roles either in the legitimate political system or in the dissent movement.

Thus, women's rights have yet to find expression among the dissenters. The fundamental issue of civil rights may be so all-encompassing that the woman's question appears trivial, but in my opinion the foreignness of the concept of women's liberation is probably the basic reason for its failure to become an issue. While the revolutionary movement under the Czarist regime did generate a movement for female equality, the rebirth of the women's movement in the West has not found an echo in the Soviet Union or Eastern Europe. My émigré respondents assured me there was no need for one. Women had been liberated as much as they could be.

Perhaps the relation of women to the Communist political system may be best summed up in the words of one émigré dissident: "What can one person do against a system like that? They are strong and they can squash you. Resistance is futile." Women in Communist societies may have a greater sense of practicality than men. Tied down to a job, and preferring home and family to high risk and an uncertain future, the vast majority of women have opted out of the Communist political structure both as contributors to it and as opponents, except when the regime calls them forth to participate.

6 / Leadership Guidance: Legislation and Decrees

Leadership guidance involves actions taken by governments to modify the existing conditions of a client group, in this case, women. In determining an appropriate response, the governments have to assess the relative value of the various demands or needs presented by the environment. Communist leadership response to the needs of women may be divided into two time periods: the postrevolutionary phase, when the objective was to break up the old social order, and the maintenance phase, in which the regime constantly reviews the various options whereby it may maintain itself in power and promote economic development.[1]

In taking action, any leadership essentially performs in two ways: (1) it prescribes by law, decree, and resolution; and (2) it promotes through propaganda, education, and socialization. In the case of the Communist countries, the two functions vary with the different time periods, depending on national economic and social requirements. Initially, Soviet legislation regarding women was truly revolutionary and transforming, as such legislation now is in China. However, the authoritarian posture inherent in the Communist ideology, coupled with the European Communist leaderships' continuing attachment to traditional cultural standards, has resulted in an increasingly conservative attitude regarding sex roles. A brief comparative examination of Party and government regulatory and socialization policies in the two time periods will substantiate this thesis. This chapter will be devoted to Communist legislative policy, the next to Communist socialization policy.

THE POSTREVOLUTIONARY PHASE

The postrevolutionary phase is characterized in all Communist regimes by a pursuit of labor and marriage policies designed to mobilize women into the work force and loosen their ties with the home. Included in this type of legislation would be: Party resolutions and laws pertaining to the secularization of marriage, easement of divorce, and permission for abortion; laws establishing preschool and child care facilities; and laws determining the conditions of women's work and the extent of female employment. The dates and nature of the laws are given by country in table 38. In addition, every Communist constitution drawn up during the postrevolutionary period granted women de jure equal rights. The emphasis was on revolutionizing the status of women by weakening their ties to the traditional home and promoting their allegiance to the new state.

It is to be remembered that, except for Yugoslavia, there was nothing voluntary or native about the onset of communism in Eastern Europe. It is thus impossible to divorce the impact of the Communist takeover from the influence exerted by the conquering Soviet Union. From the start, all East European policies concerning women, including Yugoslav policy, had their origins in Soviet experience. Hence, the discussion that follows will concentate on post-revolutionary policy in the Soviet Union and China as exemplary proscriptive leadership guidance during this period.

THE SOVIET UNION

Following the Russian Revolution, the Bolshevik regime inaugurated a relatively relaxed policy toward marriage and divorce and granted permission for abortion through its 1919 legislation. The 1926 marriage law has been mentioned in a different context. It was pointed out earlier that Kollontai's suggestion for the gradual disappearance of the family and the institution of communal living never met with much enthusiasm and that she herself modified her more radical views in favor of the government's assuming responsibility for motherhood in the form of state subsidies.[2] But the marriage law itself was a fundamental milestone in the Soviet regime's prescriptions about women.

Barely a month after the Bolsheviks' seizure of power, in December 1917, revolutionary legislation permitted divorce and decreed that marriages registered by the civil authorities were the only valid marriages. It also promulgated equality of the sexes in marriage. But the law neglected to consider what would happen to women if and when their husbands left them.[3] The New Economic Policy (NEP) had brought the end of labor conscription. As women were the most unskilled part of the labor force, women were the first to suffer from job cutbacks. "Registered women" had a right to alimony. But the responsibility of the state to the woman if a couple had neglected to register their marriage was unclear. The solution proposed by the All Russian Central Executive Committee in October 1925 was to legalize unregistered marriages. An unregistered marriage was defined as living together in a joint household and

Table 38—Communist Legislation and Regulations regarding Women in the Soviet Union, Eastern Europe, and China

Legislation	USSR	Bulgaria	CSSR	GDR	Hungary	Poland	Romania	Yugoslavia	China
Post-Revolutionary Phase									
Secular marriage and divorce	1917	1945	1948[a]	1946	1949	1947	1946	1946	1950
Family law	1918	1947 1949	1950	1946	1952	1950	1953 1954	1946 1947	
Equal rights	1918	1944 1947	1948	1946 1949	1949	1947 1952	1948	1948	1949
Protective labor legislation, protection of women	1922	1947	1948	1950	1950	1950	1948	1949	
Child care	1918	1945	1948	1950	1950	1950	1948	1947	
Social insurance	1919 1925	1945	1948	1950	1950	1950	1948	1948	1951
Abortion permitted	1920	1956	1953	1956	1953	1956	1958	1952	1957
Maintenance Phase									
Change in marriage and divorce laws, family law	1936 1944 1968	1961 1966	1962	1958 1965		1964	1958 1966	1960 1965	
Abortion proscribed	1936 1944			1968			1966		

Abortion modified	1955	1973	1972	1973	1970	1969
Abortion reinstated	1953	1971	1972	1969		1973[b] 1974
Extension of social legislation, family allowances	1971					
Extension of education			1965 1972	1967		1973
Extension of protective labor legislation	1965	1960 1961	1966	1972	1965	
Restatement of civil rights	1971 1977	1968	1967	1969	1970	1973 1978
Extension of child care facilities, protection of motherhood	1971	1970	1968			1973[b] 1974
Rulings on recruitment of women into administrative positions	1970	1970	1969	1970	1973[c]	1974[b] 1972[c]

Source: The data for this table have been gathered from many sources and the reader is referred to the bibliography.

[a]Czechoslovakia, Poland, Hungary, Germany, Romania, and Yugoslavia all had secular marriage before the Communists came to power. The laws went into effect after World War I. For example, Czechoslovakia's law was passed in 1919.

[b]These laws were passed at the republican rather than federal level.

[c]Party decrees rather than regulations.

announcing this to a third party.[4] Women living in an unregistered marriage would have the same right to alimony as their registered sisters.

The law had its conservative and revolutionary features. Certainly, the recognition of unregistered marriages as legal was highly unusual. But, in fact, such recognition extended the responsibility of society to include most sexual liaisons. Living together without a marriage contract carried the same legal consequences as the registered marriage. Moreover, if the couple separated, the wife could demand that the husband's family support her. As might be expected, the main thrust of the protest was against the disposition of property upon divorce, particularly in the countryside, and the section of the code having to do with this aspect was modified to meet peasant needs at least partially. Thus, the law facilitated the formation and dissolution of sexual relationships while at the same time providing closer legal watch over them in terms of family responsibility for alimony payments.

In its labor policies, the new Soviet regime also showed "progressive" as well as conservative tendencies. Soviet legislation of the twenties and even the thirties was in many respects far-sighted, particularly with regard to the directives for drawing women into higher education and technical schools, preparing and promoting women kolkhoz members, and various directives to improve the work and living conditions of female workers and peasants.[5] When women seemed to be hesitant to try the world of work, the regime substituted quotas for women in vocational schools. In 1924, a woman foreman occasioned much publicity because it was questionable whether women were "suited" to such jobs. By the thirties, however, the regime was encouraging women into engineering by means of an open admissions policy in engineering institutes. The result was that by 1936, women comprised one-third of the labor force and 41 percent of those in institutions of higher and technical education.[6]

In the postrevolutionary period, the Soviet government further initiated protective labor legislation for women, and the protection of women was made an official commitment of the Soviet government in Article 122 of the 1936 Soviet constitution. The Soviet meaning of protection of women at work was spelled out in successive pieces of early legislation. In 1922, the Soviet Labor Code set down provisions protecting women's health at work and outlawing types of work that might endanger their ability to have children or seriously injure their health.[7] The legislation was much needed at the time. During the late twenties and early thirties *Rabotnitsa* contained frequent reports of women who had so overstrained themselves physically that they had ruined their health or damaged their uteri.

As can be seen, protection was based on physical and sociological sex differences. The physical differences concerned woman's lesser strength and her biological functions of pregnancy and childbirth. Some jobs were automatically excluded as unsuited to woman's physical condition. Sociological differences involved the recognition that motherhood was a social function and as such should be supported by society. From the outset, day care and preschool institutions were considered essential if women were to work. Mention has been made of Kollontai's and the *Zhenotdel*'s role in ensuring that these be built. In 1936, when abortion was abolished, a complementary law was passed that increased material aid to women in childbirth, established state aid to large families, and expanded the network of lying-in homes, nurseries, and playgrounds for children. Women were also granted leave before and after childbirth.[8]

However, the same legislation carried the seed of future discriminatory policies. By designing certain job categories as health risks for women, the government unwittingly created a woman's place in the economy similar to her traditional place at home. The legislation established not a prescription for bringing women into men's jobs—for the men withdrew from those that women entered—but a policy of sexual pluralism in the economy.

Soviet policy on the emancipation of Moslem women in Central Asia took shape gradually. The marriage and divorce laws of 1917 applied to Central Asia but could not be immediately enforced. In 1924, the RFSFR Criminal Code outlawed polygamy, *kalym* (bride price), and child marriage. In 1927, the Central Executive Committee of the USSR formally divested the traditional Moslem *shariat* and *adat* (courts) of all vestiges of legality and officially ended the Moslems' ability to interfere in the sphere of property, the family, and other relationships.

Penalties against expression of "the relics of the tribal order" were severe, and special decrees were enacted to promote greater equality between the sexes. These included the right to initiate divorce, the right to equal inheritance of property, and the right to equal witness in court (the Moslem ruling had been that two women witnesses were equal to one male witness). To ensure that women received these rights, special units of the *Zhenotdel* were assigned to help women with legal problems. Women thus were among the first and most frequent users of the new Soviet legal system.[9]

Parallel with the laws and decrees on marriage, property, and the family came decrees and Party resolutions opening educational institutions for women in Central Asia. According to Khudzhume Shukurova, the first of these decrees was signed in 1919 by the Party committee for the region. It required the opening of apprenticeship schools for sewing, weaving, and knitting; the organization of Moslem women in professional "cadres"; the opening of labor schools and youth and lying-in houses; the training of native midwives; and the construction of children's orphanages.[10] Such measures were not without their effect. In 1921, in Fergana Oblast, the handicrafts and textile industries reportedly had 6,385 female employees, of whom 4,900 were Moslem women. That same year, thanks to the work of the *Zhenotdel,* Tashkent Evropeiskii Universitet graduated 30 women.[11] *Zhenotdel* members were again responsible for encouraging women to go to work or seek an education. It is significant that the first *Zhenotdel* workers were Russians or Slavs. Moslem women were liberated not on their own initiative, but from without, by "Europeans" as they were called then and are still called today. This liberation extended even to a women, Kumikhon Iakovova, finishing a mechanic's course on tractors in 1926.[12]

The "European" intervention in the emancipation of Central Asian Soviet women underscores Soviet thinking at that time, which partially persists to this day. The postrevolutionary legislative phase of every Communist government has been directed toward ending the old order. In European Russia, the Civil War and the February Revolution had largely achieved the collapse of the old order before the Bolsheviks took power. In addition, traditional Russia had already experienced considerable transformation through the advance of industrialization at the end of the nineteenth century.

The emancipation of women was more radical and revolutionary in Soviet Central Asia than in European Russia precisely because of the deep roots of Islam and the feudal character of the area. Russian imperial power was ascendant in Central Asia beginning only in the mid-1880s. The ambivalence expressed by the "natives" toward the colonizing values of Russianization is well portrayed in the novel *Ali and Nino,* written about Baku at the turn of the century. The author, obviously sympathetic to the Moslem attitude, relates the love story of a rich Moslem youth and a European girl from Georgia. The book paints a vivid picture of the two distinct worlds—Asia and Europe, Islam and Christianity—that formed the young man's environment. While appreciating what Europe has to offer, Ali in no way feels inferior to the Europeans, despite their technology. When he consults the Islamic mullah about his love, the old man tells him: "A wise man does not court a woman. A woman is just an acre on which the man sows. Must the field love the farmer? . . . Never forget that a woman is just an acre."[13] The tragedy of the story is that Ali loves his wife in the European meaning of the word. Yet when the Red Army reaches the gates of Baku, he sends his wife back to Europe and goes to his death with his fellow Moslems, resisting the advancing Europeanization of his land by Soviet power.

Moslem women, then, were a key to the Soviet conquest of Central Asia. In making their status nearly equal to that of Moslem men, the Soviets were undermining the old order, which they had to do if they wanted to consolidate Soviet control. It could not be expected that Moslem men would interpret the Soviet takeover of the region differently than they had viewed the actions of the Czarist predecessors. During the Civil War, the Bolsheviks avoided a direct assault on Islam.[14] When they finally turned their attention to it, women became the focal point of their effort in a decision by the Orgbureau and Central Committee Plenum in late 1924 and 1925 entitled "The Immediate

Tasks of the Party and its Work with the Female . . . Toilers of the East.'' Inevitably, the effort ran into the opposition of Moslem men, but the retrenchment that followed *khudzhum* in the late twenties did not efface the fact that *women* were seen as an important instrument through which one order could be destroyed and a new one erected.

China

The Chinese Communists understood the role of women in the revolution perhaps even better than their Soviet comrades. During the Civil War, the pattern of later legislation became apparent in the ''red'' or ''liberated'' areas, where the Communists were determined to change the traditional structure of the family and the kinship-oriented nature of social organization. Changes in Chinese family behavior had long been in process when the Communists came to power. But during the previous regime, it had proceeded largely on a course of spontaneous evolution. The Communists made it a matter of determined policy. There is some indication that divorce and marriage were made relatively easy in the ''red'' areas. Women were encouraged to speak out against their husbands in the belief that a rebellious wife would make a good fighter for the revolution. There was even talk that the Communists encouraged communal wives.[15]

The comprehensive assault on the traditional family did not come until the end of the Civil War. One of the first acts of the new leadership was to promulgate the 1950 marriage law. According to that law, arbitrary and compulsory marriage was made illegal. Parents were no longer allowed to interfere with their children's marriage. Bride price was abolished in every form. Much like the 1926 Soviet law, all a couple had to do when they wanted to get married was to register with the local government. The marriage was considered legal if both parties consented and no compulsion had been exercised by third parties, i.e., the parents. The law outlawed polygamy and child brides and permitted the remarriage of widows. Finally, a minimum age for both partners was set.[16]

The 1950 marriage law implied far more than mere legislation regarding the way two people decided to live together. For over two thousand years the traditional Chinese family had been the most important social institution in Chinese society. As its basic constituent, it had enjoyed a large degree of autonomy in three ways: it was the primary unit for economic production, the primary unit for the protection of property, and perhaps most important, the major means of social control. By the twentieth century, the family system had outlived some of its functions, but the evolutionary development it had experienced during the years immediately preceding the Communist takeover had been uneven. Some sections of the country, mainly the cities, had faced the change, and were molding the family along European cultural patterns. Large segments of the peasantry, however, clung to the old ways.

In their attack on the family, then, the Chinese Communists were attacking the old feudal society. They strongly stressed the inhumane aspects of the traditional system—the ''bitter past'' as they called it—in order to foster the attitude that the old family was wrong or bad. In this respect they were following in the earlier footsteps of the Soviets in Central Asia. And like their Soviet counterparts, the new Chinese leadership saw in family reorganization the key means by which to engineer a social revolution and transfer loyalty from the family unit to the Party and state. Because such an objective was consciously planned, as was the eventual Soviet assault on the family order in Central Asia, direct intervention took the place of spontaneous evolution. Hence, there was much artificiality in the changes wrought by propaganda and indoctrination. While Westerners might consider the law merely ''progressive,'' the legalization of marriage and divorce in China was more than that: It meant in effect the creation of a new morality to replace the old Confucian morality and the first step in the assumption of state control over family life. In this sense, the changes in family life instituted by the Chinese Communists were more revolutionary than what occurred in Central Asia. In the old Moslem *umma,* marriage had been a public matter, regulated by Islamic law. The establishment of Soviet order meant the replacement of one form of law with another. But the Chinese family had never been subject to public regulation. Thus, the 1950 legislation did not replace former law with new law, but supplanted the Confucian ethic with Communist legality, a radically different approach altogether.

Some perspective is gained by comparing the Communist marriage act of 1950 with the Nationalist family code of 1930. The Nationalist code did not give women special privileges or advantages over men by the possibility of divorce, nor did it give women custody of the children. These remained with the husband. Furthermore, it did not emphasize the formal legalization of marriage and divorce. Instead, it recognized a marriage as being valid when performed in the presence of two witnesses in an open ceremony.[17] Thus, the nationalist family code might be best considered transitional legislation, aimed at producing change slowly. By contrast, the Chinese Communist law was an open call to revolutionary transformation. It is perhaps no coincidence that it was passed at the same time as the Land Reform Act, which implemented the dispossession of the formerly landed gentry and gave the more depressed sections of the peasantry their own plots. Both acts were aimed at the complete ''overturning'' of the old order through the simultaneous use of economic and social means.

The parallel collectivization of Chinese agriculture affected family structure and authority even more profoundly. One of its side effects was to erase the father or male head of the family as chief producer or organizer of farm activities. His role was assumed by a staff of planners and managers. Second, the status of women was raised to the degree that they were paid wages equal to those of men. Chinese women could see how much they were contributing to the family income and gained a feeling of achievement in the contribution.

As regards the marriage law, the major instrument for weakening the traditional family system appears to have been divorce. Those who divorced their "reactionary" husbands were held up by the Party as models of *fanshen,* or the successful overthrowing of feudal claims. Formally granting to women the possibility to shape their own identities has much merit. However, the fact that their "liberation" was planned as part of China's necessary social transformation brought untold hardships to the women themselves. As Vera St. Erlich made clear in her study of the changing Yugoslav family, the shift from the patriarchal system to the modern family unit left women in a precarious situation. Inevitably, the old, stable relationships were broken up and a kind of class war ensued within the Chinese family on lines similar to what had occurred in Soviet Central Asia.

As was the case in Soviet Central Asia, women were among the primary users of the new Chinese court system and represented 75 percent of the initiators of divorce cases.[18] A Shanghai paper reported that during the first six months after the law went into effect, 90 percent of all cases handled by a Peking civil court were divorce cases, while a survey of eight major Chinese cities revealed that divorce suits constituted an average of 48.9 percent of all civil cases. Grounds cited for divorce included polygamy, adultery, desertion, forced or parent-arranged marriage, physical cruelty, and child marriage.[19] If these statistics are at all representative, they provide a partial indication of the extent of the revolutionary effect exerted by the 1950 marriage law.

As in Soviet Central Asia, the problem was that the new regime promised more than it could reasonably fulfill. In October 1951, the Chinese minister of justice announced that tens of thousands of women had met a tragic death during 1950–1951. United States Air Force research indicates that some 90 percent of all female deaths in certain parts of China during this period were murders or suicides. According to the Air Force study of Chinese documents, 60 percent of those who met with a tragic end were young women under the age of 25, the majority of whom had embraced the new morality and were productive workers in the economy. As bits of evidence were pieced together from the local Chinese press, it appeared that the main reason why husbands murdered their wives was because the wives demanded a divorce. The highest correlation between cause of divorce and murder was the accusation of cruelty on the part of parents-in-law or husbands.[20]

The primary reason for women committing suicide appears likewise to have been divorce. In the majority of cases, officialdom was slow in granting the divorce or ruled that there were insufficient grounds. Women who were refused divorce ran the risk of being ostracized by their community. The refusal was not unnaturally viewed by both men and women as an indication of the guilt or moral turpitude of the women, who thereby suffered considerable loss of face or status. "Struggle" meetings were reported where young couples were accused of being "promiscuous" by local women's associations. In addition, once a woman had determined on divorce and left her husband's household, she frequently had nowhere to go. It was not always possible for her to return to her parents, and since China had always lived in households, there were no hotels where she could go. The regime had not had the time to create the necessary infrastructure to take care of divorcees. Thus, women were driven to suicide when their desire for "freedom" ran headlong into lack of support by the ruling Communist "cadres."

Finally, the whole concept of free sex clashed with traditonal values. Conservatives in the people's militia were frequently reported to beat up women whom they caught in illicit sexual relations. On occasion, they apparently brought adulteresses before mob courts. These beatings in many instances were not considered "cruel," because it had been customary in old China for men to beat their wives, and judges evidently took no particular exception to similar incidents on which they had to rule. The Communists also were reported to have tried to trick or force a woman into marrying a Communist Party member rather than a person of her own choice by putting the desired husband under surveillance or threatening the woman with imprisonment. "Struggle" meetings, which should have been used for the liberation of women, were used to lay bare love affairs or to permit husbands to take revenge on rebellious wives. As a result, the abolition of the old, strict habits of female chastity and the ending of the old taboos providing for the separation of the sexes worked to the disadvantage of women, particularly female Communists, who were considered fit prey for male passions because the Communists were perceived as the purveyors of free love.[21] Thus, the marriage law revolutionized women's status with one hand and with the other took away the traditional protective infrastructures that had surrounded women in the past, leaving them prey to all the expressions of frustration and resentment the law occasioned.

The mobilization of women into the economy for "productive" work, in my view, was far less revolutionary than the marriage law. Most women in China already worked in agriculture. They now were encouraged to enter industry. A draft for a labor law prepared by the Communist Party of China was submitted to the First Congress of Soviets held in May 1930. Among its provisions were the exemption of women from unhealthy occupations; prohibition of their employment in any work where carrying heavy loads was necessary; an injunction to prevent women under 18 and expectant and nursing mother from working on night shifts; and paid maternity leave. Equal pay for equal work also was stipulated. During the 1950s the Communist regime proceeded to put much of this program into effect, by Party ruling if not by law. A labor insurance law passed in 1951 provided social security and death benefits, and in particular provided for a 56-day maternity leave with pay for women workers. All factories with over 500 workers were required to set up medical insurance to be administered by the trade union.

To a seemingly greater extent than in the Soviet Union, occupational differentiation of the sexes was abolished in China. Much was made of the first three female bus drivers in 1951, and an all-woman air show was held on Woman's Day 1952. Women were encouraged to go into coal mining and tractor driving as well as the more traditional fields. The government's effort may be compared to the Soviet effort in the thirties. While women constituted only 8.9 percent of those employed in industry in 1952, a 74 percent increase in the employment of women in this sector was reported for that year over 1951. Also, by 1951, women constituted 60 percent of all textile workers.[22] However, the majority of women remained on the land. Men, on the other hand, were recruited into the cities. Official data for 1952 reveal that 60 percent of the rural hands were female.[23] Since the majority of women had always worked the land, the social impact of their slow movement into industry was probably less traumatic than the loosening of age-old family ties.

EVALUATION OF POSTREVOLUTIONARY POLICIES

The discussion of Soviet and Chinese postrevolutionary policies toward women suggests four general conclusions. First, the relevant legislation in both countries provides classic examples of the costs and benefits of social engineering at its revolutionary peak. Certainly, part of the motive for the 1917 and 1926 Soviet marriage laws, the Soviet program among the Moslems, and the Chinese Marriage Act of 1950 was a sincere desire to raise the status of women. Engels's dictum was that the first class division was based on sex. Eradication of this division demanded a change in the nature of the family and family relationships. The attempted political revolution within the home constituted the basis for a wider social transformation by transferring primary allegiance from the family to the state in three ways: (1) by destabilizing family relationships; (2) by downgrading the importance of fatherhood and, by comparison with the past, marriage in general; and (3) by creating a mini–class war within the family unit.

As we have already seen, by 1926 a certain retrenchment from the free-and-easy legislation of 1917 was visible in the Soviet legislation affecting both registered and unregistered marriages. The real retreat occurred in the 1930s in both Central Asia and European Russia. After 1953, the Chinese also appear to have retreated to more traditional attitudes regarding women and the family. On 11 May 1968 the *People's Daily* carried an article criticizing Liu

Shao-chi's line on the women's movement. Liu Shao-chi was accused of opposing women's participation in the Revolution, promoting "bourgeois" women's rights in politics, and confining the women's movement to nurseries and children's welfare. The implication in the article was that the women's movement had lost its momentum.

Both the Chinese and Soviet regimes ran into the inevitable conflict between the revolutionary necessity to create social upheaval and the need to provide a basis of legitimacy with a minimum measure of popular consent. The attack on Liu might be interpreted as evidence of cleavage within the Chinese leadership over the direction the women's movement should take within the overall framework of rapid economic development. After 1926, the Soviets did indeed begin to prosecute upholders of the "old tribal order" in Central Asia, but in the end a considerable amount of the old order was left intact. The male Party leaders, together with the women Party members (as noted in the discussion of the 1926 marriage law in the Soviet Union), were not ready to destabilize society to such an extent that its basic social unit would be destroyed before they had determined its replacement. In the shifting sands of change, something had to remain firm. Industrialization could not take place if the regime could not maintain order.

Second, the primacy of the goal of social change made women the victims of this process. The divorce law in the USSR (before the 1926 modification and, in the case of illegitimate children, up to the 1968 reform) left women without a means of support and frequently without a roof over their heads. With the withdrawal of patriarchal protection, free love brought sexual exploitation as habits and customs ingrained over the centuries were ruthlessly torn away. In the USSR, the necessity of child support obliged women to seek work under adverse conditions, particularly during the NEP period in Soviet Russia. "Emancipation" did not come without a price, as the violence perpetrated on women in Soviet Central Asia and China attests. No doubt, changing the family structure would have been less costly had it been less socially engineered and more evolutionary, as was the case in Eastern Europe during the interwar period. The scars left after such effort can only be vaguely estimated from continued reports in both the Soviet Central Asian and the Chinese press of the survival of old habits. The retreat from revolutionary tactics in both the Soviet Union and China indicates the strength of the cultural input from the environment in which the women's revolution was attempted. Perhaps the unisex dress in today's China and the Soviet determination to keep sex out of the media are symptomatic of the continuing felt need to regulate sexual behavior rigidly in light of previous experience. The result of the clash between revolutionary legitimacy and cultural persistence was at best a partial transformation in the status of women, with women paying the price.

By contrast, in Eastern Europe the laws on marriage and divorce passed by the new Communist regimes after the Soviet takeover caused far less trauma. In all countries, divorce had become widely accepted during the interwar period, although it was frowned upon for religious reasons. The populations were more literate and more exposed to modern (Western) culture. Industrialization was in various stages of development in all the countries. Most importantly, although the family in the peasant villages was one of extended kinship ties, it carried virtually no institutional implications in terms of economic production, protection of property, or social control. Most of Europe had lived under the concept of the rule of law for centuries. Hence, the introduction of Communist legal norms did not pose a problem as it had in China. Nor did Communist law represent a fundamentally different concept of law, as did Soviet law as compared with the Islamic *shariat* and *adat*. In this sense, the Communist legislation was a continuation of a process, not a definite break with the past. What family revolution there was, was in progress, accelerated (particularly in Yugoslavia) by the trauma of World War II.

Third, the Soviet-Chinese postrevolutionary experience points to the importance of infrastructure. Both regimes "liberated" women, but then failed to create the infrastructure that would give them a new place in society as rapidly as circumstances demanded. Hence, the frustration evidenced in the tragic deaths of thousands of Chinese women and in the double burden East European and Soviet women have to bear to this day in terms of home and career. In the conflict between the old and new, the new could not easily keep its promises. And women were caught in between. It is no wonder that they have tended to adhere to their more traditional roles.

Fourth and last, Soviet and Chinese policies toward women in the postrevolutionary period were deliberate measures to politicize them. Not only were women called into the economy out of the home, but this mobilization was interpreted as a political act, an act in favor of the new regime. Hence, the leadership's legislation and rulings regarding women in this period had definite meaning. Women who did not seek a divorce, who went to work, who wanted an education, were progressive; those who were divorced, did not go to work, did not want an education, were considered remnants of the old order. Obviously, every woman in the USSR and China did not fit the progressive mold, given the majority's previously confined and in most cases impoverished life styles. Massell provides ample evidence of the resistance of women in Central Asia to change. Soviet women opposed the 1926 marriage law. Probably for most the change was radical, too imposed, too artificial. But social censure followed those women who retreated. As one Yugoslav women lawyer told me, "I would love to take off several years and spend time with my family, but I am afraid of what other women would say. I would be abandoning my liberation."

In summation, the Soviet and Chinese experience in changing the status of women in the postrevolutionary period suggests that attitudes cannot be changed by revolutionary fiat, particularly when, as was the case with women, attitudinal change is not the primary objective of the revolution. Modernization affects every traditional social group in differing degrees. The social-engineering approach to the problems of women adopted by the Soviets and Chinese during this period meant that women bore the brunt of modernization in these societies while reaping comparatively few of the benefits that a real change in status might have brought.

THE MAINTENANCE PERIOD

A dividing line between the postrevolutionary mobilization phase and the maintenance period in Communist societies is difficult to define with a hard-and-fast rule. Essentially, the second period begins when the revolutionary experiment ends and the regimes proceed to balance economic requirements of growth with the perpetuation of their power bases. In the Soviet Union, I would put the beginning of the maintenance phase at the end of the First Five-Year Plan or coincident with the Sixteenth Party "Victory" Congress. At the latest, the second phase began with the termination of the Great Purges in 1939. The end of the First Five-Year Plan spelled the end of radical transformation and brought retrenchment in preparation for war. After the war, Soviet society assumed the prewar pattern: conformism accompanied by economic recovery. Certainly, there was no new experimentation in the area of solutions to women's problems. In Eastern Europe, the postrevolutionary phase ended in 1956, when Communist power became a permanent phenomenon.

In China, it is not yet clear whether the maintenance period has begun. Other experimental periods have followed the Great Leap Forward, including the Cultural Revolution and the more recent assault on Confucianism. The Cultural Revolution once more stressed the mobilization of women, as do similar exhortations today. However, tradition and lack of facilities have proved stronger than government edict. The considerable objection to the commune system was an important factor in the subsequent official endorsement of the continuance of the family as a unit. Hence, in terms of the end of experimentation regarding approaches and solutions to the problem of women's liberation, we are probably not far wrong in assigning 1959 or 1960 as the threshold date for the maintenance period in China, the Cultural Revolution representing but a slight interruption. I would stress that this date obtains only as far as women are concerned. The Cultural Revolution most certainly affected other aspects of Chinese life profoundly, and its ramifications have yet to be thoroughly understood. The impact of the death of Mao is another factor that remains to be evaluated. Thus, China contines to be in the postrevolutionary phase (at least up to the death of Mao), except perhaps as regards regime policies toward women.

If Communist policies regarding women in the postrevolutionary phase had a "liberating" or "progressive" cast, in the maintenance phase they become increasingly conservative. A key factor in the rising conservatism in the Soviet Union and Eastern Europe has been the negative demographic trend, which was discussed in chapter 3. The following section will concentrate on Communist policy evolution in three areas: (1) the increasing occupational differentiation by sex in Eastern Europe and the Soviet Union; (2) changes in family legislation—i.e., in marriage and divorce policies—as well as the expansion of benefits and child care facilities to encourage motherhood; and (3) regime efforts to recruit women into administrative positions.

INCREASING OCCUPATIONAL DIFFERENTIATION BY SEX

The 1970 revision of the Soviet Labor Code specifically states in Article 68: "It is prohibited to employ female labor on arduous jobs with unhealthy working conditions and underground jobs except for a few underground jobs (non-physical labor on jobs connected with sanitary and communal services)."[24] The next article forbids the employment of women for night work except where there is a special need on a temporary basis. According to Article 70, a pregnant woman shall be transferred to an easier job for the entire period of her pregnancy, as shall be nursing mothers if they are unable to carry out their normal work. Both shall continue to receive their previous average pay. Finally, Article 71 grants women a maternity leave of 56 calendar days both before and after giving birth. Should it be a complicated pregnancy, post-natal leave can be extended up to 70 days. After that, a woman may choose to be absent for a period of up to one year without pay. In the early seventies, there was some discussion of increasing this leave, but it was left at one year.

Soviet labor legislation has been a model for the East European countries. As can be seen from Table 38, every Communist country enacted protective labor legislation ensuring that women do not engage in any labor that might endanger their capacity to bear children or that is unsuitable to women as women. While there have been infringements of this legislation,[25] women in all the East European countries and the Soviet Union are forbidden to undertake arduous physical work.

The job categories closed to women because of these and similar stipulations vary from country to country. In the Soviet Union, women are forbidden to serve in the armed forces, although they may serve in the merchant marine. In Romania and China they do serve in the armed forces. In both countries,

women soldiers are much in evidence, but they are not expected to be front-
line fighters. In China, women in the People's Liberation Army (PLA) are
mostly involved in logistics, medical, and office work. More importantly,
as far as status is concerned, they do not hold higher administrative posts
in the army.[26] In Yugoslavia, women do not serve in the regular army, but
they receive equal training with men in the national guard or People's Army.
Two former women Partisans now hold the rank of general. Soviet and Chinese
policies encourage women to become tractor drivers, while Romanian
law forbids women to drive tractors, on the grounds that it has been
scientifically proven that the vibrations of the tractor seriously shake up a
woman's uterus and thereby raise the risk of damaging her ability to bear
children. Women are also universally protected from working in harmful
conditions, such as in factories where there is a great deal of noise or where
polyvinyl chloride is used. Underground work is forbidden except in China,
where there are women miners.

Perhaps the most interesting section of the Soviet and East European legislation regarding women at work is that which demands that a woman be
transferred to easier work once a medical certificate has been issued giving
official notice of pregnancy. Changing a woman's place of work because it
might not be a healthful environment for pregnancy raises the question as to
the potentially disruptive effect such changes might have on enterprise productivity. In an interview with Rosalea Speteanu, director of "Miraj," I asked
how such regulations worked out in practice. She said she knew most of her
workers by sight and generally had a good idea who might be pregnant even
before she was told. Most of the younger workers were recruited from among
the children of older workers, so relations among workers and management
were in a very real sense "all in the family." In addition, the medical staff
was required to make a report every week. Thus, Director Speteanu was able
each week to look at her target projects for the weeks ahead and to plan how to
reassign women to the special jobs reserved for pregnant women. Since the
number stayed relatively stable from year to year, estimates could easily be
incorporated into the yearly plan. Also included in the plan were provisions
for the hiring of additional workers to take the place of the expectant mothers.
According to the director, these new workers were not necessarily laid off
upon the mother's return, because the cosmetics industry was a growing concern and most temporary workers could be kept on at a different job.[27]

In understanding the regulations on pregnant women it is important to
remember that the economic enterprise does not bear the cost. The wages of
the women who change their place of work and then go on leave are paid out
of social security. Still, while a relatively unskilled worker who became
pregnant might not cause too much disruption in factory productivity, a highly
skilled woman might not be so easy to replace, particularly if she had acquired

considerable experience. If official data are any indication, the threat of possible pregnancy could offer an additional explanation why women have advanced relatively slowly in industrial management positions. Such legislation, coupled with recent rulings that management cannot now prefer a nonpregnant job applicant to a pregnant applicant, would seem to foster a natural reluctance on the part of management to hire women in responsible posts.

As of this writing there is no comprehensive labor legislation regarding women in China, so no comparison can be made between current Soviet–East European and Chinese policies in this area. In 1956, during the de-Stalinization period, Liu Chao-chi stated that "one of the urgent tasks facing our state at present is to begin the systematic codification of a fairly complete set of laws."[28] But Mao preferred campaigns to law, and legal reform has only just become of concern to his heirs. While there apparently is no specific proscription against women working in any field, the Committee of Concerned Asian Scholars and other visitors to China have noted the division between jobs for women and jobs for men. When committee members asked why differences between male and female employment continue, they were usually told that women are "by nature" better suited to some tasks, and these tasks generally include the nurturing, meticulous, subservient jobs. The committee did note a policy of wage differentials that discriminated against women. In communes, pay for men tends to measure from 1 to 2 points higher than pay for women because men's work is more arduous or because of previous experience before the Communist takeover.[29] If there is a general policy setting strength as a criterion for higher pay, then these differences will persist. With no clear legislative policy, it would seem difficult to point to a standard by which to change existing inequities in employment patterns or pay open to women.

In terms of providing for women work conditions that are adapted to their biological function, protective labor laws may be necessary. Every society has enacted them. But it seems indisputable that such laws inevitably discriminate against women if they determine what types of jobs women may or may not do. In the Soviet Union and Eastern Europe, the legal proscriptions that have created male and female jobs imply more than the insurance of women's health. For one thing, they vary from country to country. For another, they have contributed to the feminization of certain job categories and the persistence of wage differences between the sexes. Equal pay is given only for equal work, but some work—and frequently the higher paid work—is closed to women. Moreover, the legislation that requires women to change their work place as pregnancy nears its term would seem to be a two-edged sword. On the one hand, it provides protection to the expectant mother; on the other, it clearly argues against the movement of women of childbearing age into critical posts where they may have to be replaced. A case could be made that the

East European and Soviet position regarding women at work has placed primary emphasis on protecting women as the nation's potential childbearers rather than on making them equal members of the work force.

FAMILY LEGISLATION

Legislative policy regarding the family in the Communist countries is directly related to the demographic problem. The law and regulations governing marriage, divorce, maternity, and abortion reflect the various leaderships' differing perceptions of the severity of the demographic crisis.

Abortion and Divorce

The Communists hold that the change in property and economic relations inaugurated during the post revolutionary phase undermined the psychological basis for having children. If you are not breeding sons to continue ancestor worship or as workers for your plot of land, then many sons become a liability rather than an asset. There are extra mouths to feed and bodies to clothe. While radical social transformation does indeed affect attitudes toward childbirth, an important contributing factor in the case of the Communist countries was the early permissive policy on abortion and marriage. The crisis in the Soviet Union came to its first peak in the mid-1930s, when the birthrate fell so low among the Russian nationality that official birth statistics were suppressed until well after World War II.

In 1936, abortion was made illegal in the Soviet Union except for medical reasons. Restrictions were put on divorce, and marriage was made more permanent. The law also increased material assistance to mothers. But it was the draconian 1944 law that attempted to stabilize the Soviet family and encourage childbearing. This law included three provisions to promote large families and glorify motherhood. First, it granted state aid to mothers in relation to the number of living children. Subsistence grants were given on the birth of the third child and each subsequent child, instead of at the birth of the sixth child as stipulated in the 1936 law. Second, it increased the privileges of mothers and expectant mothers, providing longer maternity leave, higher food rations, state nurseries, and kindergartens. Third, it instituted the Motherhood Medal, the Order of Glory of Motherhood, and the honorary title of Mother Heroine to encourage large families.[30] Abortion was made a criminal offense. Divorce became extremely costly. A fee was charged for filing the intention to get a divorce and for a public announcement in the newspaper. The court fee ranged from 500 to 2,000 rubles for one or both parties. Given the low wages of the average worker, the cost of divorce virtually put it out of reach. At the same time, enforcement of child support became even more stringent. The goal was to hasten the formation of a "Soviet family of a new type."

One of the most negative aspects of the 1944 law was the reintroduction of bias against illegitimate children, or children born out of wedlock, through the famous "blank spot" on the child's birth certificate. The law forbade either a voluntary or court-ordered declaration of fatherhood of a child born to an unwed mother. Where the father's name should have been placed on the birth certificate, a "blank spot" was left. However, through the same law the unwed mother could receive an increase in grants for illegitimate children up to twelve years of age, or she could choose to put her child in a home, where illegitimate children were given priority in admission.

After Stalin's death the government moved away from the rigid conservatism of the 1944 law. Abortion was legalized again in the 1950s, and through piecemeal reform legislation maternity became less of an onerous burden. In the early 1960s Soviet female lawyers spearheaded a fight for more thoroughgoing reform of the family and marriage codes. It took 14 years, from 1954 to 1968, to withdraw the "blank spot" from the birth certificate and push through a less restrictive divorce policy. The end product was the enactment of the Basic Principles of Family Law on 27 June 1968.[31] Perhaps what is most significant about the fight is that it was led by women lawyers and, in the debate which attended the passage of the principles, women endorsed the proposed legislation with apparent enthusiasm in letters to the newspapers. Men tended to be less positive, particularly as regards the ending of the "blank spot."[32]

While the 1968 principles modified the harshest aspects of the 1944 law, they introduced several features aimed at strengthening the relationship between sex and the family, with the objective of promoting family stability. Article 9 provides that marriages are to be performed in a ceremony. Prior to registration a young couple has to wait one month to appreciate the seriousness of the marital undertaking. Article 14 lifts the most serious obstacles to divorce by lowering the fees, but requires that divorce proceedings take place in court, except in cases involving criminal conviction or where one of the parties has disappeared. A husband may not introduce divorce proceedings while his wife is pregnant or for one year after childbirth. Annulment, however, can be granted "where there is no intention of establishing a family." Childbearing and marriage are thus linked closely together.

Article 17 abolishes the "blank spot." The mother may now fill in her own name or the name of the father, or both. The courts have jurisdiction to enforce the revelation of paternity. Whether they do or not, the named father is required to pay alimony. The article strengthens the mother's position by relieving her of the necessity of being the sole supporter of the unwed child and at the same time discourages extramarital behavior on the part of the male partner, who becomes liable for the consequences.[33]

If there is any doubt as to the law's intention, it is erased in the preamble, which declares that the family is the primary "social cell" in which societal and personal interests are harmoniously combined. Gone, then, is any question of the disappearance of the family or its weakening through the substitution of parallel social services. While the Soviet law made considerable progress toward strengthening woman's equal position in the family, especially as regards common ownership of personal property acquired during the marriage, the stress on the importance of marriage, and the linking of sex and marriage and childbirth and marriage, would seem to indicate strong regime support of both traditional sexual values and traditional sex roles.

In particular, as Peter Juviler's research has indicated, the stigma has not been erased from the illegitimate child. Not all putative fathers are liable for support, and the extramarital child has a legal father only if the father voluntarily declares himself. Those who do not have a legal father have to rely on state payments that are much lower than the support a father would provide, not to mention the fact that the illegitimate child is deprived of the right of inheritance. Alimony payments are generally lower than legal prescription because of various forms of payment evasion. Finally, social pressures against illegitimate children are not only still strong, but encouraged by the leadership.[34]

Further evidence of official promotion of traditional sex values may be found in the Soviet courts' treatment of rape. The laws on the statute books severely censure rape. For example, rape accomplished by a group of persons may be punishable by death. In practice, however, the victim does not always get a fair hearing. For one thing, she is required to bring the case into court herself and in so doing, as in other countries, runs the risk of social castigation. Second, in 1964, the USSR Supreme Court directed lower courts to look with special care into the relations between rapist and victim. Doctors testifying to alleged rape were instructed to inspect carefully the alleged scene and to examine and question the victim with care. Rape convictions have been overturned upon findings of "inconsistent" testimony on the part of the victim or the baring of suspicions about her previous moral conduct. Courts have been careful to look into the victim's reputation. The net balance of such recent court rulings, in Juviler's view, has been the favoring of women over men de jure, but the application of a double standard de facto in court.[35]

In Eastern Europe, legislation on marriage and the family has generally followed the Soviet formulations. As table 38 indicates, basic marriage and family codes were passed immediately after the Communists assumed power. These were essentially patterned after the Soviet law of 1944 and included such positive features as the equality of the wife in marriage and the statutory joint ownership of property acquired by either spouse during the marriage.[36] Again, as can be seen from table 38, virtually every East European country revised its family code in the sixties to make divorce easier and to give more legal recognition to the child born out of wedlock.

Similarly, Eastern Europe followed the Soviet example in instituting abortion on demand in the 1950s. Despite the evidence of Soviet experience, the results of the legalization of abortion were apparently not anticipated by the East European leaderships. As chapter 3 documents, the number of abortions soared, and in some countries exceeded the number of live births by the mid-sixties.[37] The modification of abortion policy and family codes was not long in following.

In Romania, the leadership evidently considered that sex in marriage was the optimum method for increasing the population. In 1966, divorce was virtually outlawed and abortions were forbidden except for therapeutic reasons. The East German family law of 1966 contains similar provisions. It abolishes abortion and states that a marriage may be dissolved only "if the courts have established that the reasons put forward are so serious as to permit the conclusion that the marriage has lost its meaning for the partners, their children, and consequently, also for society" (Article 24). Marriage itself is defined as a "life-long union based on mutual love, respect and faithfulness, understanding and trust and unselfish help for each other . . . to give rise to founding a family which finds its fulfillment in living together." Couples contemplating matrimony are urged to "examine seriously" whether they are suitable for each other and whether they understand the seriousness of their act. The emphasis on "life-long union and founding a family" goes even farther than does the Soviet statute in emphasizing the traditional goal and purpose of matrimony.[38] Article 6 states that the family "remains the basic unit of society."

The East Germans reinstated abortion in 1972, permitting the termination of pregnancy during the first trimester for any reason whatever, but restricted it to the endangerment of the mother's life after that period.[39] These stipulations are in line with similar legislation on the subject in virtually all other Communist countries.

Bulgaria's abortion policy followed East Germany's. In 1956, abortion on demand was permitted. In 1967, the law was amended to allow abortions only for medical reasons. In 1970, abortion on demand was reinstated. In Czechoslovakia, abortion was legalized in 1958. In 1960, fees for abortion were abolished as discriminatory, but in 1963 they were required again, in an effort to discourage the numbers demanding abortion. The legislation also made it necessary for a woman seeking an abortion to go before a commission of doctors to explain why she wanted it. Doctors were compelled to play the role of social worker and evaluate the reasons why a woman refused to give birth. Data gathered in 1969 indicate that only 20 percent of the abortions sought were on medical grounds. Twenty-nine percent of all applicants had three or more children, 14 percent were unmarried, and 10 percent cited housing problems.[40] Doctors resented being put in the position of having in effect to make social policy. Were three children sufficient? How serious was the housing problem? In the ensuing years, an effort was made to discourage abortions through the expansion of the use of contraceptives and through the development of marital counseling centers. However, as has been pointed out, contraceptives were in short supply and the state had not yet begun a really comprehensive program of sex education and family planning in the schools. Although many psychiatrists were apparently against forcing a woman to have a child if she did not want one, in 1973, regulations went into effect instructing the commissions that abortion was forbidden, except for medical reasons, in the case of childless married women and women with only one child. Prior to that time, in 1971, a government population commission was established to appraise the population situation and to coordinate the activities of the various government organizations implementing population policy.[41]

Hungary and Yugoslavia also modified their abortion laws. As of 1969, abortion in Yugoslavia was restricted to the medical grounds of the deformity of the fetus and preserving the life or mental health of the mother, and to the social grounds of rape, incest, and poverty of the mother. In Hungary, abortion was limited to the same grounds in 1973. Poland's law was not modified, because the original legislation permitted abortion only on the grounds given above.[42]

Abortion remains illegal in Romania. However, doctors and patients have resorted to illegality in an effort to ease women's situation. In 1976, the regime began to crack down on the medical profession, accusing it of "moral degeneracy."[43] One doctor was found guilty of performing 14 abortions and was sentenced to 14 years in prison,[44] while another, who had performed 168 abortions since 1967, was given a 9-year sentence.[45] The Woman's Council was mobilized as the government gave every indication that it would use all its power to see that Romania reached the ambitious population target of 24 million by 1990.

Family-planning programs have been actively encouraged only by the Polish and Yugoslav governments. East Germany recently embarked on such a program, and apparently contraceptives are becoming more readily available there. However, for the majority of the European Communist countries, abortion is the primary tool of population regulation.

In China, public policy toward the family appears likewise to have become more conservative. Although the 1950 marriage act permitted divorce, the aim now apparently is to discourage it as far as possible. On a recent visit to China, Ruth Sidel attended a meeting of a Chinese neighborhood committee investigating a marital quarrel. A young couple came before the committee, the woman demanding a divorce. Testimony was heard. After discussion, the committee sided with the husband, who did not want a divorce. The wife's reasons were judged insufficient. She was instructed to talk again with her husband. She did so and returned to say she would try to continue the marriage. The committee told her she was not alone, that she could rely on the committee membership and her husband for help. The case was closed.[46]

The Chinese legalized abortion in the fifties, during their extensive campaign to lower the birth rate. Each street and village was organized so that every woman could be regularly visited and questioned on what contraceptives she was using and how many children she had. The aim was to pressure her to volunteer to have fewer children. Contraceptives were made widely available, and severe public censure was incurred if a couple had more than three children.

The campaign has continued with varying degrees of intensity to the present time. Pressure is exerted on young people to maintain traditional Chinese sex norms. Thus it happens that when a husband and wife work in different cities, the wife reports she is using no contraceptives, an indication that the instance of extramarital sex is low. In addition, late marriages are encouraged, with 24 or 25 seen as the appropriate age for women to marry and 28 or 29 the correct age for men. Chinese women are told that late marriage and birth control are forms of serving the people. Practicing planned birth includes studying and applying Mao's thoughts in a "lively way." Birth control is thus a political act, a positive expression of a young couple's commitment to build the new China.

The campaign appears to have paid off. According to Sidel's account, in one section of Peking, doctors at a health station serving a population of 49,500 performed only 4 abortions in 1970, and none were reported in the first nine months of 1971.[47] Although China has not published any population figures since 1953, it claims that population growth has stabilized at about 1.1 percent.[48] China's experience in limiting the birth rate contrasts with the Soviet and East European drive to increase it. In China, contraceptives are available, and the Chinese themselves claim to have developed their own birth control pill. In the European Communist countries, contraceptives have been hard to find. In China, there has been a nationwide effort to organize the population into units small enough for every woman to be educated in family planning and "correct" marriage habits. In all the European Communist countries except Poland and Yugoslavia, sex education and family planning are still considered "taboo," although lively discussions on whether and how to introduce sex education in the Soviet suburbs have been going on in the USSR over the past two years.[49]

Yet, in three areas there is agreement between the Eastern and Western versions of communism. First, the Chinese seek family stability through the discouragement of divorce, as do most of the European Communist countries. Second, the Chinese discourage abortion as a remedy for unwanted children, although for decidedly different reasons. Third, in both East and West, similar policies express the belief that women are not "mistresses of their own bodies." The laws do not give them inalienable rights, as did the recent United States Supreme Court decision on abortion. Divorce and abortion are seen as tools of population control, since childbirth in the Communist view is ineluctably bound up with marriage. When population growth is to be stimulated, abortion is made more difficult, divorce becomes costly or impossible, and the family and motherhood are exalted. When population growth is to be discouraged, the woman is told that her patriotic duty lies with proper family planning, and she is questioned and "educated" until she complies. The woman is the object and the victim of these changes.

Clearly, a negative birth rate has enormous social and economic consequences, causing serious dislocations in society. If a country gives women the inalienable right to decide whether to have children or not, and they decide not to, that decision is tantamount to national suicide. Overpopulation also is a critical problem, creating housing, clothing, and food crises. The Communist regimes' pronatal regulation of their populations through family and abortion legislation has been far from successful, as the statistics and data on population growth in the European Communist countries indicate. The success of Chinese antibirth policies is similarly uneven. The birth rate has been more reduced in the cities than in the villages, where traditional attitudes and less literacy prevail.[50] As elsewhere, women in Communist societies evidently refuse to accept the state's dictates on such a highly personal matter as the decision to bear a child.

Pregnancy and Welfare

In 1953, Soviet regulations introduced the payment of wages to mothers when they stayed at home to care for sick children under the age of 14. Mothers received full pay for 7 calendar days if they were married, for 10 if they were unmarried. A system of income maintenance composed of lump payments at the time of the birth of a child increased as the number of children increased. A family allowance program made payments to families after the birth of the fourth child, but these amounted to only 4 rubles (about $4.00) a month. The inadequacy of both programs in terms of the amount of money the families actually received and the number of eligible families was clearly obvious by the mid-sixties. In 1966, less than 1 percent of all families in the Soviet Union qualified for the family allowance.

In 1971, Soviet government issued a new version of the family income supplement, budgeting 1.8 billion rubles a year for it, as compared with the roughly 400 million rubles it had spent on family allowances in 1969. However, as my respondents were quick to tell me, while the supplement reaches a larger number of families, it is still pitifully small. For a family to qualify, the average income per family member must not be higher than 50 rubles a month, and the supplement cannot be made in addition to benefits already being received. For those who qualify, the payments are 12 rubles a month to the mother, if she works or studies, or to the father, if the mother does not work or study, for each child under the age of 8.[51]

Eastern Europe was not long in following the Soviet lead. In 1967 and 1970 respectively, Hungary and Romania passed laws that substantially extended maternity leave from work and increased the number of sick days a mother could take off while her child was ill. In Hungary, the leave period was extended to 3 years with a decreasing pay schedule; in Romania, 7 years.[52] The two laws were pioneers in this type of legislation in the Communist countries. For the first time, it was formally recognized that housework had a social value and women were paid to stay at home.[53] Czechoslovakia subsequently passed a housewife's allowance. East Germany modified its pregnancy policy only in 1972, extending pregnancy leave from a total of 12 weeks to 18 weeks, and increasing birth payments for each child to 1,000 marks. In addition, a joint decision of the Socialist Unity (Communist) Party Committee and the National Executive of the Trade Unions provided for grants of credits to young married couples "to finance the purchase, building or enlargement of a private home, to pay for the furniture and to exempt them from repaying part or all of the credit at the birth of one or more children."[54] While it does not establish a family allowance, the decision provides incentives for a young couple to have children.

China's policies again follow the general pattern, but are less radical. The mother is entitled to change to light work in the fifth or eighth month of pregnancy, depending on where she lives. This stipulation is particularly important for working farm women who are doing heavy manual work. In the cities, maternity leave is given for 56 calendar days, but in the country it varies. Some communes give no leave, others give a 30-day leave with a return to light work after that time and to regular work after 4 months, and still others give the full 56 days. In the city, maternity leave appears to be paid for by the government; in the country it is not.[55] Because the Chinese leadership is more interested in lowering the birthrate than in increasing it, it stands to reason that few incentives will be given women to stay at home. For example, there is no year-long paid leave of absence from work to take care of a newborn infant, as was common in all the European Communist countries until East Germany, Romania, and Hungary extended theirs. In point of fact, in the recent campaign to recruit more women into the labor force, Communist "cadres" have been criticized for voicing opinions that suggest that marriage and work do not mix, such as "Women cannot do much after they are married" or, "Women are very capable in household chores but not in politics."[56] The trend in China is to deemphasize childbearing and stress productive work.

The incentives outlined above have produced uneven results. In Hungary, by 1970, 70 percent of all eligible mothers were taking advantage of the 1967 law, but 60 percent of these were staying at home for only a year and a half, half the permitted leave time. The majority of those who did stay at home were evidently the unskilled or semiskilled. Women with professional careers were least likely to want to take that much time off.

As discussed in chapter 3, the demographic results have been far from spectacular, although the birth rate in all the East European countries increased some in the mid-seventies (see Figure 8). Urbanization and, to a more limited extent, the availability of abortion help to explain the fall in the number of live births, but there is no clear correlation between the regimes' provision of incentives to childbirth and an increase in the number of live births. Indeed, the Romanian statistics provide an interesting comment on the relationship between the availability of abortion and the birth rate. Romania is the only country that now categorically forbids abortions. Yet, until recently, the birth rate was steadily sinking back to its pre-1967 level. The evidence suggests, then, that positive incentives notwithstanding, the European Communist leaderships have yet to create an environment that would encourage women to bear children.

The reaction of women in these countries to their leaderships' pronatalist policies has been ambivalent. Both Poland's Magdalena Sokołowska and Hungary's Judit Sas thought family allowances that encouraged mothers to stay at home were a good thing if there were complete freedom of choice. If the options opened to parents were, for example, adequate child care services, having a husband stay at home part of the time if he chose to, or having the wife stay at home all of the time if she chose to, then these women thought the pronatalist rulings would be in the woman's interest. As it was, however, they thought there was a strong likelihood that such measures would tend to increase the already existing economic sexism for the sake of demography. In Hungary, I was told, the Party is considering a proposal that would enable the father to stay at home and baby-sit in place of the mother. In terms of changing sex roles, this was the most radical suggestion I heard during my research in Eastern Europe.

The purpose here is not to cast judgment upon the Communists' population policies in the maintenance period, but to understand their impact on women. The revolutionary promises of economic and social freedom for women were not fulfilled. Mobilizing women into the work force while insisting on the preservation of the nuclear family with an insufficient infrastructure could not "liberate" women in the sense of giving them equal status with men. They simply acquired two burdens instead of one: home and work. Neither the pro- nor the antinatalist policies have attacked the root of that fundamental dilemma. At the present time, there seems to be no solution to it in either the Western or Communist world. To a degree, the West appears to have opted for an either/or policy: *either* women stay home and raise children *or* they go to work. No woman who has tried to do both simultaneously can say that she has had an easy time. In the Communist world, the governments have had to force women to do both. There is no labor that can be imported. But when women do both, one of the two jobs suffers. If women choose the maternity leave and stay at home for a number of years to raise children, their careers suffer. If they stay at work, particularly work of high responsibility, they will want to have fewer children. What neither the Communist nor democratic leaderships appear to have given any serious thought to are (a) alternative work patterns that might ease the burden and (b) alternative sex roles that might be more supportive of the working women. The differences between East and West, in this respect, is that the West affords women more options. Women can choose to work or not. In the Communist countries, women must work. The loss of the wife's earnings is a loss the average family can ill afford.

PROMOTION OF WOMEN TO EXECUTIVE POSITIONS

All Communist regimes are sensitive to the fact that women are not rising to decision-making positions. By the end of the postrevolutionary phase, it was clear that mobilizing women into the economy and giving them training did not automatically assure a concomitant rise to high-status positions. Thus, the recruitment of women to leadership posts is the third area in which there has been movement in official policy in recent years.

In Czechoslovakia, the reestablished Czechoslovak Women's Union proposed a four-point program to solve the woman's question without taking women out of productive work and returning them to the home. Among the four points was "to investigate why more women do not hold top jobs and positions in public life." A recent survey by Jaraslava Bauerová of 500 women in leading positions revealed that the absolute majority of them performed the same lower functions to which they had been appointed at the average age of 35. It was also found that, on the average, women in these positions devoted less time to housework than the all-state figure—three hours a day—but that the older the woman, the more the burden of housework fell upon her. A further finding was that although these women had more support at home than the national average, this support was insufficient. According to the survey, the greatest obstacle to self-improvement was lack of leisure time.[57] Aside from urging the further development of paradomestic communal services, Bauerová's study made no suggestions on how to move women out of their niche in the lower economic administrative jobs.

Pioneering efforts in this direction were taken by Hungary and Bulgaria in 1970, when Hungary enacted a decree requiring that women be brought into higher positions because female educational attainment had reached virtually the same level as that of men.[58] A Politburo plenum in Bulgaria set down similar provisions that same year. In 1973, Romania followed with its female executive recruitment program.[59] As might be expected, recruitment implementation policies vary from country to country.

In Hungary, the law calls for every sector of the economy to develop a plan aimed at enabling all men and women capable of it to attain a higher level of education. The decree specifies three selection criteria for those to be trained in management: (1) faith in socialism; (2) expertise in the field; and (3) administrative talent. The Hungarian factory women's councils are responsible for seeing that the law is upheld in every enterprise and that there is no discrimination on the basis of sex. A Romanian Central Committee decision projects an analogous training and recruitment procedure for women, but goes further by expanding the number of job categories in which women can work and by increasing the number of women attending the Party academy, which provides the political education requisite for Romania's potential leaders.

In 1976, the Romanian Communist Party reaffirmed its commitment to the promotion of women, particularly within the Party. A December resolution by the Political Executive Committee established a 25 percent quota for women in all the regional, local, and enterprise Party committees.[60] At a talk before the counties' regional and local First Party secretaries, Ceaucescu subsequently stipulated that at least one woman be elected secretary in each county Party committee. He argued that women would be promoted to leadership in the Party in proportion to their participation in the national economy.[61]

The Bulgarian approach has been radically different, recalling Soviet methods in Central Asia in the twenties. As Ms. Tropolova, first secretary of the Bulgarian Women's Committee, explained, the committee recommended to the Party and government that women needed special training if they were to overcome the centuries-old handicap of nonparticipation in decision-making. A pilot program was undertaken in Sofia to train women in executive leadership, and the national program began in 1976. Qualifications for admission include nomination by Party representatives. Not all women who express interest are admitted; they must be specified by the Party. My Hungarian and Romanian respondents thought the Bulgrian program discriminatory because it was directed especially at women. Ms. Tropolova disagreed. In her opinion, women need that extra preparation to give them confidence in their ability to perform in an executive capacity.

Symptomatic of the Hungarian, Bulgarian, and Romanian efforts to promote women has been the elevation of women into the respective Politburos. Four European countries now have female role models in their highest political body. All of these women, except Romania's Mme. Ceaucescu, are heads of the national women's committees. In line with the greater visability accorded these committees is the enlargement of the area of their responsibility, as discussed in chapter 5. However, caution should be exercised in evaluating the promotion of women to the Politburo and the importance of women's organizations in general. As discussed earlier, the recent reorganization of most East European national women's councils weakened them appreciably politically, even as advisory bodies.

While East Germany has not passed a decree like those mentioned above, in 1967, as a special encouragement to women to seek higher education, the East German government initiated special courses for which women can qualify through their place of work. If they do not have the proper entrance requisites, it is the task of the enterprise's educational system to see that they attain them.[62] To cut down on the amount of time women spend at work, Hungary initiated a free Saturday for women in 1972.[63] That same year, East German legislation reduced women's work week to 40 hours instead of the 43½ hours required of men.[64] (The 40-hour week is not yet standard in any country except the Soviet Union, so that time spent at work by most East European women is considerably more than that spent at work by most women and men in the United States.) The Czechoslovak study by Bauerová suggests that a reduction in the gainful work week for women could give them more leisure time for self-advancement. However, such a measure might hinder more than help. If the job requires a full work week, and most jobs of high responsibility do, then a legal reduction in the women's work week might automatically exclude women from certain managerial positions by making them ineligible.

In China, the promotion of women through the cultivation of women "cadres" has been an official policy since 1968, when newspapers carried slogans and provincial revolutionary committees made proposals "to bring fully into play the role of revolutionary women." The success of the campaign may be judged by the increase in female representation in the Chinese Central Committee between the Ninth and Tenth congresses, and from isolated reports from various towns and provinces that show an increase in the proportion of female membership in revolutionary committees. The Chinese press has also cited an increase in women in executive positions in factory Party committees in Kwantung, Tientsin, and Liaoning provinces.[65] Such statistics are far too scattered to give any real picture of the degree to which post–Cultural Revolution attempts to recruit more women into leadership positions have been successful. As has already been pointed out, visitors to China are made aware that leadership groups with which they come into contact view the absence of women from positions of higher-level decision-making as a serious problem. But the fact remains that, according to these same visitors, female representation in leadership committees is low.[66]

Only the Soviet Union maintains the claim that discrimination on the basis of sex has been eliminated, and thus has adopted no new policies aimed at advancing women into executive positions. All the women I interviewed in the Soviet Union admitted that there could be more women in decision-making positions at every level, but none saw their absence as critical. Rather, they appeared inclined to think that time will take care of the matter and that, if women really want to advance, they have every opportunity.

The built-in bias of the Communist political system finds expression in all of its policies. In none of the programs aimed at recruiting women into high-status positions is the initiative of women themselves sought; on the contrary, women remain passive. The Party seeks them out and makes the selection the leadership deems appropriate. It seems likely that women see these new programs as further intervention into their lives which those who are chosen cannot refuse, but which those who are overlooked may be happy to escape. It is questionable, therefore, whether such policies are adequate to gain their objective. What is needed to change women's status is active consent, not passive submission.

The foregoing review of Party and government actions regarding women in the Communist countries suggests general findings as to the leaderships' attitudes on raising the status of women. (1) If one accepts Rossi's theory for the integration of women into modern society,[67] the model that best characterizes the Communist leaderships' position has been the pluralistic variant. It is true that, through an aggressive mobilization policy in the postrevolutionary phase, women have moved into fields previously dominated by men. But this movement has constituted only partial assimilation to men's roles. In the maintenance phase, revised labor and health legislation perpetuated the pattern of excluding women from some occupations in order to channel them into others. Because of the drop in birthrate in the European Communist countries, motherhood became the focal point of a growing pronatalist policy that was also aimed at stabilizing the family in its nuclear form. Hence, in the maintenance phase, the emphasis on woman's place at work and "noble motherhood" (as the East German legislation terms maternity) has tended to preserve traditional occupational and social differentiation.

(2) In both the postrevolutionary and maintenance phases, the integration of women into the modernizing economy was promoted through the unquestioned endorsement of the nineteenth-century vision of female emancipation: employment of women in industrial production. A rapid drop in national birth rate as a result of the mobilization was not part of that vision, however, and forced the European Communist leaderships to shift their position in the direction of returning women to the home and reinstating traditionalism in female identity (no divorce, no abortion) when the demographic situation was perceived as critical. Moreover, the failure of women to move automatically into positions of high status was not foreseen or planned, and the regimes have had to elaborate policies to handle that problem as well.

(3) Party and government policies in all the Communist countries have shown no clear change in objectives regarding the role of women in the

maintenance, i.e., postmobilization, phase. More importantly, the policies have produced no identifiable objectives regarding woman's role in the future. The key issue in the Communist countries, as in the United States, is how to make women equal de facto as well as de jure. Yet in the maintenance phase, regardless of the level of economic development, conservatism, not creativity in public policy toward women, has been the dominant leadership attitude.

(4) While law and Party prescription appear to be effective instruments of the social transformation of women in the postrevolutionary phase of Communist development, their ability to produce change in women's status evidently weakens in the maintenance stage, when consolidation, not transformation, becomes the major regime goal. The tendency for leadership prescription to be a less effective agent of change as Communist regimes become more institutionalized in appropriate modernizing patterns explains the Communists' apparent startling successes in "liberating" women in Central Asia and China by comparison with the more mundane gains of East European women, whose life styles have not been altered so dramatically.

7 / Leadership Guidance: Propaganda and Socialization

The lack of a creative blueprint in the Communist leaderships' legislative and regulatory policies during the maintenance phase is evident in their conduct of the promotional function. In this chapter I will compare the Communist propaganda, social research, and socialization policies of the maintenance and postrevolutionary phases. It should be noted that in the case of the People's Republic of China, some policies in these three areas have remained unchanged. Moreover, the section on social research will perforce center on Eastern Europe and the Soviet Union because China has yet to acknowledge sociology as a valid discipline.

PROPAGANDA

EASTERN EUROPE AND THE SOVIET UNION

The most marked change in Communist propaganda in Eastern Europe and the Soviet Union since Stalin's death, and particularly since the early sixties, has been the increasing emphasis on femininity. The feminine ideal presented in Soviet and East European periodicals today is far removed from the militant, stern, mannishly dressed proletarian heroines of yesteryear. According to the editors of *Sovietskaia zhenshchina* [*Soviet Woman*], the ideal modern woman should be "a harmoniously developed person: intelligent, hardworking, patriotic, and feminine." When I pressed for a definition of the last term, I was told that it meant beautiful, pretty, soft, sympathetic, appealing to men ("please, not sexy"), and a good mother. An editor of *Femea*, the Romanian magazine for women, also stressed the qualities of softness, good grooming, and motherhood in her concept of *feminine*. She added that she was pleased to see the attention Romanian women were paying to dress in recent years. Thus, in contrast to the strident revolutionary Marxist women's magazines of the turn of the century, contemporary East European and Soviet periodicals aimed at women contain sections on good grooming, dressmaking, fashion, and child care.

A typical issue of *Sovietskaia zhenshchina* contains some respectful reference to Lenin; vignettes or lead articles on women in the USSR, Eastern Europe or elsewhere; a section on leisure time, a fashion section; a page on how to sew or knit; and a section on the parent's role in bringing up children. A typical portrait of an ideal young woman from the magazine is that of Svetlana Sushanskaia, a textile worker. Svetlana is depicted as having the ability and need to work honestly and well. As she grew up, "her thoughts became more profound—how could she live better and more justly?" She found her answer in being nominated deputy to the USSR Supreme Soviet. The article continues:

There is yet another aspect of our lives without which a person, and especially a woman, cannot live a full life—love. But that is sacred and you don't ask about that even in the longest and most confidential conversation. At times it is talked about, and at other times—not. Svetlana has an unusually soft, gentle smile and her eyes shine with a warm understanding light. Her love will be a happy one, no doubt.[1]

Traditional femininity is expressed well in that excerpt: warmth, understanding, softness, gentleness. The picture of Svetlana that accompanies the article is of a pretty young woman with short curly hair, her faced wreathed in a smile.

In the same issue is a poem entitled "Wrinkles," by the Uzbek poetess Zulfia, which urges respect for older women:

A wrinkle is a furrow in a field
which has delivered an abundant yield . . .
The birthmarks of a fearless generation,
our heritage, our treasure, and our pride.[2]

As in American popular magazines, whenever an outstanding woman is presented to the readers of Soviet and East European women's periodicals, the woman's family life is emphasized as much as her professional life, or else it is incorporated into it. Happy children are shown in newly constructed kindergartens with watchful, smiling mothers looking on. Women are almost always described as industrious, kind, or gentle, and are shown on outings with their families as well as at their place of work. The idea conveyed to the reader is that you can remain "soft and gentle," a good mother, and at the same time be a dedicated, hard-working, conscientious worker. That is the essence of the definition of *woman-worker:* devotion to motherhood and career.

The presentation of the ideal woman as worker and mother is common to all the East European countries. The program of the Romanian Communist Party issued after the Tenth Congress in November 1974 gave this definition of woman's role in Romania: "Women make an essential contribution to material and spiritual production in our society, to strengthening the family, to the development of the nation, to maintaining the youthfulness of the people, to rearing and educating the young generation."[3]

Maria Dinkova's short study of Bulgarian women lays out two functions for women: their role in social production and motherhood, which she defines as their basic "social function."[4] In Dr. Herta Kühig's introduction to *Equal Rights for Women in the German Democratic Republic,* eight pages are devoted to women at work and eight to women in the family. To be fulfilled as a woman means to marry, to have children, *and* to work. By and large, in the words of a Czech sociologist, "An employed woman means an employed mother."[5] This is the only option presented to women in Communist societies. The idea that women should not work, but stay at home, is negatively portrayed, particularly in East German and Czechoslovak sources. A Polish survey in a Warsaw evening paper found that school children tended to look down upon mothers who did not work.[6] In the Soviet Union, some attention has recently been paid to nonworking mothers which may indicate the start of a new trend. *Pravda,* for example, came out with an article urging that photographs of mothers of many children be more prominently displayed.[7] And one of the most recent issues of *Sovietskaia zhenshchina* contained a lead article on a mother of ten who worked on a collective farm. The article suggested that having ten children might be personally more rewarding than working on the farm.[8]

The stress on motherhood is only one aspect of the Communist regimes' new-found interest in femininity. The promotion of femininity is obvious in the streets, in the stores, and in the women executives I met in my visit to Eastern Europe. To be well dressed, to look chic, is a sign of prosperity and success in the Communist world. As was mentioned in chapter 4, relative to their earnings, women spend a great deal of money on clothes and cosmetics. According to Elena Ivanova, director of the Chief Administration of Home Service Industries in Sofia, under whose jurisdiction fall most of the communal services for the capital, dressmakers are flourishing in the Bulgarian capital, despite the availability of ready-made clothes. Women prefer to pay more to dress to their individual tastes.

Cosmetic shops and beauty parlors have proliferated in every major city. There are institutes of beauty to make women look beautiful, which for a modest sum will instruct women about facial and hair care. One such institute in Moscow caters to over 35,000 women a year, and the Soviet cosmetics industry claims it has more than doubled its sales in the past ten years. According to official statistics, in 1971, Soviet women spent 830 million rubles on cosmetics, buying some 134 tons of lipstick and 147 million bottles of perfume weighing two and a half thousand tons.[9]

Because women are the main consumers of cosmetics, Director Speteanu of Romania's "Miraj" factory, is wholeheartedly in favor of her predominately female work force. "Men," she explained, "buy only for holidays, birthdays, or anniversaries. In general, they do not know what they want and buy for effect. Women are more informed and take more interest in the product, If women are the principal buyers, then women must also design the product."

One explanation of the reversal in the attitude of the Western Communist regimes toward feminine dress is related to increased prosperity. The Soviet Union and Eastern Europe are beginning to enjoy a modicum of affluence, and dress has traditionally been a symbol of affluence. In societies where scarcity is still more prevalent than abundance, Djilas's New Class wants to be distinguished from the masses. In Romania, for example, a pretty young sales clerk wistfully eyed the appearance of a woman shopper and commented: "If she is dressed beautifully, she must be rich." A Soviet woman engineer told me she was shocked at what she considered the sloppy dress of most American women. "It cannot be that they cannot afford to dress well," she said. "Maybe they just don't want to look and feel like women."

Another explanation is based on demography. A pronatalist policy appears to demand emphasis on femininity. It might be argued that officialdom could just as well stress the revolutionary duty of women to bear or not to bear children through the militant, sexless approach of Communist China. But the time for such propaganda seems to have passed in the Western Communist countries. The Revolution has faded into history. An appeal of this nature would probably not awaken a revolutionary spirit, particularly in Eastern Europe, where, except in Yugoslavia, communism was dictated from the outside, not self-imposed.

A third explanation opens up a different dimension of the leaderships' attitudes toward female role identification. It could be argued that instead of developing blueprints oriented toward the future, the Communist regimes in the West have molded their present on social and cultural standards projected from the past. It would be hard to find adequate documentation for such a proposition, and what is offered here is only speculative. Nevertheless, the traveler to Eastern Europe and the Soviet Union is struck by the impression that once one crosses the "iron curtain," the clock is set back, and one is living in the shadow of the nineteenth century. In Moscow, the subway stations are veritable underground palaces. Stalin did not build a proletarian transportation system; he created an aristocratic environment that every proletariat would be able to enjoy. There is much ritual in the continual replay of the Russian classics of theater, ballet, and opera. The sighs of Tatiana (dressed in a pure white, frilly dress) as she dreams of Oniegin recall *Sovietskaia zhenshchina*'s saccharine comment: "Love, that's sacred." The heroines of the Soviet cinema and popular literature are reminiscent of the Natashas and Olgas of the Russian classics. In the Balkans and Eastern Europe, the evening promenade still takes place, with the walkers, particularly the women, dressed in their best. In cities where architecture spans the centuries, the atmosphere is especially redolent of a bygone era.

There is more emphasis on culture and being "cultured" (*kul' turny*) in the European Communist countries than in the West. And being cultured does not mean proletarian culture; it implies the aristocratic elitist culture of the past. One Romanian woman who had visited America said that what she missed most there was an atmosphere of culture. In all the European Communist countries, going to the theater or the opera has cultural significance. A person may go because he happens to like the theater, but more frequently he will go to get culture. Children are taken to the opera or museum to get culture. One is expected to fill one's leisure time with cultural activities. Culture is also a sign of status. In a discussion of the problem of mass culture being possibly a lack of culture, one Bulgarian sociologist I interviewed stated that he thought the dangers of mass participation in culture might be avoided through a cultural education program. He was especially aware that the advent of a shorter work week and the concomitant increase in leisure time might completely destroy "culture" as he knew it. But he thought Bulgaria would have to go through a period, "similar perhaps to what you are having in America," in which mass culture would appear to be no culture at all. Then a true culture, based on mass participation, would assert itself. In the European Communist countries, culture is something to be displayed as it was at the end of the nineteenth century. Indeed, the aim of communism is to bring "culture" to the masses by appropriate educational uses of the mass media and by building palaces underground and parks of rest and culture above. Communism for the various leaderships is not the advent of some unknown future society; it is the reincarnation of nineteenth-century aristocratic values that, under communism, will be available to all, not just a few.[10]

The cultural image of the nineteenth-century European woman is one of the gentle, soft, motherly, nonaggressive, generous, pure Victorian female who is the heroine of so much recent Soviet literature. Vera A. Dunham has shown in her study of postwar Soviet fiction that the self-sacrificing woman, the woman who, when she reaches a position of authority, humiliates herself before her husband and gives up equality for domestic happiness, represents what being a woman is all about by Soviet leadership standards.[11] While married love is not necessarily seen today as the highest form of love, the woman who shows the Victorian feminine qualities, or at least converts to them at the end of the story, is ideal. In other words, the official cultural image of women in Eastern Europe and the Soviet Union is immersed in nineteenth-century mythology. Sociologists in Eastern Europe may condemn the survival of "bourgeois myths" about women in their societies, but it would appear that the European Communist leaderships have opted for these very same myths.

CHINA

China represents a totally different picture. The absence of formal legislation has meant that the Chinese leadership has depended on propaganda, campaigns, and discussion groups to educate the population in the new norms of behavior. The breadth and scope of these methods are unique to China. Significantly, it was the actress Chiang Ch'ing who drew upon both the imperial operatic tradition and the republican heritage of popular drama as instruments to educate the masses, revise previous works, or compose new ones to create the "model" repertoire that became the hated symbol of the Cultural Revolution. The only Western analogy to this repetoire is the medieval mystery play, which was written at a time similar to the present period in Chinese history, when a high rate of illiteracy prevailed. Among these Chinese plays are *The Red Detachment of Women, The White-Haired Women,* and *Azalea Mountain,* all of which depict women as militant fighters for the Revolution, ready to sacrifice home and children for the cause. "Real love," both men and women are told, "exists only when the revolutionary spirit and your love of an individual are in harmony."[12] "Besides the love of two persons, there are other loves, greater loves: the love of work, the love of country, the love of people."[13] Like the plays, Chinese magazines and broadcasts have tended to present women as militants rather than as wives and mothers. Indeed, the Chinese promotion of women recalls the early Soviet period, adding confirmation to the thesis that the Chinese postrevolutionary phase may not yet be over.

Campaigns are another feature reminiscent of the Soviet Union in the late 1920s and thirties. Beginning with the birth control and marriage campaigns of the 1950s, Chinese women have been systematically subjected to pressure to go into "productive work," to join the Party, and to take more active roles in public affairs. (The campaigns will be discussed briefly under socialization.) What is significant about the Chinese campaigns is that they have been utilized over a period of thirty years, longer than in any other Communist country, and, until the death of Mao, showed no signs of being discarded as a means of mobilizing the people.

Discussion groups have also been a traditional feature of Chinese communism. The "speak bitterness" meetings of the Civil War and the campaigns of the 1950s, were aimed at transforming women's attitudes about the nature of the family and their place in it. Discussion groups demanded individual involvement through public confrontation, and hence might be expected to force commitment to new behavioral norms.

The emphasis on female militancy should not obscure the conservatism that has come into Chinese propaganda policies regarding women. The family has been accepted as the basic social unit, and as the main carrier of the continuity of a culture, the family is a culture's most conservative element. The retrenchment that followed the campaigns of the 1950s saw women's magazines extolling the virtures of home and children, and the evidence suggests that the commune experience will not be repeated. Perhaps a certain compromise has been reached. Chinese women continue to be portrayed in a revolutionary fashion in the Chinese media, but the traditional roles are still much in force and, as the Committee of Concerned Asian Scholars observed, are not subject to question.

One explanation of the Chinese leadership's ongoing revolutionary approach to women is that the objectives of Chinese communism do not lie in Chinese history. The need of the leadership was to forge a modern nation by creating new ties of loyalty, by bringing the scientific revolution to a people who for centuries had experienced only prescientific thought, and by appropriating Western technology to develop an industrial society. As chapter 6 indicated, changing family relationships was critical to breaking old patterns of thought and loyalty. In European Russia and Eastern Europe, the nation, the scientific revolution, and the "bourgeois" nuclear family preceded the industrial revolution. In China, these occurred virtually simultaneously. Hence, the advent of Communist power in the West was less an *overturning* of a previous life style than a forced and violent redirection of a process already under way. The European regimes may justifiably look back on nineteenth-century cultural values as desirable in themselves since these values were formative to Communist ideology and the development of the Communist state. What took place in Western communism was a process of selection by which some values were retained as "progressive" or meaningful in terms of the new Communist society, while others were rejected as "bourgeois." For example, the identification of women as gentle, soft-spoken, warm, and understanding became a building block of communism, while the idea of woman's place as uniquely in the home was rejected as "bourgeois." The present Chinese campaign against Confucianism suggests a more total rejection of pre-Communist values on the part of the Chinese leadership. Many writers have proposed that Maoism incorporated traditional Chinese concepts of authority and obedience to superiors, but substituted the state for the head of household as the object of obedience.[14] However, the very fact that the state, not the head of the household, is now presented as the fitting subject of "filial piety" means that every member of the household must turn outward to public life. If women remain enclosed within the home, their loyalty remains with the family. Hence, the emphasis in Chinese propaganda continues to be on the militant revolutionary female ideal at this stage in the country's development.

What changes will occur once China becomes consolidated as a modern Communist nation-state are open to speculation. If European Communist propaganda is any indication, the Chinese leadership may well return to the past for a definition of the *Chinese* Communist woman. However, given the simultaneous occurrence of the three fundamental processes of modernization and the evident need to reject what does not contribute to them from the past, the official Chinese attitude would seem less likely to take the highly conservative turn it has taken in Eastern Europe and the USSR.

RESEARCH ON WOMEN

East European and Soviet research on women provides less concrete evidence of the continuing strength of tradition. Rather, certain assumptions that appear to be unassailable are posited as the basis of research. On the positive side, the numerous East European and Soviet sociological studies on women that have been cited in this book are proof of official support of investigations designed to identify the problems in the life style of contemporary women and the endorsement of a search for solutions. The assumptions that are never questioned, however, are the assertion that only under socialism are women really liberated, woman's dual role as childbearer and mother, and the conviction that biological and psychological differences are sex-linked.

WOMEN AS CHILDBEARERS AND WORKERS

Studies of women at work inevitably involve the woman's role at home, how much time is spent on housework, and how many women with more than three children are employed. When, as in Magdalena Sokołowska's study, it is found that absenteeism is higher among women with young children, the source of the phenomenon is found in the home. As unpublished study by a Romanian woman psychologist showed greater evidence of neurosis among working women at three sample factories than among working men. She attributed the cause to the "double shift." The most commonly stated solutions to this problem follow strict ideological lines: (1) more rapid development of communal services to end housework forever; (2) the assumption of household duties by the husband; and (3) the elaboration of a family model in which both husband and wife can live happily.

The fundamental question posed is what role the family plays under socialism. To say that it is the basic social unit is not enough. What is its function? Two approaches are discussed here to indicate the type and range of research in this area. One is a study by Vlasta Fišerová, a member of the Department of Philosophy and Sociology of the Czechoslovak Academy of Sciences, and the other is a study by Zoya Yankova of Moscow's Institute of Sociology.

Ms. Fišerová sees the modern family as a community of leisure. In her view the literature shows that the greater part of one's leisure time is spent with other members of the family. The space and degree of freedom for spending the time that every individual has at his disposal are to a large extent determined by the various roles realized within the family group. According to Ms. Fišerová, in Czechoslovakia these roles are most often sex specific. Data from her survey, "The Leisure Time of the Ostrava Population," indicate that women have, on the average, eleven hours per week less leisure time than men, even though the family as a productive economic unit has virtually ceased to exist. While the author does not go so far as to say the family's function today is only to fulfill leisure-time activities, she does state that the Ostrava survey shows a relationship between family life style and type of leisure-time activities. Since most free time is spent within the family, free-time contacts outside the family are limited. The Ostrava study revealed that there can be severe tensions within the family over the use of leisure time, and that these in turn may be correlated with the "disintegration" of the family. The author recognizes that the family performs the basic functions of childbearing and childrearing, but she suggests that seeing the family as a leisure-time community makes it possible to understand better its role in fulfilling certain basic needs such as emotional balance and companionship.[15] These needs are on an entirely different level than the economic needs that determined earlier family structures. Important in any analysis of the changing structure of the family, in Ms. Fišerová's view, is the identification and definition of the specific needs the family group supplies.

Zoya Yankova's book *The Twentieth Century and the Problems of the Family* is less abstract. In the first part, she assesses the impact of working women upon the stability of the family. Using data from research directed by Professor N. G. Yurkevitch, she finds a positive relationship between the satisfied working woman-mother and family stability. She dwells on one particular point in the survey. In response to the question, "Does the fact that a wife-mother works negatively influence the strength of your marriage?" she found that among the happily married, 10 percent of the men and 13 percent of the women thought it did, but that the answer "yes" ranked highest (37 percent) among the unhappily married men and second highest (25 percent) among the unhappily married women.[16]

Moscow sociologist Yankova does not attempt to draw a causal relationship between happy work and happy marriage. However, she evidently wants to demonstrate that when the marriage is unhappy, the fact of the wife's working becomes a problem, especially from the man's point of view. By contrast, in a marriage that is happy, both spouses are likely to be satisfied in their work.

As Yankova sees it, the key to the relationship between work and marriage lies in the nature of marriage itself and in the changes that have occurred in family structure in this century. Critical to modern marriage, she finds, are *moral values (moral'nyie tsennosti)*. Citing the work of Leningrad sociologists on the orientation of Leningrad youth to marriage, she points out that for young people the moral factor in marriage outranks intellectual, emotional, and material values. She goes on to compare premarital relations in "capitalist" and "socialist" societies and states that in most cases in the socialist countries, premarital relations occur only in the presence of a serious, firm "feeling of love," and with the intent to marry. She concludes that the stability of the family rests on the "moral education" of young people. She does not recommend sex education as a solution, because in her view the relations between boys and girls and men and women can be resolved only "as the result of the affirmation of high moral norms in the context of society as a whole."[17]

We have returned to the traditional moral values on which the permanence of marriage is based and to the need for moral education to provide stability. If Yankova's opinions seem conservative, it must be remembered that they also reflect the official posture regarding the meaning and purpose of marriage.

What is the woman's role in this type of marriage? In my interview with Dr. Yankova, she stressed two classes of functions in family life that vitally affect women: (1) that which forms a woman's personality; and (2) that which impedes the development of her personality. She termed the education of children one of women's duties in the home that contribute to the development of personality. Other such duties include new ideas in cooking and the organization and management of leisure time. She cited repetitious housework as an example of the latter category. The aim of family living is in her view to enable each member to reach self-fulfillment. Particularly for women, one way of achieving that aim is to eliminate housework. The state has done its part by building stores that sell semiprepared foods and by establishing kindergartens and other communal facilities. But one of the most important changes still needed, in her view, is a change in men's attitudes toward sharing household chores.

Other surveys by Soviet sociologists indicate that the male role at home increases as the educational level of the couple rises (see the Golod and Kharchev study mentioned in chapter 3). In fact, the whole direction of Soviet research seems to point to a terminus toward which the modern family is evolving in terms of size, sex-role differentiation in the home, income and cultural interests, and standardization of customs and family behavior. A survey carried out in the Tartar Autonomous Soviet Socialist Republic (ASSR) traces intergenerational changes in family relations from the more traditional patriarchal structure in the older rural Tartar families to greater equality in the younger urbanized families.[18] In Leningrad, sociologists are working on a dynamic family model that will incorporate all the changes in life style a modern family experiences, from marriage, through middle age, to the death of one and then the other partner. In Moscow, the Institute of Sociology's model is the static, "happy family" paradigm of the Moscow suburbs survey discussed in chapter 4. The "happy family" model incorporates such elements as "democratic" decision-making, equal sharing of household tasks by all family members, and open communication between all members. I was told that democratic decision-making applies to children as well as adults, and that the sharing of household tasks includes children too.

The model does not seem much different from the American democratic family ideal. When I asked what the particular "socialist" contribution to family life was, I was told it was that women are liberated under socialism and can work where they choose. Indeed, the chief factor in the thinking about women's liberation that East European and Soviet sociologists insisted upon was that there can be no other equality unless there is economic equality, unless the wife contributes a significant amount of the family income. My Soviet colleagues, especially, could not conceive of multiple options for women and for men in terms of life styles. For them, self-fulfillment comes through gainful work and the family. And their research conclusively demonstrates that happy, gainful work and a happy family are related.

The danger in positing a single "happy family" model and a single role option for women—that of the wife-worker—is that surveys based on these or any other unchallengeable assumptions can become self-fulfilling prophecies. The universality of the Soviet findings raises doubts about their validity. The sociologists I interviewed appeared to be devoting their attention entirely to seeing the model of the small, well-integrated nuclear family work as the ideal "basic social unit," but they were not asking whether such a unit might in fact be irrelevant 30 or 40 years hence. Nor were they wondering whether the model could be applied to all families, even if all had an equal education, since frequently husbnd and wife live apart because they have jobs in different cities. Finally, the urban bias of the model was not considered.

One of the stated aims of communism is the elimination of the difference between city and country, but in the Soviet Union the elimination appears to be in favor of the city. The isolated nuclear family is specific to the city. Vera St. Erlich made a strong point when she listed as one of the advantages of the traditional extended rural patriarchal family the support it gave its members, the protection it afforded its women, and the identity it provided for each individual in it. The East European and Soviet sociologists look upon this type of family as obsolete, but they have yet to give sufficient thought to the development of infrastructures that might diminish the isolation of the modern urban nuclear family.

Not that Soviet sociologists do not recognize that this isolation exists. The study of the Moscow suburbs discussed in chapter 4 demonstrated that Muscovite families generally do not know their next-door neighbors and that their contacts and friendships are made at work. When the respondents were asked what they would suggest to make their apartment living more neighborly, the majority wanted some kind of meeting place within the apartment complex where people could get to know one another.[19] But the literature provides little evidence of serious attention being given to breaking down the isolation of the family through designing smaller apartment complexes, landscaping, or the development of community activities.

One last comment on Soviet family research. According to Golod and Kharchev, new studies in the Soviet Union indicate that the first four years of a child's life are the most crucial. During them, it is important that the child have a mother's care. For this reason, some pressure is developing to have the mother paid to stay at home during this time. Dr. Yankova, however, does not agree with the studies. In her view, there are two sides to the question: the men more frequently range themselves in favor of the mother staying at home, but the women prefer to use the day care centers and nursery schools. As she sees it, the family, school, and community are interrelated and mutually supportive in the following relationships:

family⎯⎯⎯⎯⎯⎯⎯→ school⎯⎯⎯⎯⎯⎯⎯→ community

The schools are not there merely for educational purposes but for the upbringing of the child as well. The family helps the school by providing individual attention to the child's emotional needs, while the school socializes him to the community. Dr. Yankova cited a Hungarian study which shows that children in social institutions receive better physical training and generally a better diet, but are not prepared for real life. Children who live at home are "closer to reality" she said. They become acquainted with the tensions and problems of daily life and learn how to cope with them through watching their parents. While she thinks that motherhood is necessary for a woman to attain self-fulfillment, she does not agree that this means being obliged to stay away from work for four years. In this connection, she stressed that equality does not mean sameness (*"ravenstvo niet tozhestvo"*). For her, equality in the home depends on mutual understanding. It means an equal division of labor, but not necessarily men and women doing the same job. It also means equal decision-making, but not in the same place. Again giving the conservative opinion I had come to expect in the Soviet Union, Dr. Yankova expressed the belief that decision-making in the home could be exercised by women, while that in industry was the men's province.

Sociologists interviewed in Eastern Europe differed about the possibility of positing one model of a happy family and its relationship to school and community. Some were hesitant to discuss the nature of family happiness, now or in the future. The Yugoslav survey that has frequently been cited in this book seems to be based on a model similar to the Soviet one, although the authors call it the "syncratic" rather than the democratic family. The Bulgarian studies previously mentioned also posit a democratic form as the end product of family development. Czech studies point to the necessity of shared duties and mutual support if a family is to be happy,[20] while the East Germans hold up life-long marriage as the aim of every citizen. Hungarian and Polish sociologists, however, indicate that one cannot make objective statements about happiness. Hungarian sociologists in particular stress that happiness is an individual affair and cannot be produced on a mass scale.

Sociology in the European Communist countries supports the leaderships' stress on family stability, pronatalism, and the roles of father and mother as the scientifically demonstrated proper adult roles for men and women. East European researchers are a little more adventurous than their more conservative Soviet colleagues in considering the kinds of needs the modern family can fulfill, but no doubt is expressed that the family is the only place where certain needs can be fulfilled, such as the need for companionship during leisure time (Fišerová) or the need to develop a rounded woman's personality through the education of children (Yankova). Most countries hold the married state as the norm for adults. In fact, modern society does not truly accord unmarried persons or celibates a "place." In both Communist and Western society, celibacy is generally considered an abnormal condition. The original Marxist goal was to abolish marriage by radically transforming sex and family relations. The studies of marriage in Soviet and East European research, however, reveal just the opposite of this position. With their emphasis on the moral content of marriage, its permanency, and noble character, they refer back to the Judaic-Christian tradition for which nineteenth-century Marxism had little sympathy.

SEX DIFFERENCES ON THE JOB

The second focus of East European and Soviet sociological research is investigation of sex differences in leadership styles and the influence of the different emotional and physical capacities of the two sexes upon job performance. Both East European and Soviet researchers are frank in admitting that the level of knowledge regarding the different qualities a man and a woman might bring to a leadership position is low. However, they are convinced that men and women *do* bring different capacities to their work.

Ilieva, Trifaniv, and Tsaneva's study of Bulgarian women is a case in point. One chapter of their book deals with the physical and hygienic problems of women in the labor force, another with the psychological characteristics of what the authors term "sexual dimorphism." In the first chapter, they present a great deal of data to document women's lower physical capacity. They then produce statistics demonstrating that women become ill 30 percent more frequently than do men, that they are more prone to anemia and to illnesses of the nervous system. According to the authors' figures, absence from work because of illness reaches its peak in women between 30 and

39 years of age, when women are overtaxed both at home and at work. Their data also show that married women tend to be absent from work more often than unmarried women or men. The authors next introduce tests which show that women are less adaptable to the schedule change required by night or late-shift work, primarily because of family responsibilities, but also because biologically women are seen as less adjustable. Finally, the authors discuss the problems of women with automation, line work in the factory, and other aspects of industrial work. They conclude chapter 1 by recommending that close attention be paid to improving the conditions under which women work, ending the equation of man with machine, and ensuring preventive safety measures in working conditions, particularly among women between the ages of 30 and 50.[21]

Ilieva, Trifaniv, and Tsaneva's display of data regarding types of illnesses to which women are prone, absenteeism from work, and the relationship between job tension and the burden of responsibility at home supports Magdalena Sokołowska's earlier pioneering study of the Polish working woman. In particular, Sokołowska stresses that the cumulative burdens caused by pregnancies, miscarriages, deliveries, confinements, nursing, and the menstrual cycle compose only the background of what she terms the psychophysical condition of women. Against this background other factors, such as contentment in marriage and a woman's relationship to her job, come into play to determine a woman's state of health and ability to work. Sokołowska calls for an updating of protective labor legislation to bring it into line with changes that have occurred in women's life styles and habits.[22]

Chapter 2 of Ilieva, Trifaniv, and Tsaneva's book deals with the psychological differences between men and women. The fundamental assumption is that psychological "dimorphism," or psychic differences by sex, do exist and that these predispose women to one type of work and men to another. Before saying what these differences are, the authors first discuss the "social-psychological" factors that may account for woman's place in the labor force: (1) historical conditioning whereby women have been socialized into some types of work and men into others, going all the way back to when women first worked in agriculture and men hunted; (2) class differences, such as in existing capitalist countries, where women are exploited by being kept out of "upper-class" jobs; (3) differences in the difficulty of work where physical strength may be needed. In the author's view, the first two factors have been eliminated under socialism. The third will be eliminated by the scientific-technical revolution.

Nevertheless, these authors feel that all differences in jobs based on sex are not going to disappear with the culmination of the scientific-technical revolution. Thus, they turn to traditional arguments about the way women think. They agree that most women under socialism work because they want to bring in a second income. But women's secondary reason for working usually depends on their level of education and the type of job they have. East German studies show that girls draw technical and industrial pictures in the course of a certain test in the same proportion as boys. The reason they do not go into engineering is that they are more interested in the domestic and social sides of life. Similarly, women are equal to men as regards the ability to concentrate for a prolonged period of time. The reason they do not seem to go into creative and organizational types of work is not because of any impaired ability in this sphere, but because of family burdens. Engaging in creative work requires freeing the mind from peripheral concerns. Being more domestically and socially inclined, women find such freedom much harder to achieve.

Next the authors analyze specific psychomotor tests given to boys and girls by various Soviet psychologists. From the results of these tests the authors conclude that the psychic structure of women is not different from that of men, but that their psychic orientation is. A woman's emotional makeup is composed of ups and downs, while a man's is more even.

Summing up all their data, and applying it to different types of work, the authors assert that women will always be found in those spheres of industry that have been automated and that demand psychosensor and psychomotor capacities. Women, in their view, show better coordination of movement than men, especially better visual-motor coordination. Moreover, the accuracy of women's memory for visual and moving things is better than men's. Thus, women will be found in those jobs that combine their superiority in the psychomotor and visual fields with their social qualities: they will be secretaries, telephone workers, laboratory assistants, and nurses. Women's further progress in the more intellectual professions, such as architecture, medicine, planning, and economics, will depend on the degree to which they are liberated from the burdens of home. Women do not have the same capacity for work as men, because of their uneven emotional makeup. Hence, the burden of job and housework deprives women of the energy necessary to do continuous intellectual work. The authors' conclusion is that the scientific revolution will overcome the obstacles regarding physical strength that now stand in the way of women doing some jobs, but that sexual dimorphism, while not directly closing women out of some professions, will exert an inevitable and permanent influence on women's choice of career. Thus, the main objective of a proper labor policy for women, in the authors' opinion, is to gear women's work to their biological limitations, i.e., to require less physical strength and to compensate for the menstrual and birth cycles.[23]

The work of Ilieva, Trifaniv, and Tsaneva represents the more liberal view of sex differences on the job among East European and Soviet sociologists. However, the old "nature" argument remains: women will not do certain things because their biological nature argues against it. And psychological differences, in the opinion of these authors, are linked with biological differences.

Other researchers use the "nature" argument more obviously. A new book discussing the psychology of the sexes is about to appear in Bulgaria. It addresses itself to the question of the special qualities women and men bring to leadership positions. The author, a man, singles out humanism (Ilieva, Trifaniv, and Tsaneva's "social qualities") as the most important different quality a woman brings to a leadership post. He concludes that women should be employed in positions where "humanism and empathy" are important considerations, while men should work where rational thinking is the criterion.[24]

This line of thinking supports the pluralistic attitudes expressed in Party and government public policy decisions. In the future Communist society, women will be doing their traditional emotional thing, and men their rational thing, as they always have. The Bulgarian research has been presented at length because it appears to be representative of the general approach of Soviet and East European sociologists to the problem of women at work. In general, these researchers have tended to emphasize what they term the "affective-sympathetic" nature as feminine and the "rational-organizing" character as masculine, despite data, such as that cited by Ilieva, Trifaniv, and Tsaneva, showing that the "rational-organizing" ability is common to both sexes.

Traditional views of sex-linked characteristics die hard. A recent study of the kinds of traits psychiatrists in the United States consider male or female showed psychiatrists assigning passive-emotive characteristics to a "feminine" cluster and aggressive-rational traits to a "masculine" cluster.[25] The problem is that those traits designated as specifically "feminine" are precisely those that have been assigned to subordinate and oppressed groups throughout the centuries. As Helen Hacker has shown in her research, traditional descriptions of the American Negro's character are virtually identical to contemporary images of the "feminine" woman.[26]

The evidence indicates that the Communist regimes continue to give strong endorsement to this type of divided thinking. Moreover, the demographic factor does not seem to operate in this area, since both the Chinese and the European Communist leaderships support a clear division of sex traits. It is a sobering commentary that those countries which pioneered in the liberation of women now appear to accept as scientific truth the doctrine of "separate but equal."

SOCIALIZATION

Communist socialization policies provide the firmest evidence of the leaderships' conservative stance on sex roles.

THE SOVIET UNION AND EASTERN EUROPE

Communist sociologists argue that the socialization a child experiences in his family is the major determinant of his adult attitudes. In their view, the division by sex of aptitudes and appropriate careers generally takes place automatically in the family.

My research provided some substantiation of this view. When I asked a group of children in the Central Asian town of Fergana what they wanted to be when they grew up, the three girls answered in turn: "A teacher," "A nurse," "A doctor." The boy wanted to be a pilot. Hungarian sociologist Judit Sas set 70 first-year Budapest University students the task of writing down a complete description of everything they would be doing on a certain day ten years hence. In virtually every response, traditional role stereotyping prevailed (see chapter 4).[27] Sas concluded from this that early family socialization ingrains patterns of sex behavior and performance expectation that education is unable to eradicate. The Bulgarian sociologists I taked with are preparing a more elaborate survey along similar lines. They plan to ask more structured questions, but their aim is to determine to what extent socialization at school may alter attitudes previously formed within the family.[28]

The process of socialization begins with the family, but does not end there. In the Communist countries, as elsewhere, education is a strong reinforcer and conditioner of attitudes acquired at home. Mollie Schwartz Rosenhan has made a content analysis of Soviet children's readers. Basing her research on 21 variables related to categories of behavior, she found "striking" differences between the characteristics ascribed to males and females in the books she investigated.

In the textbooks reviewed, the Soviet adult male was presented as altruistic and politically involved, concerned with his own advancement. Antisocial behavior might be manifested by male children, but never by adult males. A boy was rarely shown engaging in nurturing behavior or doing household tasks.

The Soviet adult female was depicted as bound up in traditional household and nurturing tasks. She was more emotional, supportive of the advancement of others, but less concerned about her own advancement. She tended to be careless, politically naïve, as well as politically uninvolved. In stories about the Russian Revolution or the prerevolutionary period, women were shown in supportive and nurturing roles, contrary to the historical fact that revolutionary women in czarist Russia played a prominent and frequently aggressive part in the revolutionary movement. The textbooks depicted only men as being truly concerned about the Revolution.

Women's place in the working world was clearly identified in these readers. Women were persistently identified as mothers and grandmothers, while men were seldom shown to be fathers or grandfathers. Males were identified in 26 different types of jobs, females in only 12. Some of these female jobs were what traditionally might be expected: teacher, factory worker, doctor, secretary, milkmaid, worker in a chicken house. Some were less obvious: tractor driver, construction engineer, operator of a thresher. But the males were draftsmen, policemen, test pilots, and more importantly, Party leaders. As in American elementary readers, women were seen as indoor, passive creatures, while males were active outside the home. Significantly, the higher the grade level of the textbook, the fewer the adult females represented.[29]

Romanian and Yugoslav texts reveal the same tendencies. In a third-grade history reader, Romanian heroism is portrayed by heroes, not heroines. Patriotism is depicted as a primarily male characteristic, with women supporting the patriots as wives and mothers. In a Hungarian first-grade reader that teaches the alphabet, under one letter there is a picture of a boy with a hole in his sock. He asks his little sister to mend it. When she dutifully does so, the next picture shows the boy kissing her and saying, "I like you."

One explanation for the differentiation of sex roles in educational texts might be the pronatalist policy of the European Communist regimes. But Judit Sas believes that the reason lies deeper than that. Many textbooks, she thinks, are written without conscious bias. The prejudice expressed in the presentation of women as mothers with jobs rather than as career women with home and family is unconscious, the result of centuries of tradition. Two Czech and Hungarian studies likewise stress that the concepts of womanhood and family are the product of a long historical process. In particular, the Czech author notes conflict between the functional demands of the two basic systems of modern industrial society: the family relationship system and what she calls the "socioprofessional" system. Industrialization, she argues, has not always and everywhere figured as the necessary and sufficient condition for the existence of the conjugal nuclear family. In fact, there is no immediate connection between the two. In her view, the old belief in the ability of the social sciences to reconstruct the past and provide a scientific basis for changes in family structure "overestimated the influence of moral ideas at the expense of the impact of actual conditions on family life." These moral values are impeding the development of scientific theory regarding the family today, as the survival of old myths continues to condition thinking about the ongoing development of the family (witness the persistence of traditional sex stereotyping in textbooks).[30]

An objective appraisal of the degree of conscious or unconscious bias in the portrayal of sex roles in Communist textbooks is difficult, to say the least. It can be argued that a great deal of the bias is deliberate. At a kindergarten in Tashkent, for example, the play corner contained sex-specific toys for boys and girls. Mention has already been made of the Soviet requirement that girls in the secondary grades take home economics while boys are taught skills one learns in an American "shop" class. In Albania, home economics for girls was introduced in 1959 and was directed particularly at girls from urban families.[31] Mention has also been made of the tendency in the Soviet Union for men to be admitted to universities more readily than women, as well as the propensity on the part of women in the Soviet Union and Bulgaria to consider social service careers more favorably than men, and for men to be drawn to the technical fields.

The existence and persistence of trends such as these cannot, however, be considered an indication of voluntary choice on the part of young women, or as independent of reinforcement from the educational environment. A case in point is a Soviet textbook that teaches Communist morality to teen-agers. The Soviet double standard in sexual behavior comes across in such a way that it cannot be considered accidental. "In the absolute majority of cases, the behavior of young people depends upon the girl." Stressed is the fundamental "duty" girls owe to society to marry and to have families. "It is important to remember that *no matter* [italics mine] what they become—doctor, teacher, or textile worker [note the woman's place at work]—girls will become wife and mother." The book goes on to say that a wife and mother cannot have the respect of her husband if she does not conduct herself properly before marriage. These admonishments are presented in the context of some excellent common-sense advice on possible tensions arising in marriage because women have equal opportunities and equal rights. For example, the husband is urged to realize that his wife needs assistance in the home and to help where he can. He is also urged to be understanding of his wife's problems at work, as she is to be of his.[32]

Soviet data support the contention that traditional family upbringing is reinforced by school socialization. Soviet girls tend to get better grades on the whole, but they are less frequently numbered among the high achievers. E. K. Vasil'eva found in her study of girls' and boys' behavior in the Leningrad schools that girls tend to hold the important jobs in the Pioneers or Komsomol *aktiv* and to be class monitors and student leaders. And girls are less likely to be the troublemakers in school.[33]

Soviet sociology traces the origins of female ascendancy in secondary school to two factors. The first is the predominance of female teachers at the elementary and secondary school levels, as was shown in figure 6, chapter 2.[34] The second is that girls are socialized at home to the role of housewife and mother and toward "less arduous production activity." Girls are encouraged to be dignified, moderate, restrained, and balanced. In the words of one sociologist: "While the pugnacity of boys is not congenital . . . the nature of the previous upbringing, the style of the old pedagogy and the reliance on it in the school predetermined greater mobility . . . and less strict self-control . . . among boys than among girls.[35]

According to this explanation, the earlier maturation of girls, as evidenced by their greater self-control and ability at self-appraisal, combines with the feminization of the teaching profession at the lower grades to encourage more compliance among girls toward their teachers than among boys. Like Judith Bardwick and other experts in this country,[36] Soviet sociologists find greater compliance in girls toward adults, and a greater need for interpersonal rewards. Boys, by contrast, tend to compete for dominance among themselves and thus develop more internalized standards of behavior. When girls become adults, their compliance carries over to their husbands and children.

Thus, as in American schools, girls in Communist societies tend to be socialized into the continued identification with traditional behavior patterns oriented toward domesticity and rule maintenance. Bulgarian and Hungarian sociologists indicated to me that they were far from satisfied with the results of the "old pedagogy" and were investigating new methods designed to combat sexual stereotypes. Polish sociologists feel that some progress may have been made. One Polish survey, for example, determined that women and men rate approximately equally on every human characteristic except emotion and empathy, where women rate significantly higher than men.[37]

Premarital or even extramarital sex in terms of a relationship over time is strongly censured in the Soviet Union. According to a former Moscow woman lawyer interviewed in Israel, a case of premarital sex that is discovered is a matter of concern to the school, the Komsomol organization, the block organization, the work place, even the Party organization. A girl is made to feel ashamed of having demeaned herself and not worthy of a decent career and future. Public pressure, supported by organized Party pressure, encourages a young woman to hesitate before trying a taste of "free love," which might wreck her whole life. Leningrad sociologist V. Minskaia provides statistical evidence that the majority of sex crimes are accomplished in the context of what she terms the "surprisingly hasty or rash entry of young persons into proposed intimate relations," Such meetings bear an accidental and short-lived character and usually take place in the street, in the park, the public transportation system, or in settings like the rush of a party or an evening with friends. In 70 percent of the sex crimes, 50 percent take place one to two hours after intital contact and 20 percent occur after one to two days. "Often both partners are in a drunken condition."[38] Because young people are constrained to associate sex only with marriage, marriages are built on what the former lawyer considers "an unhealthy basis." Sex outside marriage may be possible in high circles, but is condemned among the average citizenry. Finally, quarrels are cases for the extralegal comrade's courts. Sooner or later, according to the former Soviet lawyer, the young people wake up to the fact that neither is suited to the other. Divorce and remarriage may fulfill official socialization norms, my respondent thought, but they do not produce stable families.

In terms of adult socialization, Peter Juviler has found a very mixed pattern of Soviet legal norms regarding women, as well as stark contrasts in attitude over whether motherhood or the professional woman should be exalted. For example, in the Soviet judicial profession, one-half of the People's Court judges are women and there is a high percentage of women in other legal jobs. Thus, in cases involving women, women may encounter a sympathetic ear. In cases of rape and homosexuality, the courts appear to discriminate in favor of women, but, as was pointed out in the earlier discussion of rape law, they also take the defendant's prior conduct into consideration. The courts generally discriminate against women in the case of prostitution. Mothers who have been convicted of promiscuous behavior face the penalty of deprivation of parental rights. Adultery is not considered a case of promiscuous behavior but is a cause for divorce. In Central Asia, the battle over *kalym* goes on. Punishments range from two to five years' confinement for accepting bride price and two years for paying it. Yet the practice persists, especially if the father has many daughters to marry off. Abortion after the third month of pregnancy is a criminal offense. But codes concerning the destruction of an unwanted child vary from republic to republic. In some cases, it is considered abortion, in others manslaughter, and the penalties vary. The law is also unevenly applied to pregnant women who have been sentenced to exile. The RSFSR code delays exile until the child is a year old and it outlaws capital punishment in the case of pregnant women.[39] The position of a woman who is pregnant or becomes pregnant in Gulag, according to Solzhenitsyn's accounts, is desperate. An abortion can be fatal, yet if a woman bears the child, she runs the risk of being separated from it.[40]

The application of the law suggests the continuation of a largely puritan atmosphere in the Soviet Union. Although the puritan environment has its roots in the Russian past, the regime, in my opinion, is responsible for its unchallenged official position today.

In sum, both Eastern Europe and the Soviet Union stress generally the same traditional sex stereotypes in their socialization policies. The difference may lie in the somewhat softer approach of the East European regimes, which have been more tolerant of rock-and-roll, hand-holding in the streets, and other manifestations of "decadent bourgeois" behavior. Moreover, as the section on social research indicated, the East Europeans appear somewhat more questioning of sex roles than the Soviets. Nevertheless, convention remains the handmaid of socialization in Eastern Europe as it is in the USSR.

CHINA

In China, the present sex norms may be described as both the product of and reaction to the Confucian ethic. As we have seen, the freedom of women to get a divorce and to marry whom they choose was considered by Party members, as well as the bulk of the population, as an invitation to promiscuity and the end of female chastity, so valued by the Confucian system. The strict sexual code would seem to serve two functions. (1) It promotes the cause of birth control: serving the people takes precedence over personal desires, sexual and otherwise. (2) It channels women's energies away from the family toward the Revolution. Thus, in the Chinese case, conservative sex norms would appear to operate in favor of rather than against changing sex roles.

The chief vehicle of adult socialization has been the campaign. In the course of Chinese Communist history, three major campaigns specifically oriented toward radically changing women's roles may be identified: the 1950s campaign for the marriage law and birth control; the Cultural Revolution, when women were repoliticized; and the campaign since 1972 to mobilize women into productive work and recruit female "cadres." (The 1958 Great Leap Forward attempted to radicalize sex roles but was a short-term experiment.) The campaigns have been implemented mainly through a series of rewards offered to women for correct performance.

In the first campaign, the government rewarded village women for fertility limitation by offering them educational opportunities and upward mobility. The introduction of the First Five-Year Plan brought an end to the mass mobilization of women in 1953, perhaps because such revolutionary struggles appeared counterproductive to economic development. As has been mentioned, the women's movement subsided in the next decade and socialization reverted to more traditional lines. The official line was that women had been liberated because discriminatory wages and family domination had ended. Women were now able to rise as individuals to high-status positions. In fact, career openings for women declined because of the negative economic situation, and many women were forced to leave the labor force for lack of jobs.

During the Hundred Flowers Campaign, women with high-status positions complained that wives of Party members were being given preference because of their political pull. While individual women might be successful, the status of the majority had not changed that much. The propaganda of the period turned increasingly traditional: respect for the aged, emphasis on the importance of kinship obligations, reverence for the male head of the family, and even the importance of women to reproduction and the maintenance of the household returned. However, women were still encouraged to adopt an antinatalist prowork attitude through their contacts with organized groups in schools and work places, which opposed large families, and regime pressure to "serve the people," which provided motivation away from identification with the traditional roles of wife and mother.

The Cultural Revolution somewhat reversed the trend. In August 1966, *China's Woman* published a self-criticism of its performance over the previous six years. The editors accused themselves of "massively proselytizing such 'bourgeois' and revisionist fallacies as 'women live for the revolution and husband and children,' 'to have a warm small family is happiness itself';

and to bear children is woman's natural duty.'' The so-called absurd views, the journal said, "intoxicated" women with motherhood and family.[41]

After a second period of retrenchment, in 1972 the press renewed its campaign of criticizing women for their unquestioning obedience to husband and male authority in politics, and their failure to assert themselves politically as women.[42] Equality through work, education, and pay was reemphasized to encourage women toward a new role identification. As increasing numbers of women graduate from the new lower-middle schools, it is assumed that more and more will want to compete for status positions with men rather than bear children.[43] However, current reports suggest that the campaign may be less extensive than it was initially. The persistence of slogans urging women to enter productive work suggests that they are not taking jobs, while other slogans accusing men of wanting to keep women in the home indicate the strength of popular feeling regarding woman's place there.

Girls as well as women have been the object of regime socialization. Because of the disruption of the educational system during the Cultural Revolution, it is difficult to assess the school's role in the political socialization of young people. Ruth Sidel reports that the treatment of boys and girls was virtually identical in the schools she visited,[44] and films on China shown in this country depict girls engaging in paramilitary exercises along with boys. But very little concrete information is coming out of China on what is happening in the schools today.

There is more evidence of the impact of the various campaigns on the behavior of China's young people. During the height of the Cultural Revolution, children were apparently encouraged to denounce "reactionary parents."[45] In the wake of the Revolution, urban girls and boys were sent to the countryside to be reeducated and to learn of Chairman Mao's special concern for the position of women. No difference seems to have been made between male and female in terms of who was sent to the rural areas, but an article in a Szechuan provincial paper demanded that better care be taken of the city girls sent to the villages, an indication of the conditions under which the girls were forced to live. Some young women were apparently sent into the army, for a Hunan paper published a picture of a group of smiling girls with the caption "We crack horsewhips, we are happy on the high plateaus; we reform our world outlook."[46] In other newspapers, the girls have been given less favorable publicity and have been accused of "thinking only of going back to the cities," while others are described as having love affairs too early and marrying too soon.[47] The uprooting of urban young women has had its costs, and the scanty evidence suggests that "girls still will be girls," despite attempts to reeducate them in their special duties.

Thus, as she emerges into the maintenance phase, China presents a rather ambivalent picture with regard to the socialization of women. On the one hand, there is continuing need to politicize women in order to enlist their support for the new order. On the other, there is the need to assure stability and continuity, for the securing of which values the family is aptly suited. It would appear, then, that the Chinese are trying to find a balance between traditional and new female role identification. What this balance is, however, remains to be seen.

The comparison between Chinese propaganda and socialization policies and those of Eastern Europe and the Soviet Union supports the likelihood of greater female participation during moments of revolution and social upheaval. Women's liberation *is* a status revolution. It involves a change in the hierarchical relations between the sexes, which have traditionally assigned women second place. To make women equal with men means to completely redefine these relations in terms of the needs of both men and women, as Yankova asserts toward the end of her book.[48] This redefinition is revolutionary precisely because it upsets centuries-old male-dominance behavior patterns. Moreover, no one is able to predict with certainty what will happen when this revolution takes place. Wherever the Communist regimes have tried to mobilize women, a reaction has set in. In Soviet and East European literature, fears for the stability of the family and concern for population growth have been expressed. In both Central Asia in the 1930s and China in the 1950s, female mobilization suffered retrenchment because of concern that the revolution in sex roles would hamper economic production. The documentation presented here suggests that when a regime desires social crisis for a purpose, as China did in the fifties and during the Cultural Revolution, and as the Soviet Union did in the 1920s, it develops policies that deemphasize the family unit and radicalize sex roles. However, when a regime enters the maintenance phase, it adopts policies directed toward strengthening the family, promoting traditional sex stereotyping, and directing women away from public involvement. The male-female relations that are challenged in the postrevolutionary stage revert to a new status quo in the maintenance phase. Significantly, while the Chinese Cultural Revolution attempted to overturn many political arrangements and to tear down divisions between elite and followers, it basically left male-female relations alone.

The aim of the Party leaders would seem to be to utilize women in areas of public and private life where the regime needs them most. The stereotyped criteria of masculine and feminine that are evidently being applied by medical and psychological research raise questions about the validity of the aim. Eastern Europe leads the way in the serious investigation of the status of women. Whether the investigations will produce fundamental changes in propaganda and socialization policies remains to be seen, since the researchers do not make policy. Up to now, women have been the useful tools of social engineering in all the Communist countries. Where attitudinal change affects birth rates and economic targets, the regimes promote equal status for women. Where such change opens up unknown risks and social upheaval, the regimes extol the virtues of family stability and happy motherhood. Research has uncovered no fundamental commitment so far on the part of either the Western or Chinese Communist regimes to socialize their populations to a real change in attitude regarding sex roles and the status of women in their societies.

8 / The Female Self-Concept

The final variable described in chapter 1 was the female self-concept: how most women perceive their role or identity in Communist societies. The most fruitful method of measuring attitudes is, in my opinion, the survey. The many surveys emanating from Communist sources provide a great deal of information on women's self-identificiation. However, as has been noted throughout the book, the tendency for Communist researchers to apply a similarity of approach in Eastern Europe and the Soviet Union makes a supplementation of these sources necessary. The Bulgarians, in particular, appear to rely heavily on Soviet methodology in their research, but the specialists in other countries with whom I talked had received a good part of their training in the Soviet Union and tended to follow Soviet thinking on the problems of women. Hence, it seemed useful to attempt a series of interviews with women in the East European countries and the USSR to see what attitudes regarding woman's role in Communist society would surface during our talks. As mentioned in chapter 1, I visited the area twice, in the fall of 1974 and during the summer of 1975. I was not at all sure what my reception would be. Prior to the trip, I contacted women whose names I had seen frequently in the course of my investigations in this country. I also wrote to the national women's committees of the countries I planned to visit. In my letters, I stated my interest in interviewing women in leadership positions and indicated I would appreciate any help I might receive. The response was most gratifying. Given the unfortunate short duration of my trips, it would have been impossible to achieve any results without the help my contacts gave me.

In the course of my journeys, I interviewed more than 100 women, sometimes in formal business settings, at other times on a chance-meeting basis on buses, subways, in the streets, and in stores. Because the majority of the women I interviewed at their work places held executive posts, I operated under the assumption that their assessment of official Party and government

179

policy reflected leadership attitudes, while more personal comments indicated their own views.

My investigation of female attitudes focused on three areas: (1) Was there a positive identification with the new female public and economic role, or did women tend to identify themselves primarily through the traditional role? (2) What was their identification with the Communist regime? (3) What was their sense of political efficacy and political participation?

Before I take up these questions in turn, something should be said about the problems of interviewing women and women elites in Communist countries. Interviewing elites in any country presents a challenge. There is a tendency for the interviewee to want to give you her views as she sees them, not within the framework in which you have structured your interview. If there is a series of prepared questions, the interviewer frequently finds herself departing from the text as the interviewee expounds on a subject of particular relevance to her.

In the Communist countries, I encountered the additional problem that many of the questions I asked appeared to make little sense to my respondents. For example, there is a concept of personality in Communist sociology, and a concept of achievement, but there is no understanding of a self-concept. Hence, the answer to a question such as ''How do you view your role in the organization in which you work?'' usually was a detailed description of the interviewee's job, not how she looked at herself on the job. Again, women have been told endlessly that they are liberated in Communist societies. To ask what liberation means is thus a meaningless question. A liberated woman by definition is a woman living in a Communist, or in their terms ''socialist,'' society. But the interviewee will doubtless go on to say that there are still many problems to overcome and will describe these. In the light of these semantic difficulties, many questions that I prepared were never used, and I simply tried to structure the conversation to cover the topics in which I was interested.

There was also the difficulty of distinguishing between personal opinion and official line. Soviet and East European émigrés generally will advise you that no woman living in a Communist country will tell a foreigner what she really thinks. To do so would be counterproductive to her career and position. Yet, while there was an understandably remarkable similarity in much that I was told throughout Eastern Europe and the Soviet Union, I was able to learn a good deal indirectly. I particularly found social scientists more than willing to discuss research and survey results in detail.

Finally, I was unable to visit China in person. Hence, the attitudes of Chinese women have by and large been left out of this chapter. What information I have been able to glean from reports of visitors to the People's Republic has been included where appropriate.

ATTITUDES TOWARD NEW SEX ROLES

Women are not required by law to work in the Communist countries, but every constitution gives them the *right* to work. As the data have shown, most women now do work in Eastern Europe, China, and the USSR. The question of why they work and whether they enjoy the work they do has been a matter of concern to East European Communist sociologists since the possible correlation between the demographic problem and the "double shift" was officially recognized. The frenzy felt by some women in trying to be a model mother and model professional is described with great sympathy and, for the Soviet Union, remarkable candor in Nataliia Baranskaia's controversial short novel, *Nedel' iia kak nedel' iia* [A Week Like Any Other].[1]

Surveys in most of the East European countries and the Soviet Union give us a good deal of information on women's attitudes toward work. The pioneer in this area was Poland, where J. Piotrowski and A. Kurzynowski published the first sociological study on women and work in a Communist country. Kharchev and Golod's late 1960s analysis of survey data in Leningrad and Kostroma mentioned in previous chapters follows Piotrowski's questionnaire. Kharchev and Golod give four major categories of reasons why women work: (1) the desire to participate in the work of society; (2) the desire to be in a collective; (3) the desire to be materially independent of one's husband; and (4) the necessity for additional income for the family. According to the answers of their respondents, the greatest percentage of women (53.5 percent) indicated that they worked for additional income, followed by the desire to be in a collective (21.5 percent), the desire to participate in the work of society (13.6 percent), and finally the desire to be materially independent of one's husband (11.4 percent).[2] Kharchev and Golod's findings confirm Piotrowski and Kurzynowski's research in Poland, where "financial considerations" were given as the primary motive behind women working in that country.[3]

In the spring of 1969, Moscow's Institute of Social Relations conducted a survey for *Sovietskaia zhenshchina*. Of the 421 women surveyed, 58 percent said they were "very happy" to work. Once again the principal reason cited for liking to work was to earn money to support the family. However, when the financial motive was eliminated from the possible answers, the distribution of other responses proved quite significant.

As can be seen in table 39, multiple responses were permitted. Even so, when the data were controlled for financial reasons, the most important secondary reason given for why women work was sociability. The work place has superseded the home as the place where things happen. While the desire to receive a pension and to improve one's living standard might be expected to be popular answers, the percentage who evinced interest in work for its own sake is noteworthy. Admittedly, the table displays a rank order of choices, but the fact that a third of the respondents indicated they found their work interesting is an important finding. Golod and Kharchev discovered a relationship between satisfaction with one's work and the conditions of work, such as the presence of an understanding factory or enterprise administration and the type of "collective" in which a woman found herself.[4] In other words, sociability appeared to be a necessary component of finding one's work interesting. Women might continue to work if they were unhappy, but their happiness depended on being in a sympathetic collective. A young Yugoslav teacher explained it in a similar way. "You never know," she said. "If you have a job, you have security, your pension, your future. Then, if you get a divorce, you know you will have something on which to live. Besides, no one can stay home with the children the whole day. It's so boring. And all you have to talk to are your neighbors. If they work, there is no one. Your friends are at work." She thought that no young Yugoslav woman today would not want to work.

All the women with whom I had formal interviews said their work was absorbing and assured me they would continue to work, even if their husbands could support them. Because these women held prominent positions in academe, industry, or government, they were among those who "had made it" professionally and their attitude was expected. Many of them, however, expressed some concern for those in factory jobs, whose work was dull. The Moscow Institute of Social Relations survey suggests that even if these did not find the work itself a challenge, they found the factory surroundings more interesting than home, as did the Yugoslav teacher.

The Bulgarian survey mentioned in earlier chapters provides a second dimension on the attitudes of women in Communist societies toward work: when they like to work (see table 40). While Bulgarian women appear to have accepted work as part of their life style, the most desired time periods within which to work are prior to the birth of children or part-time work. Work as a

Table 39—Soviet Women's Answers to the Question, "Why Do You Work?"

Reason	No.	Percentage (to the nearest hundredth)
To be in a collective	227	54
To receive a pension	180	43
To improve one's standard of living	160	38
To feel useful to society	147	35
The work is interesting	140	33
Total number of women surveyed	421	

Source: *Sovietskaia zhenshchina*, July 1968.

Table 40—Bulgarian Women's Answers to the Question, "If All the Material Needs of Your Household Were Guaranteed, Would You Continue to Work?"

Answer	%
No	6.1
I would work as long as I had strength and opportunity	8.6
I would work until I qualified for a pension	10.3
I would work, but not a full day and with part-time wages	22.1
I would work from time to time	22.0
I would work until I had children	36.7
I would work after the children had grown up	14.0

Source: People's Republic of Bulgaria, Ministry of Information and Communication, *Zhenata v stopanskiia, obshchestveniia, kulturniia zhivot a v semestvoto* (Sofia: Central Statistical Office, 1971), p. 20.

lifetime career appealed to only a small percentage of women and ranked sixth among the seven possible responses and last in terms of work options. In a sense, then, the Soviet elementary readers are accurate in portraying adult women as mothers with a job, rather than as career women with family responsibilities. If the Bulgarian survey is any indication, work is seen as a necessity, and some type of supplementary, marginal job is preferred over an all-absorbing career. Children would seem to come first in the thinking of these women.

It must be remembered that this survey was taken in both rural and urban Bulgaria. Among urban Bulgarian women, the percentage favoring a full-time career was higher, suggesting that urban opportunities were considered to be preferable to work on a collective farm. Dunn's study of Soviet rural women supports this finding. Soviet women apparently view farm work as something a woman should not do. When they have the chance, they move to the city.[5]

In my interviews with women, the primary reasons given for working were economic independence and the self-respect that accompanies it. Personal independence was particularly stressed by the Uzbek women interviewed. Becoming a family breadwinner may have played a greater part in bringing to Central Asian women a new sense of self and new status in the hitherto highly male-dominated family. Visitors to China found that Chinese women likewise valued the sense of self-respect that earning their own money gave them. Linda Gordon suggests that another, deeper reason may be involved in the Chinese women's response. The female vice-chairman of a revolutionary committee described the situation this way: "We, the former housewives, responded to the call of Chairman Mao. We would no longer stay at home, but would contribute to building socialism by setting up a small factory to . . . meet the needs of the people. . . . We had to wage acute ideological struggles at home, since before liberation we were oppressed not only by the three big mountains but a fourth—the authority of husbands.''[6] Work was not just a means of bringing home an additional income; it was a means of showing what a woman can do. It brought a sense of achievement and usefulness.

Women interviewees were also self-confident about their abilities to work. In general, respondents thought women make better students (and statistics bear them out) and take their education more seriously than men. They also perceived women as working harder on the job and as being more patient, more conscientious, and more adaptable to changing work conditions than their male coworkers. Perhaps the most radical comment came from a woman in Moscow. She seemed little concerned that so few women had reached leadership positions. Technology would take care of that problem when it eliminated physical work. Then, women would become the leaders because they were naturally more clever and more down to earth in solving problems than men.

In addition to this generally positive consensus regarding women's work role, the majority of the interviewees appeared to agree with their leaders' dictates concerning where women might work and the relationship between family and work. Most favored the trend toward the feminization of certain types of industry and job categories, even though they admitted, as in Bulgaria, that the process had depressed women's wages. But they seemed genuinely to believe that a job which the government determined might impair a woman's health or her ability to bear children should not be open to her. In the past, women had ruined their health because of the strains of heavy physical labor, and they were now glad to have legal protection. Indeed, a major source of concern was how to improve factory conformity to the law through more efficient control of women's working conditions by the factory women's committees.

Interviews with émigrés provided further confirmation that women tended to favor health restrictions on certain types of work. One woman expressed the opinion that Soviet protective labor laws were excellent. The problem was that they were not carried out all the time. When I mentioned the proscription against women tractor drivers in Romania, and asked why they should be permitted in China and the USSR, she said that research might vary, but that if science did conclusively show that certain types of work were injurious to women's health, then they should be prevented from filling these positions. She felt that men also should be protected, but that there were dangerous jobs which had to be performed. If no way could be found to do them without risk to health, then the men would have to do them. A Bulgarian woman doctor agreed rather reluctantly with this position. It was dangerous for everyone to work with polyvinyl chloride, she said, but someone had to work with it. It was worse that women should be the victims, because they were the bearers of the future generation, so the lot fell to men. Of course, she favored all efforts that would eliminate dangerous work conditions altogether.

Some women thought occupational differentiation by sex a matter of gender preference. The women director of a kindergarten in Tashkent indicated that the Party and government were very much interested in reversing the complete feminization of elementary and preschool education, and were giving men incentives to train in this area. At the time of my interview, however, Tashkent University had had no male registrant in elementary education. "Of course, men are welcome in any field, as are women," she explained. "But men simply do not have the patience needed with small children. That's a woman's job." When it was mentioned that historically, before women had been allowed to receive an education, teachers for every age level had been male, she smiled and said that was true, but that men had never taught really small children.

Other women thought sex differentiation essential for economic or social reasons. As discussed previously, Director Speteanu of Romania's "Miraj," said she felt it was necessary that the majority of her employees be women because women were the main consumers of her products. A young female engineer at a large silk factory near Fergana said that women are better than men at designing and making fabrics, for the same reason. Although I was not taken to the design room and so did not see how many women designers were working there, the majority of the employees at the silk looms appeared to women. A female gynecologist in Moscow suggested that it was only "natural" that women should prefer to consult women doctors on women's problems. Their native shyness made them hesitant to talk about female illnesses with men. She indicated that in her clinic a definite sorting took place. Women tended to consult women on health matters and men consulted men, although she hastened to add that there was, of course, some mixing.

The exception to what appeared to be the general acceptance of the feminization of occupations was agriculture. The women sociologists I interviewed said that the preponderance of women in the countryside was not conducive to their progress. While the absence of men meant that peasant women perforce became involved in rural decision-making, respondents stressed that the rural environment did not offer women opportunities for advancement. The lack of social and education facilities gave women no time or place to gain the necessary skills. Both men and women respondents in the various countries considered the problem a serious impediment to the further emancipation of women. However, Hungarian sociologists were inclined to think that it was only temporary, a product of the first generation of rapid and intensive industrialization, and would disappear as agriculture became mechanized and children left the land for jobs in the cities.

Finally, none of the interviewees expressed particular concern about the relatively few women in executive positions. They knew the percentages were higher than those in the Western world and tended to attribute to cultural backwardness the slowness of women to rise to administrative posts. Members of the national women's councils in Bulgaria and Romania took great pride in acquainting me with the Party's decisions regarding the promotion of women mentioned earlier. Equality would come, but not overnight, they argued. Ms. Grzecic of the Hotel Libertas was convinced that the opportunities were there, but that most women did not want to make the sacrifice. When asked whether a sacrifice was necessary for women, since men do not make a sacrifice when they work toward high positions, she replied that any important job requires sacrifice. However, a woman's sacrifice is necessarily greater because she has two problems to resolve: the proper adjustment of her family life and overcoming the popular attitudes regarding woman's seriousness of purpose at work.

Among the younger respondents, I found less enthusiasm both as regards the progress women have made and the possibilities of women attaining high-status positions. A female doctoral candidate in her twenties was quick to protest when I congratulated her on her achievements and said we would soon be reading that she had become an academician. "Oh, no!" she exclaimed, "that's only for old men with beards." A young female doctor saw nothing unusual in her career—"Doctors are employees like everyone else." The lesser degree of enthusiasm may be attached to the fact that the younger generation has not experienced the dramatic changes in women's status that occurred in the postrevolutionary phase. Thus, the basis of their comparison is considerably foreshortened, with the immediate past and immediate future tending to be perceived as identical in prospects.

Women who had left the Communist countries evinced a generally negative attitude about women in high positions. Some expressed the opinion that because of political intrigue and the nature of administrative jobs in those countries, no "good" woman would want an important job unless she were thoroughly committed to a career. They tended to look upon administrative and decision-making positions as being the province of already corrupted and corrupting individuals who had compromised with the injustices of the system. In view of their émigré status, a negative attitude among these women was to be expected. To what degree they represent the more general attitudes of women living in Communist societies is questionable. The fact that they emigrated or left their country is an indication of disaffection with the system. The data presented in chapter 5 suggest that women living under communism generally tend to have a negative perception of their involvement in politics. The explanation offered by the émigré women provides one insight as to why.

Several studies in Eastern Europe and the Soviet Union support the finding that women, for whatever reason, do not see themselves as high-level executives. In a small survey in the Soviet Union's Akademgorod, only 23 percent of those surveyed, half of whom were women, saw women in management roles, while 77 percent attributed management characteristics to men.[7] Czechoslovakia's Eva Bartová participated in a world-wide sample of public opinion entitled, "The Conception of the World in the Year 2000." Table 41 represents the distribution of male and female responses in the sample regarding expectations of there being more women in leading positions in the future. It illustrates several important dimensions regarding the attitudes of both men and women in the European Communist countries toward women in prominent positions. In the first place, only in Soviet-dominated Czechoslovakia and Poland is a negative desire recorded for men as far as women in leading positions is concerned. In Poland it is as high as minus 26 percent. Second, the desire of women to have executive careers is lowest in Poland and Czechoslovakia. By contrast, the desire of Yugoslav women to be in leading positions exceeds their expectations by a margin greater than that in any other country.

Third, the process of socializing men and women to accept women in leading positions seems to be most complete in the Scandinavian countries. Holland comes next, while this socialization seems least complete in the Communist countries. However, the desire of men in all the survey countries to have women in high-status posts is lower than their expectation and lower than either desire or expectation on the part of women. This attitude may be attributed to the survival of traditional male concepts regarding woman's place, as is most evident in the case of Spain and Japan. If it were true that in

Table 41—Answers of Men and Women to the Questions, "Do You *Wish* That in the Future There Will Be More Women in Leading Positions?" "Do you *Expect* That in the Future There Will Be More Women in Leading Positions?"

	Men		Women	
Country	Wish (%)	Expect (%)	Wish (%)	Expect (%)
Czechoslovakia	−2	+17	+36	+34
Poland	−26	+51	+47	+63
Yugoslavia	+26	+40	+67	+42
Finland	+62	+94	+88	+92
Holland	+40	+84	+55	+82
Norway	+79	+97	+95	+98
Spain	+48	+88	+96	+87
Japan	+17	+52	+66	+73

Source: Eva Bartová, "Postoje k problém ženy a rodiny: Několik úvah nad výsledky jednoho mezinárodního výzkumu," *Sociologický časopis* 8, no. 1 (1972): 48.

Note: + = yes; − = no.

comparison to the Scandinavian countries, a larger percentage of women occupied leading positions in Poland, the ČSSR, and Yugoslavia, then one could argue that female expectations and wishes are lower because the desired quantity of women in high-status positions has already been reached. But the data indicate the contrary. In Spain, for example, the high desire and expectation of both sexes for more women in leading positions reflects the almost complete absence of women from these posts. But in the "socialist" countries, some women do occupy high-status posts. The fact remains, however, that *both* men and women in these countries, including Yugoslavia (where one might expect considerable difference in view of Yugoslavia's less authoritarian political system), generally express little desire and limited expectations in this area.

Why should women neither want nor expect to attain leading positions in their country's economy or government? The argument that has been put forward most often by Communists and Westerners alike is that women do not want leading positions *because* of family responsibilities. Table 42, however, challenges this line of reasoning. The data show that in every country surveyed, women would very much *like* to be more tied to their families in the year 2,000 than they are today (mean = +83.3), but *expect* by a considerable margin to be less so (mean = −38.9). Men show the same pattern, although on the average they appear to be less bound to traditional thinking in terms of a narrower mean spread between hope and expectation (men, 105.9; women, 122.2). Poland, Holland, and Spain represent the extremes of the distribution, with Poland being the most radical case. In these countries, both women and men seem to want closer family ties but expect a drastic reduction in them. The expectation of looser ties is particularly high in Norway and Poland, and highest of all in Spain, especially among men.

Clearly, if the survey is at all representative, most people realize that the family is undergoing radical change, which they tend to view with apprehension or at least with a negative attitude. It would appear from table 42 that the fact of change is more readily accepted in Czechoslovakia and Yugoslavia, but that in traditionally Catholic Poland, change is desired very little by both sexes, although women seem to be a shade more conservative. When table 41 is compared with table 42, it becomes evident that family responsibilities are not a reason for women not wanting to assume leading positions. Both men and women expect that families will in the future be less of an obligation than they are now. Indeed, the attitude of women in the survey toward assuming leading positions would seem to have little correlation with their expectation of family burdens. In the non-Communist countries, women generally appear to desire both close family ties *and* greater participation in leading positions. In the Communist countries, the pattern is varied. Yugoslavia follows the Western trend. In the Polish sample, women's *desire* to participate in leading positions is much less than that of women in the non-Communist nations, but

Table 42—Answers of Men and Women to the Questions,
"Do You *Hope* That in the Year 2000 People Will Be More or
Less Tied to Their Families Than They Are Today?"
"Do You *Expect* That in the Year 2000 People Will Be More
or Less Tied to Their Families Than They Are Today?"

| | Men | | Women | |
| | *Hope* | *Expect* | *Hope* | *Expect* |
Country	*(%)*	*(%)*	*(%)*	*(%)*
Czechoslovakia	+20	−20	+46	−17
Poland	+96	−51	+97	−51
Yugoslavia	+46	−20	+64	−36
Finland	+85	−12	+98	−20
Holland	+94	−02	+98	−27
Norway	+81	−56	+88	−58
Spain	+67	−70	+79	−60
Japan	+97	−12	+97	−18

Source: Eva Bartová, "Postoje k problem ženy a rodiny: Ně kolik úvah nad výsledky jednoho mezinarodního výzkumu," *Sociologický časopis* 8, no. 1 (1972) : 52.
Note: + = more tied; − = less tied.

their *hope* for closer family ties ranks at the top of the scale. In Czechoslovakia, however, women appear to have slight hope of closer family ties and rank only a little higher as regards desire for high-status positions. Thus, Bartová's study suggests that the future of family relationships cannot be considered a determining factor in women's reluctance to rise to leading positions in the Communist countries.

Two other factors may offer more valid explanations of the negative perception of high-status positions on the part of women in the "socialist" countries. The first involves fears about female stability or competence in that kind of role. The mayor of the Leningrad city district frankly admitted she had had no prior preparation for her job. She had been educated in linguistics. She had had to work extremely hard to catch up with her more experienced colleagues in the beginning and expressed gratitude for the help her advisers had given her. Director Ivanova in Sofia said she had at first felt swamped with work. Both she and Director Speteanu had been trained as engineers and had had no previous managerial experience. They also indicated that in the beginning they had put in long, hard hours. Finally, Ms. Grzecic, a specialist in her profession, stressed the amount of time and work it had cost her to make her career a success. Table 41 indicates that most women would prefer not to undergo such a struggle to achieve a prominent position. In the words of a Yugoslav female lawyer, "It would be nice to stay home and take care of the children for a while."

Paradoxically, the Party may be urging women to seek high-status positions when they do not want to go that far themselves. Since they have not yet totally integrated the idea of a career into their concept of womanhood, they prefer the image of mother with a job, rather than that of the serious professional with a family. In this connection, it is noteworthy that none of the female administrators with whom I talked in the Soviet Union and Eastern Europe attributed their success to their personal abilities but stressed the role of the Party in their promotion. A Bulgarian sociologist indicated that she had received her degree after she was 40. If it had not been for the Party, she would never have had a higher education.

The second factor can in no sense be documented, because no public opinion poll would be permitted to test it. Women in the Soviet-dominated East European countries, such as Poland and Czechoslovakia, may have little desire to participate in public decision-making because they do not identify with its political structure. Particularly in the case of the Polish women with whom I talked, I came away with a sense of frustration. Whatever was tried, researched, or talked about would not change anything, my respondents told me. If the Catholic tradition is a factor in Poland,[8] then the desire for closer family ties indicated in table 42 suggests that 30 years of communism have not succeeded in changing the fundamental attitudes of Polish men and women regarding the family. On the other hand, in 1956, the Catholic church was an ally of the reform movement, and it is possible that the continued insistence on traditional norms is another aspect of popular dissatisfaction with the present social and political reality. This is, of course, pure speculation. However, it should not be forgotten that, except for Yugoslavia, communism was imposed by the Soviet Union upon Eastern Europe. The permanence of Soviet control was reiterated by Soviet military intervention in 1956 and 1958. It would be unreasonable to assume that women have remained immune to the existence and nature of Soviet domination. Their attitudes toward family, work, and life in their respective countries must in some way reflect an awareness of this basic political fact. Noninvolvement or apathy may reflect passive protest.

ATTITUDES TOWARD TRADITIONAL SEX ROLES

The primary focus of most women remains the family, and the Communist countries are no exception, as my interviews indicated. When I discussed with women their own families or my family in the United States, the reserve I had encountered when work was the topic disappeared. In Fergana, I received an impromptu invitation to the home of a woman language teacher at a local institute. My hostess had two children. Rather than discuss her work at the institute, she insisted that her children perform for me. Quite obviously, they were the adored center of the household, and the mother appeared to take more pride in telling me about her son's success in English than about her professional life. A Romanian psychologist confirmed that the family continued to be the center of a woman's life. The woman's main function was to take care of the household and children. The husband's income was considered primary to the upkeep of the family, while the wife's provided the frills.

In some instances, women seemed so immersed in their traditional role that they appeared to bring upon themselves additional unnecessary work. Particularly among the older generation of women, there is a feeling that if the women does not spend a considerable amount of time cooking, she is not a suitable wife. In most of the homes I visited the women almost insisted upon performing their traditional tasks. When I offered to help in some way, they immediately refused my assistance, with the excuse that everything had already been prepared or that doing the dishes was "no problem at all." I was the guest, and it was the duty of the woman of the house to wait on her guests.

A second aspect of this identification with the traditional role in the East European Communist countries is the fact that children generally do not help at home. When they return from school, they sit down to do their homework, watch television, and go to bed. Never once in my presence were children asked to set the table, wash the dishes, go to the store to shop, or do anything that it is customary for an American child to be asked to do. There is no Communist counterpart of "baby-sitting," although parents like to go out in the evening, as parents do everywhere. The mother literally takes care of the children, and if the husband does not help, she bears the whole burden. Part of each of my interviews was directed at understanding why children were so catered to. One Russian woman explained that her child had to work so hard at school that she did not have the heart to ask her to work at home. "Besides, how could she continue to get good grades, if she did not spend all her time at her books?" A Hungarian woman said that "childhood was the time to play, and children should not be burdened by having to do housework." A proud Russian father said that his children spent their free time learning English and taking private dancing and tennis lessons, activities he had not been able to participate in during his peasant childhood.

The women evidently believed that it was essentially their role alone to take care of the home. One Bulgarian woman had never let her husband or children help her in all her life. In the home I visited in Fergana, the mother and grandmother served the meal while the children sat and watched. The idea of having children help in the home is apparently foreign to the cultures of the European Communist countries. Perhaps the official propaganda makes so much of encouraging the sharing of household burdens because it literally is absent from most homes. If women do not demand help, they are in fact limiting their freedom of action by their own volition.

Finally, women seem to seek the childrearing role. Interviewees generally preferred to take care of their young children rather than send them to the state day care and nursery facilities. The reasons given were: there is insufficient individual attention; there is too much danger of catching cold; cleanliness is not strictly observed; a child needs the care of his mother at that age. Whatever the reason, the traditional role of mother was always stressed.

Among the several explanations for women's continuing conservative identification with their traditional roles, one involves their response to the regimes' conservative socialization policies described earlier. Women may in fact find support in these policies for their own conservative preferences and willingly accept propaganda and education on the subject. A second, and in my mind more persuasive, reason is social origin and force of habit. The vast majority of women in Communist countries who have been promoted to executive political and economic posts since World War II were socialized into the traditional life style of the countryside. As discussed in chapter 3, the majority of residents of the cities of the European Communist countries are newcomers from the rural areas. If is not surprising that they should continue in their traditional life style. What is surprising is that the younger generation of women also continues to identify with their traditional roles, if Judit Sas's research at the University of Budapest is any indication. A 26-year-old woman teacher in the Belgrade school system explained why she upheld the double standard. She had had a boyfriend for many years. They were planning to get married, but they had not yet had any sexual relations. She in fact was still a virgin. She did not believe in God, she said. She was simply following the advice of her mother, who had told her that if women were not virgins on their wedding night, the men would not keep them. Her brother apparently did not subscribe to this view and indeed was on the point of marrying a young woman with whom he had been closely acquainted for some time. But my respondent saw her fiancé as holding "very strict" views. Inquiry revealed that both of this young woman's parents had been born in a small village in rural Yugoslavia.

A third reason is derived from the way in which individuals in Communist societies are channeled into jobs and careers. Universities and technical institutes fill quotas for positions in the different faculties and departments. It was shown in the case of the Soviet Union that young men seem to be admitted more readily to higher educational institutions than young women, who may have to wait a year or so and in the meantime go to work. Once a young person is admitted into a particular course of study, the entire course of his life is determined. One Romanian woman was unable to choose between computer science and psychology, but she knew that when she made her decsion, she could never change her field. There is an element of finality in entering a university, particularly in the smaller East European countries, where opportunities are not very broad. While young people do not have to worry about unemployment, they have relatively few options as to where they can go or what they can do after completing their education. After university, the pattern in the East European countries (excluding Yugoslavia, where the options include study and work abroad) is for the young woman to be assigned to a town in the "provinces," away from her friends and acquaintances, unless she gets married and manages to stay in the university town. If she is from the provinces, her fear of moving into the larger, unknown world of the big city may encourage her to stay there. From the first job, the individual works his way up through a hierarchy of professional levels until the very top is reached. But he knows what the top is, what his chances of reaching the top are, and what the price will be.

Another aspect of career patterns in the Communist countries is the fact that a subordinate does not generally originate an action, a modification of work practices, or a research topic. At the scientific institutes, research topics are part of the Five-Year Plan and are determined at the appropriate policy levels. Subordinates are expected to participate in the investigation of these topics by doing the research project assigned to them. Doctoral candidates do not pick their subjects, but are given a choice from a narrow selection. Hence, the subject may or may not be one which interests the student, but it is never his own. The fact that research is seldom self-initiated may help to explain the general lack of enthusiasm for the work they had in progress exhibited by many of the women academics I interviewed. They, in turn, found it hard to believe that personal initiative could play a determining role in choice of project. In Hungary and Bulgaria, women respondents showed a greater interest in their research. Although the project would have to go through the proper bureaucratic channels for approval, a Bulgarian sociologist had just completed a research proposal that she hoped would receive approval and of which she would be one of the directors. Understandably, she was full of excitement and purpose. But the chance of making a proposal comes to the few, and most are recruited into work they did not select.

Such a system exists in modified degree in Western countries where the government is the main dispenser of research funds. But there is always the possibility of financing one's own research, if one wants to make the sacrifice. Such a course is impossible in the Communist countries. It may be argued that men as well as women are caught in the "directed employment" situation. However, the continued identification of the male as breadwinner means that men do not have any other option. They have to accept the system and learn to manipulate it to their advantage. Women, on the other hand, can more easily choose to forgo a career, have "just a job," and turn their attention to the family. The evidence shows that many prefer that course. If work is perceived as a life-long straight and boring path, then the family might offer the emotional outlet that is not available at work.[9]

The "directed character" of career patterns should not be overemphasized as a factor encouraging women to continue in their family role, but it must be considered if self-actualization is anything more than a phrase. A female state planning administrator in Uzbekistan indicated she had been in the same place, moving up the ladder from job to job since right after World War II. Her situation was common to many other women I interviewed. There may be more job security in the Soviet Union and Eastern Europe than in many Western countries, but there is less job challenge. Benefits other than sociability must be perceived to derive from work in order for there to be commitment. If there are none and another option is open, as the family role is open to women, a rational behavior model suggests that that option will be preferred.

In summary, the concept of work outside the family appears to have become permanently accepted into the life style and consciousness of women in Communist societies. Work, however, does not yet mean to the majority full-time dedication to a career or profession. On the contrary, the family continues to be the center of a woman's life. The ambivalence about work comes in the way women perceive the proper management of their public and traditional roles. Some of the women I talked with admitted conflict in themselves. "How can you eliminate centuries of oppression in one or two generations?" they asked.

IDENTIFICATION WITH THE COMMUNIST LEADERSHIPS

It was expected that the majority of the interviewees would express strong positive attitudes toward the Communist leadership of their respective countries. Most of the respondents were, in fact, women who had experienced the benefits of the system. What was more significant was the fact that the subjects were able to criticize their social system constructively while at the same time suggesting that the Communist system was the only one capable of solving the problems confronting modern women.

Positive Identification

One of the most persuasive proponents of the Communist system was Khudshume Shukurova, Director of the Lenin Museum in Tashkent and one of the USSR's foremost specialists on women in her native Uzbekistan.[10] "If you have any understanding of our history," she said, "if you have seen the *paranja,* and appreciated what a crippling, humiliating thing it must have been for women to wear a garment which covered them from head to foot with only the eyes looking out, you will realize what Soviet power did for Uzbek women. My mother was forbidden by her husband to leave the house except with his permission. Most of us were illiterate. We could not study or hold jobs. Now we are free to walk in the streets as we please. Our faces are open to the sky. We may marry whom we choose and pursue any career we like. Does Afghanistan give such freedom to its women? Does Egypt? Does India? These achievements would have been impossible without Soviet power."[11]

Director Shukurova's position recalls Myrdal's portraits of Chinese village women exulting in being liberated from the "bitter past." In each case, the present would appear to present a happy contrast to the previous era. The Chinese women interviewed by Myrdal and Sidel expressed their appreciation for what the Communist regime had done for them. As Shukurova did, they stressed the injustice and cruelty of the old traditions. Of Mao's "four mountains," which the Chinese people must conquer, the fourth represented the ugliness and oppressive character of woman's position in the old society, her limited opportunities, her slave status. In Uzbekistan, the new national dress is considered a symbol of Uzbek women's liberation. With its open collar, surrealistic pattern, absence of belt, and short skirt, the national dress represents everything the old dress was not: freedom of movement and opportunity. Uzbek women are thus reminded of how far they have come from their old confinement everytime they put it on. Chinese women must have experienced similar feelings when foot-binding came to an end.[12]

While Central Asian and Chinese women may attach greater importance to the visible signs of women's changed life styles, the European women I interviewed focused on the leaderships' actions. The female mayor of the Leningrad district was strongly supportive of both early and present Soviet policy toward women. She praised the child care system and the concern for women's health and well-being evidenced in Soviet legislation, she said, from the beginning of Soviet power. Director Ivanova expressed her gratitude to the Party for its role in promoting Bulgarian women. She herself had come from a working-class background and without communism would never have even dreamed of getting where she was.

The Communists' achievements in providing education for women were among the benefits of the system most frequently mentioned by the women I interviewed. One of the most frequently expressed beliefs was that only under "socialism" were women able to work or be educated in significant proportions. Even those who had lived and worked for a while in the West were of the conviction that socialism alone had liberated women. One Hungarian sociologist said that no one in Budapest had asked any questions when she went off for a year of work in the West, leaving her family behind. But her European hosts were much amazed that she could do a thing like that.

NEGATIVE IDENTIFICATION

Awareness of the negative aspects of woman's position in Communist societies was expressed in several ways. The most pervasive criticism was of the "double shift." It was candidly admitted that there were not enough child care institutions, that shopping was difficult, that consumer goods were not in large supply. But only one woman expressed doubts that the government was doing its best to remedy the shortages and hardships. She thought the leadership might be developing the kindergarten network not in women's interests but in the state's interest: to keep the much-needed female labor on the job. She criticized the facilities for not being able to take care of children after work hours or when illness struck. A Czech émigré to the United States was of the same opinion. She said that it was very hard to be called out of work when a child fell ill. You had to go fetch him at the kindergarten or nursery, take him home, and then care for him until he was well again. In the meantime, you lost all that time at work. She thought the state should design its child care institutions to treat minor illnesses at the facility, so that the mother would not have to bear alone the responsibility for nursing the child back to health.

A more sophisticated criticism was that while "formal-legal equality" and economic equality had been achieved, social equality still lay in the future. Social equality was generally defined as being two-headed: equality in the home based on an ideal democratic family model, and equality in public life based on the expansion of social services and the presence of women at all levels of political and economic life.

The question, "What does liberation mean to you?" brought varying responses. Most considered emancipation to mean that a woman could make her own decisions about her life and help her husband make his without outside pressure. A few women gave more formal and less personal views: A liberated woman should "know" herself, liberate herself from old-fashioned prejudices, and gain self-confidence and equality at home. She should be competent in her profession and mistress of its qualifications. She should not forget she is a woman and take care of herself. She should love and be loved. Finally, she should not forget that as a woman she is a mother. Women, according to one respondent, bring to the world sensitivity and the capacity to understand "problems of the heart," qualities which men do not have. Women bring grace, coquetry, and inspiration. A liberated woman should develop these qualities and use them to do good in the world. Such answers implied an awareness of the concept of self-actualization, even though the term was not used.

Society's role in this process is seen as providing the social services to free women from household drudgery and the economic possibility for women to advance their interests as they choose. More importantly, society provides the climate in which traditional attitudes can change. Opinions as to whether the Party really wanted to change the dominant social value system were generally positive. A Hungarian sociologist thought the Party did want to secure real equality between men and women but did not know how. Until recently, in her view, the economic problem of industrialization had been paramount in

Hungary. More importantly, it is difficult to effect a change in attitudes without clear objectives. "What is equality in the family?" she asked. "What characteristics will women bring to management? What advantages will accrue to an industry or an institute if a woman is at the head?" These were questions, she felt, which the Party and government would have to answer before they could develop the means to change current attitudes.

Zoya Yankova sees the solution to social equality in diminishing the amount of time women spend in the home. As discussed earlier, her research has emphasized that women should concentrate on that type of housework which contributes to the formation of their personality, namely, childrearing and the organization of leisure time. The state should eliminate such personality-deforming tasks as repetitive housecleaning tasks by expanding social services. She stressed that this solution does not equate equality with identical male and female behavior patterns. In her view, women are better at human relationships and men are better at normative decision-making. An enterprise needs both types of leadership. The state should encourage women to assume their proper leadership role once it has freed them from the frustrating and negative burden of housework. Social equality will come only under communism because Commuists alone, as the vanguard of the people, are in a position to educate both men and women to new attitudes.

THE ÉMIGRÉS

The women who had emigrated from the Communist countries expressed little sympathy for the Party and government, as might be expected. Both were seen as "they." Initially, the émigrés described woman's low profile in Communist political life with the term used by women living under communism: the "double shift." But further discussion elicited a different response based on a very negative perception of the Party *apparatchik*. According to one émigré, the first secretary of a local party committee earned a salary equal to that of what we might call an assistant professor at a university. The salary was considered excessive because the job carried no particular qualifications and produced no useful product. Once a man went into Party work, he was no longer perceived as working in his profession. In the subject's opinion, most people in Communist societies consider the Party or government bureaucrat to be a socially useless, noneconomically productive person. Real engineers who practice their profession deserve their salaries, but these are way below what a Party functionary receives.

Moreover, an *apparatchik* experiences the benefits of the exclusive stores, the possibility of obtaining articles from abroad, a select apartment, and all the other trappings of a privileged position. The wife of a local Party secretary, one interviewee alleged, likes to order the most expensive dresses from a private dressmaker who has the fabrics imported from Europe. "No one else in town has access to such luxuries." Not only are Party functionaries seen as socially useless, they are also described as parasites living off the rest of the population and contributing to the corruption of the whole system.

In the émigrés' view, most women do not want to be involved in this sort of intrigue. Their families are too important to them. The system is something to be endured, not something in which one can actively participate and retain one's integrity.

Thus, not only is politics viewed as unattractive or, better to say, unsuitable for women, but the time one has to spend on it is seen as cutting into woman's valuable time for managing her affairs at home. The question as to why more women do not join the dissident movement elicited the response discussed in chapter 5, reflecting traditional attitudes about the female personality.

This line of thinking is applied to revolutionary women of the nineteenth century as well. Even the most active and aggressive of these are seen as having had a negative experience in domestic life—an overprotected childhood, an unhappy marriage, the death of a loved one—or else they simply were sickened by the "bourgeois" life they were leading. In each case, the choice of revolution or dissent replaced the love that in more ordinary circumstances would have been shown toward a man or the family. Men, on the other hand, are perceived as being able to express love and dissent at the same time. It is not an either/or choice in the same way as it is for women, because for men the involvement is rational, not one-sidedly personal and emotional. It is also ideological, being bound up with what is seen as normal male power-seeking and other aggressive drives. Involvement in the dissent movement implies a total emotional commitment on the part of women. The depth of this commitment is a sufficient explanation for most of the émigrés as to why women are not widely represented among the dissenters, except in the roles of wives and mothers. While many women in the Communist countries may see the Party and government as "they," women are less likely to go into opposition of their own accord, because commitment to family is the norm for the large majority of them.

Although the female émigrés I spoke with view the Soviet political system as a contaminating environment, they share with women in the Communist countries their enthusiasm for what the Communists have done for women through legislation and the provision of communal facilities. In one émigré's view, a girl who gets an abortion in Israel or the United States is a social outcast, but this is not true in the Soviet Union. Others criticized the absence of preschool facilities and the prevailing attitudes toward women who have large families.

The émigrés' comments taken together appear to reflect a sense of injustice about the Communist system which does not include Communist policies toward women. The injustice covers such areas as the monolithic state, the

tyrannical and ruthless bureaucratic Party hierarchy, religious and racial discrimination, and a host of other ills, but not discrimination on the basis of sex.

Indirectly, the attitudes of the émigré women confirm the positive identification with the Party and government of the successful women interviewed
within the Communist countries. First, émigré women tend to view the Party
and government as having taken progressive steps with regard to women.
Second (and this thought will be developed in the section on political participation), the émigrés agreed with the respondents living under communism
that women are normally committed to immediate family concerns. Action
against the regime is taken at the expense of family, and only women with a
negative experience in that domain will choose to do so.

In sum, both émigrés and residents of the "socialist" countries surprisingly
appear to agree that the Party is the prime instrument of female emancipation
under communism. Female emancipation is taken as given. Women have
nowhere further to go. However, the liberating efforts of the Party and state
on behalf of women appear to be accepted on the condition that they not be
carried too far. Because they occurred in a franker atmosphere, my interviews
with the emigrants strengthened consideration of the possibility that perhaps
the majority of women living under communism are not at all convinced that
they want to be liberated in the sense defined earlier. Gratitude is expressed to
the leadership only as long as woman's traditional role is not seriously undermined. If this finding has any validity, then Dr. Yankova's insistence on the
need for the deployment of the educative powers of the Party and state to bring
people to new attitudes becomes crucial.

SENSE OF POLITICAL PARTICIPATION
AND POLITICAL EFFICACY

Attitudes relating to political participation and political efficacy were the
most difficult to observe. First, the absence of voting, in the Western sense of
the term, sets boundaries to the ability to identify the visible consequences of
political action. Second, one cannot stay long in a Communist country without gaining a strong impression of the enormous educative power of the state
to which Dr. Yankova made such positive reference. The Party and government set the tasks; the rest of the population executes them. It will be recalled
that the Communist regime's authoritarian posture, as noted in chapter 5, is an
important source of women's political passivity.

Without exception, all the women I interviewed stressed the increased
importance and prestige women have acquired under communism. The most
frequent comment was that it would have been impossible to build socialism
"without us." Next in frequency was, "There can be no question of women

returning to the home, even if they did not have to work. Society needs women workers and the Party and government know it.'' Women in Bulgaria and Romania see proof of the Party's recognition of women's contributions in their promotion of women to the highest political organs.

Yet, this sense that women have made a difference in the industrialization of their countries was never coupled with any open statement related to "women's power." Most of the interviewees started off with an expression of reservation: "You must understand these are only my views." "Of course, I do not make policy. That's for the Party to decide." "I'm speaking only as a professional." The women interviewed were eager to relate what the Party has done, how the Party has understood women's problems, but even those in executive positions who were Party members (as in most Communist countries they must be if they are to attain high-status posts) did not express an identification with Party decisions. In most cases, I had to ask directly whether the subject was a Party member. This information was never volunteered. Again, specific questions were needed to gain information about a subject's work in the Party. Without such questioning, Party activities probably would not have been brought up at all. Whoever or whatever the Party is, it was never identified in the respondents' conversation with themselves, nor as part of that aspect of life which is visible to the public—the elected offices and managerial positions the Party distributes. These are not perceived as "political" in the same sense that we in the West consider them political. Communist leaflets discuss the role of women in government administration as that of women in "public life." The enterprise managers I met in Bulgaria and Romania were deputies to their respective national assemblies, as were the representatives of the women's committees. It is taken as a matter of course that individuals in prominent social or economic positions will be deputies. Being a deputy was not seen by the respondents as a full-time job in the same way that being a United States senator is a full-time job, nor was it viewed even as a part-time job commensurate with that of a state legislator. And, of course, service in the national legislature was never mentioned as a step in the ascent to political power.

My interviews confirmed that "politics" is accepted as taking place in Communist countries behind the scenes, far from "public life." Political decisions are not made in the legislative assemblies or the local soviets. They are made at the appropriate level of the Party hierarchy. The exception to this rule is Yugoslavia, where predictably women's participation in elected office at all levels of government is much lower than is the case with the other European Communist countries. But in Yugoslavia the legislatures have gradually acquired real decision-making capabilities, and wherever power politics is really operative, female participation is low.

The finding that the Party is felt to be outside the workaday world and above the lives of ordinary people raised the question as to how women looked upon the Party. Do they consider that they have a political input into its decisions? This type of investigation could not be carried on. Attempts to probe women's desires for political participation generally resulted in my being given figures about female membership in the Party or in the discussion being turned to other channels. Emigrant women, however, offered many interpretations about women's attitudes toward the Party. Once again, their views must be taken in the context of their decision to leave their countries. Their opinions are doubtless more negative than are those of the women who live under communism and certainly of those who became Communist Party members.

Reference has already been made to the émigré's perception of the Party *apparatchik* as a parasite who makes his living off the hard work of others. The Party was also described as a political arena that promises a privileged life at the cost of personal corruption. The impression conveyed was that women in general wanted no part of such a life unless they were seriously bent on a career, since career advancement could be made only at the price of Party membership.

Such statements, however, are only a partial explanation of why women in Communist countries are apolitical. Women, according to the émigrés, are more "moral" or idealistic than men (as the Virginia Slims Poll shows American women like to think),[13] but they are also more practical: "Why should women join the dissent movement?" one respondent asked. "What good will it do? You cannot change Soviet power." "Assuredly," said another, "there is more freedom in the Soviet Union now than there was under Stalin. Fewer people are going to Gulag. But Soviet power has not been weakened. It has only changed its character. There is less violence, but the Soviet state no longer needs violence. It can get what it wants by administrative measures." A third stated that it was futile for women to join the Party and work for changes from the inside. "You cannot change the system."

Since the system is perceived as immutable, it makes no sense to the emigrant women to have anything to do with it. It is best to stay away. Women, in their opinion, do not join the Party because they want to in most cases. They join because the Party recruits them. The decision is the Party's and not a product of any particular female client demand. Those who are given posts in the Party organization are objects of pity. "It's not her fault. She really is a nice woman."

Nice women, the émigré respondents alleged, do not go into politics. The reasons given probe the heart of the problem.

1. If a woman starts a meteoric rise in the Party, whether she is married or not, it is taken for granted that she has a "protector" in the Party apparatus. She has "sold" her independence and self-respect for his protection. Two problems then confront her. First, her protector might fall into official disfavor and then, of course, she would too. Second, she is seen by other women

as "fallen," as having been bought, as not "nice." It is all right on the local level, where Party work, gainful work, and home are closely connected. But the only way to move farther up the political ladder, my respondents urged me to believe, is by the old tried-and-true method of virtual prostitution. Furtseva, they charged, would never have been admitted to the Politburo if Khrushchev had not been her protector. Women, the émigrés were convinced, do not want to enter politics, because politics creates for them an insoluble dilemma. If they love their husbands but their husbands are not politically important enough to be their protectors, then they prefer to maintain the marriage rather than enter politics. The émigrés noted that the wives of politically important males also are generally apolitical. If women do find a protector, they risk social ostracism as well as a broken marriage. Not one of the émigré respondents I spoke with thought it possible for a woman to rise in Soviet politics on the basis of her merits and achievements alone.

2. Another aspect of the issue is even more revealing. All the émigré respondents thought it impossible for a woman to be in a top political position without a protector because sex would then become a problem. Introducing a woman into decision-making circles meant breaking down male solidarity and fostering competition for the woman's favors, unless it was certain that she was attached. My respondents did not see any way in which a woman could be in politics without a husband or a "protector." Men would not leave her alone until she found one, and until she did, the process of decision-making would be crippled. The discord introduced into male decision-making by the presence of women was stressed time and time again. "Even in discussions among colleagues, it is different when men talk to men and when they talk to women. Always they are considering a woman as a woman."

The reverse side of the coin, as we have seen, is that sex or love is given as the main reason for women's opposition to the system. It was not admitted that women could enter politics for any other reason. For a "nice" woman, love and her emotions seem to be everything. To go into official politics and rise in the Party hierarchy means to transgress love, or, in other words, to cease to be a true woman.

It must be repeated here that opinions are at issue, not facts, and that the opinions are those of women who have left their countries. There is a decidedly conservative bias to their views. Woman's traditional role is offered and no other role is considered possible. However, when one compares the views of these emigrants with the data on women in politics given in chapter 5, there would seem to be some ground for arguing that although these attitudes are certainly not shared totally by women in the Communist countries, they may represent some of the women's more fundamental "gut" feelings. Politics is still a man's world. Certainly, there is no exception to the proposition that a woman at the height of Communist political power must have a protector. Anna Pauker was allegedly French Communist leader Maurice Thorez's mistress. Madame Mao would surely not have exercised the power she had if her husband had not been the ruler of China. Her power died with her husband. Nor would Chou En-lai's wife have been as much in evidence politically had her husband not been prominent. In the rest of the Communist world, there is no woman at the pinnacle of power. Perhaps the absence of women there does indeed reflect a female conviction that political prominence for women under communism demands male sponsorship. We who are outside the system are not in a position to say.

3. A final factor in Communist women's sense of political participation was suggested by the general thrust of the émigré's words. It is the possible relationship between a strict moral code and attitudes toward women's political role. A true Marxist-Leninist thinks in only one way in his personal life and in his public life. There are no shades of meaning, no nuances. The Soviet slogan is that "private life belongs to society." In China, behavior in one's personal life, such as late marriage or reduced family size, is an indication of public support of the Revolution. A straight and narrow private life promotes a straight and narrow commitment to the authority of the Party and state. A single personal code of conduct is matched by a single public code of obedience. In this connection, one émigré respondent commented that she had observed a relationship between the awakening of an anti-Soviet attitude and the broadening of an individual's tolerance or acceptance of other ways of life. Sexual experimentation was a part of dissident expression.

The strict moral ethic puts women in a subordinate role, making them victims of what one émigré termed "her biological situation." As we have seen, both men and women in Communist countries are indoctrinated in this ethic in school. Many of them have had it instilled in them from childhood by parents who were newcomers from the village. Hence, if women are perceived as unable to compete with men in politics except on the basis of their biology, the perception may make the fact. Political competition then becomes reduced to sexual competition. Where some might excuse a man for going into the Party to achieve his career aims (with the exception of the despised *apparatchik),* men and women would view a woman who did the same in terms of the strict ethical code and condemn her. The inherent double standard inevitably places women outside politics, where she is seen as woman competing with man, not as one human being competing with another.

The Communist regimes' continued emphasis on the traditional feminine role in sex and marriage may indeed have been a critical factor in silencing the development of political consciousness among women in Eastern Europe and the Soviet Union. We have already seen in the case of China that when the government wanted female participation, it attacked woman's traditional role.

The highly conservative attitudes of the émigré women I interviewed, women who admitted they were products of Communist socialization, reflect an official conservatism regarding woman's place in Communist society.

If Communist women are poorly motivated for political participation, their sense of political efficacy is even less developed. Only members of the Bulgarian National Women's Committee gave me the impression that they thought they had some input into political decisions. The secretary spoke at some length on the committee's right to initiate legislation and its right to call a delinquent enterprise into court if it had discriminated against women. While few women feel they have some weight in decisions, the majority probably would echo the words of one Romanian woman: "I am so tired of being told what to do all the time."

Mayor Starodub of the Leningrad city district indicated that women's delegations frequently come to her with a specific problem. It is her duty when the complaint comes to see that something is done about it. But she does not see herself as a woman representing women or helping them in any way other than as a man would do, or as she would do for men. None of the other women deputies I interviewed seemed to feel that their being women made much difference in the way they performed their duty in public office. (The behavior of women in public office in the United States has likewise been found to differ little from that of their male counterparts.)[14] The authoritarian nature of the Party means that women in it accept orders, as do men, and there is probably little thought on the part of either men or women joining the Party that they will make their own particular contribution. In chapter 5 I discussed the possibility of women making indirect inputs into the system and the resultant tangible rewards—the Soviet marriage law of 1968, increased housing throughout Eastern Europe and the USSR, more domestic appliances, and the expansion of child care facilities. But the women I interviewed gave little indication that they might themselves have been effective in producing these rewards. The Party changed attitudes and ended traditional prejudices. Women in the Party did not appear to see themselves as instruments toward this end.

The chapter's findings may be summed up in the following statements.

1. Women in Communist societies appear to have accepted work as part of their life style, as a job, not a career, and continue to find their female identity in the traditional role of homemaker.

2. Female attitudes toward the Communist system and its leadership, as far as what these have done for women is concerned, are positive. However, these attitudes are passive and accepting rather than active and initiatory.

3. The sense of political efficacy and motivation on the part of women in

the Communist countries is low, indicative of an apolitical female consciousness.

4. Politics are seen primarily as a man's world which women enter cautiously because of their "biological situation."

5. A Party career is viewed negatively, and the more idealistic women prefer to shun it.

6. The female self-concept remains firmly anchored in tradition.

9 / Perspectives on Equality

The picture of women in contemporary Communist societies may be summarized along three lines of thought.[1]

First, Marxism as an ideology of economic revolution has proved wanting as a conceptual vehicle for feminism. The track records of the Communist countries in employing women are just that: measures of female employment patterns in all walks of life. But liberation does not automatically follow upon high employment.

Second, a central issue in female liberation, which to date no country has resolved, is the nature and scope of the family in industrial society. What types of behavior and roles characterize the modern institution, and to what degree must traditional sex-role differentiation persist? Communist regimes have opted for a high degree of traditional role-playing in their conceptualization of the nuclear family. The emphasis on the woman as first mother and then worker has created tension between the demands made upon her at home and those made at work. The guaranteed right to work has meant that women must perform a minimum for four roles—wife, housekeeper, childrearer, and worker—and no Communist state has yet succeeded in creating an infrastructure of social services necessary to reduce this load.

Third, while communism has been successful in implementing the feminist demands of the nineteenth century for women's entrance into the productive work force and public life, it has failed to modify the nineteenth-century program to meet twentieth-century conditions and attitudes created by such factors as the threat of nuclear war, the pill, and the impact of technology on all aspects of daily life.

These three points may be summed up in a fourth and final proposition: The Soviet and Chinese variants of Marxism have demonstrated that feminism cannot rely on male ideologies for its rationale, motivation, or goals. Throughout history, women have served the patriarchal establishment, whether as supporters of the status quo or as revolutionaries seeking to replace one variant of male political order with another. Women are continuing this support in the Communist countries. High levels of female employment are necessary in countries where immigration and birth rates are low or where the early stages of industrialization demand large inputs of physical labor to offset a weak technology. Abortion and marriage policies that aim at breaking up traditional patterns of loyalty or that support official population goals equally serve the interests of the state. The fact of the matter is that in no Communist country do we find policies toward women—or men for that matter—directed at their self-actualization. The sole aim established for both sexes is service to the state. While the Chinese slogan, "serving the people," may have greater merit than serving private interest, the meaning of the term is one that continues to be defined by the Chinese ruling group. Likewise, the definitions of patriotism and *partiinost'* (Party-mindedness) are the prerogatives of the Soviet leadership.

With heavy-handed paternalism, the Communist regime tells each citizen that there is only one way to the future, one meaning of women's liberation, one goal: to work. Neither men nor women have many options in life style. But if men are limited in their choices in Communist societies by the constraints of educational opportunities, influence, and party loyalty, women are even more limited by the dual commandment to work and bear children. What is not allowed either sex is sufficient space to develop according to individual inclination. Women fall into a lower category because they bear the special responsibility of producing the next generation, and every Communist country puts this responsibility ahead of a woman's development as an individual.

Thus, while Communist systems have had great success in mobilizing women into the work force, educating them, and moving them into what the West has considered high-status professions, women as a group tend to be more apolitical and less visible in positions of political, economic, and social power in the Communist countries (with the possible exception of China) than in the West or the developing nations.

In assessing the relationship between the six variables of the model presented in chapter 1, primary importance in the intrasocietal environment, in my opinion, lies with the political structure. A monopolistic regime can go only so far in "liberating" any group, for then the requirements of monopolistic absolutism logically impede it from going further. In its pedagogic posture the Communist state does not enter into a dialogue with the pupil; it tells him what to do. The regime may preach, propagandize, and recruit as it deems necessary. Women remain politically apathetic. Without their own power base, they cannot gain the positions of political leverage that obtain through control of key positions in the economy, Party, or state apparatus. The American experience shows that even when women do have their own organizations, political leverage is difficult to achieve. But there is the possibility of achievement. Under Communist regimes, women cannot achieve anything unless authority permits it. As we have seen, at times authority encourages political involvement; at others it promotes domestic happiness.

If the political structure is crucial to the intrasocietal environment, the female self-concept is critical in women's relations with the leadership. This study suggests that tradition and economic position are major determinants of the self-concept and that there is little feedback from women into the environment or to the leadership. The picture is essentially circular. Women in Communist societies cannot attain high-status positions if the economic and social conditions for their advancement are not changed to permit the rearrangement of domestic priorities and if they fail to join the Party. Women cannot overcome the traditional male image of them when they themselves in part internalize this image and thus are poorly motivated to achieve in the political and economic worlds. And women cannot compete in the political arena if their economic position is inferior to that of men and if their own identity is largely formed by traditional attitudes. This study further indicates that women's self-concept must free itself from environmental influence if motivation is to be roused toward greater participation in the political and economic hierarchy. When women remain passive and acquiescent, the leadership can make policies as it chooses. Since the 1960s, the Western Communist regimes have been making policies that encourage passivity by stressing femininity in the traditional sense of the term.

To put such findings as these in perspective demands an objective approach to sexual equality, one that is independent of "capitalist" or "Communist" modes of development. What I would like to propose is a concept of the multistaged evolution of equality, as suggested in figure 11.

In traditional society, sex-role differentiation is marked, with men performing the prestigious status and power functions and women performing lesser functions, although these vary from society to society, as American anthropologist Margaret Mead has pointed out.[2] Industrializing societies of both the capitalist and Communist types have encouraged women to assume male roles while losing none of their "female" roles, by entering man's industrial world. But adoption of male roles in many ways is a step backward for sexual equality. In traditional society, woman plays a complementary role to man's, a role integrated into the productive world of work through her participation in raising crops or, in the case of the wealthy, her help in managing the family estate. Industrialization creates a dichotomy between home and work, with the home losing its economic importance and productive work being centered in the factory or enterprise. Women left in the home become increasingly alienated from the world of work. More importantly, their home skills are ill-adapted for use in the new industrial complex. When women move into the industrial world, they move where their skills can be utilized. With low literacy and low technical experience, they tend to find employment in those industrial sectors which require low-paid labor, such as

Traditional Society	Industrializing Society (Capitalist, Communist, or Socialist)	Industrialized Society (Capitalist, Communist, or Socialist)	Postindustrial Society
Women in inferior status			Women question their status
Women are possessions of dominant males	Women are mobilized by outside groups	Women are concerned with consumer satisfaction	Women have leisure time to consider personal fulfillment
Roles of men and women are complementary	Women attain men's roles while losing none of their traditional roles		Sex-role differentiation gradually disappears
	Revolutionary activity liberates women from traditional family structure Women's life styles are integrated into industrial paradigm	Industrial paradigm: Emphasis is on the nuclear family and material needs	Search is undertaken for new paradigm

FIGURE 11. Relationship of Industrialization to Equality between the Sexes

textiles or the social services. In time, these sectors become feminized: men move out to higher-paying and more prestigious jobs. An industrializing economy demands the formation of a skilled and specialized labor pool. Entering the labor force with the handicap of lower educational and technical skills, women naturally suffer in the competition for the higher-status jobs. "Women's place is in the home" becomes the slogan to inhibit women from competing in the marketplace of power and prestige. In the capitalist countries, women have retaliated by demanding that they have the right to perform all male industrial roles. Under communism, women have been accorded most male jobs, but their advance to positions of status and power has been markedly impeded by the drudgery of daily living and by official pronatalist and profamily policies.

During the industrialized phase, women encounter what may be considered a second setback to the achievement of equality: the revolution of rising expectations. The main objective becomes better living conditions, more of life's available amenities. Private consumption is the goal. Women during this stage not unnaturally concentrate their attention on the home and thus contribute to the increasing sex-role differentiation in the industrial world. Nevertheless, women make some advances toward equality during this phase, insofar as society accepts their presence to a greater or lesser degree in every walk of life.

The last stage is the postindustrial society. Here, the question is not how to better one's material standard of living, but how to improve the quality of one's life. Self-actualization becomes a key goal. The present woman's movement in the United States exemplifies this new stage. The demand is for androgyny: Women and men should be free to perform whatever role a particular situation requires, regardless of sex. Several factors deriving from the industrialized stage have created social conditions that support this demand.

1. The pill has separated sex from fertility, transferring to women the vital decision whether to bear children or not. The woman's pivotal role in this fundamental decision weakens the primacy of the male as traditional biological decision-maker and hence undermines his special claim to be chief political and social decision-maker.

2. The invention of the atomic bomb, as well as the experience of two world wars, has called into question the validity of the traditional male value of aggressiveness. The "female" role of peacemaker and expert in interpersonal relations becomes non-sex-differentiated.

3. The increasingly rapid pace of change, as Alvin Toffler indicates,[3] has made the female virtue of accommodation more valuable than male steadfastness or stubbornness.

4. The relative assurance of an adequate living standard has encouraged both men and women to consider the pursuit of nonmaterial objectives as a life style. Women thus have the time to think about where they are and where they are going.

The use of a concept such as "stages in the progress of female liberation" puts the experiences of the various Communist countries in perspective. The Chinese can be said to be in the first phase of industrialization; Soviet Central Asia is moving into the industrialized stage; and the rest of the Soviet Union and Eastern Europe are well into that stage. No Communist country has yet crossed over into the postindustrial society, the stage reached by the United States and Sweden.

It may be anticipated that as the Soviet Union and Eastern Europe move into the postindustrial phase, their populations, too, will be increasingly less preoccupied with satisfying material wants and more attuned to the quality of life. Thus, Communist women may be expected to become more conscious of the problems and prospects of self-realization.

The difficulty that I see impeding men and women in Communist societies in their aspirations for self-actualization in a setting where sex-role differentiation no longer pertains is the authoritarian, pedagogic nature of the Communist regimes. Initially, when women are moving out of the domestic environment of traditional society, the command nature of the Communist regimes can produce changes in their status with relative efficiency, because the kinds of change involved are susceptible to rule-making and administrative action: breaking up the traditional family and religious organizations; moving women into the labor force; providing equal educational opportunities. However, the further advance of women toward equal status brings into question the whole structure of the male political hierarchy and hence is something that can be won by women only through their own efforts.

A share in political leadership cannot be mandated, as history has shown us in the cases of religious and racial minorities. The Communist regimes, with their monolithic ideology, which permits only one view of the future and the place of men and women in it, together with their monolithic political organization, are ill equipped to enable women to arrive at the level of consciousness and group cohesiveness needed to make the requisite demands for equality.

As modernization progresses, change in status is more effectively realized by the group seeking such change. The fact that Communist politics provide no possibility of independent group activity for men and women is a decisive factor in the "leveling off" of women in middle-hierarchy jobs in the Soviet Union and Eastern Europe. That China has not yet reached this leveling-off point may be explained by her position at the beginning of the industrialization time span. In this regard, the present study confirms the proposition of a threshold of mandated change, outlined in chapter 1, before which authoritarian regimes greatly facilitate progress toward sexual equality, and after which they begin to impede the very objective they claim to have come to power to realize.

When equality is seen as an independent developmental process, the question of whether capitalism or socialism liberates women becomes irrelevant. Sexual equality is not a matter of competition between public or private ownership, or between two types of political systems, but is dependent primarily upon two variables: the stage of modernization and the degree of authoritarianism in a given society, as shown in figure 12. If the concept of a multistage evolution of equality has any validity, it holds out a challenge both to the woman's movement in the West and to the progress of women in the East.

1. Western women's movements should divest themselves of their Marxist economic revolutionary leanings and concentrate on giving priority to women's interests, regardless of the economic base of society. As long as women view their own interests as secondary, and revolution, universal suffrage, world peace, or democracy as primary, they may gain legal and economic recognition, but the achievement of equal status will continually be postponed.

2. There are limits to the ability of authoritarian states to command equality. "The revolution from above" goes only as far as the revolutionaries in control desire. The more open a society, the more likely it is to foster diverse interests. A paternalistic, pedagogic regime may have the best intentions, but equality implies a situation where the ruled can talk to the rulers without danger to life or threat to one's security. As Ludvík Vaculík stated in 1967, when the state is all-powerful, the ruled are passive. They are subjects, not citizens.[4] Modernized open societies appear to provide the most favorable climate for the status revolution. Women should therefore be skeptical of all acts that concentrate the power of government. Concentration of power implies paternalistic hierarchies, where women have always found themselves at the lower end of the status scale.

3. The Communist and American approaches to women's liberation may be seen as complementary. Neither by itself has revolutionized women's status. On balance, the changes wrought in the life style of women in the Communist countries cannot be denied. They have moved into virtually every area of society. The governments of these nations have taken an active part in mobilizing women into the modern world. The leaderships, particularly in Central Asia and China, where women were significantly oppressed by traditional society, are justified in taking pride in their achievements. But women in these countries still are inferior in status. In the United States, women have legally and politically received equal rights. But just as the political movement floundered for lack of economic base, so the economic emancipation of women is meaningless without political expression. Finally, the self-concept of women in both democratic and Communist societies continues to be tied to traditional myths. The majority of women in both cultures do not yet see benefit in changing identities to adapt to changing social realities.

Consciousness generally lags behind reality. Yet consciousness can change reality. The experience of the Communist countries suggests the limits of

Regime Type	Early Stage of Modernization	Late Stage of Modernization
Highly authoritarian	Progressive with respect to sexual equality; marked by high degree of mobilization	Regressive with respect to sexual equality
Pluralistic	Regressive with respect to sexual equality; marked by low degree of mobilization	Progressive with respect to sexual equality

FIGURE 12. Sexual Equality by System and Stage of Modernization

guided change. Where leaderships know the direction of modernization, they have examples before them of the pitfalls to be avoided, and they have a rich past as a standard for the future. But they can bring women only as far as their vision takes them. In Western society, women are not guided to change. They must change themselves. Once freed from the bonds of preindustrial and industrial traditionalism, they will be in a position to change their status and in the process liberate men as well.

Appendix 1

Men and Women in the Central Governments, Political Parties, and Mass Organizations of East Germany, Hungary, Poland, Romania, and Yugoslavia for Selected Years

EAST GERMANY, 1972

Government Officials	_Men_	_Women_
National Executive Organs		
Council of State		
Chairmen	3	0
Deputy Chairmen	18	0
Chiefs	14	2
Members	35	6
Ministries		
Ministers	27	1
State Secretaries	29	0
Deputy Ministers	27	4
Department Chiefs	38	7
Deputy & Administration Chiefs	88	1
Commissions, Committees, Councils, Secretariats, Offices		
Chairmen	33	0
State & Deputy Secretaries	19	0
First Deputy Chairmen	9	0
Deputy Chairmen	43	2
Department Chiefs	22	1
Judiciary		
Chief Justices	11	0
Justices	29	9
Chairmen & Deputy Chairmen	7	0
District Court Directors	12	2
District Prosecuting Attorneys	13	1
People's Chambers—_Volkskammer_ (Legislature)		
Members of the Presidium	8	1
Chairmen	24	1
Members	317	115
Representatives	67	20
District & Local Government Officials		
District Councils		
Chairmen	13	1

215

Government Officials (continued)	*Men*	*Women*
First Deputy Chairmen	14	0
Deputy Chairmen	0	0
Secretaries	13	1
Members	143	19
Chairmen of County Councils	184	8
Mayors of Principal Cities	17	4
Deputy Mayors	7	0
District Mayors	8	0

Party Officials

Socialist Unity Party		
Politburo Members	16	0
Secretariat Secretaries	8	0
Members of the Central Committee	114	20
Other Organs of the Central Committee		
Chiefs	36	4
Deputy Chiefs	43	2
Directors	6	0
Deputy Directors	16	0
Chairmen of District Commissions	40	18
Regional Party		
Secretariats of SED Districts		
Members	194	11
Departments of SED District Directorates	126	6
Stadtkreis (Municipal) First Secretaries	46	4
Landkreise (Rural) First Secretaries	163	6
Nongeographic Directorates		
First Secretaries	29	0
Christian Democratic Union of Germany		
Chairmen	1	0
Deputy Chairmen	3	0
Members of the Presidium	18	1
Secretaries	10	0
Department Chiefs	12	0
District Chairmen	15	0
National Democratic Party of Germany		
Chairmen	1	0
Secretaries	5	1
Department Chiefs	7	0
Members of the Executive Committee	17	2
District Chairmen	15	0
Liberal Democratic Party of Germany		
Chairmen	2	0
Deputy Chairmen	2	0
Secretaries	7	0
Department Chiefs	7	0
Members of the Political Committee	18	1
District Chairmen	15	0
Democratic Peasants' Party of Germany		
Chairmen	1	0
Deputy Chairmen	2	0
Members of the Presidium	15	3
Department Chiefs	9	0
District Chairmen	15	0

Mass Organizations	Men	Women
President	1	0
Vice-Presidents	5	1
Secretaries	27	7
First Secretaries	14	2
Department Chiefs	35	4
Members of the Presidium	59	16
Chairmen of the District Committees	29	0
Chairmen & Deputy Chairmen	32	12
Members of the National Executive Committee	129	108
Commission Members	15	13
Members of the Central Council & Bureau	139	59
Organizations Concerned with Foreign Relations		
Presidents	17	1
Vice-Presidents	55	5
Secretaries	15	2
Secretaries-General	14	1
Chairmen & Deputy Chairmen	13	0
Professional Associations		
Presidents	7	0
Vice-Presidents	17	0
Secretaries	18	1
Religious Groups		
Chairmen	5	0
Bishops	17	0
Sociocultural Organizations		
Presidents	2	0
Vice-Presidents	10	2
Secretaries	12	0
Sports Organizations		
Presidents	40	0
Vice-Presidents	10	0
Secretaries-General	36	3
Chairmen	21	0
Economic Organizations		
General Directors	133	3
Presidents	4	1
Vice-Presidents	13	0
Academies, Universities & Other Institutions		
Presidents	7	0
Vice-Presidents	18	0
Rectors	43	1
Information Media		
Newspapers & Periodicals: Chief Editors	58	2
Publishing Houses: Directors	19	0
Radio & TV: Directors	5	1
Representation Abroad & in International Organizations		
Ambassadors	28	0
Counselors	30	0
Commercial Counselors	17	0
Military Attaches	14	1
Trade Missions		
Chiefs	33	0
Deputy Chiefs	14	0
Organizations	3	1

Representation Abroad (continued)	*Men*	*Women*
Members	18	2
Vice-Presidents	3	1
Secretaries	4	0

HUNGARY, 1971

Central Government Officials		
	1	0
Presidential Council	2	0
President	20	1
Vice-Presidents		
Members	19	1
Council of Ministers	15	0
Ministers	50	0
First Deputy Ministers	185	15
Deputy Ministers	65	5
Department Chiefs		
Deputy Chiefs	17	0
Commissions & Related Committees		
Chairmen	18	2
Deputy Chairmen	32	1
Department Chiefs	9	1
National Assembly		
President	1	0
Vice President	1	1
Clerks	3	3
Deputies	273	79
Administrative, Legal & Judicial Committees		
Chairmen	11	0
Secretaries	8	2
Members	142	36
Supreme Court Judges	13	1
Supreme Court President	1	0
Supreme Court Vice-President	3	0

Party Officials: Hungarian Socialist Workers' Party		
Leadership		
First Secretary	1	0
Secretaries	6	0
Politburo Members	12	1
Central Committee Members	94	9
Other Committee Chairmen	7	0
Components under the Central Committee		
Department Chiefs	9	0
Deputy Chiefs	20	0
Members	23	2
Regional Administration		
Party Committee		
First Secretaries	19	1
Secretaries	56	2
Executive Committee	148	21
Megye (County) Government		
Chairmen	19	0
Deputy Chairmen	52	1
Secretaries	18	0

Party Officials (continued)	*Men*	*Women*
Municipal Party & Government Officials		
Party Committee		
First Secretaries	3	0
Secretaries	6	1
Executive Committee	17	4
Megye (Town) Government		
Chairmen	5	1
Deputy Chairmen	12	2
Secretaries	5	1
Mass Organizations		
President	28	3
Vice-Presidents	48	14
Secretaries General	21	4
Secretaries	60	12
Chiefs	24	5
Chairmen	17	0
Educational Institutions		
President	1	0
Vice-Presidents	2	0
Deputy Secretaries General	2	0
Members of the Presidium	14	0
Executive Committee		
Chairmen	8	0
Secretaries	7	0
Members	87	4
Academy of Sciences		
Secretaries	10	0
Deputy Secretaries	10	0
Universities		
Rectors	19	0
Prorectors	42	1
Deans	30	0
Professional and Cultural Organizations		
President	8	0
Vice-President & Deputy	26	1
Secretaries General	8	0
Secretaries	12	0
Chairmen	9	0
Religious Leaders (all types)	50	0
Information Media		
Radio and TV		
Directors	5	0
Editors	2	0
Chiefs	8	2
Foreign Correspondents	34	2
Newspapers & Periodicals		
Editors-in-Chief	31	2
Deputy Editors-in-Chief	5	0
Editors	39	4
Representation Abroad		
Ambassadors	76	0
Representation in the UN	31	3

Representation Abroad (continued)	*Men*	*Women*
Representation in International Organizations		
President	8	0
Vice-Presidents	6	3
Secretaries General	9	1
Directors & Directors-General	12	0
Chiefs	11	1
Foreign Trade Agencies: Directors	37	0

POLAND, 1970

Central Government Officials

Council of State		
Chairmen	1	0
Deputy Chairmen	4	0
Secretaries	1	0
Members	10	1
Council of Ministers		
Chairmen & Deputy Chairmen	24	0
Ministers	23	0
Secretaries & Secretaries-General	7	1
Directors & Deputy Directors	32	1
Chiefs	6	0
Other Government Agencies		
Officials	20	0
Ministries		
Vice-Ministers	86	0
Directors & Deputy Directors	212	5
Chairmen & Vice-Chairmen	17	0
Chiefs & Deputy Chiefs	93	0
Commanders & Deputy Commanders	69	0
Commandants & Deputy Commandants	33	0
Sejm (Legislature)		
Marshals & Vice Marshals	3	0
Secretaries	9	4
Deputies	395	65
Chairmen	23	4
Deputy Chairmen	53	11
Judicial Organs		
Supreme Court Presidents	5	1
Supreme Court Justices	5	0
Province Courts		
Presidents & Vice-Presidents	21	2
Prosecutors	19	0
District Arbitration Commissions		
Presidents	15	2

Regional Government Officials

National Councils		
Chairmen	17	0
Deputy Chairmen	53	0
Secretaries	17	0
Municipal Councils		
Chairmen	25	0

Regional Government Officials (continued)	*Men*	*Women*
Deputy Chairmen	40	1
Secretaries	12	1

Political Parties: Officials

Democratic Party (SD)		
Chairmen	29	0
Vice-Chairmen (or Deputy Chairmen)	28	0
Secretaries	19	3
Members of the Central Committee	101	6
Polish United Workers' Party (PZPR)		
Central Organs: Secretariat		
Secretaries & First Secretaries	9	0
Members	12	0
Commissions		
Chairmen	2	0
Deputy Chairmen	4	0
Members	55	4
Central Committee Members & Candidates	172	7
Central Committee Departments		
Directors	17	1
Deputy Directors	45	1
Province Committees		
First Secretaries	79	1
Secretaries	109	1
Executive Members	151	7
Control (or Supervision) Committee Members	284	47
Revision Committee Members	119	11
Chiefs & Deputy Chiefs	46	1
Directors & Deputy Directors	193	6
Chairmen & Deputy Chairmen	68	0
United Peasant Party (ZSL)		
Presidents & Vice-Presidents	4	0
Secretaries	21	1
Revision Commission Members	24	3
Main Party Court	22	4
Members & Candidates of Supreme Committee	121	18
Chairmen & Deputy Chairmen	55	0
Directors & Deputy Directors	10	0

Mass Organizations

Chairmen	203	28
Vice-Chairmen & Deputy Chairmen	146	19
Secretaries & Assistant Secretaries	65	11
Directors & Deputy Directors	23	4
Commanders & Deputy Commanders	25	3
Members of the Presidium	95	15
Economic Organizations & Information Media		
Directors	136	1
Directors General & Deputy Directors General	44	0
Editors-in-Chief	79	2
Deputy Editors-in-Chief	70	5
Secretaries	34	4
Scientific & Technical Organizations		
Presidents & Vice-Presidents	5	0

Mass Organizations (continued)	*Men*	*Women*
Members of the Presidium	36	0
Secretaries	18	0
Chairmen & Vice-Chairmen	20	1
Directors	56	1
Universities		
Rectors	34	0
Vice-Rectors	75	2
Deans	156	7
Religious, Cultural & Professional Organizations		
Ordinaries	23	0
Suffragans	30	0
Seniors & Deputy Seniors	11	0
Chairmen & Vice-Chairmen	130	10
Presidents & Vice-Presidents	83	3
Secretaries & Secretaries-General	78	16
Members	154	23

Representation Abroad		
Ambassadors	64	0
Chargés d'Affaires ad interim	13	0
Representatives	18	0
Chairmen & Deputy Chairmen	60	2
Presidents & Vice-Presidents	19	0
Secretaries & Secretaries-General	29	1
Committee Members	41	8

ROMANIA, 1973

Government Officials: National Government		
Council of Ministers	44	0
Heads of Ministry	23	0
Deputy Ministers	69	0
Council Chairmen	12	0
Committee Chairmen	4	0
Grand National Assembly		
Assembly Chairmen	12	0
Assembly Deputies	464	71

Party Officials: Romanian Communist Party		
Secretaries	7	0
Presidium	9	0
Executive Committee Members	23	2
Central Committee Members	318	33
Central Auditing Commission		
Members	45	1
Deputy Section Chiefs	35	1
Regional Party & Government Officials		
County Committee		
First Secretaries	39	0
Secretaries	43	2
People's Council, Executive Committee		
Chairmen	39	0
First Vice-Chairmen	36	0

Party Officials (continued)	*Men*	*Women*
Vice-Chairmen	140	5
Municipal Party & Government Officials		
Municipal Committee		
First Secretaries	13	3
Secretaries	46	2
People's Council, Executive Committee		
Chairmen	16	3
First Vice-Chairmen	11	0
Vice-Chairmen	30	3

Mass Organizations

Chairmen	44	5
Vice-Chairmen	43	15
Secretaries	27	7
Executive Bureau		
(or Committee) Members	87	20
Central Council		
(or Committee) Members	384	192
Cooperative Organizations		
Chairmen	3	0
Vice-Chairmen	14	2
Secretaries	2	0
Executive Committee Members	49	9
Educational Organizations		
Chairmen	29	0
Members of the Presidium	35	3
Full and Corresponding Members	286	9
Directors of Institutes	38	2
Universities		
Rectors	6	0
Prorectors	18	1
Deans of Faculties	39	2
Cultural, Professional & Social Organizations		
Chairmen	17	1
Vice-Chairmen	56	3
Secretaries-General	9	1
Secretaries	19	0
Religious Leaders	37	0
Economic, Financial & Commercial Organizations		
Chairmen	8	0
First Vice-Chairmen	4	0
Vice-Chairmen	16	0
Directors General	51	1
Deputy Directors	21	0
Information Media		
Chairmen	2	0
Vice-Chairmen	6	2
Directors General	2	0
Deputy Directors	6	0
Newspapers and Periodicals		
Editors-in-Chief	58	1
Assistant Editors-in-Chief	56	6
Secretaries-General	20	1
Directors	23	1
Ambassadors	89	0

Representation Abroad	*Men*	*Women*
Organizations in International Relations		
Chairmen	12	0
Vice-Chairmen	13	2
Secretaries	9	0
Representatives	12	3

YUGOSLAVIA, 1974

Federal Government

Office of the President of the Republic		
Presidents	1	0
Chiefs	4	0
Assistant Chiefs	3	0
Council of the Federation		
Presidents	1	0
Members	94	11
Council of National Defense		
Presidents	1	0
Secretaries	1	0
Members	27	0
Coordinating Commission for Constitutional Questions		
Chairmen	1	0
Deputy Chairmen	1	0
Members	10	0
State Presidency		
Presidents	1	0
Vice-Presidents	1	0
Secretaries-General	1	0
Assistant Secretaries-General	1	0
Members	20	0
Counselors & Chiefs	4	0
Council Chairmen & Presidents	15	0
Council Secretaries	4	0
Council Members	43	0
Federal Executive Council		
Presidents	1	0
Vice-Presidents	2	0
Members	22	2
Secretaries	1	0
Chiefs	2	0
Committee Presidents	7	2
Committee Members	20	0
Commission Chairmen	8	1
Commission Members	21	1
Commission Secretaries	2	0
Assistant, Deputy & Undersecretaries	5	0
Federal Economic Council		
Presidents	1	0
Secretaries	1	0
Federal Legal Council		
Presidents	1	0
Social Committee Service		
Presidents	2	0
Federal Administration		

Federal Government (continued)	*Men*	*Women*
Federal Secretaries	10	2
Deputy Secretaries	8	1
Assistant & Undersecretaries	60	3
Counselors	39	3
Inspectors	2	1
Directors, Commanders & Chiefs	45	2
Assistant Directors	11	0
Federal Organizations		
Directors	19	1
Deputy & Assistant Directors	10	3
Counselors	3	0
Federal Assembly		
Presidents	1	0
Vice-Presidents	6	0
Secretaries-General	1	0
Counselors	2	1
Chiefs	1	1
Service Secretaries	3	0
Commission Presidents	28	2
Commission Vice-Presidents	7	0
Commission Secretaries	4	2
Chamber Presidents	4	1
Chamber Vice-Presidents	5	0
Chamber Secretaries	3	2
Chamber Members	567	76
Chamber Counselors	0	2
Committee Presidents	29	6
Committee Secretaries	1	1
Federal Judiciary		
Court Presidents	3	0
Court Secretaries	1	0
Court Judges	41	2
Public Prosecutors & Defenders	2	0
Assistant Prosecutors & Defenders	5	0

Republican & Provincial Administration		
Executive Council		
Presidents	8	0
Vice-Presidents	13	2
Secretaries	20	0
Members	110	8
Council Presidents	4	0
Commission Presidents	22	2
Chiefs & Directors	9	0
Commission Secretaries	1	0
Committee Presidents	13	0
Committee Secretaries	4	0
Republican & Provincial Administration Secretaries	85	4
Assistant, Deputy & Undersecretaries	77	2
Directors, Commanders & Chiefs	44	2
Council Presidents	6	0
Council Vice-Presidents	6	0
Assistant Directors	4	0
Commission Presidents	11	0
Commission Secretaries	1	0

Republican & Provincial Administration (continued)	_Men_	_Women_
Assembly and Provincial Assembly		
Presidents	9	0
Vice-Presidents	16	0
Secretaries	19	0
Chamber Presidents	41	3
Chamber Vice-Presidents	21	7
Chamber Secretaries	25	2
Commission Presidents	40	0
Commission Vice-Presidents	1	0
Committee Presidents	37	1
Members	8	0
Judiciary		
Judges	85	12
Public Prosecutors & Defenders	16	0
Court Presidents	24	0
Court Secretaries	3	0
Assistant & Deputy Prosecutors	2	0
City Government		
Presidents	50	5

Political Parties		
President	1	0
Secretary	1	0
Executive of the Presidium	25	4
Department Heads & Center Directors	10	0
Assistant Department Heads & Directors	2	0
Commission Chairmen	10	1
Commission Secretary	1	0
Commission Members	20	1
Committee Members	10	2
Conference Permanent Section Members	59	11
Republican Leagues		
Central Committee Presidents	7	1
Executive Committee Secretaries	9	1
Executive Committee of Central Committee	59	12
Central Committee Members	340	46
Commission Presidents	90	11
Commission Secretaries	1	1
Commission Members	77	12
Committee Presidents	11	4
Committee Members	47	18
City Conference Permanent		
Members	702	63
City Conference Presidents	21	0
City Conference Secretaries	21	2

Mass Organizations		
Confederation of Trade Unions		
President	1	0
Vice-President	1	0
Secretaries	6	0
Presidium Members	38	2
Committee Presidents	0	1

Mass Organizations (continued)	Men	Women
Commission Presidents	7	0
Trade Union Council Presidents	9	0
Trade Union Council Secretaries	12	0
Federation of Reserve Officers & Veterans Associations		
Republican Committee Presidents	7	0
Republican Committee Vice-Presidents	7	0
Federal Committee Presidents	11	0
Secretaries-General	0	0
Secretaries	3	0
Secretariat Members	10	2
Presidium Members	22	2
Commission Presidents	2	0
Reserve Officers & Veterans Association Presidents	9	1
Reserve Officers & Veterans Association Secretaries	8	0
Federal Conference of S.A.W.P.		
Presidents	1	0
Vice-Presidents	4	1
Secretaries-General	1	0
Secretariat Members	8	0
Committee President	6	0
Presidium Members	34	2
Section Presidents	5	0
Commission Presidents	5	1
Commission Secretaries	1	0
S.A.W.P. Presidents	15	1
S.A.W.P. Secretaries	7	1
Conference of Social Activity for Women		
Presidents	1	0
Vice-Presidents	0	2
Secretaries	0	1
Secretariat Members	1	4
Conference Presidents	3	8
Student Association Presidents	6	0
Student Association Secretaries	3	0
Youth & Student Federation		
Presidents	21	0
Secretaries	2	1
Commission Presidents	2	0
Commission Secretaries	1	0
Youth & Student Association Presidents	6	1
Commercial Organizations		
Presidents	1	0
Deputy & Vice-Presidents	8	0
Secretaries-General	1	0
Economic Chamber Presidents	8	0
Economic Chamber Secretaries	8	0
Council Presidents	1	0
Office Heads	5	0
Directors	5	0
Directors General	6	1
Assistant Directors	12	0

Scientific Organizations	Men	Women
Presidents	5	1
Vice-Presidents	4	1
Secretaries	4	1

International Organizations		
Ambassadors	96	7
Diplomatic Missions to Other Organizations	3	1
Assistant & First Ambassadors	1	3
Commission Presidents	5	1
Red Cross Presidents	1	0
Red Cross Vice-Presidents	1	0
Red Cross Secretaries	0	1
Interparliamentary Union Presidents	1	0
Interparliamentary Union Vice-Presidents	3	0
Interparliamentary Union Executive Secretaries	1	0
Interparliamentary Union Secretaries	1	0

Mass Information Media		
Editors-in-Chief	22	3
Assistant Editors-in-Chief	4	1
Directors	23	0

Universities		
Presidents	0	1
Vice-Presidents	1	0
Secretaries	1	0
Rectors	8	0
Prorectors	5	4

Professional Organizations		
Presidents	18	2
Secretaries-General	2	2
Secretaries	3	0

Institutes		
Directors	18	2

Sources: United States, Department of State, Reference Aid: Directory of Albanian Officials, R 74-22 (Washington, D.C.: Government Printing Office, June 1974); idem, Reference Aid: Directory of Czechoslovak Officials, A 67-30 (Washington, D.C.: Government Printing Office, November 1967); idem, Reference Aid: Directory of East German Officials, A 72-40 (Washington, D.C.: Government Printing Office, December 1972); idem, Reference Aid: Directory of Hungarian Officials, RA 71-18 (Washington, D.C.: Government Printing Office, June 1971); idem, Reference Aid: Directory of Polish Officials, A 70-3 (Washington, D.C.: Government Printing Office, February 1970); idem, Reference Aid: Directory of Romanian Officials, A 73-24 (Washington, D.C.: Government Printing Office, August 1973); idem, Reference Aid: Directory of Yugoslav Officials, A 74-30 (Washington, D.C.: Government Printing Office, October 1974).

Appendix 2

Leading Women in the Political and Cultural Life of
the People's Republic of China, 1949–1970

Abbreviations:

ACDWF = All-China Democratic Women's Federation
ACFDY = All-China Federation of Democratic Youth
ACFIC = All-China Federation of Industry and Commerce
ACFTU = All-China Federation of Trade Unions
ACWF = All-China Women's Federation
Cadre = Communist Party Member
CC = Central Committee
CCP = Communist Party of China
CCPCC = Communist Party of China Central Committee
CDNCA = China Democratic National Construction Association (before 1949)
CPG = Central People's Government
CPPCC = Chinese People's Political Consultative Conference
CYL = Communist Youth League
ECMAC = East China Military and Administrative Committee (Civil War Period)
KMT = Kuomintang
MFW = Municipal Federation of Women
MPC = Municipal Party Committee
MPG = Municipal People's Government
NDYL = National Democratic Youth League (Civil War Period)
NPC = National People's Congress
P = purged
PLA = People's Liberation Army
PPC = Provincial Party Committee
PPG = Provincial People's Government
YWCA = Young Women's Christian Association

Name	Year of Birth	Cadre	PLA	Education	Husband
Chang Chia-yün					
Chang Chieh-ch'ing					P'eng Chen: veteran revolutionary
Chang Ch'ien					Ch'en Yi
Chang Ch'in'ch'iu			Long March	Sun Yat-sen Univ., Moscow	Su Ching-kuan: PLA; reorganized health system
Chang Hsaio-mai	1901				Hsu Ping: economist; Party functionary
Chang Hsi-t'ing					
Chang Yun				Futan Univ., Shanghai	
Chiang Ch'ing	1914	1933	political instructor, Civil War; advisor to PLA on cultural work, 1964	Experimental Drama Acad., Shantung	Mao Tse-tung

Career	CC	NPC	P	Government Position
ommune member, Shou ien, Anwei Prov.				vice-chairman, Anwei Prov. Rev. Comm., 1968
king MFW		1964	1964	
CDWF		1964		vice-minister, Textile Industry, 1949
		1964		
cretary, Ipin MPC, zechuan				vice-chairman, Szechuan Prov. Rev. Comm., 1967
CDWF; Peking MPC	1969	1954, 1958		vice-chairman, Comm. for Implementation of the Marriage Law; chairman, Peking Women's Federation, 1957
CDWF, Shanghai; rved on various ommittees & elegations	1956–1958	1954, 1958, 1964		Shanghai MPC, 1949; Peking MPG, 1953
ctress, "model plays," 966	Chief, CC Central Office, 1949–1950; member, 1969, 1975	1964, 1969	1976	director, Cinema Dept., Dept. of Propaganda; leader in Cultural Revolution

Name	Year of Birth	Cadre	PLA	Education	Husband
Ch'ien Cheng-ying	1922		X	Eng. Dept., Tatung Univ., Shanghai	Ch'en Ta-hsieh
Chuang T'ao					
Fan Chin					Huang Ching: physicist; scientist
Ho Hsiang-ning	1878	X		Tokyo Girls Art School	Liao Chung (d. 1925): architect; KMT-CCP alliance
Ho Tse-hui				Doc. of Sci., Berlin; Curie Inst., Paris	Ch'ien San-ch'iang
Hsia Chih-hsu	1907	X		Labor Univ., Moscow, 1929	Chao Shih-yen: CCP leader; executed in 1927
Hsieh Hsueh-hung	1900	1947		Dept. of Soc. Sci., Shanghai Univ., Moscow Oriental Univ.	
Hsieh Ping-hsin	1902	X		Yenching Univ., Peking; Wellesley College, USA	Wu Wen-tsao: educator; professor, Central Nat. Inst.
Hsu Kuang-p'ing	1907 (d. 1968)	X		Peking Girls Normal College, 1925	Lu Hsun: writer

Career	CC	NPC	P	Government Position
)WF; engineer		1962	1965	engineering jobs in government; minister of Water Conservancy and Power, 1975
ia-Japan Friendship)c.; China Afro-Asian ety		1954		Responsible Person for CCP central organ., 1963
nalist; ACDWF; director, *ng Daily News*, 1962–1966		1954	1966	director, Propaganda Dept., Peking, member, Peking MPC
T post; ACDWF; member, rd of Directors, Bank hina, 1950				
)WF; physicist (discovered techniques in splitting ium atoms)		1957		
ius posts in PPC in 1930s in CCPCC from 1937		1954 (1st NPC), 1964 (3rd NPC)		director, Admin. Office, Ministry of Light Industry, 1954; vice-minister, 1960
h organ.; Red Cross; i-Soviet Friendship)c.; 13 years in Taiwan in (released in 1939)	1969	1954	1957	
er-journalist; ACDWF; in & Writers Assoc. gations		1975		official delegate to International Writers Conference
er; president, Shanghai nen's Assoc.; editor, *ocratic Weekly*, 1945;)WF				chief, Women's Section, 2nd CPPCC, 1954; participant in official delegation on women

Name	Year of Birth	Cadre	PLA	Education	Husband
Hsu Ming					K'ung Yuan: economis
Hua Yin-feng	1932	1950s			Chang Nai-ch'i
Hu Tzu-ying					
K'ang K'e-c'hing	1912	1920s	prewar Red Army College		Chu Te
Kung P'eng	1920	1940s	8th Route Army		Ch'iao Kuan-hua: vice-minister of Foreign Affairs
Kung P'u-sheng	1917	X		Yenching Univ.; Columbia Univ., USA	Chang Han-fu: ambassador; Foreign Affairs Ministry
Kuo Chien	1913	member, CYL			
Kuo Ming-ch'iu	1917				Lin Feng: journalist
Li Chen	1910	1926	Long March		Kan Szu-ch'i: army

Career	CC	NPC	P	Government Position
CDWF Executive Comm.		1964	1967 (suicide)	secretary-general, Fushun MPC
armer, pig breeder; lected agricultural abor model; deputy head, ungyang State Farm				vice-chairman, Chekiang Prov. Rev. Cmm., 1968
CDWF, 1949–; CDNCA; hanghai municipal and Party rganizations		1954 1958 1964		delegate to 1st–3rd CPPCCs
rmy until 1949; ACDWF & ceremonial jobs fterward		1954, 1958, 1964; Standing Comm., 3rd NPC, 1965		
ewspaper reporter & ditor; intelligence				director, Dept. of Intelligence, Min Inst. of Foreign Affairs, 1949–1955
uman Rights Council, UN; ed Cross; ACDWF				International Section, Ministry of Foreign Affairs; director, International Section, 1965–
CDWF; chairman in Shanghai olitics, then Chinese epresentative to women's nternational congresses				
CDWF; director, Policy esearch School, 1965		1954		Northeast People's Comm., 1950
hild bride at age of 6; rmy (promoted to major-eneral in 1955)	1949, for army			deputy, chief procurator, PLA military procurations

Name	Year of Birth	Cadre	PLA	Education	Husband
Lin Ch'iao-chih					
Li Po-chao	1911	CYL, 1920s	Long March	Chungking #2 Girls Normal School; Sun Yat-sen Univ., 1927–1930	Yang Shang-k'un: magistrate & veteran
Li Te-ch'uan (originally Christian)	1897	CYL, 1958			Feng Yu-hsiang: "the Christian general d. 1948
Liu Wang Li-ming					Lui Chan-en: former president, Shanghai Univ.; killed by Japan
Liu Ya-hsiung	1921			Peking Girls Normal School	
Lo Ch'iung					
Lo Shu-chang	1907			elementary	
Ou Meng-chueh	1903	1923–1924		Kwangtung Univ.	T'an T'ien-tu: vice-chairman, CPPCC; Kwangtung PPC, 1965

Career	CC	NCP	P	Government Position
ynecologist; active in MA; head, Obstetrics & ynecology, Hsieh Ho ledical College, Peking		1954, 1958, 1964 1975		
ournalism; theater; CDWF; member, Acting IPC; vice-president, nd CCPCC		1954, 1958, 1964	1967	
WCA, Peking; chairman, Vomen's Christian emperance Union; ACDWF; arious ceremonial ctivities		1954, 1958, 1964, 1975	1964	KMT delegate to 1st CPPCC, 1949; delegate to 4th CPPCC, 1964
JSA; Chinese Women's emperance Union; ACDWF				Local Work Comm., 2nd CPPCC, 1957
secretary, Changchun CCP Municipal Comm.; urban work; physical education; ACWF; 1949	1960; Control Comm., 1962	1954, 1958, 1964	1967	1st CPPCC, 1949
director of propaganda, ACWF; Secretariat, ACWF		1954, 1958, 1965	1967	1st CPPCC, 1949
school teacher; prewar women's movements; after war opened pharmacy in Shanghai; ACDWF; CDNCA; ACFIC		1954, 1958, 1975		1st CPPCC, 1949; vice-minister, Food Industry, 1957–1958; vice-minister, Light Industry, 1958–1965; 1st minister of Light Industry, 1965
as student worked for PPC, 1926; ACDWF, 1949; PPC, 1955–1967; Kwangtung PPC, 1966–1967	1956–1958	1954, 1964	1967	delegate to 1st CPPCC, 1949; People's Control Comm., Kwangtung PPG

Name	Year of Birth	Cadre	PLA	Education	Husband
Ou T'ang-liang					
Shen Tzu-chiu	1930			Normal School, Japan	Hu Yu-chih: journalist specializing in languag education & culture
Shih Liang	1908			Wuchin Girls Normal School; Shanghai Pol. Sci. & Law College	
Shuai Meng-ch'i	1907	1920s		Soviet Union	
Sung Ch'ing-ling	1890			Wesleyan College for Women, Macon, Georgia	Sun Yat-sen
Teng Chieh		1923			
Teng Ying-ch'ao	1903	1925	Long March	Tientsin #1 Girls Normal School	Chou En-lai

Career	CC	NPC	P	Government Position
)YL; ACFDY; ACDWF; World d. of Democratic Youth; Party activist has held rious jobs at world ngresses, served on such ernational committees as ? World Peace Council		1954, 1964; Standing Comm., 1965		member, 1st & 2nd CPPCCs; NDYL, 1949–1963; vice-chairman, Chinese People's Comm. for World Peace, 1965
iter; art teacher; editor of ɔmen's Life; active in ɔmen's movement; director, ?pt. for Propaganda & Education; a chairman in CDL; ?WF	vice-head, Women's Section, 1960–1965	1954, 1958, 1965		CPPCC delegate, 1949, 1954; Chekiang PPG, 1951
ʌyer-instructor; helped ganize Nat. Salvation ssoc., Shanghai, 1937–?45; worked in community ɔmen's movement; CDL ember of Politburo; pported marriage law; CDWF	1949, Prep. Comm. for drafting constitution	1954, 1958, 1964		CPPCC delegate, 1949, 1954, 1964; Ministry of Justice, 1954–1959
tive in labor movement, ʌanghai, after 1949; CDWF activist; del. to ɔmen's congresses	president, 8th CCP Nat. Cong.; Control Comm., 1956–1969	1954, 1958, 1964		
ter 1949 served in many ɔnorary posts		1954, 1958, 1965, 1975		del. to 1st & 2nd CPPCCs; vice-chairman, Central People's Gov., 1949–1954
ʳorked her way up as ʌdre in Northeast ?gion in industry & roduction posts			1967	del. to all CPPCCs; vice-chairman, Ministry of Light Industry, 1958–1963; acting minister, 1959; vice-minister, Petroleum Industry, 1963–1965
ʲomen's movement (unbinding ?eet), France, 1920; ACDWF; ?r. Edgar P. Snow's maid ?rvant; vice-chairman, ?omm. to Implement ɅΛarriage Law	1945, 1956–1958, 1969, 1975	1954, 1958, 1965, 1975		delegate to 1st CPPCC, 1949

Name	Year of Birth	Cadre	PLA	Education	Husband
Teng Yu-chih				Nanking Univ.	
T'ien Wei					Wang Ku'ang
Ting Ling	1904	1931	8th Route Army	Chounan Middle School & Normal School for Girls, 1923	(1) Hu Yeh-p'i writer; (2) Ch' Ming, reporter writer
Ts'ai Ch'ang	1900	1919	Long March	Chounan Girls School	Li Fu-ch'un: industrial planner, Politburo
Ts'ai Shu-mei					
Ts'ao Meng-chun				Changsha Girls Normal School	(1) Tso Kung, curator, Peking Library; (2) Wang K'un-lun propagandist & literary critic
Ts'ao Yi-ou					

Career	CC	NPC	P	Government Position
ACDWF; activist in women's movement; Red Cross (nationalities admin.); Sikang Autonomous PPC, 1950; Szechuan PPC, 1959	president, 9th CCP Nat. Cong., 1969; member CC, 1969	1954, 1958, 1964		delegate to 1st CPPCC, 1949; vice-governor, Sikang Prov., 1954–1955; vice-governor, Szechuan Prov., 1955–1968; member of Tibetan government; vice-chairman, Szechuan Prov. Rev. Comm., 1968
journalist; director, Broadcasting Bureau; Kwangtung PPC, 1964–1966		1966		head, Kwangtung Cult. Rev. Group; director, Kwangtung People's Radio Station, 1966
writer-publisher-journalist; taught Chinese literature at Red Army College, 1936–1937; ACDWF; editor, *Lit. Gazette;* vice chairman, Union of Chinese Writers, 1953–1957; declared in rightist clique and expelled from all posts in 1957		1957		
physical education instructor, 1919; Women's Work-Study Society, France; organized CCP in France; active in women's work for CCP, 1920; CCP underground; ACFTU, 1958; ACDWF Presidium; women's work among workers	1924, 1945, 1956–1958, 1969, 1975; president, 9th CCP Nat. Cong., 1969	1954, 1958, 1965, 1975; vice-chairman, 10th NPC		member, Kiangsi PPC; CPG, 1954
worker, representative of Tientsin #4 Printing & Dyeing Plant	1969, 1975	1975		
ran nursery school before 1949; editor, *Modern Woman;* ACDWF; worked on marriage law (honorary delegation member)		1954, 1958, 1964		delegate to CPPCC, 1949, 1954
worker in Higher Party School	1969, 1975	1958, 1964, 1975		

Name	Year of Birth	Cadre	PLA	Education	Husband
Tseng Chih	1931	1933			T'ao Chu: PLA; member of Politburo; purged in 1967
Tseng Hsien-chih				Waseda Univ., Japan	Yeh Chien-ying: did cadre work; PLA; government admin.; CC Presidium, 1959
Tung Pien					
Wang Hsueh-ying					
Wang Kuang-cheng (sister of Wang Kuang-mei)					
Wang Kuang-mei		1948		Yenching Univ., postgrad. in physics	Liu Shao-ch'i (Wang Kuang-mei was his 5th wife)
Wang Yu-chen					
Wen Hsiang-lan		1954			
Wu Hsueh-ch'ien					

Career	CC	NPC	P	Government Position
en's work in Canton; nistrative secretary, on PPC; secretary, ngtung PPC		1964, 1975	1968	member, Canton MPC, 1956
WF; 4th CPPCC Presidium, ; ACFIC; ACDWF; ACWF		1954 1964		delegate to 3rd CPPCC, 1959
tor and chief editor, *Women of China*, 1952–1966; secretary WF; branded "black gangster,"		1958, 1964	1966	
				ACDWF delegate to 2nd, 3rd, & 4th CPPCCs; on 4th CPPCC Standing Comm.
ty head, Admin. Office, ghai #1 Medical College			1967	
mpanied husband on his travels	Foreign Affairs Section, CCPCC, 1946; General Office, CCPCC, 1948	1964	1967	
retariat, CCP; Hupeh PPC, 5; ACFDY		1964		
r peasant; director, icultural Production op, 1952	alt., 1969, 1975			Honan Prov. Rev. Comm., 1969
YL; youth activist & aratchik; ACDWF & orary delegtions; Chinese ple's Inst. of Foreign airs, 1964		1964		4th CPPCC Standing Council

Name	Year of Birth	Cadre	PLA	Education	Husband
Wu Kuei-hsien		X			
Wu Yi-fang	1892			Michigan State Univ., USA	
Yang Chih-hua	1898	1924			Ch'u Ch'iu-pai: general secretary of CCPCC, 1935
Yang Ch'un					Li Ch'ang: veteran cadre; CC Section for Cultural Relations with Foreign Countries
Yang Fu-chen		1949			
Yang Yün-yü	1914				

Career	CC	NPC	P	Government Position
Rev. Comm., #1 Northwest State Cotton Mill; activist in study of Mao's works	1969; 1975, alt. member of Politburo			member, Shensi Prov. Rev. Comm., 1968; vice-premier, State Council, 1975
teacher; professor; president, Chinling Girls College, 1928; del. to UN conference, San Francisco, 1945; director, Education Dept., Kiangsu PPC; vice-chairman & chairman, Assoc. for Promoting Christianity, 1961; ACWF		1954, 1958, 1964	1962, 1964	delegate to 1st CPPCC; member, Kaingsu PPC, 1955
CYL, 1922; May 30 movement, Shanghai; Moscow, 1928 & 1935; Yenan, 1941; women's work in trade unions; vice-chairman, ACDWF, 1957; women's work in ACFTU; member delegations abroad		1954, 1958, 1964; Standing Comm., 1965		delegate to 1st & 2nd CPPCCs
member, Land Reform Comm.; ECMAC, 1950–1954; ACDWF; deputy director, Textile Admin.; CCP Medical College, Peking, 1961; vice-president, Chinese People's Assoc. for Cultural Relations & Friendship with Foreign Countries		1954, 1958		South Kiangsu People's Admin. Office, 1950–1952
poor peasant; weaver; Responsible Person, Rev. Comm., Shanghai State-run #1 Cotton Textile Mill, 1967; served on ACFDY & government committees	1969, 1975	1959, 1964		leading member, Puto Ward Rev. Comm., 1967; member, Shanghai Mun. Rev. Comm., 1968
ACDWF; judge, Peking People's Court, 1952; in women's delegations & honorary delegations		1964; Standing Comm., 1965		

Name	Year of Birth	Cadre	PLA	Education	Husband
Yeh Ch'un					Lin Piao
Yu Ai-Feng				M.D.	
Yu Chih-ying					

Sources: Donald W. Klein and Anne B. Clarke, *Biographic Dictionary of Chinese Communism, 1921–1965,* vol. 2 (Cambridge, Mass.: Harvard University Press, 1971); *Peking Review,* 24 January 1976, pp. 9–11.

Career	CC	NPC	P	Government Position
journalist; correspondent for *Lit. Gazette,* 1957; activist in Cultural Revolution; leading member, Cult. Rev. Group, Military Comm., CCPCC, 1967; member, Admin. Unit, Military Comm., CCPCC, 1968; member, Presidium, CCP 9th Nat. Cong.	1945, 1956– 1958, 1969		1971	
professor & director, Research Group in Obstetrics & Gynecology, Tientsin Medical Inst., 1965; head, Tientsin #2 Roving Medical Team, 1965; ACWF		1959, 1964; Standing Comm., 1965; 1975		
del. to Conference of All-China Fed. of Labor, 1949; ACFTU activist		1958, 1964		

Appendix 3

Women in the United States Congress, 1920–1970

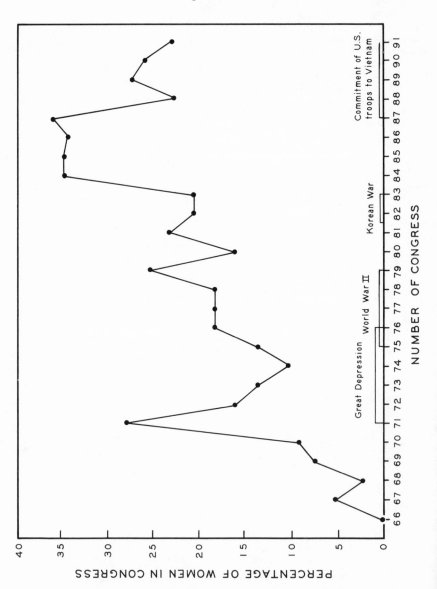

Appendix 4

Women in Cuba

The status of Cuban women differs little from that of women in the other Communist countries. Like its counterparts, the Cuban Revolution was committed to the emancipation of women, but the data presented in tables A.4.1–A.4.5 indicate that Cuban women still have a long way to go.

In terms of economic status, Cuban women in 1974 constituted only 24 percent of the labor force, or of those engaged in salaried work. As in the other Communist countries, jobs have been feminized by sector and branch. Women constitute more than 50 percent of the labor force in education, health, and the textile and plastics industries. The number of women reported working in agriculture is low because much of the work is not salaried. But as elsewhere in the Communist countries, women constitute a sizable proportion of the agricultural labor force.

Table A.4.1.   Occupations of Cuban Women, 1953 and 1973

	% of Women Employed	
Occupation	*1953*	*1973*
Education	15.0	30.0
Health	2.0	17.5
White collar/commerce/retail	20.0	15.0
Agriculture	5.0	12.0
Light industry (including textiles)	12.1	7.0
Tobacco	6.0	5.4
Domestic servants	30.0	0.0
Services and food-processing	5.4	7.5
Professions	1.5	3.6
Manual labor	3.0	0.0
Sugar-processing	0.0	2.0
Overall	100.0	100.0

Sources: Figures derived from graphs made from Population Census of 1953, tables 50 and 54; *JUCEPLAN Statistical Bulletin,* 1971; and conversations in January 1974 with Digna Ceres, secretary-general of the *Frente Feminina,* as cited in Carolee Benglesdorf and Alice Hageman, "Emerging from Underdevelopment: Women and Work," *Cuba Review* 4, no. 2 (September 1974), p. 7.

249

Table A.4.2. Percentage of Women in Total
Cuban Work Force by Occupation,
1953 and 1973

Occupation	1953	1973
Education	80.0	55.0
Health	10.0	60.0
Retail trades	8.0	32.0
Agriculture	2.0	5.0
Light industry	9.0	40.0
Tobacco industry	35.0	44.0
Textiles	45.0	75.0
Hotels and Restaurants	30.0	38.0
Communications	15.0	38.0
Plastics	0.0	75.0
Total work force	13.7	24.0

Sources: Same as for table A.4.1.

Table A.4.3. Cuban Women Working for Wages, 1953 and 1973

	1953	1973
Total number	256,000	520,000
Percentage of total female population	13.7	24.0

Sources: Same as for table A.4.1.

Cuba's marriage, divorce, and fertility rates are among the highest of any Communist country, but its high birth rate is accompanied by a relatively high infant mortality rate: 27.5 per thousand, as compared with 16.0 in the GDR, 43.3 in Yugoslavia, and 86.8 in Albania. The divorce rate is equal to or higher than that in the Soviet Union. There are no statistics on abortion, and the annual rate of increase is officially given as equal to that of China, 1.7 percent in 1970–1973.[1]

The ideological commitment of the Cuban regime to an improvement in women's status may best be compared to that of the Chinese leadership. In 1969, a widespread campaign began to bring women into the salaried labor force, in consonance with a resolution of the First Congress of the Communist Party of Cuba (CPC) to the effect that "the struggle to enable women to enjoy full equality is the task of the whole society. It is an economic and cultural task; it requires the efforts of the Party and state, of the administration and schools, of the Young Communist League, and of all social and mass organizations, especially the Federation of Cuban Women (FMC) and the Central Organization of Cuban Trade Unions (CTC)."[2] The Cuban family code incorporates provisions establishing equality between man and wife, both economically, in terms of joint ownership of property acquired during the marriage, and psychologically, in its stipulations that "both partners must care for the family they have created" and that both husband and children "must participate . . . in the running of the home, and cooperate so that it will develop in the best possible way."[3]

Cuban sources suggest four phases in the ideological position of the regime toward the problem of women. The first, lasting from 1959–1963, centered on "overcoming the effects of the double exploitation of women under neo-colonialism." The focus appears to have been primarily on education and the raising of political consciousness. The second phase, 1964–1970, was directed at mobilizing women into the work force either through a basic education program or through training in new skills. As part of the campaign to bring women outside the home, women were recruited on a massive scale as volunteers in the sugar harvests of 1969 and 1970.

The third phase was inaugurated in 1970 with the enactment of a vagrancy law, Article 1 of which stipulated that all citizens who are physically and mentally fit have the social duty to work. But this phase also saw the recognition of the "double shift" for women and the introduction of measures to ease their domestic burdens.

The fourth phase, which began in 1974, was marked by the passage of a maternity law in 1974 and a family code in 1975, and was directed at solving the problems of women as both workers and mothers in Cuban society.[4] During this period particular attention was devoted to developing the day care and communal services networks.

Thus, since the Communist takeover, the Cuban ideological approach to the emancipation of women has run the gamut from revolutionary persuasion, through semi- and then full coercion in the vagrancy law, to an accent on pragmatism in recent years.

Politically, the position of Cuban women is comparable to that of women in the other Communist countries. In 1974, women represented 15 percent of the Communist Party membership, or the mean percentage of female representation in the other ruling parties, but only 6 percent of the Communist Party leadership.[5] The percentage of women in the National Assembly after the 1976 elections was 22.2 percent, or again the mean percentage of female participation in the national legislatures of all Communist countries. The percentage of women participating in the 1975 Central Committee was just under the mean percentage of female membership for the other Communist states, 8.8 percent. Cuban women seem to have fared less well in representation at the local government level. In the 1976 elections, women represented 13.4 percent of the candidates and only 8 percent of the elected delegates (856 of 10,725). By contrast, the percentage of women participating in the local soviets in the Soviet Union is around 45. Apparently, the Cuban regime has been able to bring women into the higher echelons of the Communist government and Party administration, but has been unable to influence attitudes at the local level to any significant degree. It must be remembered that since the recent electoral reforms, local elections have provided a certain amount of choice. The exception, as might be expected, is in the executive arm of the national government, where only 2 of the 45 members of the Council of Ministers are women, and no woman is an officer. The two women are heads of ministries that correspond to the woman's place in government mentioned in chapter 5.[6] In the Council of State, 1 woman is an officer, and 4 others serve on the 31-member body (or 13 percent). This rate of participation again conforms to the general pattern in the other Communist countries.[7]

In terms of leadership guidance through laws, decrees, and party resolutions, the Cuban regime has varied slightly from the overall norm. Its vagrancy law has already been mentioned as a means to coerce women into the labor force. However, it should be pointed out that this law was

Table A.4.4. **Female Membership in the Communist Party of Cuba, 1962–1975**

Date	Total No. of Members	Women	%
November 1962	5,414	838	15.5
March 1963	16,002	2,118	13.2
February 1964	32,537	3,534	10.9
December 1973	170,000	22,000	13.0
November 1974	186,995	23,900[a]	12.8
September 1975	202,807	29,000[a]	15(-)

Source: William M. LeoGrande, "The Political Institutionalization of Mass-Elite Linkages in Revolutionary Cuba," Ph.D. dissertation, Syracuse University, 1976.

[a]Estimates based on data on total number of members and percentage of women.

Table A.4.5. Female Membership in the Government Bodies and Central Committee of the Communist Party of Cuba

	Delegates or Members		Officers or Candidates	
	No.	%	No.	%
		(Officers)		
1. National Level				
a. National Assembly	107	22.2	—[a]	—
b. Council of State	4	12.9	1	12.5
c. Council of Ministers	2	4.4	0	0
2. Central Committee	11	8.8	0	0
		(Candidates)		
3. Local Level	856	8.0	—	13.4
a. Matanzas Province pilot project, 1974	—	3.0	—	7.6

Sources: Granma Weekly Review, 12 December 1976, 12 December 1975, 8 December 1974, 31 October 1976, and 8 December 1974.

Note: I want to thank Dr. William M. LeoGrande for his help in compiling this data.

[a]Data not available.

not specifically directed at women. Women happen to be the group most affected by it, since far more women than men are not gainfully employed. Family and welfare legislation has paralleled that of all Communist countries, but with certain important innovations. The maternity law gives women a paid leave of absence of only 18 weeks and an unpaid full year's leave after that, In this respect it is less generous than its Soviet models and the East European modifications. However, the father is also permitted to take one day's paid leave per month during the first year after birth to look after a sick child. Except for Hungary, where the practice is still experimental, no other Communist country permits fathers time off for child care. The Cuban family code makes the father, as well as the mother, responsible for the care and upbringing of their children, in contrast to similar legislation in the European Communist countries, which is not so specific. Finally, in cooperation with local governments, the Ministry of Domestic Commerce, and the Federation of Cuban Women (FMC), the Cuban regime has been developing a system called *Plan Jaba,* which gives priority shopping service to any member of the family of a woman who works.

The family in which husband and wife both work is given two options. The "predispatch plan" enables them to drop off a list at the grocery store on their way to work in the morning and to pick up the groceries on the return trip home. The "immediate dispatch" plan permits the person doing the shopping to go to the front of the line at each counter.[8] With some 145,000 working women allegedly benefiting from the plan in 1974, it is not clear how a store can give each working woman priority, but the regime claims that shopping time has been reduced. The concept is certainly novel and one which no other Communist leadership has tried.

It would seem from Cuban sources that the regime has much to do in the area of propaganda and socialization. There is frank recognition of the "survivals of neo-colonial attitudes" among women, coupled with the authorities' "lack of understanding of the problem of the working mother."[9] There is also official concern for the difficulties of promoting women to leadership positions. Recognition has been made of the material problems, such as the transfer of a husband from his job if a woman is promoted, as well as of the psychological problems, such as "Women are not demanding enough of themselves." However, as the Second Congress of the Federation of Cuban Women frankly stated: "On many occasions promotion is blocked because of continued backward criteria and negative attitudes, which block appraisement of the true qualifications and possibilities of the woman, her organizing abilities, her sense of responsibility and discipline, blocking her access to the levels of leadership."[10] Here, too, in the area of self-concept, an indigenous conservatism on the part of both women and men is reflected in the low percentage of women serving as delegates at the local level and in the low level of their employment in the salaried labor force as compared with women in the European Communist states.

In sum, the status of Cuban women is probably most comparable to that of women in Communist China. The postrevolutionary phase has ended. As in China, the regime has had to modify its aim of rapidly mobilizing women into the working world. But, perhaps even more than in China, Cuba's approach to the problem of women maintains a revolutionary and experimental thrust. Certainly, the regime does not seem to have settled into the conservatism typical of the European leaderships. The explanation may lie in the leadership's perception of Cuba as the Communist outpost against North American imperialism, or in the fact that the Cuban Revolution was initially, and in large degree remains, an indigenous movement. At the present time, although the position of Cuban women does not substantially differ from that of women in the rest of the Communist world, the momentum is still upward. The Revolution is near enough for women to see the difference in what went before and what came after.

In the long run, however, Cuba's failures are those of all Communist states: the government defines the objectives and tells women and men how to behave. The Federation of Cuban Women, like Communist women's organizations elsewhere, is the main instrument for achieving government goals, and there is no other independent woman's movement. Without substantial modification of the authoritarian nature of the system, continued improvement in the status of Cuban women must perforce follow the same leveling-off course as has been seen in Eastern Europe and the Soviet Union.

Notes

CHAPTER 1

1. Maurice Duverger, *The Political Role of Women* (New York: UNESCO, 1955), appendices.

2. For further data on women in political positions in Canada and the United States, see Karen O'Connor and Nancy McGlen, "Legal and Political Status of Women Cross Culturally Considered" (paper presented at the annual meeting of the Midwest Political Science Association, Chicago, Ill., 21–23 April 1977).

3. See, for example, Mohaly Vajda and Agnes Heller, "Family Structure and Communism," and Helen Benston, "The Political Economy of Women's Liberation," in *Women in a Man-Made World*, ed. Nona Glazer-Malbin and Helen Youngelson Waehrer (New York: Rand McNally & Co., 1973), pp. 292–305 and 119–41.

4. The fascination of the Marxist solution to women's emancipation is apparent not only in the recently published eulogy by Soviet women written by William M. Mandel, *Soviet Women* (New York: Anchor Books, 1975), but more importantly in the thinking of female representatives of the so-called Third World. At a conference on "Changing Sex Roles" held in Dubrovnik, Yugoslavia, 17–20 June 1975, African delegates were split over the question of whether capitalism or socialism would liberate women more efficiently. The Algerians took the socialist side, while a delegate from Zaire promoted a more capitalistic view. American women who have visited the People's Republic of China have come back impressed with the strides made by women in that country. See Ruth Sidel, *Women and Child Care in China* (New York: Hill & Wang, 1972).

5. Everett E. Hagen, *On the Theory of Social Change* (Homewood, Ill: The Dorsey Press, 1962), p. 185.

6. Jeane Kirkpatrick, *Political Woman* (New York: Basic Books, 1974), pp. 8–9.

7. Alice Rossi, "Equality between the Sexes: An Immodest Proposal," *Daedalus*, Spring 1964, pp. 607–52; and Carolyn Heilbrun, *Toward a Recognition of Androgyny* (New York: Alfred A. Knopf, 1973).

8. Athena Theodore, "The Professional Woman: Trends and Prospects," in *The Professional Woman*, ed. Athena Theodore (Cambridge, Mass.: Schenkman Publishing Co., 1971), pp. 4–14.

9. Cynthia Epstein, "Encountering the Male Establishment: Sex-Status Limits on Women's Careers in the Professions," in ibid., pp. 55ff.

10. Karl Deutsch, *Comparative Theories of Social Change* (Ann Arbor, Mich.: Foundation of Human Behavior, 1966), pp. 61–64.

11. Barbara Jancar, "Women Under Communism," in *Women and Politics*, ed. Jane Jaquette (New York: John Wiley & Sons, 1974), pp. 220ff.

12. The examples are too numerous for me to list them all. Suffice it to mention but a few here: Athena Theodore, ed., *The Professional Woman;* Jessie Bernard, *Women and the Public Interest* (New York: Aldine, Atherton, 1971); Esther Boserup, *Women's Role in Economic Development* (New York: St. Martin's Press, 1970); Mary Daley, *Beyond God the Father* (Boston: Beacon Press, 1973); Germaine Greer, *The Female Eunuch* (New York: McGraw-Hill, 1971); Shulamith Firestone, *The Dialectic of Sex* (New York: Bantam Books, 1972); Steven Goldberg, *The Inevita-*

254

bility of Patriarchy (New York: William Morrow, 1973); Elizabeth Janeway, *Man's World, Woman's Place* (New York: Dell Publishing Co., 1971).

13. Among these should be mentioned Norton T. Dodge, *Women in the Soviet Economy* (Baltimore: The Johns Hopkins Press, 1966); Mandel, *Soviet Women*; David Mace and Vera Mace, *The Soviet Family* (Garden City, N.Y.: Doubleday & Co., 1963); Donald R. Brown, ed., *The Role and Status of Women in the Soviet Union* (New York: Teachers College Press, 1968); Bernice Madison, *Social Welfare of the Soviet Union* (Stanford: University of California Press, 1968); and Barbara Jancar, "Women and Soviet Politics," in *Soviet Politics and Society in the 1970s,* ed. Henry Morton and Rudolf Tökés (New York: The Free Press, 1974), pp. 118–60.

CHAPTER 2

1. The ratio of men to women in the Soviet Union in 1950 was 73:100. Czechoslovakia lost around 15 percent of its population through the expulsion of the Sudeten Germans. Poland lost an estimated 12 million in population through war casualties, the extermination of the Jews, and population and territorial exchanges, or well over 25 percent of its 1941 population. Hungarian and Romanian losses were lower, but Hungary's war toll included the deportation of an estimated half-million Jews and the liquidation of another 570,000, 200,000 military casualties, and the expulsion of 200,000 Germans and 63,000 Slovaks. Some of these losses were offset by other minorities migrating into the country as a result of the postwar settlement. In 1949, 11.6 percent of the population was over 60 years of age. The number of Germans who fled East Germany before 1945 is not known, but an estimated 3.5 million left for the West before the Berlin Wall was built in 1961, representing around 19 percent of the 1946 population. In 1964, the East German census recorded 1.3 million fewer individuals, including new births, than in 1950. After Poland, Yugoslavia suffered the heaviest war casualties, which have been estimated at 10.6 percent of its 1941 population. Sources of these statistics include: B. R. Mitchell, *European Historical Statistics* (New York: Columbia University Press, 1975), pp. 19–32; the relevant pages of the U.S. Government-sponsored handbooks of the East European countries and the Soviet Union (Washington, D. C.: Government Printing Office, 1971–1973); Robert J. Kerner, ed., *Yugoslavia* (Berkeley: University of California Press, 1949), pp. 390–91; and John Dornberg, *The Other Germany* (Garden City, N. Y.: Doubleday & Co., 1968), p. 17.

2. *Yearbook of Labour Statistics, 1973* (Geneva: International Labour Office, Statistical Office of the United Nations, 1973).

3. For example, see Maria Dinkova, *The Social Progress of Bulgarian Women* (Sofia: Sofia Press, 1972), p. 17.

4. *Women in the Contemporary Life of Romania* (Bucharest: Meridiane Publishing House, 1970), p. 30.

5. Atanas Liutov, ed., *Zhenata-maika, truzhenichka, obshchestvenichka* (Sofia: Partizdat, 1974), pp. 46–66.

6. The university selection process is based not only on sex but on the political reliability and "class origin" of the candidate. The preferential admissions standards given those considered reliable, at the expense of talent or ability, has been a subject of grievance among dissenters for some time. See International Committee for the Support of Charter 77 in Czechoslovakia, "White Paper on Czechoslovakia" (Paris, 1977), chap. 6, pp. 127–50 (mimeographed).

7. Norton T. Dodge, *Women in the Soviet Economy* (Baltimore: The Johns Hopkins Press, 1966), p. 228.

8. "Romania and International Women's Year," *Romania* 26, no. 4 (April 1975): 13.

9. *Soviet Life,* March 1975, p. 12.

10. *Sovietskaia zhenshchina,* October 1974, pp. 14–16.

11. Dodge, *Women in the Soviet Economy;* Barbara Jancar, "Women and Soviet Politics," in *Soviet Politics and Society in the 1970s,* ed. Henry Morton and Rudolf Tök-2es (New York: The Free Press, 1974), pp. 120–24; and virtually all the sociologists with whom I talked during my trip to Eastern Europe.

12. Nikolina Ilieva, Trifon Trifaniv, and Nikolina Tsaneva, *Izpolzvane na zhenskite trudovi resursi v NRB* (Sofia: Partizdat, 1973), p. 180; Czechoslovak Socialist Republic, Federal Statisti-

cal Office, *Statistická ročenka ČSSR, 1969* (Prague: SNTL-ALFA, 1969), p. 122; Union of Soviet Socialist Republics, Council of Ministers, Central Statistical Office, *Zhenshchiny i deti v SSSR: Statisticheskii sbornik* (Moscow: Statistika, 1969), p. 18; *Statisztikai évkönyv, 1973* (Budapest: Központi Statisztikai hivatal, 1973), pp. 109–10; *Romania 26*, no. 4 (1975): 12; *The Working Women in People's Poland* (Warsaw: Ministry of Labour, Wages, and Social Affairs, 1975), pp. 8–9; Ibrahim Latitić, ed., *Women in the Economy and Society of the SFR of Yugoslavia* (Belgrade: Federal Institute for Statistics, 1975), pp. 10–11; Herta Kührig, *Equal Rights for Women in the German Democratic Republic* (Berlin: GDR Committee for Human Rights, 1973), p. 148.

13. *The Working Woman in People's Poland*, p. 20.

14. Latitić, ed., *Women in the SFR of Yugoslavia*, p. 5.

15. *The Working Woman in People's Poland*, pp. 20–21.

16. Dodge, *Women in the Soviet Economy*, pp. 174–76.

17. "Zhenshchiny v SSSR: Statisticheskie materialy," reprinted from *Vestnik statistiki*, no. 1 (1974), p. 74.

18. See, for example, *Literaturnaia gazeta*, 22 January 1969, where a professor of pediatric surgery at Moscow University claimed that sex definitely entered into the rules of the game as far as admission to medical school was concerned.

19. *Izvestia*, 30 August 1975.

20. Latitić, ed., *Women in the SFR of Yugoslavia*, p. 10.

21. *The Working Women in People's Poland*, p. 9.

22. *Women in Poland* (Warsaw: Central Statistical Office, 1975), p. 14.

23. Latitić, ed., *Women in the SFR of Yugoslavia*, p. 18.

24. Dinkova, *Bulgarian Women*, p. 19.

25. *Women in Poland*, p. 14.

26. *Bulletin of Statistical Work*, no. 23 (1956), reprinted in *Hsinhua Fortnightly* (Peking), no. 2 (1957), pp. 87–89, as cited in *China News Analysis* (Hong Kong), no. 215 (7 February 1958), p. 1.

27. Barry Richman, *Industrial Society in Communist China* (New York: Random House, 1969), pp. 304–5; Janet Weitzner Salaff, "Institutionalized Motivation for Fertility Limitation," in *Women in China: Studies in Social Change and Feminism*, ed. Marilyn B. Young, Michigan Papers in Chinese Studies no. 15 (Ann Arbor: Center for Chinese Studies, University of Michigan, 1973), pp. 124–25.

28. People's Republic of China, Directorate General of Budgets, Accounts, and Statistics, *The China Yearbook, 1934* (Nanking: Bureau of Budgets, Accounts, and Statistics, 1935), p. 270.

29. Reported in *People's Daily* (Peking), 14 March and 6 March 1973 respectively.

30. Committee of Concerned Asian Scholars, *China: Inside the People's Republic* (New York: Bantam Books, 1972), pp. 270–74.

31. Salaff, "Institutionalized Motivation for Fertility Limitation," p. 125.

32. Czechoslovak Socialist Republic, Federal Statistical Office, *Statistická ročenka ČSSR, 1969*, p. 131.

33. *Pravda*, 19 August 1971.

34. Elizabeth Janeway, *Man's World, Woman's Place* (New York: Dell Publishing Co., 1971), chap. 13.

35. William Mandel, "Soviet Women and Their Self-Image," *Science and Society* 35, no. 3 (Fall 1971): 296.

36. Dodge, *Women in the Soviet Economy*, pp. 184–95.

37. Miro A. Mihovilovic, principal investigator, *Reports and Studies: The Influence of Women's Employment on Family Characteristics and Functioning* (Zagreb: Institute for Social Research, University of Zagreb, 1971), pp. 28, 67.

38. Latitić, ed., *Women in the SFR of Yugoslavia*, p. 5.

39. "Zhenshchiny v SSSR," p. 9.

40. Latitić, ed., *Women in the SFR of Yugolavia*, p. 5.

41. Komlós Pálné, ed., *A nők a statisztika tükrében* (Budapest: Hungarian Woman's National Council, Kossuth könyvkiadó, 1974), pp. 26–28; Ilieva, Trifaniv, and Tsaneva, *Izpolzvane*, pp. 195–209; and Mihovilovic, *Reports and Studies*, pp. 217–30.

42. Computed from statistics given in the United Nations, Department of Economic and Social Affairs, Statistical Office, *Demographic Yearbook, 1973*, pp. 760–80.

43. "Zhenshchiny v SSSR," p. 11. For a detailed analysis of women in science and technology in the USSR, see Gerhard F. Schilling and Kathleen M. Hunt, *Women in Science and Technology: US/USSR Comparisons*, Rand Paper no. P–5239 (Santa Monica, Calif. The Rand Corporation, June 1974).

44. Dinkova, *Bulgarian Women*, p. 19.

45. *Women in the Contemporary Life of Romania*, pp. 37–38.

46. "Zhenshchiny v SSSR," p. 11.

47. Norton T. Dodge, "Women in the Professions," in *Women in Russia*, ed. Dorothy Atkinson et al. (Stanford, Calif.: Stanford University Press, 1977), p. 222.

48. People's Republic of Bulgaria, Ministry of Information and Communications, *Zhenata v stopanskiia, obshchestveniia, kulturniia zhivot a v semestvoto* (Sofia: Central Statistical Office, 1971), p. 50.

49. Liutov, ed., *Zhenata-maika, truzhenichka, obshchestvenichka*, p. 57.

50. Richman, *Industrial Society in Communist China*, p. 396.

51. Janet Wetizner Salaff and Judith Merkle, "Women and Revolution: The Lessons of the Soviet Union and China," in *Women in China: Studies in Social Change and Feminism*, ed. Marilyn B. Young, Michigan Papers in Chinese Studies no. 15 (Ann Arbor: Center for Chinese Studies, University of Michigan 1973), p. 169.

52. See appendix 2.

CHAPTER 3

1. Jerzy Berent, "Some Demographic Aspects of Employment in Eastern Europe and the USSR," *International Labor Review*, no. 101 (February 1970), p. 178.

2. Zdenek Juráček, "Differenčni plodnost výsledky sčitání lidu z r. 1961," pt. 2, *Demografie* (Prague), no. 3 (1961), p. 213.

3. Miro A. Mihovilovic, principal investigator, *Reports and Studies: The Influence of Women's Employment on the Family Characteristics and Functioning* (Zagreb: Institute for Social Research, University of Zagreb, 1973), p. 153.

4. Ibid., p. 133.

5. People's Republic of Bulgaria, Ministry of Information and Communications, *Zhenata v stopanskiia, obshchestveniia, kulturniia zhivot a v semestvoto* (Sofia: Central Statistical Office, 1971), p. 39.

6. Mihovilovic, *Reports and Studies*, p. 272.

7. Atanas Liutov, ed., *Zhenata-maika, truzhenichka, obshchestvenichka* (Sofia: Partizdat, 1974), p. 43.

8. Both the Yugoslav and Bulgarian surveys cited in this chapter, as well as Sokołowska's work on Polish women and that of Judit Sas.

9. Magdalena Sokołowska, *Kobieta pracująca* (Warsaw: Wiedza Powszechna, 1963), pp. 131–95. In her study of French working women, Andrée Michel also cites the obligations that women have in the family as the most permanent obstacle to their working. Andrée Michel, *Travail féminin: un point de vue* (Travaux et Recherches de Prospective: Schéma général d'aménagement de la France: La Documentation Française, 1975), pp. 94–120.

10. This impression is derived from my own observations and talks with emigrants from the Soviet Union.

11. Colette Shulman, "The Individual and the Collective," in *Women in Russia*, ed. Dorothy Atkinson et al. (Stanford, Calif.: Stanford University Press, 1977), p. 379.

12. *Demografiai évkönyv, 1973* (Budapest: Központi Statisztikai hivatal, 1973), pp. 417–18.

13. *Czechoslovak Statistical Abstract, 1972* (Prague: Orbis, 1972), pp. 43 and 50.

14. V. Perevedentsev, "We're Always on the Go," *Literaturnaia gazeta*, no. 36 (3 September 1975), p. 10. The average annual out-migration of the rural population in 1973 was 18 for every 1,000 rural residents. The author stresses that most of this migration was from the RSFSR.

In Central Asia, Armenia, and Georgia, out-migration averaged between 4 and 6 for every 1,000 rural residents.

15. Statistics from "Current Problems of Urbanization in Romania," *Romania* 25, no. 7 (31 July 1975): 12. For Romanian Communist Party's policy on housing, see *Programme of the Romanian Communist Party,* draft (Bucharest: N.p., 1975). pp. 72–73. Some 3–3.5 million dwellings, of which 2.5 million will be in towns, are planned for construction by 1990.

16. "Zhenshchiny v SSSR: Statisticheskie materialy," reprinted from *Vestnik statistiki,* no. 1 (1974), p. 14.

17. Herta Kührig, *Equal Rights for Women in the German Democratic Republic* (Berlin: GDR Committee for Human Rights, 1973), pp. 152–54.

18. In China, the same picture obtains. The kindergartens and schools are generally located in the cities. Rural mothers have to assume almost total responsibility for the preschool child. The leadership has undertaken a campaign to mobilize women into work, yet there is no infrastructure in the villages to care for children whose mothers are at work. A locality in Fukien reported in the fall of 1972 that many women had not turned up for the harvest because there was no one at home to look after the children. Child care facilities are desired, but the regime simply cannot afford to institute them. *People's Daily* (Fukien), 2 July 1972, as reported in *China News Analysis,* no. 919 (11 May 1973), p. 5.

19. A. G. Kharchev and S. I. Golod, *Professional'naia rabota zhenshchin i sem'ia* (Leningrad: Izdatel'stvo "Nauka," 1970), p. 92.

20. Ibid., p. 320; Mihovilovic, *Reports and Studies,* p. 286.

21. Z. A. Yankova, "O Semeino-bytovykh roliakh rabotaishchei zhenshchiny," *Sotsial'nye issledovaniia,* (Moscow) 4 (1970): 77–81.

22. It is sometimes forgotten that there is an income tax in the European Communist countries. For example, a man who has his *Kandidat nauk* (equivalent to the Ph.D.) earns 300 rubles a month and takes home 265. A woman who has graduated from an institute, roughly equivalent to our college, earns 220 rubles a month and takes home 190. It is said that during World War II the Soviet income tax rose to 50 percent of one's salary in order to pay for the war effort. Given the generally low wages in Communist countries, the additional tax must cause added difficulties in the family budget.

23. A. Suslov, "Speech at the Solemn Meeting Celebrating the Fifty-third Anniversary of the Great October Revolution," as printed in *Pravda,* 7 November 1970.

24. Z. A. Yankova, *Nedelia* 18 (24–30 April 1972): p. 20.

25. Komlós Pálné, ed., *A nök a statisztika tükrében* (Budapest: Hungarian Woman's National Council, Kossuth könyvkiadó, 1974), p. 56.

26. Liutov., ed., *Zhenata-maika, trezhenichka, obshchestvenichka,* p. 283.

27. Ibrahim Latitić, ed., *Women in the Economy and Society of the SFR of Yugoslavia* (Belgrade: Federal Insititute for Statistics, 1975), p. 21.

28. United Nations, Department of Economic and Social Affairs, Statistical Office, *Statistical Yearbook, 1955, 1960, 1967;* idem, *Demographic Yearbook, 1971; Demografiai évkönyv, 1972* (Budapest: Központi Statisztikai hivatal, 1972), p. 385. There are no data from China because China has not published any since 1953.

29. Sokołowska, *Kobieta pracująca,* p. 144.

30. Birth rates from United States, Department of Commerce, Bureau of the Census, *The 1977 U.S. Fact Book* (New York: Grosset & Dunlop, 1977), p. 871.

31. A. K., "A Demographic Problem: Female Employment and the Birth Rate," based on research conducted by the Demographic Section of the Moscow House of Scientists, *Voprosy ekonomiki* 6 (1969), translated in *Soviet Review* 9, no. 1 (Spring 1970): 76–81.

32. This figure was given by the Population Council of New York City and was published in *Democrat and Chronicle* (Rochester, N.Y.), 21 April 1976.

33. Vladimir Szt, Kasabov, "Bulgária népessége születésgyakoriságanak kérdéséhez," *Demográfia* (Budapest), no. 2 (1974), pp. 169–83.

34. William F. Robinson, "Selected Demographic and Economic Data on Eastern Europe," RFE Background Report no. 90, 29 April 1977, Radio Free Europe Research Department, Munich, West Germany (mimeographed), p. 6.

35. *Népszabadsag,* 25 December 1976.

36. Z. A. Yankova, *Nedelia,* no. 18 (24–30 April 1972) p. 20.

CHAPTER 4

1. Two popular examples of female as well as male belief in this myth are Helen B. Andelin, *Fascinating Womanhood* (New York: Bantam Books, 1975), which has sold over a million copies in this country, and Mirabel Morgan, *The Total Woman* (New York: Pocket Books, 1975). Both serve as textbooks for courses now widely organized throughout the United States on how to be a woman and keep your husband. Presenting the same image, Carol Wald's *Myth America: Picturing Women, 1865-1945* (New York: Pantheon Books, 1975), portrays how male America has been looking at female America since 1865.

2. A great deal has been made of the extended family as being typical of the Moslem *umma* and the Orient. Recent demographic studies, however, have shown that such families rarely existed, and when they did, it was only in the palaces where there was enough to feed everyone. The mean family size of Suwa County in Japan's Tokugawa era, for example, was 5.01, indicating the statistical significance of the nuclear household. Indeed, the nuclear family is one of the enduring realities, perhaps only today being challenged in any important degree. See A. Hayami and N. Uchidu, "Japan: Suwa in the Tokugawa Era," in *Household and Family in Past Time: Comparative Studies in the Size and Structure of the Domestic Group over the Last Three Centuries in England, France, Serbia, Japan, and Colonial North America, with Further Materials from Western Europe,* ed. Peter Laslett and Richard Wall (Cambridge: At the University Press, 1972), p. 487.

3. Gregory J. Massell, *The Surrogate Proletariat* (Princeton: Princeton University Press, 1974), pp. 226-46.

4. Ibid., pp. 374-75.

5. See Richard Pipes, "Assimilation and Muslim: A Case Study," in *Soviet Society: A Book of Readings,* ed. Alex Inkeles and H. Kent Geiger (Boston: Houghton Mifflin, 1961), pp. 588-607. *Pravda* and *Literaturnaia gazeta* have recently published examples of the survivals of "obsolete" marriage and other customs oppressive to women, including *kalym,* or "bride price," in Kirghizia, Tadzhikistan (*Pravda,* 12 November 1975, p. 3), and Turkmenia (*Literaturnaia gazeta,* no. 22 (28 May 1975), p. 12.

6. William Hinton, *Fanshen: A Documentary of Revolution in a Chinese Village* (New York: Vintage Books, 1966), pp. 157-60, 396-98, 454-58.

7. See "Welcome the New Policy in Women's Work" (March 1943); "Decisions of the Central Committee of the Communist Party of China: On the Present Women's Work in the Rural Districts of the Liberated Areas" (20 December 1948); and *Documents of the Women's Movement in China* (Peking: New China Women's Press, 1950), pp. 6-26. The 1948 decision stressed that letting the "peasants'" ideology drift on its own "course" or being too hasty could be disadvantageous. However, it urged that foot-binding, infanticide, monetary marriage, and child betrothal be prohibited by law (an indication that these practices were highly entrenched at the time), and that education of the peasants should be undertaken.

8. See the report in *China News Analysis,* no. 776 (3 October 1969), pp. 61-62.

9. Jan Myrdal, *Report from a Chinese Village* (New York: Signet, 1965), pp. 252-67.

10. For a good study of the Chinese family, although now dated, see William J. Goode, ed., *World Revolution and Family Patterns* (New York: The Free Press, 1963), pp. 230-70.

11. Francis L. K. Hsu, "Chinese Kinship and Chinese Behavior," in *China in Crisis,* vol. 1, *China's Heritage and the Communist Political System,* ed. Ho Ping-ti and Tang Tsou, 2 bks. (Chicago: University of Chicago Press, 1968), 1: 583-93.

12. Vera St. Erlich, *Family in Transition: A Study of 300 Yugoslav Villages* (Princeton: Princeton University Press, 1966).

13. Sheila Fitzpatrick, remarks made at the Conference on Women in Russia, Stanford University, Stanford, Calif., 29 May-1 June 1975.

14. A. L. Pimenova, "Novy byt i stanovlenie vnutrisemeinogo ravenstva," *Sotsial'nye issledovaniia* (Moscow), no. 7 (1971), pp. 38-42.

15. Zoya Yankova el al., *XX vek i problemy sem'i* (Moscow: Izdatel'stvo "Znanie," 1974), pp. 35-36.

16. Ibid., p. 50.

17. The word is used in the sense of mutual power or rule, which in itself presents a rather

interesting conceptualization of marriage, implying equal status. "Democratic" on the other hand implies popular rule, an entirely different matter.

18. Miro A. Mihovilovic, principal investigator, *Reports and Studies: The Influence of Women's Employment on Family Characteristics and Functioning* (Zagreb: Institute for Social Research, University of Zagreb, 1973), pp. 413–26.

19. Conversation with Judit Sas, Fall 1974.

20. See my discussion of this survey in Barbara Jancar, "Women and Soviet Politics," in *Soviet Society and Politics in the 1970s*, ed. Henry Morton and Rudolf Tökés (New York: The Free Press, 1974), pp. 133–34.

21. For example, a survey conducted in Kostroma revealed that Soviet men prefer their wives not to work. Only 24 percent of the male respondents were enthusiastic about their wives working, while 64 percent of the female respondents said they felt their jobs strengthened their home life. See *Literaturnaia gazeta*, no. 39 (22 September 1971).

22. The term *demarcation line* was in use in 1964–1965, according to *China News Analysis*. Even after a person's death, a class analysis must be made to determine whether the deceased is entitled to an honorable funeral. Drawing the line means that the individuals within the family separate themselves from the other members in terms of their loyalty to the leadership rather than to the family. Drawing the line can separate parents from children, and probably has produced cases of children reporting to the authorities on their parents' activities. In essence, drawing the line divides revolutionaries in a family from the "counterrevolutionaries." For further discussion, see *China News Analysis*, no. 776 (3 October 1969), p. 3.

23. Jan Myrdal and Gun Kessle, *China: The Revolution Continued*, trans. from the rev. Swedish ed. by Paul Britten Austin (New York: Pantheon Books, 1970), pp. 137–38.

24. *China News Analysis*, no. 821 (13 November 1970), pp. 3–5.

25. As printed in the *Hong Kong Times*, 5 November 1972.

26. As quoted from Roxanne Witke, *Comrade Chiang Ch'ing* (Boston: Little, Brown & Co., 1977), and cited in *Time*, 21 March 1977, p. 59.

27. Szuza Ferge in an interview with the author, Fall 1974.

28. *Zhenata dnes*, June 1976.

29. *Otechestven front*, 27 June 1973.

30. *Literaturnaia gazeta*, 3 September 1970.

31. A. Gorkin, "Concern for the Soviet Family," *Soviet Review* 10, no. 3 (Fall 1969): 47–63.

32. Vladimir Chkalalin, "The Family and Family Relationships under Socialism," *Sovietskoe gosudarstvo i pravo* 12, no. 4 (Spring 1974): 80.

33. Questions taken from a questionnaire shown to me by a researcher on the project at Moscow's Institute of Sociology. Because the findings had not been published, I was unable to obtain the questionnaire itself. The survey was completed in 1973. My thanks go to the institute for sharing their printouts and findings with me.

34. Goode, ed., *World Revolution and Family Patterns*, p. 317.

35. G. Kiseleva, "How Many Kids Do People Want and How Many Do They Have?" *Current Digest of the Soviet Press*, 7 November 1973. The Soviet Press has carried many articles in recent years stressing the disadvantage at which parents put an only child and strongly suggesting that society may be interested in the rounded development of Soviet children while selfish parents are not.

36. Henry O. David, ed., *Abortion Research: International Experience* (Lexington, Mass. & Toronto: Lexington Books, 1974), p. 211.

37. As researched and reported by Dennison I. Rusinow in "Population Review 1970: Yugoslavia," American Universities Field Staff report DIR-1-70 (Yugoslavia), *Fieldstaff Reports: Southeast Europe* 17, no. 1 (1970): 9–11.

38. Hilda Scott, *Does Socialism Liberate Women?* (Boston: Beacon Press, 1974), pp. 151–53.

39. Rusinow, "Population Review 1970," pp. 11–12.

40. Nila Kapor-Stanulovic and Berislav Beric, "Family Planning Behavior in Yugoslavia," in *Abortion Research: International Experience*, ed. Henry P. David (Lexington, Mass. & Toronto: Lexington Books, 1974), pp. 129–36.

41. Material for the succeeding paragraph was drawn from Han Suyin, "Population Growth

and Birth Planning," *Eastern Horizon*, no. 5 (1973), and Ruth Sidel, *Women and Child Care in China* (New York: Hill & Wang, 1972), pp. 53–60. See also Ruth Sidel, *Families of Fengsheng: Urban Life in China* (Middlesex, Eng.: Penguin Books, 1974), pp. 81–97.

42. Vladimir Ilyich Lenin, *The Emancipation of Women* (New York: International Publishers, 1966), pp. 23–56.

43. As quoted in S. I. Golod, *Sociological Problems of Sexual Morality* (Leningrad: Philosophical Faculty, Leningrad University, 1968).

44. Friedrich Engels, *The Origins of the Family, Private Property, and the State in the Light of the Researchers of Lewis H. Morgan*, trans. Ernest Untermann (New York: International Publishers, 1942), *passim*.

45. Alfred Meyer, "Marxism and the Women's Movement," in *Women in Russia*, ed. Dorothy Atkinson et al. (Stanford, Calif.: Stanford University Press, 1977), pp. 91–98.

46. Lenin, *The Emancipation of Women*, pp. 98–103.

47. Ibid., pp. 38–41, 103-4.

48. No less a person than Kollontai describes herself as being limited by Victorian concepts of "true love." In her autobiography, she confesses her continued efforts to find the one man to whom she could be true. "Our mistake," she writes, "was that, each time, we succumbed to the belief that we had finally found the one and only in the man we loved, the person with whom we believed we could blend our soul, one who was ready to fully recognize us as a spiritual-physical force. But over and over things turned out differently, since the man always tried to impose his ego upon us and adapt us fully to his purposes." She urges the younger generation to understand that work and the longing for love can be harmoniously combined so that "work remains as the main goal of existence." Aleksandra Kollontai, *The Autobiography of a Sexually Emancipated Communist Woman* (New York: Herder & Herder, 1971), p. 6.

49. Lily Braun is one of the more interesting radical feminists of the nineteenth century. She was the first to develop the contradiction between creative work and women's sex role, the first to see the problems of the working mother, and she felt that capitalism might end motherhood. In her emphasis on individual fulfillment and change in consciousness, she gradually moved toward a Marxism more consistent with today, which held that intellectual development and sensual enjoyment were equally important as productive labor. For a discussion of her work, see Meyer, "Marxism and the Women's Movement," pp. 107–8.

50. See Kollontai's comments as reprinted in Rudolf Schlesinger, *The Family in the USSR* (New York & London: Rutledge & Reegan, 1947), pp. 348–57.

51. For a discussion of the debate over the 1926 marriage law, see Beatrice Farnsworth, "Bolshevik Alternatives and the Soviet Family: The 1926 Marriage Law Debate," in *Women in Russia*, ed. Dorothy Atkinson et al. (Stanford, Calif.: Stanford University Press, 1977), pp. 139–65. It should be mentioned that Western specialists such as John Hazard continue to see the 1926 law as an instrument to break up the old family patterns because registration of marriage and divorce was not required and factual wives could be recognized heirs without submitting proof of dependency or legal relationship. My argument is that in the recognition of unregistered marriages as *marriages*, the law quite obviously supports the institution of marriage, with legal consequences in terms of child support and inheritance implied. In a certain sense, it attempts to include *all* sexual relationships between man and woman under the term *marriage*. The *meaning* of marriage may have been at issue in terms of legal status, but the *concept* of marriage as the appropriate social institution to regulate sexual relations and the propagation of children was never challenged. See John Hazard, *Law and Social Change in the USSR* (London: Stevens & Sons, 1953), p. 246.

52. Kollontai has left us some indication of her disillusionment with the progress of the status of women after the Revolution: "A heated debate flared up when I published my thesis on the new morality. For our Soviet Marriage Law, separated from the Church to be sure, is not essentially more progressive than the same laws that after all exist in other progressive democratic countries. . . . When one speaks of the 'immorality' which the Bolsheviks purportedly propagated, it suffices to submit our marriage laws to close scrutiny to note that in the divorce question we are on a par with North America, whereas in the question of the illegitimate child we have not yet even progressed as far as the Norwegians." Kollontai, *Autobiography*, p. 43.

53. Decree of 8 July 1944, pp. 16–17, as printed in *Ved. Verkh. Sov. SSSR* 36, no. 297 (11 July 1944).

54. As cited in C. K. Yang, *Chinese Communist Society: The Family and the Village* (Cambridge, Mass.: M.I.T. Press. 1965), pp. 38–39.

55. Goode, ed., *World Revolution and Family Patterns,* p. 301.

56. Sidel, *Women and Child Care in China,* pp. 47–52.

57. Interview with A. G. Kharchev, International Conference of Sociology, Toronto, Canada, August 1974.

58. See *The Virginia Slims American Women's Opinion Poll,* vol. 3, conducted by the Roper Organization, Inc., 1974; and Kate Millett, *Sexual Politics* (New York: Avon Books, 1971), chap. 2.

59. For example, studies of the French election of 1974 indicate that women, or the female vote, were primarily responsible for electing D'Estaing to office. Françoise Giroud, "Presidentielle: Le choix des femmes," *L'Express,* 22–28 April 1974, p. 62. See also the 1975 votes in New York and New Jersey for the Equal Rights Amendment.

60. USSR Census, *Pravda,* 17 April 1971.

61. Hsu, "Chinese Kinship and Chinese Behavior," p. 593.

62. Sidel, *Families of Fengsheng, passim.*

63. *Documents of the Women's Movement in China,* p. 10. See also M. J. Meijer, *Marriage Law and Policy in the Chinese People's Republic* (Hong Kong: Hong Kong University Press, 1971), pp. 5–82 and 85–100, for a discussion of "feudal marriage practices" in old China.

64. For a concise description of change in Chinese family practice and attitudes during the republican period, see Dun J. Li, *The Ageless Chinese* (New York: Scribner's Sons, 1965), pp. 454–60.

65. Susan Jacoby, *Inside Soviet Schools* (New York: Hill & Wang, 1974), p. 103.

66. E. K. Vasil'eva, *Sotsial'no-professional 'nyi uroven' gorodskoi molodeshi* (Leningrad: University of Leningrad Press, 1971), p. 36.

67. Nikolina Ilieva, Trifon Trifaniv, and Nikolina Tsaneva, *Izpolzvane no zhenskite trudovi resursi v NRB* (Sofia: Partizdat, 1973), chap. 5.

68. *Pravda,* 30 October 1975.

69. *Izvestia,* 7 March 1970.

70. Ibid., 17 December 1971.

71. Ilieva, Trifaniv, and Tsaneva, *Izpolzvane,* pp. 99–100.

72. Millett, *Sexual Politics,* chap. 4, esp. pp. 303–4.

73. M. Pavlova, "Irina's Career," *Literaturnaia gazeta,* 21 September 1970.

74. Interview with editorial staff of *Femea,* Bucharest, Fall 1974.

75. Interview with Natalija Grzecic, Dubrovnik, Fall 1974.

76. Reported in *China News Analysis,* no. 919 (11 May 1973), p. 2.

77. Linda Gordon, "The Fourth Mountain, Some Giant Steps Forward, Some Small Steps Backward, and a Ways Still to Go," *Women* 3, no. 4 (1973): 14.

78. "Statement of Position on the Organization of Working Women," submitted by the First International Conference on Working Women to the Second Comintern Congress, as translated from *Pravda,* no. 172 (6 March 1920).

79. *Documents of the Women's Movement in China, passim.*

80. Magdalena Sokołowska, *Kobieta pracująca* (Warsaw: Wiedza Powszechna, 1963), pp. 194–95.

81. Ethel Dunn, "Russian Rural Women," in *Women in Russia,* ed. Dorothy Atkinson et al. (Stanford, Calif.: Stanford University Press, 1977), p. 181.

CHAPTER 5

1. *New Albania* 28, no. 2 (1974): 21; Nikolina Ilieva, "Sotsialnoto ravenstvo na zhenata v ysloviiata na izgrazhdane na razvito sotsialistichesko obshchestvo, in *Zhenata-maika, truzhenichka, obshchestvenichka,* ed. Atanas Liutov (Sofia: Partizdat, 1974), p. 29; interview with Maria Groza, executive director of the Romanian National Woman's Committee, Fall 1974;

Supplement of the Bulletin of the Institute for the Study of the USSR, May 1971; Herta Kührig, *Equal Rights for Women in the German Democratic Republic* (Berlin: GDR Committee for Human Rights, 1973), p. 144; Maria Dinkova, *The Social Progress of Bulgarian Women* (Sofia: Sofia Press, 1972), p. 39; Ibrahim Latitić, ed., *Women in the Economy and Society of the SFR of Yugoslavia* (Belgrade: Federal Institute for Statistics, 1975), p. 4; *Peking Review,* nos. 35-36, pp. 9-10, and no. 4, pp. 8-9; *Women in Poland* (Warsaw: Central Statistical Office, 1975), p. 16; Czechoslovak Situation Report no. 45 (10 November 1976), Radio Free Europe Research Department, Munich, West Germany (mimeographed), p. 4; University of Pittsburgh, School of International Affairs, Archives on East European Elites.

2. Housewives, for example, are not eligible to belong to what are termed "basic organs of associated labor" and hence are ineligible for election to the successively higher occupational bodies that elect the decision-makers. Yugoslav government official Dr. Antun Vratusa responded to this charge by saying that housewives would have direct representation in local Communist and government organs. However, that is not the same as eligibility for republican or federal office. See the discussion in *New York Times,* 9 March 1974. The full text of the 1974 constitution may be found in *The Constitution of the Socialist Federal Republic of Yugoslavia* (Belgrade: n.p., 1974).

3. I. Kapitonov, "Some Questions of Party Building in the Light of the 24th Party Congress," *Kommunist* 3 (February 1972): 35.

4. People's Republic of Bulgaria, Ministry of Information and Communications, *Zhenata v stopanskiia, obshchestveniia, kulturniia zhivot a v semestvoto* (Sofia: Central Statistical Office, 1971), p. 9.

5. Ibid., p. 88.

6. Ethel Dunn, "Russian Rural Women," in *Women in Russia,* ed. Dorothy Atkinson et al. (Stanford, Calif.: Stanford University Press, 1977), pp. 182-87.

7. Ruth Sidel, *Families of Fengsheng: Urban Life in China* (Middlesex, Eng.: Penguin Books, 1974), chaps. 2 and 3.

8. See *China News Analysis,* no. 917 (27 April 1973), p. 7; no. 919 (11 May 1973), p. 4; and no. 940 (16 November 1973), p. 5.

9. *Communist China, 1971,* Communist China Problem Research Series, no. EC52 (Hong Kong: Union Research Institute, 1973), pp. 428-30.

10. Data published in *China News Analysis,* no. 859 (22 October 1971), pp. 2-5.

11. Miro A. Mihovilovic, principal investigator, *Reports and Studies: The Influence of Women's Employment of Family Characteristics and Functioning* (Zagreb: Institute for Social Research, University of Zagreb, 1973), p. 309.

12. Gabriel A. Almond and Sidney Verba, *The Civic Culture: Political Attitudes and Democracy in Five Nations* (Princeton: Princeton University Press, 1963), p. 304.

13. People's Republic of Bulgaria, *Zhenata v stopanskiia,* p. 90.

14. Ibid., p. 89.

15. A similar development has been reported by Myrdal in China. Jan Myrdal and Gun Kessle, *China: The Revolution Continued,* trans. from the rev. Swedish ed. by Paul Britten Austin (New York: Pantheon Books, 1970), pp. 90-91.

16. For further discussion of the study, the reader is referred to Barbara Jancar, "Women and Elite Recruitment into the Central Committees of Bulgaria, Czechoslovakia, Hungary, and Poland" (paper presented at the annual meeting of the Midwest Political Science Association, Chicago, Ill., 23 April 1977).

17. Joel Moses, "Women in Political Roles," in *Women in Russia,* ed. Dorothy Atkinson et al. (Stanford, Calif.: Stanford University Press, 1977), pp. 333-53.

18. Until the recent parliamentary reform, the Yugoslav Federal Assembly had been divided into five parts: industry, politics, education and culture, health and social welfare, and the Council of the Republics.

19. Kührig, *Equal Rights for Women,* p. 145.

20. Given the importance of Party direction, it is fascinating that this organization is so little mentioned by the people or in the professional literature of the Communist countries. In book after book discussing the problems of women from a sociological viewpoint, the Party is introduced at the beginning or in the conclusion by a quote from Lenin or a recent Politburo or Central

Committee resolution, as if to indicate that the Party understood the questions being discussed in the book before it was written, and had, in fact, generated the book. But that is generally the totality of the Party's mentioned role. Official statistics are most helpful in giving the number of women mayors, deputies, and trade union officials, but they are silent on Party positions.

21. Sidel, *Families of Fengsheng*, chaps. 2 and 3.

22. See Richard Stites, "Women's Liberation Movements in Russia," *Canadian-American Slavic Studies* 7, no. 4 (Winter 1973): 468–70.

23. See Aleksandra Kollontai's discussion of K. N. Samoilova's opposition to a woman's section in the Party, "Tvorcheskoe ve rabote tovarishcha Samoilovoi," in Central Committee of the Russian Communist Party (Bolshevik), Commission on the History of the October Revolution and the Russian Communist Party (Bolshevik), *Revoliutsionnaia deiatel'nost' Konkordii Nikolaevnyi Samoilovoi: Sbornik vospominanii* (Moscow: Gosudarstvennoe izdatel'stvo, 1922), pp. 8–9.

24. Communist Party of the Soviet Union, Leningrad Municipal Committee, *Pervyi legal'nyi Petersburgskii komitet bol'shevikov v 1917: Sbornik materialov i protokolov zasedanii Petersburgskogo komiteta i ego ispolnitel'no komissii za 1917 g.*, ed. P. F. Kudelli (Moscow: Gosudarstvennoe izdatel'stvo, 1927), pp. 40, 45–46.

25. Communist Party of the Soviet Union, *Odinnadtsetyi s'ezd RKP (B): Stenograficheskii otchet* (Moscow: Gospolitizdat, 1961), p. 67.

26. The East German organization reported 1.3 million members in 1973. Kührig, *Equal Rights for Women*, p. 14.

27. *China News Analysis*, no. 919 (11 May 1973), pp. 1–3.

28. Cited in *Communist China, 1971*, p. 441.

29. *Sovietskaia Rossiia*, 21 September 1971.

30. Helen Bilak, "The Influence of Women on Women's Issues" (unpublished senior paper, Union College, Schenectady, N.Y., May 1975).

31. *1975—Trideset godina pobede nad fašizmu međunarodna godina žena OUN* [Thirtieth Anniversary of the Victory over Fascism—International Women's Year at the United Nations], *Žena danas* 30, no. 275 (1975): 16–17; and United Committee of South Slavs in London, *New Yugoslavia: Declaration and Decisions of the Anti-Fascist Council of National Liberation of Yugoslavia; Composition of the Provisional Government; Parliamentary Debates' Churchill's Speech to the House of Commons* (London: United South Slav Committee, 1944), pp. 17–23.

32. *Socialist Upsurge in China's Countryside*, Eng. ed. (Peking, n.d.), pp. 285–86.

33. See Jancar, "Women and Soviet Politics," in *Soviet Society and Politics in the 1970s*, ed. Henry Morton and Rudolf Tökés (New York: The Free Press, 1974), pp. 155–60.

34. A dramatic portrayal of this situation is given in Viktor Kravchenko's *I Choose Freedom* (London: Robert Hale, 1946).

35. For a discussion of this problem, see Barbara Jancar, "Dissent and Constitutionalism in Yugoslavia" (paper presented at the annual meeting of the Midwest Slavic Conference, Ann Arbor, Mich. 3–4 May 1977).

36. *New York Times*, 15 April 1973.

37. See RFE Background Reports "Poland/4" of 15 February 1971 and "Polish Situation/19" of 19 March 1971, Radio Free Europe Research Department, Munich, West Germany (mimeographed). Further information was secured from an interview with Stefan Markowski in Il Ciocco, Italy, July 1977.

38. For a sympathetic portrait of Soviet female dissidents, see Irena Kirk, *Profiles in Russian Resistance* (New York: Quadrangle Press, 1975), pp. 30–43, 148–61, 258–75.

39. For a discussion of religious dissent in the USSR, see Barbara Jancar, "Religious Dissent in the Soviet Union," in *Dissent in the USSR*, ed. Rudolf Tökés (Baltimore and London: The Johns Hopkins University Press, 1975), pp. 191–230.

40. The plea was carried in an open letter made available to Western correspondents in Prague, in which Mme. Kubisová recalled performances since 1970. Significantly, ten days after the August 1968 invasion, she had declared: "I will try to live, and live honorably. . . . Should I ever be prevented from singing for my people, I will place an ad for a job cooking and doing the laundry." See *Mladá fronta*, RFE Situation Report no. 7 (23 February 1977), p. 4.

41. Kirk, *Profiles in Russian Resistance*, p. 152.

CHAPTER 6

1. These time periods have been proposed by Ivan Volgues and they seem to me to make a meaningful distinction between the period when the Communist regimes are consolidating their power and that when they are primarily engaged in maintaining it.

2. A. M. Kollontai, "Brak i byt," *Rabochii sud,* no. 5 (1926), p. 371.

3. Decree of the All-Russian Central Executive Committee and Council of People's Commissars concerning Dissolution of Marriage (19 December 1917), CY, 1918, no. 10, art, 152; Decree of the All-Russian Central Executive Committee and Council of People's Commissars concerning Civil Marriage, Children, and the Keeping of Records of Acts of Status (18 December 1917), CY, 1917, no. 11, art. 160.

4. Article 12 of the 1926 code as translated into English in Rudolf Schlesinger, *The Family in the USSR* (New York & London: Rutledge & Reegan, 1947), p. 156.

5. For a partial listing of some of the directives and decrees regarding protective labor legislation and education for women, see Andrei Vyshinski, *The Law of the Soviet State,* trans. Hugh W. Babb (New York: Macmillan Co., 1961), p. 594.

6. As cited in ibid., p. 595.

7. For a discussion of the code, see John N. Hazard, *Law and Social Change in the USSR* (London: Stevens & Sons, 1953), pp. 61–63.

8. CZ, 1936, no. 34, art. 309.

9. Gregory J. Massell, *The Surrogate Proletariat* (Princeton: Princeton University Press, 1974), chap. 5.

10. Khudzhume Shukurova, *Sotsialism i zhenshchina Uzbekistana* (Tashkent: Izdatel'stvo "Uzbekistan," 1970), p. 77.

11. Ibid., p. 101.

12. Ibid., p. 173.

13. Kurban Said, *Ali and Nino* (New York: Pocket Books, 1971), p. 76.

14. For an account of the early relations between the Soviets and the Moslems, see Alexandre Bennigsen and Chantal Lemercier-Quelquejay, *Islam in the Soviet Union* (New York: Praeger, 1967).

15. Information on the evolution of the Chinese family during the republican years may be found in C. K. Yang, *Chinese Communist Society: The Family and the Village* (Cambridge, Mass.: M.I.T. Press, 1965), pp. 3–21.

16. For the full text of the law, see the appendices of *The Family Revolution in Communist China,* no. 35, Human Resource Research Institute, Chinese Documents Project (Lackland Air Force Base, Tex.: Air Force Personnel and Training Research Center, Air Research and Development Command, January 1955), pp. 61–65. For a more detailed exposition on the marriage law, see M. J. Meijer, *Marriage Law and Policy in the Chinese People's Republic* (Hong Kong: Hong Kong University Press, 1971), *passim.*

17. For a discussion of the nationalist family code, see *The Family Revolution in Communist China,* pp. 4–5.

18. *Wen-Hui Pao* (Shanghai), 20 July 1951, as cited in *The Family Revolution in Communist China,* p. 16.

19. People's Republic of China, Central People's Government, Commission of Legislative Affairs, *Hun-yin Ch'i Yu Kuan Wen Chien [The Marriage Law and Related Documents]* (Peking: Hsin Hua Shu Tien, July 1950), p. 107, as cited in *The Family Revolution,* p. 16.

20. See *The Family Revolution,* p. 36, for the statistical documentation of why women were murdered during 1950–1951.

21. Ibid., chaps. 4 and 5.

22. *People's China* (Peking), no. 5 (March 1953), p. 9. See also Aline K. Wong, "Women in China: Past and Present," in *Many Sisters: Women in Cross-Cultural Perspective,* ed. Carolyn J. Matthiasson (New York: The Free Press, 1974), p. 248; and Victor A. Yakhontoff, *The Chinese Soviets* (Westwood, Conn.: Greenwood Press, 1972), pp. 139–40.

23. *The Family Revolution,* p. 27.

24. *Labor Legislation in the USSR* (Moscow: Novosti Press Agency Publishing House, 1972), p. 41.

25. See Lotta Lennon, "Women in the USSR," *Problems of Communism,* July–August 1971, pp. 52–53. Notably in the agricultural sector, women dominate the manual jobs.

26. Katie Curtin, *Women in China* (New York & Toronto: Pathfinder Press, 1975), p. 65.

27. Interviews with members of Soviet, Hungarian, Bulgarian, and Romanian women's committees, Fall 1974.

28. As cited in Edward E. Rice, *Mao's Way* (Berkeley: University of California Press, 1972), p. 196.

29. Committee of Concerned Asian Scholars, *China: Inside the People's Republic* (New York: Bantam Books, 1972), pp. 271–76.

30. For a discussion of the law, see James H. Meisel and Edward S. Kozera, *Material for the Study of the Soviet System* (Ann Arbor, Mich.: George Wahr Publishing Co., 1953), pp. 229–30.

31. See Peter Juviler, "Women and Sex in Soviet Law: Protection, Penalties, and Obligations," in *Women in Russia,* ed. Dorothy Atkinson et al. (Stanford, Calif.: Stanford University Press, 1977), pp. 258–59. The two best-known women lawyers who fought for improvements in family legislation were Aleksandra Iosifovna Pargament and Elena Serebrovskaia.

32. For discussion of the debate in the press over the new principles, see Barbara Jancar, "Women and Soviet Politics," in *Soviet Politics and Society in the 1970s,* ed. Henry Morton and Rudolf Tökés, (New York: The Free Press, 1974), pp. 134–35.

33. In the public discussion preceding adoption of the law, women were in favor of this article, while men were generally against it.

34. Juviler, "Women and Sex in Soviet Law," pp. 260–61.

35. Ibid., pp. 245–50.

36. The exception is Bulgaria, where property is separate until divorce, at which time it is divided equally between the spouses. See (A. G. Chloros, *Yugoslav Civil Law: History, Family, Property* (Oxford: The Clarendon Press, 1974), chap. 6.

37. Estimate of David M. Heer cited in Donald R. Brown, ed., *The Role and Status of Women in the Soviet Union* (New York: Teachers College Press, 1968), p. 127.

38. For the relevant parts of the law, see Herta Hührig, *Equal Rights for Women in the German Democratic Republic* (Berlin: GDR Committee for Human Rights, 1973), pp. 55–68.

39. Ibid., p. 26, as cited in *Law Gazette,* no. 1 (1972), p. 89.

40. Hilda Scott, *Does Socialism Liberate Women?* (Boston: Beacon Press, 1974), p. 146.

41. *Population Policy in Czechoslovakia* (Prague: Orbis, 1974), pp. 72–73.

42. Henry P. David, ed., *Abortion Research: International Experience* (Lexington, Mass. & Toronto: Lexington Books, 1974), pp. 22–23.

43. *Scinteia,* 28 November 1976.

44. *Romania libera,* 6 December 1976.

45. *Scinteia,* December 14, 1976.

46. Ruth Sidel, *The Families of Fangsheng: Urban Life in China* (Middlesex, Eng.: Penguin Books, 1974), pp. 112–19. See also the transcript of two divorce cases printed in Maud Russell, *Chinese Women: Liberated* (New York: Far Eastern Reporter, Maud Russell, Publisher, n.d.), pp. 29–38.

47. Ruth Sidel, *Women and Child Care in China* (New York: Hill & Wang, 1972), pp. 53–55.

48. Figure given by the Chinese at the Conference on Population Control in Bucharest, November 1974.

49. The reader is referred to the 1975–1976 issues of the *Current Digest of the Soviet Press* for examples. The instances are too numerous to cite here. See also Helen Desfosses Cohn, "Population Policy in the USSR," *Problems of Communism,* November–December 1973, pp. 1–55.

50. Sidel, *Women and Child Care in China,* p. 57.

51. Resolution passed at the Twenty-fourth Congress of the Communist Party of the Soviet Union, 1971.

52. For discussion of these laws, see *A nők politikai gazdasági és szociálai heylzete* (Budapest: Kossuth könyvkiadó, 1970), *passim,* and *Women in the Socialist Republic of Romania,* published under the auspices of the National Women's Council of the Socialist Republic of Romania, 1974, pp. 58–62.

53. Such legislation is not unique to the Communist countries. French law earlier established family allowances that make it financially more economical for a woman with three children to stay at home than to work. According to the Hungarian legislation, a woman is paid a decreasing

amount of her existing salary until it levels off to zero in the third year, thus making it decreasingly economical for her to stay at home.

54. As quoted from the 27 April 1972 decision, translated in Kührig, *Equal Rights for Women*, p. 26.

55. Sidel, *Women and Child Care in China*, pp. 61–62.

56. "Bring into Play Fully the Role of Women in Revolution and Construction," *Red Flag*, no. 10 (1971).

57. Jaroslava Bauerová, "Rodiná problematika vedoucích pracovníc" *Sociologický časopis* 6, no. 5 (1970): 449–62.

58. The law was passed on 19 February 1970. See *A nök politikai, passim*.

59. For the text of this decision, see *Scinteia*, 18–19 June 1973.

60. Ibid., 25 December 1976.

61. Ibid., 29 December 1976.

62. As reported in *Frankfurter Allgemeine Zeitung*, 8 November 1969.

63. *Magyar Hirlap*, 30 October 1972.

64. *Law Gazette* (I. 1972), p. 313.

65. As cited in *Communist China, 1971*, pp. 428–36.

66. See Committee of Concerned Asian Scholars, *China*, pp. 271–76.

67. Alice S. Rossi, "Equality between the Sexes: An Immodest Proposal," in *The Women in America*, ed. Robert Jay Lifton (Boston: Beacon Press, 1965), p. 101.

CHAPTER 7

1. "My Young Contemporaries," *Soviet Woman*, no. 11 (November 1974), p. 3.

2. Ibid., p. 2.

3. *Draft Programme of the Romanian Communist Party for the Building of the Multilaterally Developed Social Society and Romania's Advance toward Communism* (Bucharest: Romanian News Agency, Agerpress, 1974), p. 11.

4. Maria Dinkova, *The Social Progress of Bulgarian Women* (Sofia: Sofia Press, 1972), Dinkova, pp. 10–11.

5. Jiří Dunovský, "Mateřství zaměstňaných žen a problémy péče o jejich děti v nenútnejšíň věku," *Sociologický časopis* 7, no. 2 (1971): 160.

6. Reported to me by Magdalena Sokołowska at the International Congress of Sociology, Toronto, Ontario, 21 August 1974. Sokołowska conducted the survey.

7. *Pravda*, 29 November 1972, p. 3.

8. *Sovietskaia zhenshchina*, no. 4 (April 1970), pp. 10ff.

9. Laura Velikanova, "Women, Stay Young," *Literaturnaia gazeta*, 22 September 1971.

10. See Vera S. Dunham, "Surtax on Equality: Women in Soviet Postwar Fiction" (paper presented at the Conference on Women in Russia, Stanford University, Stanford, Calif., 29 May–1 June 1975).

11. See, for example, Jaroslava Bauerová, "Rodiná problematika vedoucích pracovníc," *Sociologický časopis* 6, no. 5 (1970): 449–62.

12. Shanghai PBI, 18 May 1972, as quoted in *China News Analysis* no. 887 (14 July 1972), p. 3.

13. As quoted in *China News Analysis*, no. 944 (21 December 1973), p. 4.

14. See, for example, James R. Townsend, *Political Participation in Communist China*, (Berkeley: University of California Press, 1968), p. 194; and Franz Shurmann, *Ideology and Organization in Communist China*, 2nd ed. (Berkeley: University of California Press, 1971), pp. 8ff., where the author argues that the cadre, or revolutionary leader in an organization, has taken the place of the *pater familias* of traditional China.

15. Vlasta Fišerová, "Rodina-pospolitost volné chvile?" *Sociologický* časopis 8, no. 3 (1972): 316–24.

16. Zoya Yankova et al., *XX vek i problemy sem'i* (Moscow: Izdatel'stvo' "Znanie," 1974), p. 15.

17. Ibid., pp. 60–63.

18. Yu. V. Arutiunian, ed., *Sotzial'noe i natsional'noe: Opyt etnosotsiologicheskikh*

issledovanii po materialam Tartarskoi ASSR (Moscow: Izdatel'stvo "Nauka," 1973), pp. 140-229.

19. Both the model and the survey of family life in the Moscow suburbs were kindly shown to me by a young researcher in Moscow's Institute of Sociology.

20. Bauerová, "Rodina problematika vedoucích pracovníc."

21. Nikolina Ilieva, Trifon Trifaniv, and Nikolina Tsaneva, *Izpolzvane na zhenskite trudovi resursi v NRB* (Sofia: Partizdat, 1973), chap. 2.

22. Magdalena Sokołowska, *Kobieta pracująca* (Warsaw: Wiedza Powszecha, 1963), pt. 1.

23. Ilieva, Trifaniv, and Tsaneva, *Izpolzvane*, chap. 3.

24. A synopsis of the book was given to me by the Committee of Bulgarian Women. Unfortunately, no title or author was noted.

25. See the account of the study in Phyllis Chesler, *Women and Madness* (New York: Avon Books, 1972), pp. 77-126.

26. Helen Mayer Hacker, "Women as a Minority Group," in *Women in a Man-Made World*, ed. Nona Glazer-Malbin and Helen Youngelson Waehrer (New York: Rand McNally & Co., 1973), pp. 42ff.

27. Conversation with Judit Sas, Budapest, November 1974.

28. I gave several of my classes the same exercise, I was impressed with the general expectation that life ten years from now was going to be more or less a continuation of life as it had been ten years back. Few students varied much from the "rise at seven-go to work-return home at five-watch the evening news" type of day. While most of the women saw themselves working, they again, as in the Hungarian experiment, identified more with childrearing and housekeeping. A few, but not many, bravely asserted they would be earning more than their husbands ten years hence. What made the deepest impression on me was the seeming boredom they projected into their accounts. Entertainment was strictly limited to Saturday night, with the rest of the week being marked by a disciplined dedication to the organization, business, or other place of work.

29. Mollie Schwartz Rosenhan, "Images of Male and Female in Children Readers," in *Women in Russia*, ed. Dorothy Atkinson et al. (Stanford, Calif.: Stanford University Press, 1977), pp. 293-305.

30. Vlasta Fišerová, "Relations of the Basic Civilization Variables to Changes in Family Behavior Patterns," *Sociologický časopis* 6, no. 5 (1970): 434-35.

31. John L. Thomas, *Education for Communism* (Stanford, Calif.: Hoover Institution Press, 1969), p. 39.

32. System of Communist Political Textbooks, *Osnovi kommunisticheskoi morali* (Moscow: "Molodaia gvardiia," 1974), pp. 327-41.

33. E. K. Vasil'eva, *Sotsial'no-professional'nyi uroven' gorodskoi molodezhi* (Leningrad: Leningrad State University Press, 1973), p. 15.

34. V. Bezdenezhenykh, "V zashchitu mal'chisek," *Sem'ia i shkola*, no. 2 (1970), p. 28.

35. Iu. K. Babansky, "Optimalization of the Teaching Process: Preventing Failing Grades among School Children," *Soviet Education* 15, no. 2 (October 1973): 50-52.

36. Judith M. Bardwick, *The Psychology of Women* (New York: Harper & Row, 1971), chap. 10.

37. One of the findings of a survey conducted by Magdalena Sokołowska, who is currently conducting a similar survey in the United States as the basis for a comparative study of male and female attitudes regarding gender.

38. B. Nikoforov and V. Minskaia, "Poterpevshie—v zerkale morali," *Literaturnaia gazeta*, 14 March 1973.

39. Peter Juviler, "Women and Sex in Soviet Law: Protection, Penalities, and Obligations," in *Women in Russia*, ed. Dorothy Atkinson et al. (Stanford, Calif.: Stanford University Press, 1977), pp. 245-50, 255-59, 262-63.

40. Alexander Solzhenitsyn, *Gulag Archipelago* (New York: Harper & Row, 1975), 2: 227-50.

41. *China's Woman*, no. 8 (1966), as quoted in Janet Weitzner Salaff and Judith Merkle, "Women and Revolution: The Lessons of the Soviet Union and China," in *Women in China: Studies in Social Change and Feminism*, ed. Marilyn B. Young, Michigan Papers in Chinese Studies no. 15 (Ann Arbor: Center for Chinese Studies, University of Michigan, 1973), pp. 170ff.

42. For a discussion of these points, see Janet Weitzner Salaff, "Institutional Motivation for

Fertility Limitation," and Salaff and Merkle, "Women and Revolution," in *Women in China,* ed. Young, pp. 132-34 and 145-74.

43. Salaff and Merkle, "Women and Revolution."

44. Ruth Sidel, *Women and Child Care in China* (New York: Hill & Wang, 1972), chaps. 6-7.

45. *People's Daily* (Peking), 2 February 1972.

46. As cited in *China News Analysis,* no. 835 (19 March 1971), p. 5.

47. *People's Daily* (Peking), 16 October 1972.

48. "Family relations formed on the basis of education for personal needs of man in the family in this period [socialism] acquire the expectation of the surmounting of every kind of inequality" *(XX vek i problemy sem'i).* See also V. Varskii, "Vospitania potrebnosti cheloveka v sem'e kak neobkhodimoie uslovie podgotovki podrastaiushshego pokoleniia k budushchei semeinoi zhizni" (material from the Fourth All-Union Congress of the Society of Psychologists, Tbilisi, 1971), as cited in ibid., p. 68.

CHAPTER 8

1. Published in *Novy mir* 14, no. 11 (November 1969): 23-56. Among other things, the novel deals openly with abortion, whether women should quit work when they have children, the problems connected with work and family, and it even threatens Soviet puritan moral standards through some indirect references to sexual intercourse. The novel was sufficiently controversial, according to Susan Jacoby, to set off a storm of arguments in Moscow's intellectual circles between the defenders of the heroine Olga and her accusers. See Susan Jacoby, *Moscow Conversations* (New York: Coward, McCann & Geoghegan, 1972), pp. 217-18.

2. A. G. Kharchev and S. I. Golod, *Professional' naia rabota zhenshchin i sem' ia* (Leningrad: Izdatel'stvo "Nauka", 1970), p. 42.

3. J. Piotrowski and A. Kurzynowski, "Kobieta w przedsiebiorstwie przemystowym," *Biullettin Inst. Gosp. Spo.* (Warsaw), 17, no. 1 (1957): 19.

4. Kharchev and Golod, *Professional' naia rabota zhenshchin i sem'ia,* p. 18.

5. Ethel Dunn, "The Status of Rural Women in the Soviet Union" (paper presented at the Conference on Women in Russia, Stanford University, Stanford, Calif., 29 May-1 June 1975), *passim.*

6. As quoted in Linda Gordon, "The Fourth Mountain, Some Giant Steps Forward, Some Small Steps Backward, and a Ways Still to Go," *Women* 3, no. 4 (1973): 16.

7. For a more detailed discussion of the results, see Barbara Jancar, "Women and Soviet Politics," in *Soviet Society and Politics in the 1970s,* ed. Henry Morton and Rudolf Tokes (New York: The Free Press, 1974), pp. 138-39.

8. See Peter F. Sugar and Ivo Lederer, eds., *Nationalism in Eastern Europe* (Seattle: University of Washington Press, 1969), pp. 310-72.

9. The frustration that men feel at performing uninteresting jobs from which they cannot escape appears to find outlets other than the family; witness the high incidence of alcoholism that has been well documented in the Soviet Union and Eastern Europe. Some men may consciously choose to compromise some of their hopes and ideas and play the game within the system in order to increase their chances of escaping its drudgery, since they do not have the women's option of immersing themselves in the family. It is interesting that among the émigré women I interviewed, none ever criticized a man for joining the intrigue necessary to rise to a high position. He was expected to make a career in some fashion, and such behavior was accepted as obligatory.

10. Khudzhume Shukurova, *Sotsialism i zhenshchina Uzbekistana* (Tashkent: Izdatel'stvo "Uzbekistan," 1970).

11. Interview with Khudzhume Shukurova, Tashkent, November 1974.

12. For a highly informative discussion of foot-binding, see Howard Seymour Levy, *Chinese Footbinding: The History of a Curious Erotic Custom* (New York: W. Rawls, 1966).

13. Louis Harris and Associates, *The 1972 Virginia Slims American Women's Poll,* p. 29. Of the women surveyed, 46 percent thought women are more idealistic than men; 40 percent of the men agreed. Black women, by 49 percent, thought women are more idealistic.

14. Jeane Kirkpatrick, *Political Woman* (New York: Basic Books, 1974), *passim.*

CHAPTER 9

1. Portions of this chapter were published in *Problems of Communism*, November–December 1976, pp. 68–73.

2. Margaret Mead, "Prehistory and Women," *Barnard College Bulletin* (New York), 30 April 1969.

3. Alvin Toffler, *Future Shock* (New York: Bantam Books, 1970), chaps. 2 and 3.

4. Ludvík Vaculík, speech to the Fourth Czechoslovak Writers' Congress, June 1967, as printed in *Czechoslovak Press Survey*, no. 1946 (4 September 1967), put out by the Radio Free Europe Research Department, Munich, West Germany (mimeographed).

APPENDIX 4

1. For the sources of these statistics, see *United Nations Statistical Yearbook, 1974*, pp. 81–84.

2. As published in *Granma Weekly Review*, 1 February 1976, p. 9.

3. Family code of 14 February 1975, law no. 1289, as printed in the *Center for Cuban Studies Newsletter* 2, nos. 4, 7, and 9.

4. Carolee Benglesdorf and Alice Hageman, "Emerging from Underdevelopment: Women and Work," *Cuba Review* 4, no. 2 (September 1974): 3–12.

5. *Granma Weekly Review*, 3 December 1974, p. 2.

6. Irma Sanchez is Director of the State Committee for Technical and Material Supply, and Nora Frometa is Minister of Light Industry.

7. Statistics supplied by *Granma Weekly Review*, 12 December, 10 October, and 31 October 1976.

8. The previous information has come from Benglesdorf and Hageman, "Emerging from Underdevelopment," pp. 7–10.

9. "On Women's Equality," *Granma Weekly Review*, 1 February 1976, p. 9.

10. "Theses," Second Congress of the Federation of Cuban Women, December 1974 (pamphlet), p. 5.

Selected Bibliography

PUBLIC DOCUMENTS

Area Handbook. Individual volumes on Albania, Bulgaria, Czechoslovakia, Hungary, German Democratic Republic, Poland, Romania, and the USSR. Prepared by Eugene K. Keefe et al. Foreign Area Studies of the American University. Washington, D.C.: Government Printing Office, 1972–1973.

Area Handbook of Yugoslavia. Prepared by Gordon C. MacDonald et al. Foreign Area Studies of the American University. Washington, D.C.: Government Printing Office, 1973.

Central Committee of the Russian Communist Party (Bolshevik), Commission on the History of the October Revolution and the Russian Communist Party (Bolshevik). *Revoliutsionnaia deiatel' nost' Kondordii Nikolaevnyi Samoilovoi: Sbornik vospominanii.* Moscow: Gosudarstvennoe izdatel'stvo, 1922.

Communist Party of the Soviet Union. *Odinnadtsetyi s'ezd RKP(B): Stenograficheskii otchet.* Moscow: Gospolitizdat, 1961.

———, Leningrad Municipal Committee, *Pervyi legal'nyi Petersburgskii Komitet bol'shevikov v 1917: Sbornik materialov i protokolov zasedanii Petersburgskogo komiteta i ego ispolnitel'noi komissii za 1917 g.* Edited by P. F. Kudelli. Moscow: Gosudarstvennoe isdatel'stvo, 1927.

Czechoslovak Socialist Republic, Federal Statistical Office. *Statistička ročenka ČSSR, 1969–1975.* Prague: SNTL-ALFA, 1969–1976.

Czechoslovak Statistical Abstract, 1972. Prague: Orbis, 1972.

Demografaia évkönyv. Budapest: Központi Statisztikai hivatal, 1972–1973.

Documents of the Women's Movement in China. Peking: New China Women's Press, 1950.

Draft Progamme of the Romanian Communist Party for the Building of the Multilaterally Developed Society and Romania's Advance toward Communism. Bucharest: Romanian News Agency, Agerpress, 1974.

People's Republic of Bulgaria, Ministry of Information and Communications. *Zhenata v stopanskiia, obshchestveniia, kulturniia zhivot a v semestvoto.* Sofia: Central Statistical Office, 1971.

People's Republic of China, Directorate General of Budgets, Accounts, and Statistics. *The China Yearbook, 1934.* Nanking: Bureau of Budgets, Accounts, and Statistics, 1935.

Socialist Federal Republic of Yugoslavia, Central Statistical Office. *Demografska statistika, 1972.* Belgrade: Central Statistical Office, 1974.

———*Žena u društvu i privredi Jugoslavie.* Statistical Bulletin no. 558. Belgrade, Central Statistical Office, 1969.

Socialist Federal Republic of Yugoslavia, Federal Institute of Statistics. *La femme dans la societé et l'économie en Yogoslavie.* Statistical Bulletin no. 558. Belgrade: Central Statistical Office, 1969.

Statisztikai évkönyv, 1973. Budapest: Központi Statisztikai hivatal, 1973.

Union of Soviet Socialist Republics, Council of Ministers, Central Statistical Office. *Zhenshchiny i deti v SSSR: Statisticheskii sbornik.* Moscow: Statistika, 1969.

———, Council of Ministers, Central Statistical Board. *The USSR in Figures for 1973,* Moscow: Statistika, 1974.

United Nations, Commission on the Status of Women. *Parental Rights and Duties, Including Guardianship.* New York, 1968.

———, Department of Economic and Social Affairs, Statistical Office. *Demographic Yearbook.* New York, 1970–1975.

———. *Statistical Yearbook.* New York, 1953–1975.

United States, Department of Commerce, Bureau of the Census. *The 1977 U.S. Fact Book.* New York: Grosset & Dunlop, 1977.

Ved. Verkh. Sov. SSR 36, no. 297 (11 July 1944): 16–17.

Yearbook of Labour Statistics. Geneva: International Labour Office, Statistical Office of the United Nations, 1972–1973.

BOOKS AND ARTICLES

Almond, Gabriel A., and Verba, Sidney. *The Civic Culture: Political Attitudes and Democracy in Five Nations.* Princeton: Princeton University Press, 1963.

Andelin, Helen B. *Fascinating Womanhood.* New York: Bantam Books, 1975.

Arutiunian, Yu. V., ed., *Sotzial'noe i natsional'noe: Opyt etnosotsiologicheskikh issledovanii po materialam Tartarskoi ASSR.* Moscow: Izdatel'stvo "Nauka," 1973.

Atkinson, Dorothy; Dallin, Alexander; and Lapidus, Gail Warshofsky, eds. *Women in Russia.* Stanford, Calif.: Stanford University Press, 1977.

Bebel, August. *Women under Socialism.* Translated by Daniel De Leon. New York: Socialist Literature Co., 1910.

Balabanoff, Angelica. *Impressions of Lenin.* Foreword by Bertram D. Wolfe. Ann Arbor: University of Michigan Press, 1968.

Banus, Maria. *Poezii.* 2 vols. Bucharest: Editura Minerva, 1971.

Bardwick, Judith M. *The Psychology of Women.* New York: Harper & Row, 1971.

Bennigsen, Alexandre, and Lemercier-Quelquejay, Chantal. *Islam in the Soviet Union.* New York: Praeger, 1967.

Bernard, Jessie. *Women and the Public Interest.* New York: Aldine, Atherton, 1971.

Boserup, Esther. *Women's Role in Economic Development.* New York: St. Martin's Press, 1970.

Boulding, Elise, *Women in the Twentieth-Century World.* New York, London, Sydney, Toronto: Sage Publications, Halsted Press Division, John Wiley & Sons, 1977.

Breichová, J., Holečková, N., and Košňarová, V. *Postavení žen v ČSSR*. Prague: Státní nakladatelství politické literatury, 1962.

Brown, Donald R., ed. *The Role and Status of Women in the Soviet Union*. New York: Teachers College Press. 1968.

Buljachit', Rada, et al., eds. *Zhene Srbije u NOB* [Women of Serbia in the National Liberation War]. Belgrade: Nolit, 1975.

Buvinić, Mayra. *Women and World Development: An Annotated Bibliography*. Washington, D.C.: Overseas Development Council, 1976.

Chesler, Phyllis. *Women and Madness*. New York: Avon Books, 1972.

Chloros, A. G. *Yugoslav Civil Law: History, Family, Property*. Oxford: The Clarendon Press, 1970.

Committee of Concerned Asian Scholars. *China: Inside the People's Republic*. New York: Bantam Books, 1972.

Communist China, 1971. Communist China Problem Research Series, no. EC52. Hong Kong: Union Research Institute, 1973.

Conference on the Communal Activity of the Women of Yugoslavia. "Pregled odredaba o zaštiti žene i materinstva u zakonima o medjusobnim odnosima radnika u udruženom radu." Belgrade, October 1974. Mimeographed.

Cunnington, C. Willett. *Feminine Attitudes in the Nineteenth Century*. London & Toronto: William Heinemann, 1935.

Curtin, Katie. *Women in China*. New York & Toronto: Pathfinder Press, 1975.

Czechoslovak Social Policy. Prague: Orbis, 1974.

Daley, Mary. *Beyond God the Father*. Boston: Beacon Press, 1973.

David, Henry P., ed., *Abortion Research: International Experience*. Lexington, Mass. & Toronto: Lexington Books, 1974.

Deutsch, Karl. *Comparative Theories of Social Change*. Ann Arbor, Mich.: Foundation of Human Behavior, 1966.

Dinkova, Maria. *The Social Progress of Bulgarian Women*. Sofia: Sofia Press, 1972.

Dodge, Norton T. *Women in the Soviet Economy*. Baltimore: The Johns Hopkins Press, 1966.

Dornberg, John. *The Other Germany*. Garden City, N.Y.: Doubleday & Co., 1968.

Duverger, Maurice. *The Political Role of Women*. New York: UNESCO, 1955.

Eighth Moon. Sansan's story as told to Bette Lord. New York: Harper & Row, 1964.

Engels, Friedrich. *The Origin of the Family, Private Property, and the State in the Light of the Researchers of Louis Morgan*. Translated by Ernest Untermann. New York: International Publishers, 1942.

The Family Revolution in Communist China. Research memorandum no. 35, Human Resource Research Institute, Chinese Documents Project. Lackland Air Force Base, Texas: Air Force Personnel and Training Research Center, Air Research and Development Command, January 1955.

Ferge, Zsuzsa. *The Search for Equality: Why and How*. Budapest: Akadémiai Nyomda, 1974.

Firestone, Shulamith. *The Dialectic of Sex*. New York: Bantam Books, 1972.

Fisher, H. H., and Gankin, Olga Hedd. *The Bolsheviks and the World War: The Origin of the Third International*. The Hoover Library on War, Revolution, and Peace, Publication no. 15. Stanford, Calif.: Stanford University Press, 1960.

Freedman, Maurice, ed. *Family and Kinship in Chinese Society*. Stanford, Calif.: Stanford University Press, 1970.

Geiger, H. Kent. *The Family in Soviet Russia.* Cambridge, Mass.: Harvard University Press, 1968.

Gilman, Charlotte Perkins. *His Religion and Hers.* 1923. Reprint. Westport, Conn.: Hyperion Press, 1976.

Glazer-Malbin, Nona, and Youngelson, Helen Waehrer, eds. *Women in a Man-Made World.* New York: Rand McNally & Co., 1973.

Glos, Ing. Bohuslav. *Práce a mzdy žen: problém ženských mezd.* Prague: Lidová knihtiskarna A. Němec a spol., 1937.

Goldberg, Steven. *The Inevitability of Patriarchy.* New York: William Morrow, 1973.

Golod, S. I. "Sociological Problems of Sexual Morality." Leningrad: Philosophical Faculty, Leningrad University, 1968.

Goode, William J., ed. *World Revolution and Family Patterns.* New York: The Free Press, 1963.

Gorcick, Vivian, and Moran, Barbara K. eds. *Women in Sexist Society.* New York: Basic Books, 1971.

Greer, Germaine. *The Female Eunuch.* New York: McGraw-Hill, 1971.

Groza, Maria. "L'Accès des femmes à l'enseignement et aux professions techniques et scientifiques." SC/WS/248. Paris: UNESCO, 29 July 1969. Mimeographed.

Hagen, Everett E. *On the Theory of Social Change.* Homewood, Ill.: The Dorsey Press, 1962.

Hazard, John N. *Law and Social Change in the USSR.* Published under the auspices of the London Institute of World Affairs. London: Stevens & Sons, 1953.

Heilbrun, Carolyn. *Toward a Recognition of Androgyny.* New York: Alfred A. Knopf, 1973.

Hinton, William. *Fanshen: A Documentary of Revolution in a Chinese Village.* New York: Vintage Books, 1966.

Ho Ping-ti and Tang Tsou, eds. *China in Crisis,* vol. 1, *China's Heritage and the Communist Political System.* 2 bks. Chicago: University of Chicago Press, 1968. Vol. 1. Chicago: University of Chicago Press, 1968.

Hungarian National Women's Council. *A nők a statisztika tükrében.* Budapest: Kossuth könyvkiadó, 1974.

———. *A nők politikai, gazdasági és szociális helyzete.* Budapest: Kossuth könyvkiadó, 1970.

———. *A nőkről.* Budapest: Kossuth könyvkiadó, 1974.

Iglitzin, Lynne, and Ross, Ruth, eds. *Women in the World.* Santa Barbara, Calif.: CLIO Books, 1976.

Ilieva, Nikolina; Trifaniv, Trifon, and Tsaneva, Nikolina. *Izpolzvane na zhenskite trudovi resursi v NRB.* Sofia: Partizdat, 1973.

Ingraham, Claire R., and Ingraham, Leonard. *An Album of Women in American History.* New York: Franklin Watts, 1972.

Inkeles, Alex, and Geiger, H. Kent, eds. *Soviet Society: A Book of Readings.* Boston: Houghton Mifflin, 1961.

International Committee for the Support of Charter 77 in Czechoslovakia. "White Paper on Czechoslovakia." Paris, 1977. Mimeographed.

Jacoby, Susan. *Inside Soviet Schools.* New York: Hill & Wang, 1974.

———. *Moscow Conversations.* New York: Coward, McCann & Geoghegan, 1972.

Janeway, Elizabeth. *Man's World, Woman's Place.* New York: Dell Publishing Co., 1971.

Jaquette, Jane, ed. *Women in Politics*. New York: John Wiley & Sons, 1974.

Khan, Mazhar Ul Haq. *Purdah and Polygamy: A Study in the Social Pathology of the Muslim Society*. Peshawar Cantt: Nashiran-e-Ilm-o-Taraqiyet, 1972.

Kharchev, A. G., and Golod, S. I. *Professional'naia rabota zhenshchin i sem'ia*. Leningrad: Izdatel'stvo "Nauka," 1970.

Kirk, Irena. *Profiles in Russian Resistance*. New York: Quadrangle Press. ₁975.

Kirkpatrick, Jeane. *Political Woman*. New York: Basic Books, 1974.

Klein, Donald W., and Clarke, Anne B. *Biographic Dictionary of Chinese Communism, 1921–1965*. 2 vols. Cambridge, Mass.: Harvard University Press, 1971.

Ko, Hu. *Steeled in Battles*. Peking: Foreign Language Press, 1955.

Kollontai, Aleksandra. *The Autobiography of a Sexually Emancipated Communist Woman*. New York: Herder & Herder, 1971.

Kravchenko, Viktor. *I Choose Freedom*. London: Robert Hale, 1946.

Kührig, Herta. *Equal Rights for Women in the German Democratic Republic*. Berlin: GDR Committee for Human Rights, 1973.

Labor Legislation in the USSR. Moscow: Novosti Press Agency Publishing House, 1972.

Laslett, Peter, and Wall, Richard, eds. *Household and Family in Past Time: Comparative Studies in the Size and Structure of the Domestic Group over the Last Three Centuries in England, France, Serbia, Japan, and Colonial North America, with Further Materials from Western Europe*. Cambridge: At the University Press, 1972.

Latitić, Ibrahim, ed. *Women in the Economy and Society of the SFR of Yugoslavia*. Belgrade: Federal Institute for Statistics, 1975.

Lenin, Vladimir Ilyich. *The Emancipation of Women*. New York: International Publishers, 1966.

Lenin on Women's Role in Society and the Solution of the Question of Women's Emancipation in Socialist Countries. Moscow: Soviet Women's Committee, 1973.

Levy, Howard Seymour. *Chinese Footbinding: The History of a Curious Erotic Custom*. New York: W. Rawls, 1966.

Lifton, Robert Jay, ed. *The Woman in America*. Boston: Beacon Press, 1965.

Liutov, Atanas, ed. *Zhenata-maika, truzhenichka, obshchestvenichka*. Sofia: Partizdat, 1974.

Ludz, Peter C. *The German Democratic Republic from the Sixties to the Seventies: A Socio-political Analysis*. Cambridge, Mass.: Harvard University Press, 1970.

Macciocchi, Maria Antonietta. *Daily Life in Revolutionary China*. New York & London: Monthly Review Press, 1971.

Mace, David, and Mace, Vera. *The Soviet Family*. Garden City, N.Y.: Doubleday & Co., 1963.

Maclean, Fitzroy. *Tito: The Man Who Defied Hitler and Stalin*. New York: Ballantine Books, 1957.

McNeal, Robert Hatch. *Bride of the Revolution*. Ann Arbor: University of Michigan Press, 1972.

Madison, Bernice. *Social Welfare of the Soviet Union*. Stanford, Calif.: University of California Press, 1968.

Malewska, Hanna. *Kulturowe i psychospołeczne determinanty życia seksualnego*. Warsaw: Państwowe wydawnictwo naukowe, 1972.

Mandel, William M. *Soviet Women*. New York: Anchor Books, 1975.

Massell, Gregory, J. *The Surrogate Proletariat*. Princeton: Princeton University Press, 1974.

Matthiasson, Carolyn J. *Many Sisters: Women in Cross-Cultural Perspective*. New York: The Free Press, 1974.

Maududi, S. Abul A'la. *Purdah and the Status of Woman in Islam*. Lahore, Pakistan: Islamic Publications, 1972.

Mead, Margaret. *Soviet Attitudes towards Authority*. New York: The Rand Corporation, 1951.

Meijer, M. J. *Marriage Law and Policy in the Chinese People's Republic*. Hong Kong: Hong Kong University Press, 1971.

Meisel, James H., and Kozera, Edward S. *Material for the Study of the Soviet System*. Ann Arbor, Mich.: George Wahr Publishing Co., 1953.

Michel, Andrée. *Travail féminin: Un point de vue*. Travaux et Recherches de Prospective: Schéma général d'aménagement de la France: La Documentation Française, 1975.

Mihovilovic, Miro A., principal investigator. *Reports and Studies: The Influence of Women's Employment on Family Characteristics and Functioning*. Zagreb: Institute for Social Research, University of Zagreb, 1971.

Millett, Kate. *Sexual Politics*. New York: Avon Books, 1971.

Mitchell, B. R. *European Historical Statistics: 1750–1970*. New York: Columbia University Press, 1975.

Morgan, Mirabel. *The Total Woman*. New York: Pocket Books, 1975.

Morton, Henry, and Tökés, Rudolf, eds. *Soviet Politics and Society in the 1970s*. New York: The Free Press, 1974.

Myrdal, Jan. *Report from a Chinese Village*. New York: Signet, 1965.

Myrdal, Jan. and Kessle, Gun. *China, The Revolution Continued*. Trans. from the rev. Swedish ed. by Paul Britten Austin. New York: Pantheon Books, 1970.

1975—Trideset godina pobede nad fašizmom medunarodna godina žena OUN [Thirtieth Aniversary of the Victory over Fascism—International Women's Year at the United Nations]. *Žena danas* 30, no. 275 (1975).

New Woman in New China. Peking: Foreign Language Press, 1972.

A nökröl. Budapest: Kossuth könyvkiadó, 1974.

Pálné, Komlós, ed. *A nök a statisztika tükrében*. Budapest: Hungarian Woman's National Council, Kossuth könyvkiadó, 1974.

Pano, Nicholas C. *The People's Republic of Albania*. Baltimore: The Johns Hopkins Press, 1968.

Pioro, Zygmunt. *Zachowanie przezstrzenne rodzin "wiodących" w dużych miastach polskich*. Series of individual works, no. 154. Warsaw: Institut urbanistyki i architektury, 1968.

Pirages, Dennis. *Arc II*. San Francisco: W. H. Freeman & Co., 1974.

Population Policy in Czechoslovakia. Prague: Orbis, 1974.

Rice, Edward E. *Mao's Way*. Berkeley: University of California Press, 1972.

Richman, Barry M. *Industrial Society in Communist China*. New York: Random House, 1969.

Rigby, T. H. *Communist Party Membership in the USSR, 1917–1957*. Columbia

University Studies of the Russian Institute. Princeton: Princeton University Press, 1968.

Rowbotham, Sheila. *Women's Resistance and Revolution: A History of Women and Revolution in the Modern World.* New York: Vintage Books, 1972.

Russell, Maud. *Chinese Women: Liberated.* New York: *Far Eastern Reporter,* Maud Russell, Publisher, n.d.

Said, Kurban. *Ali and Nino.* New York: Pocket Books, 1971.

St. Erlich, Vera. *Family in Transition: A Study of 300 Yugoslav Villages.* Princeton: Princeton University Press, 1966.

St. George, George. *Our Soviet Sister.* Washington, D.C.: Robert B. Luce, 1973.

Sas, Judit J. *Életmód és czalád. Az emberi viszonyok alakulása a családban.* Budapest: Hungarian Academy of Scinece, Sociological Research Institute [Magyar tudományos akadémia, Szociológiai kulato intézetének], 1973.

Schilling, Gerhard F., and Hunt, Kathleen W. *Women in Science and Technology.* Rand Paper no. P-5239. Santa Monica, Calif.: The Rand Corporation, June 1974.

Schlesinger, Rudolf. *The Family in the USSR.* New York & London: Rutledge & Reegan, 1947.

Scott, Hilda. *Does Socialism Liberate Women?* Boston: Beacon Press, 1974.

Sedugin, P. *New Soviet Legislation on Marriage and the Family.* Moscow: Progress Publishers, 1973.

Shukurova, Khudzhume. *Sotsialism i zhenshchina Uzbekistana.* Tashkent: Izdatel'stvo "Uzbekistan," 1970.

Shurmann, Franz. *Ideology and Organization in Communist China.* Berkeley: University of California Press, 1971.

Siddiqi, Mohammad Mazheruddin. *Women in Islam.* Lahore, Pakistan: Institute of Islamic Culture, 1972.

Sidel, Ruth. *Families of Fengsheng: Urban Life in China.* Middlesex, Eng.: Penguin Books, 1974.

————. *Women and Child Care in China.* New York: Hill & Wang, 1972.

Smith, Hedrick. *The Russians.* New York: Quadrangle Press, 1976.

Socialist Upsurge in China's Countryside. English ed. Peking, n.d.

Sokołowska, Magdalena. *Kobieta pracująca.* Warsaw: Wiedza Powszechna, 1963.

Solzhenitsyn, Alexander, *Gulag Archipelago,* vol. 2. New York: Harper & Row, 1975.

State University of Tirana. *Problems of the Struggle for the Complete Emanicpation of Women.* Tirana: The Political Book Publishing House, 1973.

Steiner, Shari. *The Female Factor: A Report on Women in Western Europe.* New York: G. P. Putnam & Sons, 1977.

Stites, Richard. *The Women's Liberation Movement in Russia: Feminism, Nihilism, and Bolshevism, 1860–1930.* Princeton: Princeton University Press, 1977.

Sugar, Peter F., and Lederer, F., eds. *Nationalism in Eastern Europe.* Seattle: University of Washington Press, 1969.

System of Communist Political Textbooks. *Osnovi kommunisticheskoi morali.* Moscow: "Molodaia gvardiia," 1974.

Szczepanski, Jan. *Polish Society.* New York: Random House, 1970.

Taking Tiger Mountain by Strategy. Peking: Foreign Language Press, 1971.

Tatybiekova, Zhanetia Sausmasovna. *Raskreposhchenie zhenshchiny Kirgizki Velikoi oktiabr'skoi sotsialisticheskoi revoliutsiei (1917-1936 g.).* Frunze: Izdatel'stvo Akademii nauk Kirgizckoi SSR, 1963.

Theodore, Athena. *The Professional Woman.* Cambridge, Massachusetts: Schenkman Publishing Company. 1971.

Thomas, John L. *Education for Communism.* Stanford, California: Hoover Institution Press, 1969.

Tien, H. Yuan, China's Population Struggle: *Demographic Decisions of the People's Republic, 1949-1969.* Columbus: Ohio State University Press, 1973.

Tökés, Rudolf, ed. *Dissent in the USSR.* Baltimore & London: The Johns Hopkins University Press, 1975.

Toffler, Alvin, *Future Shock.* New York: Bantam Books, 1970.

Townsend, James R. *Political Participation in Communist China.* Berkeley, California: University of California Press, 1968.

Trotsky, Leon. *Women and the Family.* New York: Pathfinder Press, 1970.

Tsang Chiu-Sam. *Society, Schools, and Progress in China.* New York: Pergamon Press, 1968.

Tsuzuki, Chushichi. *The Life of Eleanor Marx, 1855-1898: A Socialist Tragedy.* New York: Oxford University Press, 1967.

United Committee of South Slavs in London. *New Yugoslavia: Declaration and decisions of the Anti-Fascist Council of National Liberation of Yugoslavia; Composition of the Provisional Government; Parliamentary debates; Churchill's Speech to the House of Commons.* London: United South Slav Committee, 1944.

Vasil'eva, E. K. *Sotsial'no-professional'nyi uroven' gorodskoi molodeshi.* Leningrad: Leningrad State University Press, 1973.

The Virginia Slims American Woman's Opinion Poll, vol. 3. Conducted by the Roper Organization, Inc., 1974.

Vyshinski, Andrei, *The Law of the Soviet State.* New York: Macmillan Co., 1961.

Wald, Carol. *Myth America: Picturing Women, 1865-1945.* Text by Judith Papachristou. New York: Pantheon Books, 1975.

Waluk, Janina. *Praca i praca kobiet w Polsce.* Warsaw: Kaiązka i wiedza, 1965.

Winter, Ella. *Red Virtue.* New York: Harcourt, Brace & Co., 1933.

Witke, Roxanne. *Comrade Chiang Ch'ing.* Boston: Little, Brown & Co., 1977.

Wolfe, Margery, and Witke, Roxanne. *Women in Chinese Society.* Stanford, Calif.: Stanford University Press, 1975.

Women in Poland, Warsaw: Central Statistical Office, 1975.

Women in the Contemporary Life of Romania. Bucharest: Meridiane Publishing House, 1970.

Women in the Socialist Republic of Romania. Bucharest: Meridiane Publishing House, 1974.

The Working Woman in People's Poland. Warsaw: Ministry of Labour, Wages, and Social Affairs, 1975.

Yakhontoff, Victor A. *The Chinese Soviets.* Westport, Conn.: Greenwood Press, 1972.

Yang, C. K. *Chinese Communist Society: The Family and the Village.* Cambridge, Mass.: M.I.T. Press, 1965.

Yankova, Zoya, et al. *XX vek i problemy sem'i.* Moscow: Izdatel'stvo "Znanie," 1974.

Young, Marilyn B., ed. *Women in China: Studies in Social Change and Feminism.* Ann Arbor: Center for Chinese Studies, University of Michigan Press, 1973.

UNPUBLISHED PAPERS

Barbic, Ana. "Women in Sociopolitical Life in Yugoslavia." Paper presented at the International Workshop on Changing Sex Roles in Family and Society, Dubrovnik, Yugoslavia, 16–21 June 1975.

Bilak, Helen, "The Influence of Women on Women's Issues." Senior Paper, Union College, Schenectady, N.Y., 1975.

Dodge, Norton T. "Women in the Soviet Economy." Paper delivered at the Conference on Women in Russia, Stanford University, Stanford, Calif., 29 May–1 June 1975.

Dunham, Vera S. "Surtax on Equality: Women in Soviet Post-war Fiction." Paper presented at the Conference on Women in Russia, Stanford University, Stanford, Calif., 29 May–1 June, 1975.

Dunn, Ethel. "The Status of Rural Women in the Soviet Union." Paper presented at the Conference on Women in Russia, Stanford University, Stanford, Calif., 29 May–1 June 1975.

Farnsworth, Beatrice, "Bolshevik Alternatives and the Soviet Family: The 1926 Marriage Law Debate." Paper presented at the Conference on Women in Russia, Stanford University, Stanford, Calif., 29 May–1 June 1975.

First-Dilić, Ruža, M.S. "Sex Roles in Yugoslavia." Paper presented to the Research Committee on Sex Roles in Society, Working Group 13A on Changing Occupational and Family Roles of Women, International Workshop on Changing Sex Roles in Family and Society, Dubrovnik, Yugoslavia, 16–21 June 1975.

Jancar, Barbara, "Women and Elite Recruitment into the Central Committees of Bulgaria, Czechoslovakia, Hungary, and Poland." Paper presented at the annual meeting of the Midwest Political Science Association, Chicago, Ill., 23 April 1977.

SELECTED NEWSPAPERS AND PERIODICALS

Canadian-American Slavic Studies, 1973–.
Československý časopis, 1965–.
China News Analysis, 1958–.
China Reconstructs, 1970–.
Current Digest of the Soviet Press, 1950–.
Daedalus, 1964–.
Demografia (Budapest), 1975–.
Demografie (Prague), 1972–.
L'Express, 1970–.
Femea (Bucharest), 1970–1975.
Frankfurter Allgemeine Zeitung, 1969–.
Hong Kong Times, 1972–.

International Labour Review, 1965–.
Izvestia, 1960–.
Joint Publications Research Service, 1960–.
Kommunist, 1972–.
Kommunistka, 1917–1925.
Literaturnaia gazeta, 1960–.
Magyar Hirlap, 1970–.
Nedelia, 1970–.
New York Times, 1960–.
Novyi Zhurnal, 1970–.
Novy mir, 1969–.
People's Daily, 1970–.
Pravda, 1917–.
Problems of Communism, 1971–.
Rabochii sud, 1926–.
Rabotnitsa, 1917–1925.
Red Flag, 1971–.
Romania, 1965–.
Scinteia, 1970–.
Sem'ia i shkola, 1972–.
Sociologický časopis, 1965–.
Sotsial'nye issledovaniia (Moscow), 1969–.
Soviet Education, 1973–.
Soviet Life, 1970–.
Soviet Review, 1969–.
Sovietskaia Rossiia, 1971–.
Sovietskaia zhenshchina, 1920–.
Sovietskoe gosudarstvo i pravo, 1910–.
Soviet Studies, 1969–.
Soviet Woman, 1970–.
Studies in Comparative Communism, 1969–.
Vestnik statistiki, 1970–.
Voprosy ekonomiki, 1970–.
Woman, 1971–.
Žena danas, 1970–.

Index

Abortion: Communist policies on, 140–46; as criminal offense, 174; legalization of, 141; rates of, 70–71, 250; reasons for, 144; as tool of state interest, 146, 207; in USSR, 52, 127

Absenteeism, among women, 42

Academy of Science: of Czechoslovakia, 161; of USSR, 16, 33

Adat, 127, 135

Administration: capabilities of women in, 82; promotion of women in, 28–32

Adultery, as cause of divorce, 174

Age: as factor in use of communal facilities, 48; in China, 61, 129

Agriculture, 185; feminization of, 20, 41, 55, 185; impact of collectivation of, on Chinese family, 130–31; legal definitions of women's roles in, 138; specialized training of Polish women in, 22

Akademgorod, RSFSR, 186

Akhmatova, Anna, 119

Albania, 13; demographic data on, 51; National Women's Organization of, 106; socialization in schools of, 171

Alcoholism, as major cause of divorce, 68

Alimony: and 1926 Soviet marriage law, 75; payments of, in paternity cases, 141–42

All-China Women's Federation, 108

Androgyny, 210; as goal of sexual equality, 4

Anti-Fascist Women's Front (Yugoslavia), 113

Antifeminism, 81–84; reinforced by Communist ideology, 86–87; subtlety of, 81; at work, 49

Appliances, domestic, 49–51, 53, 86

Armand, Inessa, 74, 114

Army: Chinese women in, 176; People's Liberation, 111, 138; Red, 128; Seventh Route,

60; women in, 138; Yugoslav National Liberation, 113

Authoritarian regimes, and implementation of change in status, 9, 211, 212

Authority: in China, 61, 77; in the family, 64, 184; on the job, 83; relationship of, to political participation, 208

Automobile, as status symbol, 82

Baptists, 120

Baranskaia, Natalia, 181

Bardwick, Judith, 173

Bartová, Éva, 110, 187, 189

Bauerová, Jaroslava, 149, 151

Beauty parlors and cosmetic shops, 79, 92, 156–57

Bebel, Ernst, 76

"Belgrade 8," 119

Belorussia, rural-urban migration in, 43

Berent, Jerzy, 38

Birth control, 71–73, 145, 159, 175

Birth rate, 51–54, 70, 72, 145, 148, 178; and family allowance programs, 146–47; ratio of first deliveries to total, 52–53

"Bitter past," 60, 80, 130, 195

"Blank spot," 141

Bogoraz, Larissa, 119

Bolsheviks, 75, 84, 105; female membership in Central Committee of, 112; and Islam, 59, 128; on marriage, 75, 123; seizure of power by, 123; and women's movement, 106

Bolshevism, 73, 84

"Bourgeois" bias, 1, 4, 18, 23–24, 73–74, 79, 174, 198; and feminism, 59, 105–6; and sexual values, 57, 74–76, 86, 160

Boznia-Herzegovina, 71

281

Library of Congress Cataloging in Publication Data

Jancar, Barbara Wolfe, 1935–
    Women under communism.

    Bibliography: p. 271.
    Includes index.
    1. Women—Communist countries. I. Title.
HQ1870.8.J36   301.41'2'091717   77–16375
ISBN 0–8018–2043–X